HANDBOOK ON CRIME AND DELINQUENCY PREVENTION

Handbook on Crime and Delinquency Prevention

EDITED BY

Elmer H. Johnson

GREENWOOD PRESS

NEW YORK • WESTPORT, CONNECTICUT • LONDON

Library of Congress Cataloging-in-Publication Data

Handbook on crime and delinquency prevention.

   Bibliography: p.
   Includes index.
     1. Crime prevention. 2. Juvenile delinquency—
Prevention. 3. Crime prevention—United States.
I. Johnson, Elmer Hubert.
HV7431.H373 1987   364.4′0973   86–14985
ISBN 0–313–24023–X (lib. bdg. : alk. paper)

Library of Congress Catalog Card Number: 86–14985
ISBN: 0–313–24023–X

First published in 1987

Greenwood Press, Inc.
88 Post Road West, Westport, Connecticut 06881

Printed in the United States of America

The paper used in this book complies with the
Permanent Paper Standard issued by the National
Information Standards Organization (Z39.48–1984).

10 9 8 7 6 5 4 3 2 1

We hope prevention will raise the life chance of all children, including Alex and Suzanne.

Contents

Preface

As an addition to the reference series of Greenwood Press, the *Handbook on Crime and Delinquency Prevention* is intended to be a resource for both the intellectual community and policy makers and practitioners. As one of criminology's major sectors for direct application, prevention offers special opportunities to test theories drawn from all the disciplines. Framing criminal justice policy is subsidiary to general social policy; that interdependence is demonstrated no more clearly than in prevention of delinquency and crime. Similarly, the spectrum of prevention programs has stimulated demands for their coordination through common policy, integration of theoretical approaches, and interchange among practitioners.

A reference work is a register of vital information, a chronicle of relevant ideas, and an inventory of empirical activities. The literature on prevention is voluminous, and the efforts to exploit its potentialities are diverse in their specific purposes and approaches. As a reference work, this book has been designed to serve as a platform for intelligent consideration of vital information and relevant ideas. By identifying the common features among many programs, analyses will promote understanding that has been clouded by the diversity of purposes and activities. Thereby, the high hopes expressed for prevention can be subjected to searching scrutiny that respects the responsibility for accountability to the citizens who are asked to provide indispensable psychological commitment and fiscal support to the programs.

To that end, the contributors were asked to concentrate on a particular aspect of the broad subject matter of delinquency and crime prevention. A general scheme was established for their collective effort; thus, within a division of labor, each chapter would be part of an integrated exploration. Recognizing the vast scope of information, ideas, and activities, each contributor was asked to prepare an annotated bibliography to supplement his or her use of the given literature. As an additional resource for readers wishing to examine further particular aspects of prevention, a general bibliography is provided as Appendix A.

Since prospects for effective prevention depend heavily on those persons who have great responsibilities in matching hope with realities, the concerns of policy makers and practitioners have received particular consideration in the preparation of this reference work. The chapters reflect that intention. In addition, Appendix B lists a number of agencies that serve as resources for obtaining practical information on the planning and implementing of programs in the prevention of crime and delinquency.

My colleagues have accepted formidable challenges in light of the vast scope of the field of prevention and its intersection with virtually every scientific discipline. The difficulties for profound analysis and complete coverage are suggested by the host of meanings attached to the basic term "prevention." There are many synonyms for "prevent": anticipate, avert, balk, bar, block, check, checkmate, debar, foil, forestall, forfend, frustrate, hamper, help, hinder, impede, inhibit, intercept, interrupt, neutralize, nullify, obstruct, obviate, preclude, prohibit, repress, restrain, retard, save, stop, and thwart. The synonyms could be classified to demonstrate that prevention is a code word that conceals the great diversity of basic ideas found among advocates of prevention as the most appropriate answer to delinquency and crime. To make sense out of that jungle of often-conflicting ideas, this handbook is organized around four major rationales that are implied by the synonyms: the crime control, environmental design, therapeutic, and community rationales.

The scheme of the handbook endeavors to call attention to who carries out prevention and where that work is more likely to be conducted. We have selected the police, courts, schools, and social service agencies as the most likely institutional sectors within which specialists in preventive work are to be found. The confrontations of offenders and victims are most likely to occur on the streets, in the home and family setting, in business and industrial establishments, and in what we will call public facilities.

My introductory chapter has been designed to orient the reader to the many facets of the subject matter and to establish the framework within which the following chapters make their special contributions. The book closes with an examination of relatively recent efforts to determine whether or not the hopes for prevention have been matched by demonstrable effectiveness. As for all fields of social action and intervention, prevention has fallen short in meeting the responsibilities for accountability. Comparison of the potentialities with accomplishments is a means of making prevention an increasingly effective answer to delinquency and crime. Objective evaluation of outcomes is consistent with our fundamental purpose: to provide a register of vital information, a chronicle of relevant ideas, and an inventory of empirical activities.

As editor, my primary debt is to my colleagues who accepted the challenges outlined above. I hope that the readers share my appreciation of their respective reviews of the literature and exploration of fundamental ideas. In addition, I have benefited from the support of graduate students and the secretarial staff of the Center for the Study of Crime, Delinquency, and Corrections in research and manuscript preparation. Southern Illinois University and its College of Human Resources made this enterprise feasible by giving me the opportunity of a sabbatical leave. Finally, I thank Greenwood Press for pointing to the need for this reference work and Mim Vasan, Acquisitions Editor, and Michelle Scott, Senior Production Editor, for their invaluable services.

HANDBOOK ON CRIME AND DELINQUENCY PREVENTION

1

Introduction: The "What," "How," "Who," and "Where" of Prevention

ELMER H. JOHNSON

> The policy of controlling fires by merely putting out the flames and sitting back to await more fires is rapidly being abandoned as short-sighted and wasteful. . . . In relation to the control of delinquency and crime, however, society has not progressed much beyond the stage of putting out the flames. It has waited for violations of law and then bent its efforts to pursuing, arresting, prosecuting, and punishing offenders without giving much thought to the elimination of the forces that produce them and continue to produce thousands like them.[1]

In those words some fifty years ago, two prominent criminologists presented as self-evident the superiority of prevention over the search for and punishment of criminals. The Gluecks believed that citizens were beginning to recognize "responsibilities for many of the conditions presumed to be criminogenic, and with this an awakening of desire to participate intelligently in the amelioration of those conditions."

Their enthusiasm is matched by contemporary claims that prevention is the best route for anticrime policy, but there continue to be major questions about *what* prevention is, *how* it should be carried out, to *whom* it should be directed, and *where* it can be best implemented. The contributors take up those questions from their particular perspectives. This chapter has been designed to set the stage for their more profound analyses of the questions.

THE "WHAT" AND "HOW" OF PREVENTION

The popularity of prevention has produced a great number of articles and books that are at least indirectly relevant, but a survey of that literature reveals surprisingly few attempts to define what prevention fundamentally *is*. Even those attempts usually cover only selected aspects of the topic, depending on the particular interests of the writer. Thus, we should be placed on alert that the field of prevention is too far ranging for a simple and concise definition. A variety of perspectives and applied approaches, frequently inconsistent with one another, defy that desirable objective.

A Preliminary and Generalized Definition

Broadly speaking, prevention is based on four interrelated ideas: (1) that something evil, unpleasant, or destructive is impending; (2) that this eventuality can be forestalled by human insight and ingenuity; (3) that much of the preventive activities are outside the boundaries of the criminal justice system; and (4) that human intervention should be initiated *before* the undesirable event occurs.

The feeling that undesirable events lie in the future is especially expressive of cultural attitudes in the case of crime prevention. Prevention of crime and delinquency—as well as the public fears that stimulate it—is subject to images of the threat of criminals that vary among societies and over time and place. That variation complicates the ferreting out of objective facts. Prevention, too, is an exercise in social norms whereby conceptions of the threat of crime are colored by the particular beliefs of what is threatened, who is the source of the threat, and what should be done about it.

The resolve to prevent crime is one example of the conviction among Americans that undesirable conditions can be overcome through dedicated use of education, technological advances, social reorganization, and intervention. Prevention is imbued with the conviction that science can be brought to bear to solve human problems and the faith of reformism that the flaws of the existing social order can be remedied.

Advocates of crime prevention frequently see its proactive nature to be superior to the reactive stance of usual law enforcement. The advantage pivots on the possible involvement of every facet of the institutional system, rather than on placing heavy reliance on the formal organization of the criminal justice system in the suppression and correction of criminals in action. In other words, a comprehensive attack on multitudinous sources of delinquency and crime seeps beyond the relatively narrow boundaries of criminal justice administration.

These ideas are brought into conjunction by the fundamental principle that prevention occurs *before* official actions are taken in response to the occurrence of delinquencies and crimes. The concept of predelinquency conveys the idea that before any violation of legal norms has occurred, the presence of certain symptoms indicates that a given youngster will move inexorably toward delinquency and possibly crime. In that sense prevention rests on the premise that criminal behavior can be predicted by identifying the psychological or social correlates of future criminality. The threat of crime to victims whether individuals or the social order, the enlistment of human ingenuity, and the broad-based attack on the sources of deviance—all of these are directed against the possibility that individuals will engage in future crimes.

Levels of Preventive Activities

The vast scope of preventive activities demands some framework for relating them to one another. The precedent of public health and disease epidemiology, Richard Brotman and Frederic Suffet explain, has influenced the usual formula. "In the classic epidemiological formulation," they say, "the spread of contagious disease among people depends on the interaction of an agent (the disease germ) with a host (the human organism) as mediated through a particular environment (physical and social)." Thus, *primary prevention* entails keeping the disease germ from infecting the human organism by immunizing persons not yet attacked by the disease or by quarantining those already ill. Through early case finding and diagnosis, *secondary prevention* would limit the early effects of the disease on sick patients through treatment. *Tertiary prevention* would limit disabilities or restore the sick to wellness among patients who have not reached an advanced stage of the disease process.[2]

The extrapolation of the public health model to crime prevention must be managed cautiously. Unlike disease, antisocial behavior involves an element of volition and the availability of illicit goods or opportunities for obtaining benefits through law violations.[3] The medical analogy implies that both crime and disease are a malign process within the organism persisting over time to deprive the individual of control of behavior. Criminal careers do not develop in a sequence of progressive stages and do not present clearcut symptoms limited to biological variables. Serious difficulties are raised for identifying distinctively criminal behavior when a pluralistic culture blurs the differences between "abnormal" and "reputable" behaviors. Since legal definitions of delinquency are shaped politically within sociocultural environments, the diagnoses of predelinquents are skewed by ethnic and social class prejudices to a degree surpassing that of medicine.

Primary Prevention: In endeavoring to apply these three public health concepts to the prevention of delinquency and crime, Paul J. Brantingham and Frederick L. Faust describe three general applications of primary prevention: First, they point to "psychological immunization from certain types of behavioral tendencies." Second, the physical environment would be redesigned. Third, exemplary sentences and the administration of corrective services would qualify as general deterrence.[4]

Similar to the public health conception, primary prevention of crime and delinquency would focus on the entire population at risk of becoming delinquents or criminals. The ultimate goal, Brantingham and Faust say, is to identify and alter "those conditions of the physical and social environment that provide opportunities for or precipitate criminal behavior."[5] This conception places the greatest obstacle to specificity in clarifying the meaning of the prevention and, probably because of the diversity of programmatic approaches included, draws the greatest popularity among advocates of prevention over crime-control measures. By presenting another typology of prevention, Peter P. Lejins offers more effective distinctions. Under his term "corrective prevention," he discusses the elimination of causes of criminal behavior that motivate that behavior through actions taken before crimes are perpetrated. Under this term, he includes programs to detect symptoms of crime and delinquency, preventive attention to spatial or temporal concentrations of that misconduct, and manipulation by "general societal policies affecting many different aspects of life and also affecting crime and delinquency."[6] His "corrective prevention" includes both environment-oriented and individual-oriented approaches that must be clearly recognized if the conception of "primary prevention" is to be realistic. It also removes the confusion about deterrent policies by treating them separately as "punitive prevention."

Secondary Prevention: In public health this version engages in early case finding, diagnosis, and therapeutic intervention to check the disease process among persons infected by disease. When applied to delinquency and crime, secondary prevention concentrates on persons identified as potential lawbreakers but who have not become subjects for criminal justice actions.

Secondary prevention is directed toward those persons who have been diagnosed as being at special risk of becoming delinquents or criminals. Potential delinquents and criminals have been identified variously as school dropouts, vocationally inept, victims of poverty or racism, physically and mentally handicapped, members of disorganized families, and persons suffering inner conflicts or low self-esteem. Diagnostic techniques are supposed to discover the especially crime-prone. Membership in inferior social status groups presumably would be a useful cue. Therapeutic intervention, social action programs, and environmental approaches would be among the actions taken to reduce the vulnerability of high-risk individuals and groups.

Tertiary Prevention: In public health prevention at this level, individuals suffering an advanced stage of disease are treated to prevent death or permanent disability. For crime prevention, Brantingham and Faust explain, intervention is undertaken to the lives of actual offenders to forestall their further crimes. They see tertiary prevention through punishment or treatment to be the primary goals of correctional agencies.[7]

The targeting of actual offenders risks violation of the principle that prevention is employed *before* involvement in criminal behavior. Justification for extending the scope of prevention pivots on the claim that either punishment or treatment reduces the prevalence of crimes. That extension stretches the concept of prevention beyond the breaking point for meaningful delineation of this field for analysis and practice. The distinction between prevention in advance of offenses and control of actual offenders is obscured.

According to Lejins, the threat of punishment as a preventive device is a separate type. In his "punitive prevention," the crime-control apparatus of the criminal justice system employs the threat against criminals to teach the lesson through imposition of pain that "crime does not pay."[8] That function is known as "special deterrence" in that it is directed against offenders specifically as opposed to "general deterrence" which is directed to the total population in the sense of primary prevention.

Considering the deterrent effect of punishment is appropriate to the field of prevention, at least in regard to general deterrence and primary prevention. The efficacy of deterrence through the threat of punishment has stimulated much discussion. Johannes Andenaes objects to limiting consideration of deterrence to the threat of punishment without recognizing the mobilization of the moral effects of education, socialization, attitude shaping, norm reinforcement, and so on. "Criminal law is not only a price tariff," he says, "but rather also is an expression of society's disapproval of a particular act—a disapproval which may work in subtle ways to influence behavior."[9] Thus, "punitive prevention" seeps beyond the limits of the narrow administration of legal penalties in a calculated manner.

In advancing the concept of "mechanical prevention," which he defines as the placing of obstacles "in the way of the potential offender that make it difficult or impossible for him to commit an offense," Lejins gives target hardening a place in prevention.[10] However, it is appropriate to note that, in addition to the construction and operation of devices promoting his purpose, "mechanical" refers to the assumption that standardized and arbitrary reactions can block undesirable behaviors without serious attention given to the social conditions and psychological predispositions that influenced the criminal act. Hence, both special deterrence for tertiary prevention and general deterrence for primary prevention qualify in this sense of "mechanical prevention." Furthermore, target hardening has implications for both primary and secondary prevention.

RELEVANCE OF THE HISTORY OF IDEAS

It is a self-evident fact that no sewer can be cleared by standing at the outlet and trying to purify the sewage, so long as the inlet is supplied with a constantly-increasing quantity. No more can crime be reduced by punishing or trying to reform criminals so long as conditions exist that procreate criminals and crime faster than the law can arrest and either punish or reform them. While we dispose of those existing and to exist in the best manner we can, public safety lies only in formulating and enforcing laws to remove the sources from which criminals and crime come.[11]

That defense of prevention reads as though it were written today, not in 1892. The major arguments are not new, but C. H. Reeve goes on to argue that the criminal is one who "has such an anatomical and physiological arrangement of organs, as produces a perverted moral perception, or fails to produce any of sufficient strength to enable him to avoid offense. No matter how clear his perceptions, he lacks will power to keep him honest. He is a victim of a constitutional disease.'' Reeve recommends that laws be enacted to prohibit marriage by ''a known criminal and others unfit for the relation''; and that children be removed from the custody of parents whose care will create ''a criminal mentality.''[12]

Three implications for prevention of delinquency and crime may be drawn from Reeve's comments. First, the superiority of prevention over crime control measures has been claimed for a considerable period of time. Second, since his words reflect the biologism of the criminology of his day, Reeve illustrates the coloring of crime prevention by the dominant ideas of the particular era. In other words, we have reason to trace the history of ideas that have come to be connected with contemporary efforts to forestall delinquency and crime. The fundamental premises of prevention are based on the criminological thought of the particular time which, in turn, is an expression of general social thought. As a corollary not directly attributable to Reeve's comments, the third implication is that those ideas have not emerged full-blown but have emerged in socioeconomic and political contexts.

Earlier Thoughts About Prevention

The Gluecks were not the first nor will they be the last to be advocates of prevention, although usually the advocacy was secondary to the pursuit of other considerations. For example, Jeremy Bentham and Cesare Beccaria helped establish the argument that antisocial conduct could be forestalled by the systematic imposition of criminal sanctions.

Declaring that ''the general objective of all laws is to prevent mischief,'' Bentham argued that the purpose of enacting criminal laws was to prevent all offenses, to prevent the commitment of the worst offenses, to reduce the amount of mischief, or to prevent crimes in the least expensive way. He advanced the ''principle of utility'' which meant that the purpose of the individual's conduct was to achieve maximum ''pleasure'' (''happiness'') and to minimize ''pain.'' Preventive effect presumably would be produced by a level of punishment sufficient to outweigh the profit of the offense but short of needless pain and in accord with the nature of the offense.[13]

Similarly, Beccaria envisaged the end of deliberately calculated punishments to be ''to prevent the criminal from doing further injury to society, and to prevent others from committing the like offense.''[14] Beccaria was convinced, Marcello Maestro says, that the abolition of cruel and ferocious punishments would contribute to making the people of a nation more humane and sensitive, and therefore would tend to reduce the number and atrocity of crimes.[15] The ideas of Bentham and Beccaria have been influential in developing preventive policies resting on the calculated employment of the threat of criminal law penalties to deter would-be offenders.

Another ideological thread of crime prevention is that the evil threat of criminal victimization and the social destructiveness of crime can be forestalled by human insight and ingenuity. Among the philosophical sources of this faith is positivism which, largely through Auguste Comte's contribution to the development of sociology, coupled the scientific method with social progress. The earlier applications of positivism to criminology and to social thought generally were permeated with the conservative bias that preservation of the existing social order was the primary aim.

The Positive School of criminology gave further support to this conservative view by defining criminals as essentially pathological individuals, thereby diverting attention from the social forces inherent in the definition of crime and in reactions against deviants. Cesare Lombroso, who is usually given a major role in the establishment of the Positive School, advanced the idea that the "born criminal" was a biological throwback to "ferocious" and "primitive" ancestors. Nevertheless, other than these so-called born criminals, Lombroso noted the existence of "occasional, juvenile criminals." For them, he believed: "It is no longer enough to repress crime; we must try to prevent it."[16]

The ideological thread of faith in human ingenuity has also been directed toward modifying the society itself as opposed to explaining deviation as the pathology of individuals. Thereby, the span of scientific inquiry has expanded to include social and political factors as well as biological and psychological factors.

Emile Durkheim said: "We must not say that an action shocks the common conscience because it is criminal but rather say that it is criminal because it shocks the common conscience."[17] Thus, we should not only consider what stimulates the offenders to engage in crime, but we must also obtain ideas on how to turn potential offenders from crime.

Because delinquency and crime are seen as violations of sacred norms, prevention raises the question of whether measures other than resort to the sanctions of the criminal law can be mobilized to forestall undesirable conduct. The relevance of traditional norms to contemporary life and reforming the society itself are brought into consideration. Thus, much of the preventive activities have come to be seen to be outside the span of the agencies administering the criminal law.

Emergence of Ideas Associated with Prevention

Deliberately conceived and implemented prevention was not envisaged in eighteenth- and nineteenth-century America, but already some of the inherent premises were emerging. The prevention of delinquency rests on the beliefs that children are distinctively different from adults and that they are especially vulnerable to socially undesirable influences. Under the term "modern conception of childhood," LaMar T. Empey summarizes the gradual development of the beliefs that children must be safeguarded against that vulnerability through carefully structured education and moral training.[18] From those beliefs have come a confusing array of laws and ordinances that constitute the legal definition of delinquency.

In colonial America the family was given the monopoly over managing juvenile misconduct, but, with the strains of urbanization in the early nineteenth century, houses of refuge were established to herald a greater emphasis on institution-alization to deal with wayward, orphaned, neglected, and delinquent children.

According to Joseph F. Kett, the year 1840 marked a fundamental change in American cultural beliefs about how children should be managed. Before that year the family and school environment of children, ages seven to thirteen, were likely to be casual and unstructured. "In schools," he says, "brutality and burlesque mixed with slackness and informality." Thereafter, that "accidental education" was replaced by insistence that Sunday schools, private schools, and public schools be instruments for moral education in forming character within "planned, engineered environments." The drive to regulate the child's experi-ence in the formative years was combined with a new sensitivity to protect the child from the temptations that are especially numerous at that stage of life.[19]

That combination of humanitarian concern and a drive for moral regulation characterized the "child savers" who were instrumental in developing social settlements, recreational centers, and playgrounds, and creating the juvenile court in Illinois in 1899. The objective then was to exercise the state's guardianship over children suffering adverse conditions and to prevent criminal careers by seizing on the first indications of delinquent tendencies.[20] With the collapse of the child-saving ideology, more recently the *parens patriae* principle has come under severe criticism for failure to respect the protections guaranteed by the Constitution.

The first thirty years of the twentieth century brought increasing concerns about juvenile delinquency. In seeking explanations for the delinquency, the advocates of prevention tended to believe that the root cause lay either in the abnormalities of individuals or in the collapse of the urban order. In tracing the thoughts of seven influential experts during the 1900–1930 period, Steven Schlossman offers evidence of this ambivalence.[21] Best known for his support of eugenicism in his *The Kallikak Family* (1912), Henry Goddard came to believe that filtering out psychopathic individuals would be the proper object of pre-vention. Lewis Terman, the inventor of the intelligence quotient score, aban-doned earlier attention to social factors to concentrate on inferior mental ability. William Healy, a pioneer in the application of psychiatry to prevention, tended to emphasize individuals and to express doubts about the sociological theories.

A hesitant movement away from views of mere individual pathology appeared in the writings of other experts. Ben Lindsey, a juvenile court judge who cham-pioned community responsibility for promoting child development, argued that the courts should mesh their work with other urban child-serving institutions. As for Lindsey, Thomas Eliot, who in the 1930s insisted that social theory guide public policy on prevention, showed little grasp of the parameters of such in-terrelationships. Miriam Van Waters explored the distinctive problems of girls' transition to adulthood and the impact of major socioeconomic changes on female delinquency. Her faith in the juvenile court as an instrument of rehabilitation was combined with a critique of a materialistic culture as a source of delinquency. Frederick Thrasher, noted for his research on juvenile gangs, linked delinquency to theories of the urban community. He insisted that delinquency and gang membership were normal consequences of socialization to deviant communal values.

From the diverse ideas symbolized by those authors, prevention programs fall into one of two broad categories noted by Stanton Wheeler, Leonard Cottrell, and Anne Romasco.[22] Some programs were "directed toward changing the feelings, attitudes, and eventually the reactions of individual delinquents or predelinquents," they say. The emotional problems of children, attributed primarily to inadequate family relationships, were emphasized from psychological, psychoanalytic, or psychiatric perspectives. The other category was that following sociological perspectives focusing on the broader social environment.

The federal government gradually moved into the area of prevention in this century, Gayle Olson-Raymer points out, culminating in large-scale funding in the 1960s.[23] The Children's Bureau was created in 1912; the New Deal contributed the Civilian Conservation Corps, the National Youth Administration, and Aid to Dependent Children in the early 1930s; and new youth-serving programs were introduced in the 1960s and 1970s. This accelerated federal investment in prevention stands in sharp contrast to the previous relegation of those activities to local programs and private philanthropic organizations. That investment, Alfred J. Kahn says, tended to mitigate the heavy emphasis on clinical treatment and to give unprecedented attention to planning, community development, and social action programs.[24]

THE "WHO": OFFENDERS AND VICTIMS

The "who" of crime and delinquency prevention refers to both the potential offenders whose deviant conduct is to be forestalled and their possible victims who directly or indirectly suffer the consequences. Traditionally, preventing delinquency and crime has focused on modifying the predispositions of individuals to commit illegal acts or modifying those qualities of the environment that release those predispositions.

A new orientation has shifted the field toward increased attention to the victims and the effects of images of "the crime problem" on victims and nonvictims alike. Here is the personal dimension of that problem that has been regarded excessively in terms of its impact on "society" in abstraction, diverting attention from the victims. Only somewhat recently have criminologists accorded sufficient attention to the victim as either a participant or sufferer in the criminal event. Similarly, the possibility of mobilizing potential victims in their own defense has received increasingly serious consideration. Dan A. Lewis notes that potential victims should be included in discussions of prevention because interaction among *people* is crucial to the interpretation of the events associated with crime. Fear, isolation, and precautionary behaviors, he says, stem in part from the victimization experiences because the criminal event happens to citizens and has consequences for those involved.[25]

Offenders as Targets for Prevention

Tertiary prevention, as usually conceived, singles out actual offenders as targets, but including them violates the fundamental idea that prevention is undertaken before a delinquent or criminal act. Forestalling additional offenses is offered as a justification, but the conceptual weakness remains. Secondary prevention focuses on predelinquents and casual adult offenders. Thus, the qualities of the major classes of crime—usually conceived according to legal categories—color the images of the future misconduct that is to be prevented. Primary prevention has a similar dependence on those images, but their relevance is more tenuous because reputable persons are also the focus of attention.

In expressing images of the kinds of misconduct that are to be precluded, preventive programs imply the beliefs that certain attitudes and life orientations go with criminality, that certain experiences and living conditions favor the "choice" of criminality or preferred behavior, that law violators differ in their degree of dedication to criminal ways and self-definition as criminals, and that categories of crime differ in their impact on society in general and on their particular victims. The drive for prevention is heavily charged with images that identify criminals with the violent crimes against persons: homicide, forcible rape, aggravated assault, and armed robbery. The threat of death and injury is clearcut, but those offenders form only a small fraction of all those caught in the police net.

A much greater portion of criminals engage in automobile theft, shoplifting, forgery, and other occasional crimes against property. The so-called conventional property offenders—thieves, burglars, and larcenists—constitute a significant portion of persons arrested by the police, and some of them qualify as professional criminals.

Moral offenders—identified with drug and alcohol abuse, sexual irregularity, homosexuality, and vagrancy—are heavily represented in the police and court workloads because legal norms have been brought into play in attempts to reduce the disturbing effects they have on conceptions of public morality. These law violators usually do not conceive of themselves as criminals. Occupational offenses, usually defined as white-collar crimes, raise formidable obstacles to prevention because they are committed within the regular occupational structure and raise doubts that "respectable" persons should be managed as criminals.

Victimization and Fear of Crime

There are many motivations for preventing crime and delinquency ranging from the quest of policy makers for a handle on lawbreaking to the fears of potential victims. Those fears are not necessarily the effect of what John E. Conklin has defined as "direct victimization" where individuals have personally suffered the attack on their person or property. Many more persons are "indirect victims" in that their concerns are stimulated by knowledge of such incidents, without direct victimization, and cause a change in their usual attitudes and behavior.[26]

The concerns of policy makers and the fears of individuals converge in the association of crime with images of general community disorder. "Predatory crime does not merely victimize individuals," James Q. Wilson says, "it impedes and, in the extreme case, prevents the formation and maintenance of community."[27] Wesley G. Skogan and Michael G. Maxfield report that their respondents saw early warning signals of impending danger in abandoned buildings, unsupervised teenagers, drug use, graffiti, and visible vandalism in their deteriorating neighborhoods.[28] In both senses, the concern for reducing the incidence of crime and delinquency extends beyond the boundaries of law violations per se to make them symbolic of general social disorder. In four Chicago neighborhoods, Dan A. Lewis and Michael G. Maxfield found that the fear is stimulated by a combination of concern about crime and about incivility. "To the extent that fear can be identified as a problem independent of crime rates," they suggest, "policy makers should begin to explore ways to reduce fear independent of policies directed at reducing the incidence of crime."[29] It may be that reduction of fear will be more successful than reduction of crime.

Only a small portion of the population—even that of large cities—is victimized, but the risk differs among various status groups. The level of fear, however, does not necessarily square with actual vulnerability. Summarizing research findings, Terry L. Baumer notes that, in spite of their relatively lower victimization rates, women and the elderly are considerably more fearful than men and the young because of their greater physical and social vulnerability. The fears of women are associated with sexual assaults and the possibility of serious injury through forcible rape. Their frailty, the poverty of many of them, and the residence of many in deteriorated neighborhoods have been cited as explanations for the fears of the elderly. However, blacks and the poor—both of whom are particular targets of crime—are generally more fearful than whites and the relatively well-to-do, probably because of their greater concentration in high-crime areas.[30]

The paradox of lower victimization rates and greater fear of the women and elderly, Marc C. Stafford and Omer R. Galle warn, does not justify the implication that their fears are irrational. That claim, if true, would weaken the value of crime prevention as a means of alleviating fear. They substitute data on exposure to risk according to sex and age for victimization by criminals and find the discrepancy between possible victimization and images of victimization to be narrowed. However, the discrepancy remains in spite of the greater justification for the concerns of women and the elderly.[31]

Whether or not the perceptions of risk are realistic, the consequences of fear have remarkable impact on individuals. The consequences, Peter P. Yin postulates, are dependent on whether or not victimization has been previously experienced, messages about crime from persons in one's intimate groups and from the mass media, the presence of social support, and familiarity with the neighbors rather than feeling isolated.[32]

Victimization and Prevention

In their interviews on how people explain crime as contrasted with what they do about crime, Louise A. Kidder and Ellen S. Cohn note a discrepancy between crime-prevention programs and victimization-prevention programs. They believe that crime-prevention programs are oriented to lessening the likelihood that someone will become an offender: for example, expanding job opportunities, urban renewal, closing down bars, drug abuse treatment, and reducing poverty. In their view victimization prevention consists of actions lessening the likelihood that someone will become a victim: "avoiding dangerous areas and using locks, burglar alarms, dogs, and other measures which protect a home or establishment against victimization." Kidder and Cohn argue that people talk about crime prevention in the sense of long-term attack on social conditions generating crime, but they act to protect their bodies, homes, or neighborhoods in the sense of more short-term victimization prevention.[33]

How can individuals and groups protect themselves against personal attack or property loss? Skogan and Maxfield present four categories of crime-related activities.[34] Personal precautions include limiting exposure to risk, sometimes to the extreme of near withdrawal from public life, and acting to minimize the degree of threat when confronted in criminal incidents. Household protections entail owning weapons, installing locks and other target hardening devices, obtaining watchdogs, buying theft insurance, and using property identification systems. Community involvement carries the hope that group efforts—be they formal or informal, highly organized or spontaneous—will do something about crime. Finally, there is flight to the suburbs from the high-crime inner city in which fear of crime is usually a minor factor in a complex of reasons.

Direct victimization has considerable effect in terms of personal precautions, Skogan and Maxfield report, but indirect victimization has only marginal consequences. In one exception, burglary showed slim differences between the two groups.[35] A sample of persons in a crime-prone neighborhood was differentiated according to those who had been burglarized and those who had not. Ellen J. Langer tells us that the victims did not differ from the nonvictims in subsequent preventive measures.[36]

Taking household protection measures appears to be very common in metropolises, and they are generally adopted even more than personal precautions. Local crime conditions have stimulated the installation of special locks and window bars, Skogan and Maxfield state, and the inclination to adopt these protections was about the same for victims and nonvictims. Yet, the more vulnerable households did less than most households in response to the threat of crime. Persons with strong neighborhood ties were more likely to take actions to protect the household.[37]

Persons who enjoy wide contacts in the community are more likely to participate in preventive activities. However, Skogan and Maxfield found that participation is unrelated to fear of crime and perceptions of community disorder. These findings suggest that crime and the fear of it do not necessarily increase citizen involvement in preventive efforts. Involvement is dependent to a great extent on the inclination of individuals to join groups and the possible interest in prevention in the particular group's agenda.

Flight from the inner city is an effective answer for removing oneself from the risks of victimization only when a small portion of people take this course of action, they note, and the decision to relocate reflects changes in household composition or the position of family members in the life cycle. Economic constraints and racial discrimination inhibit many residents from fleeing the inner city, reducing the significance of fear of crime in the array of motives.[38]

CRIME CONTROL RATIONALE

As frequently noted above, the thought patterns of preventive actions and programs exhibit remarkable diversity and fluidity. The number of rationales defies encyclopedic and detailed coverage, but there are general themes that permit useful exploration of the distinctions among major categories of thought. In planning the *Handbook on Crime and Delinquency Prevention*, four major rationales were identified among the concepts and premises employed in the analysis and practice of prevention: crime control, environmental design, therapeutic, and community rationales. Each of four specialists was asked to present the respective premises of those rationales in its own terms and to subject it to analysis. Their chapters are intended to provide an intellectual foundation for the chapters that later take up the institutional spheres within which preventive programs are carried out and the settings in which offenders and victims confront one another.

Principles of Crime Control

The crime control rationale is primarily oriented to countering active criminals. Any concern about prevention is subsidiary to the beliefs that punishment of apprehended criminals will deter them from further offenses and that their suffering will serve as an example to divert would-be offenders from engaging in lawbreaking. The elaboration of the thoughts of Jeremy Bentham and Cesare Beccaria about deliberately calculated and implemented punishments is central to crime control thought.

Crime control is reactive in two senses. First, the usual practice of law enforcement relies on reactions after a crime has been committed and in response to citizen complaints. Protective responses are involved in preventive control, surveillance of known criminals, analysis of crime trends, mapping of crime locations, and files on techniques employed by known criminals. Nevertheless, the fundamental reactive style is opposed to the orientation of prevention to future misconduct.

Second, crime control is predicated on the premise that delinquency and crime are "conduct" in the sense of automatic responses to environmental or internalized stimuli that can be managed by forces originating from outside the personality of the offender. The reaction is to the misconduct without seriously raising questions about why the individual broke the law. Instead of engaging in protracted and complicated analysis of the motivations or conditions that stimulated the misconduct, the criminal act becomes the grounds for imposing standardized penalties that are supposed to counter the antisocial impulse regardless of their origin. "Conduct" implies that individuals are locked into a rather limited number of alternatives and that the threat of apprehension and punishment, in and of themselves, will manage prevention. "To manage misconduct" conveys the impression of an intractable control system that compels persons to conform to preferred standards, regardless of differences in personal tendencies and situational circumstances.

In both senses of reaction, crime control is dedicated to maintaining the public order. It is assumed the legal norms enjoy the support of everyone except lawbreakers. Furthermore, the popularity of this rationale among many segments of public opinion stems from the association of urban life with social disorder, weakened social institutions, and lessened effectiveness of self-policing.

The possibility of rapid-fire and relatively simple reactions to crime and delinquency gives special appeal to crime control measures when widespread concerns and fears shape public opinion. The measures are direct without the delay of preventive strategies that depend on the complex and long-term strategies of treating the faults of individuals and reforming the defects of the social institutions. Those arguments, coupled with the fear generated among potential and actual victims, favor target hardening as a corollary of the crime control rationale.

Linkages with Target Hardening

Some advocates of crime prevention see it as managing the risks that crimes will be perpetrated by reducing criminal opportunities within the potential victim's environment. Some risks may be eliminated, but it is more likely that the risk of loss or injury can be reduced. It has been contended that attempts to catch, "cure," or punish actual criminals are less promising than making a potential target inaccessible or unattractive to criminals.[39]

The target-hardening devices are a primary means of reducing risk. Anti-intrusive devices include better locks, electromagnetic contact devices, vibration detectors, metallic foil tape, photoelectric alarms, ultrasonic space protectors, and photoelectric radio frequency devices. Visual surveillance may be maintained through closed-circuit television. Those devices are monitored at stations where security personnel are mobilized. Those devices serve perimeter protection, as well as fencing, masonry barriers, and illumination.

Those devices are most effective when backed up by security procedures that are most relevant to business, industrial, and public enterprises. Asset control refers to management procedures in purchasing, receiving, and storing goods that prevent external theft and that complicate the perpetration of fraud, embezzlement, and theft by employees. Screening and bonding new employees, monitoring the handling of money, and being alert for cues of employee behavior that stimulates theft are recommended.

ENVIRONMENTAL DESIGN RATIONALE

In keeping with "victimization prevention" as discussed above, the environmental design rationale concentrates on reducing the likelihood that people will become victims. Emphasis is placed on characteristics of the built environment that favor delinquency and crime and the modification of that environment for defense against victimization. The neighborhood environment and building design may either hinder or assist surveillance by residents to detect intruders. Prevention becomes a matter of removing the hindrances and increasing chances for surveillance.

Principles of Environmental Design

"Research on crime and the physical environment," Fred Heinzelmann reports, "has provided support for the hypothesis that the proper design and effective use of the physical environment can help to reduce crime and fear in various settings."[40] Rather than placing sole reliance on building design, layout, and site planning, however, he recommends that the manipulation of the physical environment be incorporated with other preventive strategies to produce a comprehensive approach.

In that respect, the environmental design rationale bridges target-hardening strategies, which are also emphasized in the crime control rationale, with the concern of the community rationale for increasing the belief of potential victims that they can do something to reduce crime. The residents are encouraged to feel secure by design of the physical features of buildings (perimeter obstructions, windows, doors, and so on) to complicate the access of intruders and to increase the chances that the criminal will be observed. In that respect, building and neighborhood design and target-hardening devices are combined to reduce the opportunities for crime to occur. The environmental design rationale, however, goes beyond target hardening alone to recognize the need to cultivate resident cooperation in defensive measures and to modify those patterns of their behavior that favor their victimization.

In his seminal presentation, Oscar Newman delineates the three propositions of "defensible space theory." *Territoriality* refers to the tendency of residents of a community to defend it against intruders. *Natural surveillance* refers to the capacity of residents to observe public areas of a residential complex and thereby reduce the probability of offenses and their own anxieties and fears. *Image and milieu* refers to the proposition that proper design can alter the visual impact of a neighborhood or housing project. Empirically, he proposes that large public areas be divided into smaller areas to take advantage of territoriality and that visibility both within and outside buildings be increased to expand natural surveillance.[41]

The physical design of housing units, residential complexes, and their immediate environs would be modified to decrease the opportunity for criminals and to increase the sense of sharing common interests among residents. Initially, Newman hypothesized that changes in the physical environment would be sufficient to release latent attitudes to mobilize the residents in their own defense, but later, this enthusiasm for mechanical prevention was modified to place defensible space as one of the elements in a package of crime reduction measures that would facilitate community cohesion.[42]

Situational Crime Prevention and Target Hardening

Manipulation of the environment links environmental design in some respects with the concept of situational crime prevention and target hardening. Instead of worrying about the causes of criminality and about identifying potential delinquents and criminals through study of predispositions, situational crime prevention concentrates on manipulating opportunities for a particular kind of crime. It is not necessary to consider what qualities of personality lead only some persons to loot pay telephones, R. V. G. Clarke says, if stronger steel coin boxes are installed or if the personnel of public buildings increase surveillance and the risks for culprits. The advantage of manipulating elements of the physical locale, Clarke believes, is that such an approach is appropriate for managing vandalism, automobile offenses, shoplifting, employee theft, and other kinds of offenses by persons who do not ordinarily exhibit criminal propensities and are not likely to offend when tempting opportunities are not available.[43]

Situational crime prevention focuses either (a) on the combination of social circumstances that may lead to a criminal climax or (b) on the qualities of a physical locale that increase vulnerability to criminal attack.

The first version draws on the victimological principle that the victim does not necessarily play only a passive role in the criminal incidence. "The criminal act concerns not only situations and usually, apart from cases of indiscriminate murder, focuses on the individual criminal resulting in only a partial examination of the event," Guglielmo Gulotta explains. "In fact, in certain types of crimes the victim actively participates in the development of the action, and only after the conclusion of it gets the definitive role of victim."[44] In regard to criminal homicide, David F. Luckenbill illustrates the stages through which the relationships between the criminal and victim may proceed. First, victims act in a manner that stimulates the aggression of the offender. The apparent affront can draw various responses; the criminal's choice of retaliation continues the homicide drama. Barring elimination of the victim at this stage, the victim and murderer continue a process of escalating verbal or physical retaliation and counter-retaliation. Then, the stage of a battle with various weapons is reached and the victim falls. Finally, the slayer usually awaits the police or is held for the police by members of the audience.[45]

Prevention in this instance would be increasing awareness among potential victims of the potentialities for violence or property loss that lurk in crime-prone situations. However, for environmental design, the second version of situational crime prevention is relevant because both focus on the qualities of the physical locale that increase vulnerability to criminal attack.

The assumption is that many offenses happen because individuals who are not necessarily criminalistic take advantage of tempting opportunities to steal. These opportunities have become more prevalent since World War II, Lawrence E. Cohen believes, because of more plentiful stealable objects, fundamental changes in role behavior, and new behavioral routines of probable victims. Examples of those changes are the increased participation of women in the labor force, more frequent and longer vacations, and greater leisure activity outside the home. The net effect is that the absence of family members from their residences reduces safeguards against burglary and increases the chances for victimization elsewhere.[46]

Target-handling tactics are relevant to situational crime prevention because of their emphasis on erecting barriers to criminal opportunity. Thus, as for situational crime prevention, target handling circumvents the examination of criminal motivations. Target hardening would either delay the offenders or deny them access to highly valued objects. A primary objection to this version of situational crime prevention is that success in terminating offenses in one place or against one kind of crime will merely shift the offenses elsewhere. In response, Thomas A. Repetto makes the valuable point that situational crimes have temporal, tactical, target, territorial, and functional characteristics. They are more likely to occur at certain times of the day, with repeated tactics against particular targets, with possible shifts in locations, and with changes or repetition of the type of crime. Repetto argues that patterns of criminal behavior resist the changes postulated in the displacement issue because many offenders are limited by their personality and life circumstances and because many of the offenses are opportunistic.[47]

THERAPEUTIC RATIONALE

Preventive programs following the therapeutic rationale are popular and numerous for several reasons. Their central mission is to help individuals cope with their problems, and that purpose lends a humanitarian appeal, opposing the high priority given by the crime control rationale to safeguarding of the established order, over the interests of individuals as individuals. The concern for the needs and difficulties of individuals also corrects the imbalance of the community prevention rationale which only considers institutional and group variables. Humanitarianism inclines many of us to prefer responses to the plight of troubled individuals. The therapeutic rationale meets this preference by switching attention from the deviant act to the sources of deviance within or impinging on the deviant, by conveying the optimism that there are means for intervention without excessive cost to the social order, and by linking psychology with the high prestige of medicine in undertaking prevention.

The therapeutic rationale also draws support for prevention of delinquency and crime because, under primary prevention, that particular objective can be subsumed under a wide variety of therapeutic services delivered to individuals for other purposes. Mental health, educational, and character-building organizations claim that crime and delinquency prevention is a subsidiary function to serving their usual clients. Community planners would saturate problem neighborhoods with services to underprivileged residents.

Characteristics of Therapeutic Prevention

The therapeutic rationale rests essentially on one-to-one relationships between a professional therapist and the client, such as between the psychologist and the patient or between the school counselor and the problem pupil. The intervention strategy is based on psychological theory and seeks to diagnose and treat the sources of the client's difficulties and their expression in behavior that may lead to delinquency when primary prevention is the purpose.

Treatment oriented toward the individual may be supported or replaced by group-oriented treatment, adding to the array of strategies employed. At one extreme, psychology and sociology converge in social psychology to advance the proposition that delinquency and crime are the property of groups. That is, the acquisition and persistence of misconduct are attributed to the person's affiliation with groups exhibiting criminal attitudes, beliefs, and values. Aggressive and acquisitive tendencies may be encouraged when they are rewarded by peer approval and other satisfactions sought through delinquency and criminality. The purpose of group methods is to counter that effect.

At the other extreme, group methods derive from essentially individual-oriented treatment. Group interaction among members of a client-set provides an opportunity to observe their behavior for diagnoses and to acquire other information useful to the therapist when one-to-one treatment is undertaken. One-to-one treatment is time consuming and increases personnel costs for the program. This use of groups of clients helps to reduce the impact of those disadvantages.

The applications of psychological principles vary widely, and they may be employed by specialists other than psychologists and psychiatrists. Teachers and counselors, for example, apply these principles because the school is supposed to deal with all kinds of problems that may affect predelinquents: improper use of motor vehicles, family disorganization, child abuse, sexual irregularities, drug and alcohol abuse, and mental disorder. Religious, community action, and recreational institutions also adapt psychological principles to their activities.

The psychological theories underlying the programs are too diverse for complete coverage here. In trying to summarize the recent trends in thought, David J. Murray describes psychology as eclectic. Few psychologists adhere to a single school; rather, they tend to absorb the best ideas of all schools.[48] When their interests converge on prevention, psychologists agree at a highly abstract level that something is wrong and that the explanations for this client lie somewhere in the constitution (nature) or the development (nurture) of the delinquent individual. Whatever is wrong interferes with normal personality growth and favors delinquency and crime.

From that perspective, the targets of prevention cannot be limited to legally prohibited acts but must extend even beyond status offenses to include antisocial attitudes and general lifestyle. The susceptibility of the predelinquent exceeds the span of the rather limited attention to legally defined boundaries to consider the significance of personality development to the appearance of legally prohibited behavior. This is the core of the conflict between legalistic and psychological approaches to prevention.

Psychogenic theories concentrate on the first five or ten years of life when the basic structure of personality is formed. Learning how to adjust to one's environment is a particular function of this period of life. General predispositions are established, including tendencies to engage in antisocial behavior. However, in addition to predispositions, the likelihood of delinquency of crime depends on characteristics of the sociocultural setting and on situational variables that create stress or opportunities for antisocial responses. If preventive measures directed toward individuals per se are to have real impact, Michael Rutter and Henri Giller advise, there must be "some worthwhile, and *lasting*, change in the environment."[49]

The competence of the therapists is part of the equation. They may make improvident interpretations, permitting premature airing of client grievances, encouraging client manipulation that skirts attitudinal and behavioral change, and making wooden application of diagnostic and intervention principles. The setting is also important because the therapeutic process is screened by the sociocultural environment of the given facility and must be related to the setting to which the released client returns. The management of authority is also problematic for the therapist who must find a reasonable balance between setting limits for the client and recognizing the given client's unique qualities and needs.

Brief Abridgment: Theoretical Perspectives

As already noted, a battery of theoretical perspectives has been uitilized in attempts to prevent delinquency and crime. Their wide span has stimulated recognition that the therapeutic rationale should be accommodated to a comprehensive approach. However, the following psychological variables are relevant: low self-esteem, impulsiveness, poor judgment, incompetence in relationships, ego defense, and manipulative or aggressive tendencies.

From one perspective, preventive treatment employs diagnoses and intervention which bear on the propensities of an array of personalities, exposed to crime-prone events, and which identify those personalities most likely to engage in antisocial conduct. For each of the postulated categories of delinquency or crime, offenders are believed to differ from one another in the reasons for and meaning of their misconduct. Summarizing the complexities and weaknesses of research intended to demonstrate that the personalities of delinquents differ fundamentally from those of nondelinquents, Herbert C. Quay warns that "it is time to stop considering delinquents as anything like psychologically homogeneous." He points out that "a given personality characteristic may occur more frequently or in greater magnitude in a delinquent group," but "it cannot be argued that this characteristic is pathognomic of delinquency."[50]

Psychoanalytic theory, which offers a large portion of psychology's contributions to the study of delinquency and crime, argues that they represent failures of personal controls due to faulty early training or parental neglect. Various explanations for criminal behavior have been offered: that it is the expression of neuroses, stimulated by a compulsive need for punishment, a means of substitute gratification of needs and desires, the consequence of traumatic events repressed from memory, or the expression of displaced hostility.[51]

From the second general perspective, the course of personality development is traced in order to find explanations for criminal behavior. Antisocial propensities are believed to be the products of adverse experiences, largely within the family, that distinguish the biographies of deviants from those of nondeviants.

In moral development theory, that insight is elaborated in a description of stages. At the "preconventional level," children younger than eleven years of age and many juvenile and adult offenders perceive rules and social expectations as being external to the self. At the "conventional level," average adolescents and adults understand, accept, and attempt to uphold social standards. At the "post-conventional level," a minority of adults differentiate the self from those standards and conformity is dependent on self-chosen principles.

Treatment would relate, first, the strength of resistance to the situational pressures for conformity to group standards and, second, to the individual's stage of moral reasoning. "Our review of the relevant studies on delinquency and stage of moral reasoning showed a definite monotonic pattern," William S. Jennings, Robert Kilkenny, and Lawrence Kohlberg report, "in that delinquents were consistently more likely to reason at levels lower than matched nondelinquents, and generally at a preconventional level."[52]

From the third general perspective, the explanation for antisocial behavior is sought in the situation that provoked the offense or tempted the offender. Individuals enter into crime-prone situations with predispositions that affect their responses, but the stress-provoking and tempting qualities of the situation release those predispositions favoring antisocial reaction. As Marguerite Q. Warren and Michael J. Hindelang point out, social learning theory holds that "socially maladaptive behavior" is the consequence of "contingencies in the person's environment that make such behavior productive for him or her." That theory contends that, as for conventional behavior, delinquency and crime are learned and repeated through exposure to rewards (reinforcements) that support the illicit or acceptable conduct. Withdrawing the reinforcing rewards may put an end to the undesirable behavior.[53]

COMMUNITY PREVENTION RATIONALE

The community rationale is based on the premise that the community has special responsibility for eliciting the collective commitment of its members to the values and norms that lend direction and purpose to the social organization.

A policy of community prevention is directed toward the release of communal forces in several respects. First, informal controls operating outside the sphere of the criminal justice system are brought into play. The implication is that the generation of member commitment in an environment of relatively direct experience is the community's fundamental contribution to the management of crime. The community, Rene König states, "is that point at which the community as a whole, as a highly complex phenomenon, is directly tangible, whereas without exception all other forms of society rapidly become abstract and are never so directly experienced as in the community."[54]

Second, a policy of community prevention bridges the formal structure of the political institutions and the more spontaneous and informal relationships outside the span of the governmental agencies, including those administering criminal justice. In its capacity to release the voluntaristic behavior of its members in support of the social order, the community exceeds the span of control held by political institutions that operate essentially to persuade or compel citizens through controls external to the personality.

Third, a policy of community prevention recognizes that the typical motivations for conformity to communal norms can be brought to support delinquency and crime prevention. A community's social solidarity is commonly believed to be the consequence of sentimental attachments of residents who have lived together over a long period of time. The appearance of highly urbanized, polycultural societies has not eliminated that source of social solidarity, but the new socioeconomic conditions have given increased importance to another source.

Exchange theory argues that social solidarity is the product of inducing individuals to accept the costs of self-initiated conformity because the social bonds thus created are beneficial to them. "Exchange" implies that a person for whom another has done a service is expected to express gratitude and return the service when the occasion arises. Services are essential to members of any contemporary society, but the members of metropolises are especially dependent on medical, educational, commercial, and other establishments for the delivery of those services.

Fourth, a policy of community prevention can take advantage of the community's service system and the calculative social psychology just described. An important premise is that only the state is in a position among the social institutions to lend direction and coordination to the massive and complex network of service delivery organizations that characterize urban societies. In building the social infrastructure necessary to meet the rising aspirations of its people, a nation can bring communal forces to the preventive efforts by extending a stake in conformity to a broader spectrum of people.

The release of communal forces in support of prevention is dependent on the kind of community that exists in the given society. To lend substance to the caution that prevention policy makers should consider the nature of community, three versions of community have been described in the literature: the unit of collective identity, the local self-sufficient unit, and the minimal unit of social organization.

Unit of Collective Identity

In the first version—the unit of collective identity—shared sentiments and beliefs derived from long-term association with one another in intimate and relatively small groups bind the residents of a particular physical location to one another in a spirit of moral consensus. The course of this version is suggested by our impressions of a strong kinship or family group. This version may be called the "unit of collective identity" because of its emphasis on the moral cohesion generated by the sharing of a way of life in the course of long-term association within an intimate and personally vital sociocultural universe.

The community has a geographic dimension, first, in that there are physical boundaries that separate one's "own people" and the "strangers" who are not "us," and, second, in that the natural resources of that locality are primary in meeting the basic needs of the residents. The community has a social-psychological dimension in that the sense of a common fate is cultivated by the residents sharing common experiences and social heritage. Rule-breakers are unusual and are apt to be brought into line by the threat of the withdrawal of fellowship and other benefits of group membership that are of great personal value.

Today the moral altruism assumed by the unit of collective identity is less strong in urbanized societies such as that of the United States. Since that version of community can be viewed as a vanishing phenomenon, why should we consider it? First, it may persist in some areas as a potential resource for community-oriented policy. Prevention programs may be able to establish relationships with local leaders and institutions that would envelop potential offenders in the local social-psychological milieu of commonly accepted standards of conduct and fellowship. When the normative milieu is consistent with the objectives of prevention, threats of withdrawing highly valued fellowship would make the unit of collective identity an impressive ally. Second, the unit of collective identity focuses attention on the ultimate purpose of prevention, namely, to make a wide spectrum of persons subject in the long run to the influences of conventional and regular community life. The interest in community reflects the premise that, by reducing the isolation of bureaucracies from ordinary community life, it is possible to enlist the personal conscience of potential criminals against future criminality.

Local Self-Sufficient Unit

The second version of community emphasizes the organization of human beings in cooperative relationships with one another so that collectively they are able to obtain the necessities for human life. These necessities include food, clothing, shelter, protection from famine and disease, preparation of the young for adult activities, the imparting of religious belief, security against criminals, the satisfactions of companionship, and so on. Unlike the emphasis on the social-psychological dimension of the community as a unit of collective identity, the emphasis here is on the regularized satisfaction of those basic needs through the delivery of social services. That perspective is fundamental to the rest of this discussion.

The second version of community is called the local self-sufficient unit because the given locality is believed to be capable of providing the essentials of life with only secondary reliance on resources from outside its boundaries. The local residents are dependent on one another for the satisfactions each individual seeks.

What motivates conformity to the social rules that generate the social order of the local community? The moral commitment that results when the residents feel a common identity is not the central factor; instead, the benefits that come from the satisfactions through service delivery are supposed to give the resident a stake in conformity. Membership in the community is crucial to the satisfactions because the private purposes of each member can be served only if the cooperation of other members can be obtained. The social order of the local self-sufficient community rests on the feelings of the collectivity of individuals that they have this stake in conformity.

This calculative psychology blossoms in the community as the minimal unit of social organization (discussed below). It reflects a selective participation in community life by residents as captured by Morris Janowicz's conception of the "community of limited liability."

The individual, responding to general cultural norms, is likely to demand more from his community than he will invest. But more significantly, his relation to the community is such—his investment is such—that when the community fails to serve his needs, he will withdraw. . . . The point of withdrawal may vary from community to community, from class to class, from ethnic group to ethnic group; but, for each individual, there is a point at which he cuts his losses. Seldom is the investment so great that the individual is permanently committed to a community that cannot cater to his needs.[55]

The geographical dimension for the local self-sufficient unit involves the capacity of that bounded locality to offer the raw materials for economic consumption and the range of organized relationships that produce the essential goods and services. The significance of the local self-sufficient unit for our purposes lies in the combination of restricted physical space, the capacity of that locality to deliver services essential to its residents, and thereby the cultivation of the individuals' stake in conformity in a calculative social psychology. The conception of the local self-sufficient unit opens the way for prevention agencies to become one of the local political institutions that hold the loyalty of the residents through that triple combination. Nevertheless, this version of community also has decreasing relevance because the local community is being eroded by the increasing national character of the economic system and the ascendancy of national sociopolitico structures. The local community is losing its capacity to manage the destinies of its residents.

Minimal Unit of Social Organization

Under the conditions of urbanized societies, the parental family has become progressively incapable of meeting all the necessities of its members, especially in light of the expanded range of wants. Larger than the family but smaller than the society, the village, small town, or urban neighborhood have been defined as a minimal unit of social organization capable of supplying the necessities.[56] They are the building blocks of a national society and serve as conduits for filtering down the resources offered by the national social structure. Those resources supplement those which the local community can provide.

The community as the minimal unit of social organization stands intermediate between the intimate groups—such as the family—and the broader macro system of the nation-state. The intermediary function of the local neighborhood or village is the unique feature of the concept of the community as a minimal unit of social organization. The function involves the delivery of services that generate the calculative conformity discussed above, but here there is not the insistence that the local community be capable on its own to supply the wants of its residents. Instead, its intermediary function is basic in maintaining connections of the local community with the macrosystem from which flow resources for meeting residents' needs by supplementing local resources.

The intermediary function also implies an emphasis on the social organization of the community and of the macrosystem of the nation-state. The previous two conceptions of the community focused on the relationships among residents that tied them to one another in communal bonds. The community as a minimal unit of social organization instead concentrates on the integration of the private and public institutions into a collective whole dedicated to meeting the residents' needs. Together the specialized agencies constitute a coordinated service delivery system.

The social psychology of calculative conformity is basic to the community as a minimal unit of social organization and its greater relevance to the urban situation. The underlying difficulty for the concept of the community as a unit of collective identity is its loss of authority for gaining the obedience of residents. According to Raymond Plant, the authority of traditional communities was unitary and pervasive, governing the whole life of the society. The existence of a common set of rules did not require the consent of the individual. The traditional norms permeated the entire fabric of life. In an urban society, there are many communities with which an individual may affiliate. Authority is neither unitary nor pervasive. The consent of the individual becomes crucial to obtaining authority, Plant says, because "a man may, on the whole, *choose* to join a functional community or not to do so just because its sphere of influence and activity is so much more restricted."[57]

A useful distinction is that between the horizontal and vertical axes of the local community as a minimal unit of social organization.[58] The horizontal axis is that of the relationships among the local institutions. It can hold the loyalty of the local residents because the delivery of services is personalized. If the local agencies have a reputation for being responsive and accessible to their clientele, the horizontal axis can cultivate a commitment to the local social order generated by the benefits accruing to members through the delivery of services. The vertical axis extends out from the local community through the layers of social structure that constitute the society as a whole. A metropolis is composed of all the neighborhoods within its boundaries. A province is made up of all its cities, villages, and rural areas. The nation-state includes all the provinces. Here we see the local community as the minimal unit of social organization; together the communities are the building blocks for the larger social entities and constitute settings for coordinated prevention programs.

"WHO" CARRIES OUT PREVENTION?

Several authors were asked to answer this question by analyzing the respective purposes and activities of the police, courts, social service agencies, and schools. The significance of their activities lies in the contributions of the agencies to the social organization of the community. Playing a part in prevention is secondary to the primary functions of each agency to that general end, but, as parts of the community's organization, the agencies have been given prominent roles in prevention.

The police, courts, social service agencies, and schools have been singled out for special attention because they have relationships with large categories of people—here broadly considered as their "clients"—that loom large in public conceptions of the "who" of offenders and potential offenders. They are also seen to be another version of "who"—the administrators and workers of those agencies with special opportunities to undertake prevention in their work with the first version of "who."

As outlined in our discussion of the community prevention rationale, communal forces are regarded as important resources for persuading individuals to avoid involvement in delinquency and crime and for mobilizing the community, as a minimal unit of social organization to that end. As elements of the community's organization, the police, courts, social service agencies, and schools will be considered in the respective chapters of this handbook.

Their Place in the Institutional Network

Succinctly stated, a social institution is composed of a set of interrelated culturally defined behavior patterns whereby particular functions for citizens are served through social collaboration. The concept of social institution focuses on the normative dimension of the organization of collaborative activities. The emphasis is on the cluster of norms that lend order to meeting particular needs; religious institutions specialize in the supernatural environment, schools in the socialization of the rising generation and the dissemination of knowledge and skills, and economic institutions (factories, banks, and stores, for example) in the production and distribution of material goods. These are illustrations of institutions because their respective activities are carried out within normative systems. The social institutions are relevant to the social dimension because, by affording guidelines for the individuals and groups carrying out the respective activities, the institutions lend order to efforts to achieve the particular purposes (functions) to which each is dedicated.

The police, courts, social service agencies, and schools are social institutions in that they draw on the normative subsystems in guiding the behaviors of clients and personnel, and serve the ultimate mission of all social institutions. How those agencies fit into the total preventive effort depends on their respective functions and the relationship of their functions to the general rationales for preventive work.

The Police and Prevention

The crime control rationale is particularly congenial to the police and their functions as the first line of defense against active criminality. However, increasing interest in police-community relations has brought greater recognition of their service functions and the importance of planning of which the environmental design is a component. In those respects, the community prevention rationale contributes by orienting police prevention activities toward cultivating greater public participation in law enforcement.

The identification of law enforcement prevention can be traced back at least to the establishment of the Metropolitan Police of London in 1829. The prototype of contemporary police administration firmly embodied the emphasis on prevention, as is seen in several statements by Sir Robert Peel who as Home Secretary was instrumental in creating the "new police":

It should be understood at the onset, that the principal object to be attained is the "Prevention of Crime." To this great end every effort of the Police is to be directed. The security of person and property, the preservation of the public tranquility, and all the other objects of a Police Establishment, will thus be better effected than by the detection and punishment of the offender, after he has succeeded in committing the crime. ... The absence of crime will be considered the best proof of the complete efficiency of the Police.[59]

Subsequently, the first priority in police functions has not been in accord with Peel's dictum. Police work continues to be mostly reactive in response to criminal acts; that emphasis is consistent with substantial public demand for protection from active criminality. Crime control ideology tends to be favored in police administration, and that perspective encourages the social-psychological isolation of the police from the rest of the community's social structure. Because collaboration with other community institutions is a prerequisite to effective participation in a comprehensive preventive program, the thrust of the crime control perspective and the understandable reactive nature of police work opposes a firm commitment to prevention in the broader sense.

Courts and Prevention

The courts also tend toward the crime control rationale, but secondary prevention and the delivery of social services have received support, especially for juvenile courts, through diversion, diagnosis of defendants, and use of alternatives to traditional criminal sanctions. Those court activities draw on the therapeutic rationale, but the community rationale also has implications because of the court's strategic position in mobilizing the resources of social service agencies.

The crime control rationale is particularly relevant to the courts because they are charged with the enforcement of legal norms. Intermediary between the police and correctional agencies in the criminal justice system, the courts' normative enforcement functions involve them in making the crucial decisions on the guilt of the accused and what should be done with convicted defendants. However, the normative enforcement function also involves them in monitoring the legality of their decisions and those of the police in accord with constitutional protections and procedural rules. Therein lie the possibilities of the conflict between due process and the crime control rationale.

In her chapter in this book, Nancy Travis Wolfe uses the term "social role of courts" to refer to an alternative to the crime control rationale. The relevance of the therapeutic and community prevention rationales to courts is grounded in diversion as a vehicle of secondary and tertiary prevention. Thus, the courts would be involved in the difficulties of coordinating the complex of social service agencies in a coordinated attack on delinquency and crime because the courts occupy a strategic position for diverting accused and adjudicated offenders from further criminal justice processing.

The juvenile court has been especially identified with the social role of the courts and the conflict between due process and the court operations. Humanitarian concern fueled a drive to move beyond a strict definition of delinquency to include neglected and dependent children within the ambit of governmental control in keeping with the principle that signs of delinquency justified court intervention. Those primitive interpretations of the therapeutic rationale and their justifications for interventions oriented to predelinquency were challenged by the *Gault* and other decisions of the Supreme Court. The arbitrary but benevolent authority of the "father knows best" philosophy of earlier juvenile court judges was undermined by the insistence that due process be observed.

Social Service Agencies and Prevention

The calculative social psychology, attributed above to the contemporary community subject to the conditions of urban life, has been presented as being particularly dependent on authentic and responsive delivery of social services. In that respect, social service agencies follow the community prevention rationale, which suggests the importance of welding the diverse agencies into an integrated system coping with sources of deviance in primary and secondary prevention. Since the helping professions are needed for many of the services, however, the therapeutic rationale is also prominent.

Recent decades have witnessed increased expectations about what society should deliver in the areas of economic opportunity, race relations, medicine, mental health, education, and criminal justice. The cities have suffered from internal diseconomies, bringing on what is sometimes described as an urban crisis. The deterioration of inner cities, signs of urban disorder, and the inefficiencies of service delivery stand in contrast with rising expectations.

To some extent, the criminal justice agencies have been pressed to fill a vacuum of community services not filled by other agencies. A major share of police work is in services: searches for missing persons, the restoration of children to their families, the recovery of dead bodies, the administration of first aid to sick and injured persons, the management of mental health crises, and the handling of such emergencies as fires, floods, tornadoes, earthquakes, and industrial disasters. Juvenile courts are involved in social work cases. Jails and prisons are dumping grounds for various human problems. This vacuum is greatest for lower status groups, and those services that are available are often located in offices remote from where the underprivileged live. To be a welfare client is to be exposed to the mark of failure in a society that values self-reliance and to face a maze of rules for eligibility that breed impersonal management for the sake of the agency's own interests.

Inherent in the relative inadequacies of service delivery to the lower status groups, Robert B. Coates states in his chapter on social services in this book, is the policy question: Is government responsible for providing some modicum of social service, and, if so, for whom? Assuming the validity of our argument that authentic delivery of social services gives the underprivileged a personal stake in conformity, a negative answer undercuts a key set of strategies for primary and secondary prevention. If the answer is positive, there remains the question: Who should receive those services? Stigmatization of convicted offenders opposes full-fledged services in the sense of tertiary prevention. The question implies that those offenders most likely to be assessed as proper candidates for secondary prevention will not necessarily be accepted as clients by service agencies.

Those obstacles to effective prevention do not refute the potential of social services; rather the obstacles illustrate that the realization of that potential requires confrontation of the faults in the delivery of social services when compared with the claims and hopes for serving all Americans. To that end, new strategies for reaching groups that do not usually receive services and for reorganizing the relationships among agencies have been attempted. In both senses, Coates' chapter emphasizes the community prevention rationale in discussing the means of effecting greater citizen involvement in the delivery of services.

Schools and Prevention

Urbanization has produced diverse populations concentrated in relatively compact geographical space. The social, psychological, and political implications of the effects spreading out to the American society as a whole have raised a major dilemma: How can the individuals be persuaded to feel a responsibility to the overall social organization on which they are dependent but from which they are psychologically different? The schools have been assigned major functions to provide answers and thereby have been pressed to engage in the prevention of delinquency and crime.

The schools are expected to cultivate common beliefs and attitudes among graduates coming from many subcultures and stations in life. Ideally, they are to pass on various kinds of knowledge and develop skills essential to the performance of adult roles in keeping with the smooth operation of intricate social machinery. They are to serve as a primary vehicle for socializing the young, thereby serving as a surrogate parent in cases where there is little faith that the family can produce responsible and well-adjusted personalities.

In those respects, the school is a central vehicle for primary prevention because virtually every individual attends educational institutions in the early years of life when personal traits are developed. The school may observe signs of predelinquency. Also for secondary prevention, the school may grant the teacher justification to intervene in the lives of pupils and other family members without suggestions of crime control intentions and the implications of stigmatization associated with criminal justice processing. Tertiary prevention is only a minor theme, but even then, educational institutions hold out the possibility of reintegrating convicted offenders into the community.

The relevance of education to prevention must be placed within the context of the arbitrary identification of the school as a problem solver through neutral dispensing of cultural orientation, information, and knowledge. Teachers are subject to the power-constellation and conditions of the community at large, whereas the educational functions are subject to the social issues found in the community. Forces external to the school must support the efforts of educators to be agents of the fundamental changes that would reduce the likelihood of delinquent and criminal behavior. Within the educational institutions themselves, there are the problems of misdirected curriculums, standardized and inflexible instruction, unresponsive bureaucratic administration, and discrepancies between claims and accomplishments in classrooms.

THE "WHERE": VICTIMS CONFRONT OFFENDERS

As a social institution, the school has a major role in the prevention of crime and delinquency. At the same time it also provides a site where delinquency can and does occur. This example illustrates the interrelationship between "who" initiates preventive measures for their own protection and "who" are the actual and incipient offenders that are the targets for prevention. Furthermore, the relationships between those two "who" groups are most likely to occur in certain physical-sociological locations.

The locations are physical in the spatial sense of occurrences within a home, commercial establishment, or what we may call a "public facility" or outside in what is obscurely called the "street." More significantly, the locations have special meanings drawn from normative expectations about the relationships occurring in the given sector of physical space. That sociological dimension colors the kinds of criminal incidents that are likely to occur, the fears that are aroused, the images of the potential offenders stimulating defensive acts, and the form of those actions. The last-named dimension places the "where" within the context of the social institution wherein the confrontation occurs. Here, too, the "who" and the "where" overlap.

The "where" of victim-offender confrontation will be the "streets," the home and family, and the industrial and business settings of public facilities in terms of those offenses widely accepted as "genuine crime." The emphasis is on the misconduct of individuals, but even here the institutional settings lend uniqueness to the "where" of the confrontation.

Crime on the Streets

The victimization of person and property in the open spaces of the streets and parks is particularly fear-provoking because of the possibilities of unanticipated attack by "alien strangers." The attacks violate the expectation that others act in good faith—a faith that is fundamental to regularized relationships on which satisfying participation in community affairs is founded. Crimes in public space, therefore, merit special concern, but "crime on the streets" also stirs particular moral indignation and hot debate.

It appears that the extent of criminality in previous ages has been underestimated. Changes in public tolerance of deviance, the weakened capacities of informal controls to forestall delinquency and crime, and changes in the public willingness to report offenses to the policy—all tend to obscure crime waves. Victimization surveys have documented the significantly larger body of "hidden crime" (not reported to the police) that is not reflected in official crime statistics. Within the context of hidden crime, official crime rates may increase without necessarily demonstrating the greater incidence of actual criminality.

Robbery is a general term that includes the use of firearms, other weapons, or strong-arm tactics, and it can occur in several settings: commercial enterprises, residences, or in open spaces. Our concern here is with open spaces where firearms and other weapons may be used, but "mugging" adds the use of strong-arm tactics to obtain money or other valuables. Frederick McClintock and Evelyn Gibson tell us that the sudden attacks in the open on the ordinary passerby create a feeling of insecurity disproportionate to the number of muggings that actually take place.[60]

As a code word, "crime on the streets" evokes emotional judgments of individuals about their personal safety. These judgments become raw materials for political issues in a demand for the rapid-fire solutions promised by the crime control rationale. The Omnibus Crime Control and Safe Streets Act of 1968, administered by the Law Enforcement Assistance Administration, constituted the first serious attempt to make the streets of local communitis safe for all constituencies. Thomas Cronin, Tania Cronin, and Michael Milakovich have traced the politicization of this campaign issue, the complex legislative history of the act, its administrative history of contradictory anticrime policies in spite of efforts to draw on objective expertise, the failure to deal with value conflicts inherent in conceptions of the causes of crime and of what should be done to curb it, and the persistence of the crime problem after massive investment of federal funds followed by the withdrawal of national monies. What went wrong? These authors suggest that the long-term resolution of cultural conflicts, the overcoming of structural constraints, and the delineation of criminal justice policy are essential. More specifically, they suggest the need for the clear setting of goals, intelligent leadership, strengthened planning, and effective program evaluation.[61]

The organized responses to fears of criminal violence fall greatest on the police departments and prisons where the implications of the crime control rationale become everyday realities in direct confrontations of violence with violence on the streets or in cell blocks. "Given the presumption of danger that exists for the police and in prisons," Hans Toch says, "these organizations have a problem with *the management of fear*. Staff must deal with their fears of dangerous clients, clients with fears of all-powerful staff, and some clients with fear of other clients.'' The control of violence and counterviolence raises crucial questions, reflecting on society generally, of conduct in those agencies, the abuse of legal and physical power of staffs, the negative insulation of staffs from public visibility, and the undermining of public confidence in the criminal justice system.[62]

In his chapter in this book, ''Crime on the Streets,'' John Conrad limits his consideration of primary prevention to police work according to the crime control rationale. Thus, he critiques the efficiency of American police in maintaining deterrence as public policy. Although he finds that experiments with departmental organization and technology have merit, Conrad recommends that Americans can learn some valuable lessons from the close ties that exist between the police and the community in Japan. He addresses the issue of secondary prevention by assessing the validity and reliability of the prediction methodologies for selecting out potentially violent criminals and recidivists as a prelude to selective incapacitation as a preventive strategy. His discussion is relevant to the crime control rationale and adds another dimension to the presentation above of the therapeutic rationale. He cautions that the consequences of the policy of incapacitation deserve attention. For tertiary prevention in the realm of corrections, Conrad makes a case for intensive probation supervision as a facet of the community prevention rationale. This would lend some viability to a penal system that is suffering from the effects of its grounding in the crime control rationale.

Home and Family

As the physical setting for family life, the dwelling has a part to play in the social interactions among family members and in the family's relationships with the world outside. Within the home many of the most intimate social experiences occur, the children become familiar with their culture, their personalities are initially formed, available economic means are distributed, the life chances of its members are fundamentally affected, and the emotional security of belonging to a personally significant group is supplied. The heavy reliance of primary prevention on the family lends importance to its locale. The availability of resources, the family role relationships, and the adaptability of its members shape responses to those family crises that occur within the home. The responses are relevant to the possibility of predelinquency or actual law-violating behaviors that call for secondary prevention and possibly tertiary prevention.

The qualities associated with life within the home have been sought in the therapeutic and community approaches to delinquency and crime prevention. In treatment programs and facilities, the client is more likely to move toward greater conformity to preferred expectations when the therapist operates within a setting that resembles that of a home or does include the client's home as a setting for therapy, including all family members.

On the other hand, the home and family are frequently blamed for undesirable conduct when they fail to achieve their institutionalized functions and to cope appropriately with the crises of its members. The housing of the poor raises problems of space, physical conditions, and location within the community at large. In urban slums, a considerable portion of family life is conducted outside the dwelling unit because of the closeness and drabness of the quarters. Children on the streets, through exposure to antisocial influences, is a common explanation for delinquency. It is doubtful whether bad housing is in itself a direct cause for distorted personality and antisocial behavior, but living in decayed neighborhoods does extract a price in loss of self-esteem, alienation, and cynicism. Insufficient income is closely intertwined in the problems of substandard housing, inadequate meeting of member needs, and other lacks of prerequisites for decent living.

Home burglary raises fears about violent confrontations with criminal-strangers; the unwelcome invasion of private space mingles with loss of property in the special abhorrence which these crimes arouse. Rape and homicide also arouse high moral indignation, supremely violating the expectations of privacy within one's home. Those considerations lend priority to target-hardening and environmental design measures for defense of the home.

Since the family and home are the focus of particular concern as the scene of both crime and its prevention, there is a greater chance that exaggerated claims will be made about the family's contributions to delinquency. In their chapter, "The Preventive Effects of the Family on Delinquency," Joseph H. Rankin and L. Edward Wells set out to evaluate a number of widely accepted assumptions by drawing on a body of research.

That research indicates, first, that upsetting the structure of family relationships (usually examined in terms of divorce) has a relatively minor effect as a factor in delinquency. That effect is so intertwined with other factors, which are difficult to control in careful investigations, that the strains produced by the broken home per se have marginal influence.

Second, how may family-based prevention be grounded in meaningful theoretical principles? Rankin and Wells analyze four theoretical approaches as foundations for intervention: socialization, social control, family crises, and social structure. Their critique demonstrates that underlying factors complicate preventive efforts in ways unrecognized by simplistic attacks on the family as an autonomous entity. Instead, they apply the social structure approach to argue that therapeutic strategies must be combined with recognition of the effects of social changes on the family unit. Thus, both the treatment and community prevention rationales are found to be relevant.

Third, Rankin and Wells outline the tasks of diagnosis and intervention, and reveal that assessment of the family's role in increasing the risk of delinquency must precede intervention. The variables that receive most attention will be determined by which of the four theoretical approaches is followed after diagnosis. The nature of intervention may be residential, nonresidential, or family support services. Each form of intervention has its particular setting, fundamental premises, and relationships between agency staff and clients.

Fourth, Rankin and Wells report that family-based prevention, as is true of the field of prevention in general, suffers from incomplete knowledge about the causes of delinquency and a paucity of reliable evaluation of the various strategies. Meanwhile, calling for specificity in that sphere of prevention, Rankin and Wells consider individualized treatment to be more promising than "shotgun approaches that treat all youth alike."

Business and Industry

As settings for crime and its prevention, business and industries take us into the realm of privately owned space, but, unlike the privacy of the home, the use of this space involves a greater number of persons and their greater heterogeneity of characteristics. Paradoxically, shopping centers, office complexes, and other business enterprises benefit from the patronage of clients and yet are vulnerable to the criminogenic effects of high-volume traffic. Industrial plants must distinguish crime-motivated individuals from outside the ranks of employees who would defraud or otherwise victimize the enterprise. Retail establishments must cope with shoplifters, and all business and industrial organizations face the losses through employee theft.

The settings of business and industry have the benefits of private space in undertaking prevention. "Public space may be distinguished from private space," Lyn H. Lofland says, "in that access to the latter may be *legally* restricted."[63] Clifford D. Shearing and Philip C. Stenning note that private enterprises enjoy the privileges of private property owners that permit them to control access to, use of, and conduct on their property. The growth of large-scale enterprises and their increased recognition of crime problems peculiar to their settings have produced unprecedented development of private security.[64]

The criminal victimization of businesses and industries seeps into the sphere of crime on the streets. Robbery combines elements of violence and an income-producing activity. When directed at private enterprises, it threatens both the personal security and property of victims, although the robber may only intend to intimidate the victim.

As is true for the home, the burglar is a threat to business and industrial enterprises. Retail establishments have the problem of distinguishing thieves from regular patrons, balancing security measures against the possibility of discouraging patronage, and encouraging purchases by open display of products and yet denying opportunities for theft.

The magnitude of employee theft has caused William W. McCullough to call it "America's fastest growing crime." It is encouraged by the failures of businesses to recognize it as a management problem and to see their need for effective security systems.[65] As for all occupational offenses, the perpetration and prevention of employee theft are shaped by the particular conditions of a given business or industrial setting.

Public Facilities

Libraries, museums, public transit, and parks are part of the twentieth century's unprecedented distribution of the fruits of an advanced civilization.[66] Libraries and museums bring culture, once enjoyed by only a narrow elite, to people generally. Public parks are products of a similar movement in recreation. Public transit permits access to the commercial and cultural life of metropolises to a wide spectrum of riders.

Public facilities share with privately owned facilities the paradox of benefiting from great patronage and yet thereby becoming vulnerable to the criminogenic effects of high-volume traffic. Because public facilities are publicly owned, they are committed to the principle of open access which denies them the privileges of private ownership to control access to, use of, and conduct on private property. Furthermore, a commitment to cultural democracy inhibits museums, libraries, and public parks from restricting access to heterogeneous patronage.

Unable to carefully monitor the members of a heterogeneous and large patronage, public facilities have increasingly suffered the criminogenic effects of the polyglot metropolis that shelters the criminal from detection, offers opportunities for criminal acts, and weakens inhibitions against taking advantage of opportunities. In their chapter on public facilities, Sidney E. Matthews and Elmer Johnson document the kinds of delinquency and crimes that are unique to public facilities and the implications for prevention within those peculiar settings.

THE PROMISE AND ACCOMPLISHMENT OF PREVENTION

Is prevention the ultimate answer to delinquency and crime? While its advocates seek to convince us that "yes" is the obvious reply, an examination of the many facets of prevention demonstrates that the exploitation of its promise is far from simple.

Potentialities and Limitations

Prevention promises to be the ultimate answer to delinquency and crime because, if successful, it would circumvent the painstaking efforts to root out criminals and to subject them to official processing by the police, courts, and correctional agencies. Instead of dealing with actual delinquents as symptoms of personal or social inadequacies, a coordinated attack on the basic sources of the inadequacies would be the equivalent of draining the swamps to be rid of malaria. The flow of criminals into the criminal justice agencies would be stemmed. In lieu of the negative consequences of punishment for deterrence, prevention programs could be oriented toward meeting the unfulfilled needs of "predelinquents" and casual offenders along psychological, social, and economic dimensions. Psychological intervention, expanded service delivery, cultivation of communal forces for the sake of informal controls, and reform of malfunctioning social institutions would be alternative means of convincing targets for prevention programs that they have a stake in conformity.

These several justifications imply that the inclusion of potential delinquents and criminals within the benefits of regular community life will save much of the fiscal costs of the criminal justice system.[67] A hidden assumption is that the schools, employing institutions, health and mental health facilities, and other elements of the community's social organization are already in place and are prepared to receive clients for primary and secondary prevention. The validity of the assumption is doubtful in light of serious questioning that the needs of regular clients are being met, that predelinquents and casual offenders will be accepted as regular clients, and that predelinquents and potential criminals can be identified in advance. Furthermore, it should be recognized that the criminal justice system already delivers social services, whether manifest or latent, to fill some of the vacuum left by inadequacies of community institutions.

The ultimate superiority of prevention over the usual reactive tactics of the criminal justice agencies also rests on the premise that the latent personal and social sources of criminality are touched. The tactics of usual law enforcement are seen to be futile efforts to force the genie of criminality back into the bottle. The ultimate objective of law enforcement is maximum law observance, but attainment of that purpose is beyond the grasp of justice agencies alone. They do not control the process whereby particular forms of misconduct are made subject to criminal sanctions, a substantial portion of that criminalized deviance escapes official reactions, and the agencies can manage only a portion of those persons legally defined as proper subjects for their attention. Prevention seeps beyond the borders of the formal administration of criminal law to engage the spontaneity of human motivations and to enlist the communal forces. However, the strategies employing the therapeutic and community prevention rationales have their own difficulties in circumventing their own bureaucratic tendencies to capture that spontaneity and those communal forces.

According to Denis Szabo, the prevention of crime and delinquency offers the best means of incorporating criminal policy in a social policy that is based on respect for individual rights and that is dedicated to fulfilling basic economic, social, and health requirements.[68] That comment points to a fundamental advantage of prevention: it overcomes the counterproductive effects of a heavy reliance on criminal sanctions to cope with a range of personal and social problems unresponsive to crime control measures. However, questions still remain: How can the cultural conflicts, already opposing the clarity of social policy and expressed in opposing purposes set for the criminal justice apparatus, be resolved? What can be done about meeting the violations of individual rights already attributed to social programs, including those oriented directly toward prevention? In a society with fragmented governmental authority as in the United States, how is policy to be framed for coordinated and integrated administration? In short, the means of carrying out Szabo's worthy recommendation are highly problematic.

The widespread popularity of prevention promises to expand the scope of anticrime efforts. As this chapter has demonstrated, prevention strategies range from long-term incarceration and pretrial diversion through automobile antitheft devices and fines to remedial reading instruction, recreation, and psychological intervention. Ideologically, prevention is supported by both conservatives who see citizens protected from "the ravages of human predation" and by radicals who seek a world of voluntary compliance without the intervention of criminal justice agencies.[69]

Prerequisites: Planning and Theoretical Foundations

The range of ideologies and constituencies mobilized in the advocacy of prevention helps explain the piecemeal development of programs, their expression of prevailing interests of agencies and supporting constituencies, and the permeation of those activities by political controversies. Ideological conflicts have undermined programs when delinquency and crime have been indiscriminately equated with unmitigated evil and full-fledged conformity with good. The ultimate goals of programmed intervention have been obscured by fundamental disagreement on what the potential and actual offenders are to become. In those respects, the nature of programs is shaped by the particular assumptions made about what delinquency and crime are, the nature of the threat to be countered, and how prevention is to be accomplished.

Particularism is a deficiency of criminology in its quest for an integrated body of theory. Because the field of prevention is more committed to applications than to theory building, its failures in obtaining sound theoretical foundations should be assessed against the performance of criminology in satisfying its clear mandate to explain criminality coherently and systematically. A multidisciplinary model appears to be most consistent with the vast scope of criminological subject matter and its intersection with the special interests of virtually every established branch of science. The translation of general principles into effective policies and practices is problematic for criminology in general. As one of the branches devoted to application of those theories, prevention inherits those formidable difficulties. The ultimate consequence for prevention has been summarized by Michael Rutter and Henri Giller: "We delude ourselves if we think that we have already obtained the answers. Regrettably, we have not."[70]

"The prevention and treatment of delinquency is still in its prescientific phase," Martin Gold concludes. "That is, it is guided by beliefs that are more nearly articles of faith than cogent theories, and observations on its effects more by wish than by fact." He considers this field to be prescientific because of the confusion about what delinquency is and how it should be managed, ignorance about causes of delinquency, and ambivalence in simultaneously following the goal of humane treatment and the goal of retribution. Nevertheless, he sees signs that more scientific thought and rational practice are being applied to determine the real extent of delinquency and the evaluation of outcomes. He notes the increasing employment of experimental programs in a systematic fashion, greater demands for accountability in relating explicit goals to program funding, and a trend toward more sophisticated analyses of delinquency.[71]

That tentative movement toward rationality in prevention policy and practice includes planning as a cohort of scientific methods applied to the study of community problems and the framing of strategies for overcoming them. "The best argument for planning," William Clifford says, "is consideration of the intellectual poverty of the alternative. The alternative to planning for crime prevention is the continuance of the disorganized, uncoordinated, ad hoc, and fundamentally crude anticipations of future requirements."[72]

The planning process for prevention has been summarized as a matter of problem identification, resource analysis, and strategy building intended to lower rates of delinquency and crime.[73] Problem identification implies that impartial and trained observers are able to determine the precise sources of criminality, can objectively and reliably distinguish why some persons become criminals and others do not, and can obtain the agreement of influential persons with the planners' interpretations of the proper ways of reducing chances that persons will become criminals. In resource analysis, the experts are supposed to be able to inventory accurately and in advance what funds, qualified personnel, and active participation can reasonably be expected in order to implement prevention. Since unlimited resources cannot be anticipated, the experts must set priorities among alternative lines of action. Strategy building refers to the successful formulation of rational techniques for accomplishing the specified purposes.

Considering the difficulties of theory building and the translation of general principles into practical applications, we can expect that prevention planning will fall short of ideals framed in abstraction. Wilson doubts that the knowledge of social science is sufficiently comprehensive to guide policy makers as to how to control crime under particular circumstances of time, place, personality, and conditions.[74]

DOES PREVENTION WORK?

In spite of their willingness to engage in the rhetoric of prevention, Americans are slow to accept preventive measures seriously, to undertake the long-term tasks of planning, and to realize the faults of simple, direct methods. "We are not a preventive society," Stuart Palmer asserts. "We tend to take action after a problem has assumed large-scale proportions."[75]

As is true of all forms of intervention in personal and social problems, the prevention of delinquency and crime faces the fundamental question: To what extent can human ingenuity deliberately frame a set of strategies that will convert conviction that something should and can be done into tangible accomplishments that reduce the impact of undesirable conditions? This is the test of accountability for the investment of funds and other resources.

That test is formidable because the undesirable conditions associated with delinquency and crime are highly resistant to change. Conditions favorable to criminality are embedded in the regularized operations of the society and do not succumb easily to social reform strategies. Psychological intervention confronts patterns of personality development that are difficult to disengage. Furthermore, the great diversity of prevention activities presents such a bewildering array of variables and competing self-interests that some observers doubt that the rationality of science can be effectively used for reliable evaluation of outcomes and may perhaps even be counterproductive.[76]

In that vein, Jim C. Hackler in his chapter, "Evaluation: How Does It Work?" deviates from the usual condemnation of prevention programs and turns his critique to the evaluation process itself. In evaluating the evaluators, he appropriately applies the constructive skepticism of science to assessing the soundness of the uses of scientific methods. He does not oppose the evaluative projects because the field of prevention is especially lacking in meeting the responsibility for accountability; rather, he sets out to expose the unrealistic claims of some of those projects.

Some time ago an observer compared the disjointed activities of the elements of the field of prevention to Indian rain dancers prancing feverishly to monotonous drumbeats in unsubstantiated faith that the forces of evil would thereby be exorcised.[77] The new interest in accountability has raised the standards against which the promise of prevention is judged. Those readers directly involved in prevention programs probably are caught in personal terms by the discrepancies between unsubstantiated faith and the apparent rejection of their programs by tight-lipped evaluators. Perhaps the discrepancies can be reconciled by a clearcut confrontation of past failure and the further development of a basic understanding of the elements of preventive activities.

NOTES

1. Sheldon Glueck and Eleanor Glueck, "Introduction—Philosophy and Principles of Crime Prevention," in Sheldon Glueck and Eleanor Glueck, eds., *Preventing Crime: A Symposium* (New York: McGraw-Hill, 1936), pp. 2, 22.

2. Richard Brotman and Frederic Suffet, "The Concept of Prevention and Its Limitations," *Annals of the American Academy of Political and Social Science* 417 (January 1975): 55–56.

3. Ibid., p. 56.

4. Paul J. Brantingham and Frederick L. Faust, "A Conceptual Model of Crime Prevention," *Crime and Delinquency* 22 (July 1976): 292.

5. Ibid., p. 292.

6. Peter P. Lejins, "The Field of Prevention," in William E. Amos and Charles E.

Wellford, eds., *Delinquency Prevention: Theory and Practice* (Englewood Cliffs, N.J.: Prentice-Hall, 1967), pp. 3–7.

7. Brantingham and Faust, "A Conceptual Model of Crime Prevention," pp. 290–291.

8. Lejins, "The Field of Prevention," p. 3.

9. Johannes Andenaes, "General Prevention Revisited: Research and Policy Implications," *Journal of Criminal Law and Criminology* 66 (September 1966): 341.

10. Lejins, "The Field of Prevention," p. 5.

11. C. H. Reeve, "Preventive Legislation in Relation to Crime," *Annals of American Academy of Political and Social Science* 3 (September 1892): 97–98.

12. Ibid., pp. 98–99.

13. Jeremy Bentham, *An Introduction to the Principles of Morals and Legislation*, eds., J. H. Burns and H. L. A. Hart (London: Athlone Press, 1970), pp. 165, 175.

14. Cesare Beccaria, *An Essay on Crimes and Punishments* (London: Printed for E. Newberry, 1785), p. 43.

15. Marcello Maestro, *Cesare Beccaria and the Origins of Penal Reform* (Philadelphia: Temple University Press, 1973), p. 26.

16. Cesare Lombroso, *Crime and Its Remedies*, trans. Henry P. Horton (Montclair, N.J.: Patterson Smith, 1968 reprint), pp. 245, 365.

17. Emile Durkheim, *The Division of Labor in Society* (Glencoe, Ill.: Free Press, 1947), p. 81.

18. LaMar T. Empey, *American Delinquency: Its Meaning and Construction*, rev. ed. (Homewood, Ill.: Dorsey Press, 1982), p. 48.

19. Joseph F. Kett, *Rites of Passage: Adolescence in America 1970 to the Present* (New York: Basic Books, 1977), pp. 111–113. For an analysis that relates the changes in child-rearing practices to historic periods in America, see Glenn Davis, *Childhood and History in America* (New York: Psychohistory Press, 1976).

20. Anthony M. Platt, *The Child Savers: The Invention of Delinquency* (Chicago: University of Chicago Press, 1969), pp. 138–139.

21. Steven Schlossman, "Studies in the History of Early 20th Century Delinquency Prevention," in Steven Schlossman, *Studies in the History of Early 20th Century Delinquency Prevention* (Santa Monica, Calif.: Rand Corporation, January 1983), pp. 1–24.

22. Stanton Wheeler, Leonard S. Cottrell, Jr., and Anne Romasco, "Juvenile Delinquency: Its Prevention and Control," in Paul Lerman, ed., *Delinquency and Social Policy* (New York: Praeger Publishers, 1970), p. 428.

23. Gayle Olson-Raymer, "The Role of the Federal Government in Juvenile Delinquency Prevention: Historical and Contemporary Perspectives," *Journal of Criminal Law and Criminology* 74 (Summer 1983): 578–600.

24. Alfred J. Kahn, "From Delinquency Treatment to Community Development," in Paul F. Lazarsfeld, William H. Sewell, and Harold L. Wilensky, eds., *The Uses of Sociology* (New York: Basic Books, 1967), pp. 477–505.

25. Dan A. Lewis, "Toward a Criminology of Everyday Life," in Dan A. Lewis, ed., *Reactions to Crime* (Beverly Hills, Calif.: Sage Publications, 1981), pp. 11–12.

26. John E. Conklin, "Dimensions of Community Response to the Crime Problem," *Social Problems* 18 (Winter 1971): 374.

27. James Q. Wilson, *Thinking About Crime* (New York: Basic Books, 1975), p. 21.

28. Wesley G. Skogan and Michael G. Maxfield, *Coping with Crime: Individual and Neighborhood Reactions* (Beverly Hills, Calif.: Sage Publications, 1981), pp. 92–96.

29. Dan A. Lewis and Michael G. Maxfield, "Fear in the Neighborhoods: An Investigation of the Impact of Crime," *Journal of Research in Crime and Delinquency* 17 (July 1980): 185–186.

30. Terry L. Baumer, "Research on Fear of Crime in the United States," *Victimology: An International Journal* 3, nos. 3 and 4 (1978): 255–258. Also see Robert A. Silverman and Leslie W. Kennedy, "Loneliness, Satisfaction and Fear of Crime: A Test of Non-Recursive Effects," *Canadian Journal of Criminology* 27 (January 1985): 2; Fay Lomax Cook and Thomas D. Cook, "Evaluating the Rhetoric of Crisis: A Case Study of Criminal Victimization of the Elderly," *Social Service Review* 50 (December 1976): 635–642.

31. Marc C. Stafford and Omer R. Galle, "Victimization Rates, Exposure to Risk, and Fear of Crime," *Criminology* 22 (May 1984): 173–185; also see Steven Balkan, "Victimization Rates, Safety and Fear of Crime," *Social Problems* 26 (February 1979): 343–358.

32. Peter P. Yin, "Fear of Crime Among the Elderly: Some Issues and Suggestions," *Social Problems* 27 (April 1980): 492–498.

33. Louise H. Kidder and Ellen S. Cohn, "Public Views of Crime and Crime Prevention," in Irene Hanson Frieze, Daniel Bar-tal, and John S. Carroll, eds., *New Approaches to Social Problems* (San Francisco: Jossey-Bass Publishers, 1979), pp. 250–264; also see Ellen S. Cohn, Louise H. Kidder, and Joan Harvey, "Crime Prevention vs. Victimization Prevention: The Psychology of Two Different Reactions," *Victimology: An International Journal* 3, nos. 3 and 4 (1978): 285–296.

34. Skogan and Maxfield, *Coping with Crime*, p. 16.

35. Ibid., pp. 198–206.

36. Ellen J. Langer, *The Psychology of Control* (Beverly Hills, Calif.: Sage Publications, 1983), pp. 178–183.

37. Skogan and Maxfield, *Coping with Crime*, pp. 207, 217, 221.

38. Ibid., pp. 238–240, 253–255.

39. *The Practice of Crime Prevention*, Vol. 1, *Understanding Crime Prevention* (Louisville, Ky.: National Crime Prevention Institute, University of Louisville, 1978), pp. 2–3.

40. Fred Heinzelmann, "Crime Prevention and the Physical Environment," in Dan A. Lewis, ed., *Reactions to Crime* (Beverly Hills, Calif.: Sage Publications, 1981), p. 96.

41. Oscar Newman, *Defensible Space: Crime Prevention Through Urban Design* (New York: Macmillan, 1972).

42. Charles A. Murray, "The Physical Environment and Community Control of Crime," in James Q. Wilson, ed., *Crime and Public Policy* (San Francisco: ICS Press, 1983), pp. 111–113.

43. R. V. G. Clarke, " 'Situational' Crime Prevention Theory and Practice," *British Journal of Criminology* 20 (April 1980): 136–147.

44. Guglielmo Gulotta, "The Offender Victim System," in Emilio C. Viano, ed., *Victims and Society* (Washington, D.C.: Visage Press, 1976), pp. 54–56.

45. David F. Luckenbill, "Criminal Homicide as a Situated Transaction," *Social Problems* 25 (December 1977): 176–186.

46. Lawrence E. Cohen, "Modeling Crime Trends: A Criminal Opportunity Perspective," *Journal of Research in Crime and Delinquency* 18 (January 1981): 140–141.

47. Thomas A. Repetto, "Crime Prevention and the Displacement Phenomenon," *Crime and Delinquency* 22 (April 1976): 166–177.

48. David J. Murray, *A History of Western Psychology* (Englewood Cliffs, N.J.: Prentice-Hall, 1983), p. 339.

49. Michael Rutter and Henri Giller, *Juvenile Delinquency: Trends and Perspective* (New York: Penguin Books, 1973), p. 326.

50. Herbert C. Quay, "Personality and Delinquency," in Herbert C. Quay, ed., *Juvenile Delinquency: Research and Theory* (Princeton, N.J.: D. Van Nostrand Co., 1965), pp. 150, 166.

51. Marguerite Q. Warren and Michael J. Hindelang, "Current Explanations of Offender Behavior," in Hans Toch, ed., *Psychology of Crime and Criminal Justice* (New York: Holt, Rinehart and Winston, 1961), pp. 172–173.

52. William S. Jennings, Robert Kilkenny, and Lawrence Kohlberg, "Moral Development Theory and Practice for Youthful and Adult Offenders," in William S. Laufer and James M. Day, eds., *Personality Theory, Moral Development, and Criminal Behavior* (Lexington, Mass.: Lexington Books, 1983), pp. 282, 347.

53. Warren and Hindelang, "Current Explanations of Offender Behavior," pp. 173–174.

54. Rene König, *The Community*, trans. Edward Fitzgerald (London: Routledge and Kegan, 1968), pp. 26–27.

55. Morris Janowicz, *The Community Press in an Urban Setting* (Chicago: University of Chicago Press, 1967), pp. 211–212.

56. This idea is drawn from Conrad Arensberg, "The Community as Object and as Sample," in Robert M. French, ed., *The Community: A Comparative Perspective* (Itasca, Ill.: F. E. Peacock, 1969), pp. 12–13.

57. Raymond Plant, *Community and Ideology: An Essay in Applied Social Psychology* (London: Routledge and Kegan Paul, 1974), p. 55.

58. The distinction is made by Roland L. Warren, "Toward a Reformulation of Community Theory," in French, *The Community*, p. 41.

59. The quotation was drawn from several sources by Phillip Thurmond Smith, *Policing Victorian London* (Westport, Conn.: Greenwood Press, 1985), p. 24.

60. Frederick H. McClintock and Evelyn Gibson, *Robbery in London* (London: Macmillan and Co., 1961), pp. 16–17; also see Michael Pratt, *Mugging as a Social Problem* (London: Routledge and Kegan Paul, 1980), pp. 92–93.

61. Thomas E. Cronin, Tania Z. Cronin, and Michael E. Milakovich, *U.S. vs. Crime in the Streets* (Bloomington: Indiana University Press, 1981).

62. Hans Toch, *Police, Prisons, and the Problem of Violence* (Rockville, Md.: Center for Studies of Crime and Delinquency, National Institute of Mental Health, 1977), pp. 6–7.

63. Lyn H. Lofland, *A World of Strangers: Order and Action in Urban Public Space* (New York: Basic Books, 1973), pp. 19–20.

64. Clifford D. Shearing and Philip C. Stenning, "Private Security: Implications for Social Control," *Social Problems* 30 (June 1983): 493–506; also see Theodore M. Becker, "The Place of Private Police in Society: An Area of Research in the Social Sciences," *Social Problems* 21, no. 3 (1974): 438–453.

65. William W. McCullough, *Sticky Fingers: A Close Look at America's Fastest-Growing Crime* (New York: AMACOM, 1981).

66. Other examples of public facilities include public hospitals, public schools, university campuses, airports, and sports or entertainment centers.

67. Evan a crude estimate of the possible savings through substitution of prevention

for criminal justice processing is a methodological nightmare, as illustrated by Thomas Higgins, "The Crime Costs of California Early Minor Offenders: Implications for Prevention," *Journal of Research in Crime and Delinquency* 14 (July 1977): 195–205. Attempting to relate several sources of essential data, Higgins calculates that the probable direct costs of managing the future crimes of 10,000 youths, already apprehended for their first offense, would be approximately $1 million.

68. Denis Szabo, *Criminology and Crime Policy* (Lexington, Mass.: Lexington Books, 1978), pp. 162–163.

69. LaMar T. Empey, "Crime Prevention: The Fugitive Utopia," in Daniel Glaser, ed., *Handbook of Criminology* (Chicago: Rand McNally, 1974), p. 1095.

70. Michael Rutter and Henri Giller, *Juvenile Delinquency: Trends and Perspectives* (New York: Penguin Books, 1983), p. 324.

71. Martin Gold, "Crime and Delinquency: Treatment and Prevention," in John B. Turner et al., eds., *Encyclopedia of Social Work*, Vol. 1 (Washington, D.C.: National Association of Social Workers, 1977), pp. 218, 220.

72. William Clifford, *Planning Crime Prevention* (Lexington, Mass.: Lexington Books, 1976), pp. 13–14.

73. *Juvenile Justice and Delinquency Prevention* (Washington, D.C.: National Advisory Committee on Criminal Justice Standards and Goals, 1976), p. 25.

74. Wilson, *Crime and Public Policy*, pp. 3–5.

75. Stuart Palmer, *The Prevention of Crime* (New York: Behavioral Publications, 1973), p. 9.

76. One observer criticizes American social scientists generally for their virtual obsession with numbers and other indices of "results" and "effectiveness" that causes them to miss the forest for the trees. He calls for research that addresses human concerns and the recognition that research can produce results that will serve only the self-interests of politicians. See David L. Bazelon, "The Hidden Politics of American Criminology," in John P. Conrad, ed., *The Evaluation of Criminal Justice: A Guide for Practical Criminologists* (Beverly Hills, Calif.: Sage Publications, 1978), pp. 5–18.

77. Edwin J. Lucas, "Crime Prevention: A Confusion in Goal," in Paul W. Tappan, ed., *Contemporary Correction* (New York: McGraw-Hill, 1951), pp. 397–398.

BIBLIOGRAPHY

Bennett, Georgette. *Unlocking America: Commercial Union's Keys to Community Crime Prevention*, vol. 2. Boston: Commercial Union Insurance Companies, 1980.

> Crime prevention is defined as involving an awareness that a crime can occur; anticipating its form, location, time, and victim; and taking some action to reduce its chances of happening. The pamphlet deals in practical terms with targets (crimes, people, and locations), a range of strategies for prevention, and the elements of program planning and implementation. Resources in the literature, audiovisual materials, and expert contacts are offered.

Boostrom, Ronald, and Joel Henderson. "Citizen Participation Models in Crime Prevention: Conflict or Cooperation Between the Professionals and the Public?" Paper delivered at annual meeting of American Society of Criminology, Denver, November 1983.

> The assumptions of the community hypothesis are presented as background for a discussion of three models: mobilizing the community to improve social service

delivery, to increase the effectiveness of individual security, or through environmental design. The implications for police involvement in community crime prevention are considered.

Clarke, Ronald, and Tim Hope, eds. *Coping with Burglary: Research Perspectives on Policy*. Boston: Kluwer-Nyhoff Publishing, 1984.

Residential burglary and several preventive approaches are examined by Canadian and European experts.

Coffey, Alan R. *The Prevention of Crime and Delinquency*. Englewood Cliffs, N.J.: Prentice-Hall, 1975.

Summary discussions are offered on major topics: generalized explanations for crime and delinquency; citizen involvement; preventive functions of schools, social agencies, and criminal justice institutions; diversion and special problems faced by programs that would prevent, deter, and control crime.

DeWolf, L. Harold. *Crime and Justice in America: A Paradox of Conscience*. New York: Harper and Row, 1975.

A paradox of conscience, DeWolf argues, produces contradictions in public expectations applied to criminal justice systems. America A is generous, community-minded, benevolent, and humane. He hopes it holds the potential for countering the vindictive, self-righteous, harsh qualities of the treatment of convicted criminals which are derived from America B, which he describes as tight-fisted, individualistic, self-righteous, materialistic, aggressive, impatient, vindictive, and prone to violence.

Gray, B. M. "Crime Prevention Philosophy and Practice." In Timothy J. Carter, G. Howard Phillips, Joseph F. Donnermeyer, and Todd N. Wurschmidt, eds., *Rural Crime: Integrating Research and Prevention*. Totowa, N.J.: Allanheld, Osmun and Co., 1982, pp. 197–208.

A brief review of the field of prevention precedes a description of rural programs for protecting livestock, farm products, and neighbors.

Lavrakas, Paul J., and Dan A. Lewis. "The Conceptualization and Measurement of Citizens' Crime Prevention Behaviors." *Journal of Research in Crime and Delinquency* 17 (July 1980): 254–272.

Preventive efforts by individuals are usually categorized as access control/surveillance/territoriality, individual/collective behaviors, and public-minded/private-minded activities. Lavrakas and Lewis assess the categories against data from four surveys, and they recommend a different classification.

Martin, John M. "Three Approaches to Delinquency Prevention: A Critique." *Crime and Delinquency* 7 (January 1961): 16–24.

Aside from punishment, three models of delinquency prevention are discussed: all activities contributing to healthy personalities in children, coping with environmental conditions, and services provided children singly or in groups. After critiquing each mode, Martin finds that social reorganization is fundamental.

Minor, W. William. "Skyjacking Crime Control Models." *Journal of Criminal Law and Criminology* 66 (March 1975): 94–105.

The efforts to manage the seizure of passenger aircraft in flight progressed from a deterrence model to a prevention model. Minor suggests effectiveness, fiscal cost, and social costs as evaluative criteria.

2

Crime Control: Deterrence and Target Hardening

MERLYN M. BELL and MAURICE M. BELL

Simone Weil, in observing elements in children's literature, once wrote that only "imaginary evil is romantic and varied; real evil is gloomy, monstrous, barren and boring." On the other hand, "imaginary good is boring; real good is always new, marvelous, intoxicating."[1]

The same can be said of crime and crime prevention. On film and in the novel crime appears enticing and fascinating, and it certainly occupies a favored place in newspapers, magazines, and television. A totally different reality comes across when you talk to any victim of crime. What happened was not fascinating or exciting. What he or she experienced was outrage, frustration, and trauma.

Anyone working with victims of crime is confronted by conversion of outrage into criticism of the criminal justice system.[2] "Nothing happens when the bastard is caught." "I reported the burglary, but never heard anything again from the police." "I spent two days off work appearing in court as a witness, but I was never called on, and the defendant never showed up." "I quit reporting sho-plifters, and now keep a 45 revolver under my cash register." "You guys in the police department do a good job, but you can't be everywhere." "We all know who the kids are, but no one can do anything about it." "The thing that sickens me the most is just knowing they were in my house going through our things and will never get caught. We lost things that have been in the family for generations." "Until the courts start sentencing people to longer prison terms, the problem will just get worse."

These statements of victims express their expectation that something should be done *right now* to end the perceived threat of criminals and that that action should be directed against criminals rather than against some vague social condition that has provoked their criminality. The expectations seem to be best satisfied by bringing to bear forces external to individuals per se, forces that will prevent criminal activities.

The public policy dedicated to satisfying those expectations has been called the crime control rationale. This chapter presents that rationale and explores its relevance to the prevention of delinquency and crime.

CRIME CONTROL: ITS CENTRAL PREMISES

Crime control is the descendant of the nineteenth-century utilitarian philosophers. It borrows heavily from their assumption that human beings are rational creatures, capable of assessing the costs and benefits of an anticipated action and of modifying their behavior accordingly. Jeremy Bentham applied this logic to criminal behavior: "[T]he profit of the crime is the force which urges a man to delinquency: the pain of the punishment is the force employed to restrain him from it. If the first of these is the greater, the crime will be committed: if the second, the crime will not be committed."[3] When translated into public policy, crime control has emphasized actions that increase the cost or pain of criminal activity.

For some commentators, the antithesis of crime control is the rehabilitation philosophy, which has been characterized as being "soft on crime," and serious questions have been raised about its effectiveness.[4] Instead of concentrating on environmental effects, crime control focuses on the offender and, in attempting prevention, on the would-be offender. If sufficient penalties are imposed, he or she will choose not to commit the crime. Any interest in social conditions is restricted narrowly to those that increase the risk, or decrease the opportunity, for crime.

Two Directions of the Rationale

The crime control rationale has taken two directions.[5] One, deterrence, is nearly synonymous with the crime control rationale. The other, target hardening, is often confused with deterrence. As the more frequent topic of published materials, deterrence often subsumes target hardening.[6] Deterrence and target hardening, however, are different. Deterrence focuses attention on the potential criminal and the prevention of criminal activities by threatening punishment of criminals. Target hardening focuses attention on the would-be victim and the prevention of criminal activities by controlling opportunities for crime.

Deterrence rests on the belief that the threat of punishment will convince would-be offenders that crime is not in their self-interest. With regard to the effects of the threat of punishment, general deterrence posits that punishment of actual offenders will serve as an object lesson to persuade would-be criminals to give up any idea of breaking the law. Signifying the effects on actual criminals of experiencing the penalties, specific deterrence turns attention to those individuals and the possibility of convincing them that further crime is not worthwhile. Specific deterrence is distinctive in that the person experiencing punishment is expected to assess the threat of punishment differently than the inexperienced person. General and specific deterrence have separate effects, but both are intended to prevent a future crime.

A key feature of deterrence is its dedication to managing lawbreakers as a means of reducing the collective impact of crime. Actual offenders are supposed to become subject to rapid-fire actions through measures aimed directly and specifically at them. These actions can be rapid, it is believed, because there will be no delay in assessing the socioeconomic conditions that spawn criminality or in diagnosing the significance of the criminal behavior to the perpetrator. The actions are direct in that the individual, whether an active or expectant criminal, is the object.

Deterrence manages offenders by applying measures from sources external to their personalities. An underlying belief has been that crime-prone individuals are either unwilling or incapable of managing their antisocial impulses. Perhaps they are impulsive in their tendency to act without reflection or to act suddenly without foresight. Perhaps certain individuals have a remarkable potential for hostile, destructive, aggressive, or acquisitive conduct. Simplistically applied, deterrence measures ignore differences in that potential among individuals by assuming that all of them will consider the threat of punishment before deciding to commit a crime. Deterrence calls for the rigorous enforcement of criminal laws.

Target hardening is also designed to end the perceived threat of criminals but through actions aimed against criminal opportunity. It emphasizes the belief that would-be victims can modify their environments and behaviors in ways that will reduce opportunities for crime. The key feature in this instance is the citizens' assessment of the types of crimes occurring in their area and their adoption of strategies that will reduce or eliminate their chances of being victimized.

The Thrust of Target Hardening

As with deterrence, target hardening ignores the socioeconomic conditions that spawn individual criminality but, unlike deterrence, requires knowledge of the conditions conducive to crime. Deterrence is direct in that the threat of punishment is focused on the would-be criminal; target hardening is indirect in that the focus is on the probable scene of a crime, not on the possible offender.

Whereas criminological analysis would probe the long-term conditions fanning the development of criminals, the expert in target hardening concentrates on the qualities of immediate situations that favor crime. The object is to discourage criminal acts by examining those crime-encouraging situations. The criminologist is likely to be concerned about such criminogenic factors as inadequate role models, delinquency subcultures, and limited legitimate jobs. The target-hardening expert talks about better locks, buddy systems, and television scanners.

As in deterrence, target-hardening experts have only incidental interest in the offender's personality, in why some persons are antisocial, and in whether crime-prone individuals are unwilling or incapable of managing their antisocial impulses. The crime-prone individual is of interest only as a threat to be thwarted. Type of crime is of more interest than type of criminal.

Implementation of target hardening is more often a private than a public effort. Proposed laws requiring alarm systems for businesses, for example, are not likely to pass. Security provisions in building codes in some jurisdictions have required limited target-hardening devices, but the codes are effective only if enforced. Compared with fire departments, police departments have given low priority to this new function. More promising incentives may come from other private efforts such as insurance credits for use of target-hardening devices.[7]

THE NATURE OF DETERRENCE THEORY

What is deterrence theory? In its simplest form deterrence theory asserts that the rational individual includes the threat of punishment in calculating the costs and benefits of crime. It claims that everyone is motivated to violate norms but is constrained not to do so by externally applied controls that meet three conditions.

First, the controls have to work; the culprit is caught. In technical language there is certainty. Second, the controls work immediately; one gets caught in the act or nearly so. There is celerity. Third, the controls carry sufficient sanctions; one gets punished more than the misbehavior is worth. There is severity. When there is certain, swift, and severe response to norm violations, both the actual violator and the potential violator are presumed to be deterred from future violations.

Recognizing the Complexity of Human Behavior

Jack Gibbs argues that the simplistic view of deterrence is a doctrine rather than a theory. He proposes a series of refinements, to be tested by research, necessary for developing a theory.[8] As he, and others, have suggested, simple assertions must be modified to recognize the complexity of human behavior and decision making. The following points illustrate the modifications.

One, because human beings have a finite and variable capacity for assessing all the decisions confronting them, limited rationality models have been proposed. Some writers suggest that, in decisions to undertake crime, the elements considered may be few.

Two, actual risk of punishment and perceived threat of punishment are not the same. Because individuals will have differential access to information about the actual risk of punishment, inevitably, perceptions of threat will not be uniform.

Three, since absolute deterrence is rarely the objective, the aggregate effect of threat of punishment is the issue. Thus, the limited rationality or irrationality of some persons or their variations in perception are problems only if the effect is systematic, for example, the majority of persons inaccurately perceives a serious threat as very minor. Marginal deterrence only requires that some persons respond to a new threat after rational and reasonably accurate assessment, while the remainder continue to behave as previously.[9]

Four, certainty, celerity, and severity of punishment do not carry an absolute value, nor do they occur simultaneously at maximum intensity. Consequently, the relative weight each of the concepts adds to threat of punishment is uncertain. Perhaps their contributions vary depending on the norm violation being assessed, producing a multidimensional scale of threat.[10]

Five, certainty, celerity, and severity may connote different threats. Certainty, for example, is commonly denoted as the threat of imprisonment, but it may also denote the threat of arrest, prosecution, or any legal sanction.

Appeals of Deterrence Theory

These elaborations have not detracted from the appeal of deterrence as a crime control theory. Criminological theorists, including new entrants from economics particularly, find the more sophisticated consideration of deterrence to be especially appealing because the modifications come closer to meeting three criteria for theory. (1) It was not constructed ex post facto to fit assorted findings but was logically derived by such classical utilitarians as Jeremy Bentham and Cesare Beccaria.[11] (2) It can be described simply or parsimoniously; that is, few postulates are needed to express the core elements of the theory. (3) It is generalizable; it can be applied to a wider range of behaviors than crime.

Deterrence appeals to many ordinary citizens as well as to certain experts. The utilitarian view of people as rational beings places responsibility on the individual and his or her exercise of free will.[12] The view is consistent with the values of Americans who have treasured individualism and self-responsibility since the days of the frontier.

EVERYDAY DETERRENCE

The elements of deterrence fit comfortably with the conventional wisdom of daily experience of parents, teachers, police officers, and others. Parents threaten, "if you're not good, Santa will leave rocks in your sock." Even more dire may be the consequences of being caught by someone you see every day, the next door neighbor, the drugstore manager who knows your parents. Older siblings admonish the younger: "Just don't get caught." The teacher threatens to send the recalcitrant student to the principal. The police officer threatens to send the troublemaker to the police station if his or her bad behavior continues.

Yet every parent whose children are past the toddler stage has doubts about the success of their efforts to forestall deviant behavior. What parent will not acknowledge that some mischief makers are not caught? Parents are likely to be silent when their maturing offspring describe earlier indiscretions unknown to those parents. Swift punishment is delayed by the admonition: "Wait till your father gets home." Because certainty, celerity, and severity are difficult to achieve even within the narrow confines of the family, parents have settled for marginal deterrence by responding to some mischief and ignoring the rest.

The marginality of deterrence is even more clear for the police as the vanguard of official deterrence. Any police officer, or criminal, can detail the kinds of crimes for which celerity is probable; most are minor street crimes. The very structure of police departments acknowledges the lack of celerity and certainty. If every criminal was caught immediately, detective units, as presently constituted, would no longer be necessary for laborious collection of evidence. Police clearance rates demonstrate that certainty of arrest differs among types of crimes but is generally low. For offenders who are caught promptly, certainty and severity of punishment are most likely to serve deterrence. However, attrition rates from arrest to conviction may run as high as 67 percent.[13] If there were no police, the deterrent effect of law enforcement could be tested; the few opportunities for the test indicate that there is a deterrent effect.[14]

Criminologists of opposing perspectives agree that deterrence must be given serious attention. Nils Christie calls it the "scientification of the obvious" and notes that "punishment directs action."[15] Gibbs refers to Hugh Adam Bedau's "platitudinously true" assertions when stating that "all the contradictory general observations about deterrence can be reconciled by one empirical assertion: In some situations some individuals are deterred from some crimes by some punishments."[16] More research is needed to establish deterrence as a credible and useful theory.

TESTS OF DETERRENCE

Interest in deterrence research was revived in the middle 1960s and has gained momentum since then.[17] The earliest studies compared differing threat rates by calculating certainty of arrest, prosecution, and imprisonment and severity of punishment as time served in prison. Some researchers used cross-sectional methods, comparing different jurisdictions with different threat rates. Others looked at the same jurisdictions over time. These studies were largely dependent on official data: FBI crime reports, police clearance rates, state incarceration rates. All looked for a negative association between threat levels and crime rates, that is, if certainty of imprisonment is high, are crime rates low?

Range of Evaluative Studies

These studies lead to a few tentative conclusions. There appears to be no relationship between severity of punishment and crime rates, except for homicide. There does appear to be a negative relationship between certainty and crime rates. When certainty is high, the relationship between severity and crime rates can be negative for certain crimes.[18]

Much of this research focused on homicide and the deterrent effect of the death penalty. Perhaps the classic example of this interest is Isaac Ehrlich's study which estimated that each execution saved eight lives.[19] A second type of study began somewhat later as researchers became involved in deterrence-related policy evaluations. Philip J. Cook describes these studies as examining changes that are thought to affect the threat level.[20] All are experimental in method, although few approach the demands of a controlled experiment. A variety of policy and legal changes have been analyzed, usually policing patterns, but also legal change in drunk driving laws.

Some of the better known studies are the Kansas City Preventive Patrol Project, the New York Subway Project,[21] and the evaluation of the British Road Safety Act.[22] Franklin E. Zimring has suggested that researchers have failed to exploit other ideal projects, calling the Alcohol Safety Action Program a "lost experiment."[23]

The results of policy studies are mixed and tentative. Jan M. Chaiken examined the police studies and reports that "it seems very likely that arrest probability has a deterrent effect for at least some types of crime."[24] H. Laurence Ross looked at drunk driving studies and reported that "these laws seem capable of producing important deterrent effects on drinking and driving. However, in all cases in which deterrent effectiveness was noted, it proved to be temporary, disappearing within months of its attainment."[25] Cook notes that "the link between official activities and the public's perception of them constitutes half of the deterrence story." He quotes both Ross and Chaiken:

The initial publicity given the British Road Safety Act apparently succeeded in giving the British public a greatly exaggerated impression of the true likelihood of being caught. While this impression evidently was corrected after several years of experience, many lives were saved in the interim (Ross, 1973).

Intensive police manning of the New York subways during high crime hours of the day initially caused a deterrent effect not only during these times but also during the rest of the day (when police manning levels were not changed). It has been suggested that this "phantom effect" could have been sustained by random changes in police assignments (Chaiken, Lawless, and Stevenson, 1974).[26]

The positive evaluation of deterrence research findings has been echoed by other writers. For example, Thomas Cronin, Tania Cronin, and Michael Milakovich, in their political science review of the Law Enforcement Assistance Administration (LEAA), state that "we have learned . . . from LEAA . . . that if we want to make sure crime does not pay, we have to make punishment swift and certain."[27]

Recognizing Inherent Methodological Issues

Other interpretations have been less enthusiastic. Ehrlich's finding on the deterrent effects of capital punishment prompted the formation of the Panel on Research on Deterrence and Incapacitation Effects, headed by Alfred Blumstein. Their review of deterrence research before 1976 reached a less positive conclusion that current evidence was insufficient to determine whether there was a deterrent effect.[28] In regard to capital punishment the panel went even further. Noting the "strong value content" of such legislation and the necessarily nonexperimental research methodology, the report said that "the panel considers research on this topic is not likely to produce findings that will or should have much influence on policy makers."[29]

The formidable methodological problems cannot be properly treated in the space available here, except to say that there are problems of measurement, multiple causation, causal order, and time lags. The difficulties have received attention for some time.[30] The Panel on Research in Deterrence and Incapacitation Effects details the methodological shortcomings of a number of investigations.[31] John Hagan has made a similar contribution.[32]

The problems of measurement have ranged from careful specification of the variables under study to problems with errors in official statistics. Gibbs particularly raises questions of specification by listing seven types of crime rates and analyzing the circumstances under which each would be appropriate.[33] An early criticism was the use of a single rate; now the parallel use of victimization rates is encouraged.[34] Criticism has been directed toward the effects of errors in official rates when the rates are used in the denominator of one measure and the numerator of another.[35]

Specifying multiple causation is always a murky problem, but in this case the known problems are sufficient to warrant caution. For example, when a state legislature responds to increasing crime rates by approving determinate sentencing, does the decrease in crime that follows actually result from that sentencing change? Does the decrease mark some other possible cause, such as increased funding for police? Or does the decrease in crime only mark the downswing that normally follows an upswing in crime?[36]

Perhaps the causation chain is reversed, and the original upswing caused legislative interest in determinate sentencing? What is the causal order?[37]

The confusion of a time lag between implementation and impact involves the question of whether the impact begins sometime after the implementation of the legislation or whether it begins with the "get tough" discussions that precede passage.[38] Since most such legislation has a delayed implementation affecting only those arrested after a certain date, how is the effect on the new cohort separated from the perhaps lesser effect on the old cohort? How much time must elapse for an effect to be discerned? Does enough time elapse to release other factors that would move the crime rates in another direction? This question takes us back to multiple causation.

OTHER CRITICISMS OF DETERRENCE THEORY

More sophisticated methodology, recognizing the questions raised above, will probably generate more reliable support for deterrence theory, but critics have expressed objections in addition to methodological concerns. Critics have taken several avenues. Some have what they consider to be the draconian implications for public policy. Perhaps the most central issues have centered on the latent assumption of shared values.

Involvement of Value Questions

Deterrence theory assumes that the criminal shares the values of the larger society or, if not, that he or she is aware of that value and has no contradictory value of greater weight. Several generations of criminologists have questioned this assumption. One of the earliest, Walter B. Miller, specifically addressed the situations in which the values of lower class youth brought them into conflict with the values and laws of the larger society.[39] Most recently, conflict theorists have begun by assuming that different groups have different values and that the more powerful group tries to impose its values on the others; the consequence is that the least powerful individuals often are defined as criminals.[40]

Research also has noted that values are involved either in supporting prevention by enlisting informal controls or in favoring law violations when the offender is not rejected by conventional peers. Charles R. Tittle, for example, found that the convergence of one's own values with those of conventional peers has more preventive effect than the perception of certainty of being caught by the control system.[41] In white-collar crime, the perpetrator clearly identifies with majority values, but the emphasis placed on profit and "success" is included among those values to blunt rejection of white-collar offenders by their conventional peers. Uncertainties about the appropriateness of penalizing price-fixing, kickbacks, and bribery insulate the lawbreakers against the deterrent effects of announced penalties. In light of divergent and shifting value structures, deterrence research faces serious difficulty in identifying those values that lend certainty to public rejection of criminal behavior.

Effects of Deterrent Policies

Christie has noted the draconian implications of deterrence. Specifically, he points out the contradiction between the premise that individuals must be held responsible for their behavior and the use of sanctions to maintain the authority of a strong state over its citizens. He speaks most tellingly of pains inflicted by draconian policy.[42]

These reservations have not weakened the faith of policy makers in deterrence by the growth of presumptive sentencing and the decline of parole. Public demand for higher police clearance rates and stern prosecution of cases have influenced policy makers in that direction. As we have seen, the evidence does not support the faith in deterrence. Severity of punishment, that is, longer prison terms, appears to have little or no impact without certainty of imprisonment or arrest. Severity and certainty of imprisonment are amenable to public policy change, but certainty of arrest is less so. Ernest Van den Haag has estimated that in New York City only one-third of all felonies result in arrest and less than 1 percent in a felony trial.[43]

What are the consequences of manipulating severity and certainty of imprisonment? The policy of increased use of imprisonment is expensive, particularly because it requires increased prison and jail capacity. Most states and larger jail systems already face litigation stimulated by overcrowding. New prison and jail construction costs over $50,000 per bed and beyond the capital costs there are the added operational costs.[44] Local units of government have found their burgeoning criminal justice costs even more burdensome than states have. More imprisonment also imposes an indirect tax burden because it removes potential earners from the tax rolls and it places prisoners' dependents on welfare rolls.

Offenders also suffer the negative effects of imprisonment. Long sentences are likely to raise the probability that offenders will perceive themselves as criminals, will increase their rage against injustice, and will encourage their desire for revenge. James Coleman reports that in many conversations with inmates he has never heard one argue his or her innocence, but many argue that their sentences were too long.[45]

ORIGINS OF TARGET HARDENING

Deterrence, one form of crime control, focuses on management of criminals or would-be criminals by threatening punishment. Target hardening, the other form of crime control, addresses the victim or would-be victim by attempting to control opportunities for crime. Its methods would encourage the would-be victims to modify their environments and behavior in ways that make crime harder to commit. If deterrence can be crudely described as the ''lock them up'' approach to crime control, target hardening can be described as the ''lock us up'' approach.

Shift to Criminal Opportunity

As one of the first to shift the emphasis of crime control from the criminal to criminal opportunity, C. Ray Jeffery says: ''The crime rate is the direct result of the number of opportunities for crime existing in the community.''[46] Target hardening began as a pragmatic, individual response to concern with crime.[47] If teenagers joy-rode in cars whose owners left their keys in the ignition, it made sense to remove the keys. If locks prevented entry through solid doors, what did one do about sliding glass doors? Neighbors shared suggestions, and business people shopped for security systems. As this individual response became increasingly public and collective, law enforcement, the media, and even the comics provided crime prevention tips. Automobile manufacturers designed locking steering columns and locking gas caps. Urban neighborhoods organized block watch parties.

A form of risk management evolved to assess possible losses to person or property and steps to be taken to reduce or eliminate opportunities for potential criminals.[48] A language developed with terms such as deadbolt locks, one inch throws, strike plates, and drop safes. Its focus was on lighting, visibility, windows, doors, and bars. Although in simplest form it was restricted to changes in the environment, it soon was extended to changes in people. Rape prevention seminars provided tips on how to reduce the risk to one's person. The elderly were encouraged to go out in groups. Businesspeople were urged to disguise their deposit bags.

Target hardening, Charles A. Murray says, consists of "the more prosaic ways in which the design of the physical environment can deter crime through better locks and stronger doors." He prefers the defensible space approach, first espoused by Oscar Newman, because it suggests that changes in the environment will create informal social controls that will reduce crime.[49]

Its Place in Criminological Theory

Target hardening may be prosaic, but it also has a place within criminology, a place that has yet to be clearly established, whose possibilities are only emerging. Some observers would include it under general deterrence, but they overlook the focus of target hardening on opportunities for crime, rather than on making the punished offender an object lesson. Some, like Murray, would treat it as one of the many strategies of several approaches to crime prevention. Others see target hardening as another dimension for evaluation, such as for street lighting or preventive patrol.

The several interpretations suggest that target hardening can be the central idea around which a new direction for crime control can be followed. Target hardening should not be reduced to a summation of specific methods, such as locks, alarms, and lighting, because it provides an unusual perspective in criminology. It turns the whole field around by looking at crime through the eyes of the potential victim, by paying less attention to the possible criminal, by focusing more on the crime situation, and by acknowledging the victim's part in reducing the threat of crime.

Target hardening, like deterrence, is firmly rooted in the rationality of utilitarianism. If the criminal is rational, then he or she presumably will not break into the business with the good locks, polycarbonate windows, and alarm systems, will not mug an elderly person in the midst of friends, and will back away from the house that is apparently occupied. Target hardening goes further; it assumes that the victim is also rational and will adopt reasonable strategies for crime protection. Most target-hardening advocates focus their attention on pre-

venting crimes such as burglary, theft, and shoplifting, which involve the highest
degree of rationality and which are most amenable to rational prevention. When
they extend their attention to crimes that involve irrationality, they pick those
presenting elements of rationality such as rape and robbery.[50]

METHODS OF TARGET HARDENING

Target hardening would modify physical environments and the behavior of
potential victims as a means of reducing opportunities for crime. It requires an
assessment of types of crime found in the victim's environment, of factors
facilitating successful crime, of factors persuading the criminal to turn away
from possible targets. As Jeffery suggests, it calls for innovative methods ''based
on research as to the conditions under which the commission of a crime occurs.''[51]

Context of Crime Occurrences

The importance of an accurate assessment of the crime to be thwarted is
indicated by an amusing story. An enterprising New Yorker coped with a garbage
strike by exploiting his knowledge that packages often are stolen from cars. Each
day he wrapped his debris as though it were a present and left it on the seat of
his unlocked car. It was invariably gone by morning. This New Yorker had
contextual knowledge. He knew his neighborhood, the crime risks, and the
opportunity it offered him.

Effective target hardening demands insights into the context within which
crimes are likely to happen. Lawrence W. Sherman objects to motorized police
patrol because it denies police officers the detailed knowledge of the neighborhood possessed by an alert foot patrol. ''What the patrol car officer sees is
familiar buildings with unfamiliar people around them,'' he says. ''Stripped of
this contextual knowledge, the patrol car officer sees, but cannot truly observe.''[52]
The experienced criminal has the contextual knowledge that must be countered
by target hardening as a preventive strategy. In her ethnographic study of fear
and crime in an Eastern housing project, Sally Engle Merry reports that offenders
know their territory well.[53]

Residential and commercial burglary illustrates the value of contextual knowledge. Research in Akron found that burglary incidents radiate out from the urban
core along arterials and from these into nearby neighborhoods.[54] Two adjoining
neighborhoods in Tallahassee have differing socioeconomic statuses and crime
rates; the houses bordering the higher crime area have more burglaries than the
houses further away.[55] The at-risk householder may make a worthwhile investment if he or she installs an elaborate silent alarm system. The less at-risk
householder may be well protected by remembering to lock the doors. National
data indicate that burglary often occurs without forced entry because of the lack
of target hardening by residents. In the early 1970s forty-two of every 1,000
households were objects of no force burglary. And 66 percent of those crimes

were committed by entering through an unlocked door or window. Forty-four percent of all residential burglaries were of the no force type; the average loss was $74.[56] Another study found that when residences and commercial establishments had alarms, the burglar was much more likely to give up before completing the attempt.[57]

Commercial burglary presents another picture. More than a third of burglaries are commercial; in Detroit in 1972, nearly three-fourths of all retail stores were burglarized. Estimates indicate that every tenth business was burglarized in 1975. The average loss from all commercial burglary was $422, for a total of $460 million.

Although severe, the problem of commercial burglary appears to be less serious than that of internal theft. Eleanor Chelimsky, Frank C. Jordan, Linda Sue Russell, and John R. Strack report: "Insurance companies estimate that 30 percent of all business failures are directly attributable to internal theft." As much as $16 billion is lost annually to employees—that is, perhaps $1,600 per business, four times the average loss from burglary.[58] The business owner who buys an expensive security system and then turns its control over to an untrustworthy employee has locked the fox in the chicken house.

Burglary may also be analyzed in terms of factors that facilitate victimization. Numerous studies have examined the means of entry, the kinds of items stolen, and other methods used. Merry found that criminals "adopt sophisticated strategies to identify good victims—to maximize their incomes—and to avoid detection and punishment—to minimize their risks."[59] The criminals she interviewed were particularly concerned about residents who watch regularly, not just after they hear a suspicious sound, and who are believed likely to call the police.[60] She also found that the residents did not consider the neighborhood dangerous when they knew the young people most likely to commit crimes and had a contextual knowledge of the neighborhood. Residents who saw the youths as strangers did consider it a dangerous area.[61]

Considering the Threat of Punishment

Target-hardening strategies deter by increasing the actual threat of punishment, the perceived threat of punishment, and chances of detection without apprehension. They also delay or deny access, and define lack of opportunity.[62]

Apprehension is emphasized when target hardening is intended to increase the actual threat of punishment. For example, the bank teller withdraws the marked stack of bills and triggers the silent alarm, attracting the manager's attention and subsequently the police. The cameras recording the crime might frighten off a would-be robber. Other techniques include training employees to be better witnesses of crimes, keeping suspect identification forms readily available, and prompt and accurate reporting of crimes. Southland Corporation stores have height markers at entrances so that employees can more accurately describe robbers.

Target hardening can increase the perceived threat of punishment, as opposed to the actual increase in the threat of apprehension. Store mirrors, positioned to observe shoplifters, threaten apprehension, but retailers have too many other tasks to be able to continuously observe all customers. Instead, the mirrors suggest that possibility. Similarly, the visible marking of valuables increases the likelihood of regaining stolen possessions but also threatens the thief with an increased chance of being caught.

Target hardening can increase the chances of criminal activity being detected. There is reason to believe that criminals are deterred by the chance of being seen, even when the chances of apprehension are very minimal. Citizens are urged to walk in well-lighted areas and to travel in groups. The advice rests on the assumption that the increased chance of being observed deters would-be criminals. Oscar Newman, a pioneer in the analysis of environmental opportunities for prevention, describes how shrubbery around buildings can insulate criminals from surveillance.[63] Paradoxically, the American ideal of a private residence, hidden from the neighbors' sight, becomes a liability. Obstructions to surveillance exist in other settings. Displays, posters, and counters may hide the cash register from view in business establishments. Poor lighting may also conceal the criminals: widely spaced street lights, dimly lit back entrances to businesses, inadequate hallway lighting in apartment buildings, and commercial establishments left dark after hours.

The presence of people in a building increases the probability that the criminal will be under surveillance. Studies of residential burglary report that it is more likely to occur in the house that is uninhabited.[64] Neighborhood watch programs involve others in seeing, but, as Merry's work suggests, the observers must be willing to notify the police.[65]

Delaying Access to the Target

Target hardening can also delay or deny criminal opportunity without necessarily increasing the chances of apprehension. It is thus assumed that the longer it takes a criminal to gain access to his or her target the greater his or her chances of being seen or heard. Anything that impedes access may be a deterrent; denial of access is the ultimate in deterrence. Doors can be reinforced with deadbolts, glass windows can be replaced with less breakable polycarbonate or protected with grillwork, locked cash drop boxes or safes can be installed, and audible alarm systems can be added. The approach to a business or residence or to the valuables therein can be blocked. Prevention of access implicitly assumes that the criminal will withdraw empty handed and frustrated but not necessarily into the waiting arms of law enforcement.

Target hardening as denial of criminal opportunity is less concerned with seeing or catching criminals than with convincing them that there is no opportunity. The merchant disguises a bank deposit in a paper bag. Pharmacists post the information that they have no drugs with high black market value. Personal safety experts argue that people who communicate purposeful action through physical gestures are less vulnerable.

Much of target hardening is the application of common sense: installing deadbolts with long screws in the strike plate to complicate breaking the door from the frame; keeping the cash register open and empty after hours; shutting padlocks during the day so that they are not replaced by an enterprising thief; keeping an empty house lighted and noisy so that it appears to be occupied; installing peepholes in exterior doors so that only wanted visitors are given entry; leaving purses in office drawers rather than in full view; not leaving bank deposits on the seat of an open car; replacing dead bulbs in alley lighting; locking packages in the automobile trunk; and so on.

Target hardening can be negated by human failure. Heat and motion sensor alarms are often so sensitive that the family cat can trigger false alarms and pressure alarms can be set off by the family labrador. Small businesses develop elaborate procedures to insure that their alarm is activated upon closure and then deactivated upon each day's reopening. Still, owner-activated alarms are very common. When the alarm is heard in the neighborhood, there is always the possibility that a neighbor will not call the police because that alarm is usually false. If the alarm is heard by a monitoring company and it has received too many false alarms from that source, it too may be careless in calling the police. Some police departments impose a financial penalty for false alarms, a fine for each one over a given number.

AN EXAMPLE OF A TARGET-HARDENING PROGRAM

Perhaps target hardening can best be illustrated by describing a specific program for which one of the authors has been responsible.[66] The Business Watch Program was started by the Seattle Police Department because of high commercial burglary rates. In 1980 one-third of all Seattle burglaries occurred in commercial establishments. A resident of a Seattle housing unit had a one in twenty-five chance of being a victim of residential burglary, but a Seattle businessperson had a one in six chance of being a victim of commercial burglary.

Parameters of the Business Watch Program

To reduce incidents of commercial burglary and theft, the Business Watch Program organized the merchants in formal and informal associations, provided specific security assistance to each merchant, and established closer relationships between the merchants and law enforcement personnel.

Before implementing the program, the district selected as the target was defined, its history of commercial theft was analyzed, and a sponsoring merchant was recruited. District newspapers were asked to disseminate information about the program. The neighborhood business association or a less formal group of merchants was informed. First, the sponsor and then other merchants served to legitimate Business Watch in the rest of the district.

Following the initial meeting, the staff canvassed every business to introduce Business Watch and its staff; crime prevention materials were distributed. Businesspeople were asked which crimes concerned them the most; they were told about the crime pattern in the district. Then information was obtained for a district directory on the businesses. It was a key element in the program strategy because it was tangible evidence that the police cared. Once compiled, the directory provided both the district businesspersons and law enforcement personnel with current information on whom to contact in an emergency and how to contact them.

Security surveys were offered to all businesses, and many took advantage of the opportunity. Within two years, the department had increased the number of surveys by two and a half times. The survey provided risk assessment and security evaluation; cash, merchandising, and deposit procedures; key control; burglary, shoplifting, and internal theft controls; perimeter protection and internal space control; lighting and alarm system analysis; and any other relevant aspect of property or personal loss or risk.

Written recommendations for specific improvements were made. Within weeks Business Watch staff members checked to see if the recommendations had been implemented. Sometimes earlier checks were prompted by a crime report, indicating that the business had been burglarized because of deficiencies previously discussed.

These contacts with businesspeople, and particularly the discussions during security surveys, made apparent one of the most significant security problems these merchants faced: they had no idea who their neighbors were or how to reach them in an emergency. Business Watch staff told them that their crime problems would be reduced if they knew each other and developed more concern for their community as a whole. The directory was a useful tool in combating this problem.

Other police specialists, such as personal safety and robbery seminar leaders, and alarm and hidden camera personnel, were introduced to the merchants. Business Watch personnel began to report back to the precincts the particular crime problems in the district. Merchants were quicker to report crimes and suspicious activity.

All these steps were iterative, and new districts were added every two months. Twenty districts and 3,000 businesses within the city are now involved. Even given this level of activity, Business Watch is not expensive, having only two full-time positions, a small printing and motor pool budget, and the supporting services of other units within the department. The results are positive; participating districts have experienced 25 to 50 percent reductions in burglary.

ASSESSMENT OF TARGET HARDENING

Nearly all the research on target hardening stems from small studies that evaluate a single project with even less adequate methodology than that of deterrence studies because of the limitations of small projects. Often the concern is whether or not a pilot residential block watch program is sufficiently effective to justify expansion with city funds. With half a dozen similar projects to evaluate before budget hearings, sophisticated methodological questions are difficult to carry out for the immediate answers demanded.

Elements of Evaluation

Adequate evaluation of the Seattle Business Watch Program should involve at least an analysis of increases in the three independent variables: level of business security, degree of district cohesiveness, and quality of interaction between the police department and the district. Variations in the independent variable should be related to changes in the rates for commercial burglary, theft, and shoplifting and should test whether the effects of the independent variables are additive or include interaction. The analysis should use pre- and post-intervention data to determine what portion of the variation in those crimes can be explained by the independent variables or by alternative variables, such as changes in patrol assignments and reporting patterns.

As with many such programs, that quality of evaluation was not accomplished, but five findings deserve consideration. After Business Watch intervention in six districts, burglary rates decreased 40 percent. In one very large district only four out of the fifty-six post-intervention burglaries occurred in businesses that had had security surveys. In half the districts, new business associations were formed. An early post-intervention survey of merchants indicated that 54 percent believed that police efforts had improved in their area and that 40 percent were more likely to report crimes. Burglary rates continue to decrease in participating districts, while, in Seattle as a whole, commercial burglary has increased.

Because most target-hardening research is designed to determine funding, many reports are given limited distribution, thereby obstructing nationwide collection of information. Hundreds of crime prevention studies probably exist, but most are known only within the immediate community. Furthermore, target hardening covers many diverse activities and is so new that categorization of the findings into general principles would be difficult. The primary advantage of such a catalogue would be the specification of new questions.

Consider a random assortment of such findings, drawn from more widely available literature. The adoption of dramatically improved airport security has virtually eliminated hijacking within the continental United States.[67] Review of the numerous studies of street lighting projects shows no effect on crime but a reduction in fear has taken place.[68] The effectiveness of locking mechanisms for auto ignitions depends on the quality of the product.[69] Although the presence of alarms was negatively related to completed burglaries, other target-hardening devices, such as lighting and security inspections, were not.[70] Security surveys appear to reduce victimization for participants but do not reduce their fear.[71] In spite of a general agreement that some elements of target hardening are helpful, there is a scarcity of reliable evidence in support of that faith.

Dynamics of Criminal Behavior

Two serious methodological problems for both deterrence and target hardening involve the dynamics of criminal behavior. First, do the criminals just get smarter? Does the effect decay? Second, do the criminals simply take their activity elsewhere? Is crime displaced?

To illustrate the first question, we may ask whether bigger and better bicycle chains only result in bigger and better chain cutters. After a recent local burglary, the thief left behind the logging chain which he had used to rip the grille off the store entrance. Many safecrackers no longer bother to open their targets inside the store; they bring a winch to lift them off their platforms and into their truck. The introduction of polycarbonate windows has brought more smash and grab burglaries. The use of a large rock pops the window out of its housing. With the advent of phone access credit charges the more easily detected and thwarted theft of plastic has been replaced by the theft of carbon imprints, complete with names and numbers. Computerization of banking records and transfers has created a whole new field of criminal activity; locking systems and security for computer access is of concern wherever these machines are used.

The second question implies that the ingenious criminal may not have to become more sophisticated if he or she only moves on to more innocent territory. If criminals are indeed rational, then why burglarize in a neighborhood characterized by window bars and alarms? One reason may be that many residential burglaries are committed by neighborhood youth, limited both in their mobility and experience. On the other hand, the rational criminal may move on, not because an area is less vulnerable, but because another area provides better pickings. Determining whether or not target hardening results in displacement of criminal activity from one area to another will require the same level of methodological astuteness that is required when assessing deterrence.

The capacity of target hardening to manipulate illegal opportunities remains in doubt, but it does appear to reduce fear. A report makes that point: "An improved lighting program need not be judged only on the basis of measurable crime reduction. If streets and parks appear more secure and inviting, they can enhance the community, help foster a sense of participation and contribute to an improved quality of life."[72]

James Q. Wilson and George L. Kelling argue that many of the innovative efforts of the last few years, such as foot patrols, have not reduced crime but have increased order maintenance and reduced fear.[73] They speculate that disorderliness and incivility, the rowdy teenager and the obnoxious panhandler, are the paramount concerns of most citizens. If these symptoms of lowered order maintenance exist alongside the evidence of decaying neighborhoods, then increased crime is not far behind. If increased order maintenance is the key element, target hardening plays a limited role, Wilson and Kelling argue.

CONCLUSIONS ON CRIME CONTROL

As long as crime is perceived to be a serious threat, the two major directions of crime control will appeal to the public: deterrence, which addresses the criminal and the control of his or her antisocial behavior; and target hardening. Crime control ignores the possible root causes of criminality in society or the individual. Its methods are the imposition of certain, swift, and severe punishment that is supposed to turn actual and potential offenders away from crime.

The second crime control direction, target hardening, addresses the victim and the control of criminal opportunities. It, too, ignores the root causes of criminality, but, unlike deterrence, the methods are directed to modify the immediate environment and behavior of would-be victims.

Deterrence carried to the extreme would lock all criminals into fortress prisons; target hardening carried to the extreme would lock all law-abiding citizens into fortress businesses and homes. Deterrence calls for a public or governmental response; target hardening calls for a private response. Deterrence can be a severe drain on the public treasury; sophisticated target hardening can be very expensive for business or residence.

Evidence on deterrence is still inconclusive, and even fewer reliable conclusions are available on target hardening. The evidence that is available calls for changes in public policy and private response. Deterrence appears to have more impact on crime when there is certainty of imprisonment and arrest, and less when severity of imprisonment is the only consideration. Current public policy emphasizes imprisonment, but increasing the certainty of arrest through higher clearance rates and lower attrition between arrest and conviction merits more attention.

Target hardening appears to share with other strategies one important effect: it may reduce fear of crime. Nearly twenty years of experimentation and research have been fed by that possibility. Only recently have Wilson and Kelling suggested that fear of crime is generated first by disorder and then by crime. They believe that crime control strategies reduce fear in part because these strategies encourage improved order maintenance.[74] New strategies of prevention could combine increased community responsibility for order maintenance and increased citizen protection against crime. Deterrence and target hardening should play an important, if limited, role in that new strategy.

NOTES

1. Simone Weil, *Gravity and Grace* (London: Routledge and Kegan Paul, 1952), pp. 62–63.

2. These quotations were collected by Maurice M. Bell from crime reports and conversations with victims during the course of his work as Business Watch Coordinator for the Seattle Police Department.

3. Franklin E. Zimring and Gordon J. Hawkins, *Deterrence: The Legal Threat in Crime Control* (Chicago: University of Chicago Press, 1973), p. 75.

4. Douglas Lipton, Robert Martinson, and Judith Wilks, *The Effectiveness of Correctional Treatment* (New York: Praeger, 1975).

5. C. Ray Jeffery, *Crime Prevention Through Environmental Design* (Beverly Hills, Calif.: Sage Publications, 1971). Jeffery, one of the earliest proponents of crime control, would support this distinction only if deterrence were limited to general deterrence. He argues that specific deterrence is a failure because of its ties to the failure of punishment to reform.

6. Philip J. Cook, "Research in Criminal Deterrence: Laying the Groundwork for the Second Decade," in Norval Morris and Michael Tonry, eds., *Crime and Justice: An Annual Review of Research* (Chicago: University of Chicago Press, 1980), pp. 211–268. See, for example, Cook's discussion of hidden cameras, airport security, and private protection activities.

7. The National Crime Prevention Institute, *The Practice of Crime Prevention*, Vol. 1: *Understanding Crime Prevention* (Lexington, Ky.: National Crime Prevention Institute Press, 1978), pp.–4–10. According to the Lexington Crime Prevention Institute, UL approved alarms can bring a 70-percent reduction in insurance.

8. Jack P. Gibbs, *Crime, Punishment, and Deterrence* (New York: Elsevier, 1975), pp. 5–11.

9. Cook, "Research in Criminal Deterrence," pp. 216–237. He offers a brief review of these complications and refinements.

10. Gibbs, *Crime, Punishment, and Deterrence*, pp. 144. Gibbs would complicate this scale even further by adding perceived, presumptive, and objective threat.

11. Zimring and Hawkins, *Deterrence*, p. 1. They list other contributors.

12. Nils Christie, *Limits to Pain* (Oslo: Universitetsforlaget, 1981), p. 46.

13. Kathleen Brossi, *A Cross City Comparison of Felony Case Processing* (Washington, D.C.: Institute for Law and Social Research, 1979).

14. Johannes Andenaes, *Punishment and Deterrence* (Ann Arbor: University of Michigan Press, 1974), pp. 50–51. Andenaes cites two examples: the Liverpool police strike in 1919 and the Danish occupation in 1944. In both instances, the radical reduction of police services was associated with a sharp climb in the crime rates.

15. Christie, *Limits to Pain*, p. 30.

16. Gibbs, *Crime, Punishment, and Deterrence*, p. 11.

17. This chapter cannot provide a comprehensive review of deterrence research. The reader is referred to Zimring and Hawkins, *Deterrence*, Gibbs, *Crime, Punishment and Deterrence*, and Cook, "Research in Criminal Deterrence." Also see Alfred Blumstein, Jacqueline Cohen, and Daniel Nagin, eds., *Deterrence and Incapacitation: Estimating the Effects of Criminal Sanctions on Crime Rates* (Washington, D.C.: National Academy of Sciences, 1978).

18. Allen E. Liska, *Perspectives on Deviance* (Englewood Cliffs, N.J.: Prentice-Hall, 1981), p. 99; H. Frances Pestello, "Deterrence: A Reconceptualization," *Crime and Delinquency* 30 (October 1984): 593–609; Raymond Paternoster and Leeann Iovanni, "The Deterrent Effect of Perceived Severity: A Reexamination," *Social Forces* 64 (March 1986): 751–777.

19. Isaac Ehrlich, "The Deterrent Effect of Capital Punishment: A Question of Life and Death," *American Economic Review* 65 (June 1975): 397–417.

20. Cook, "Research in Criminal Deterrence," pp. 243–359.

21. Jan M. Chaiken, "What Is Known About Deterrent Effects of Police Activities," in James A. Cramer, ed., *Preventing Crime* (Beverly Hills, Calif.: Sage Publications, 1978), pp. 109–135. Also see Richard A. Berk and Phyllis J. Newton, "Does Arrest Really Deter Wife Battery? An Effort to Replicate the Findings of the Minneapolis Spouse Abuse Experiment," *American Sociological Review* 50 (April 1985): 253–262.

22. H. Laurence Ross, "Interrupted Time Series Studies of Deterrence of Drinking and Driving," in John Hagan, ed., *Deterrence Reconsidered: Methodological Innovations* (Beverly Hills, Calif.: Sage Publications, 1982), pp. 71–97. This chapter reports several of these studies, including the one in Great Britain.

23. Franklin E. Zimring, "Policy Experiments in General Deterrence: 1970–1975," in Blumstein, Cohen, and Nagin, eds., *Deterrence and Incapacitation*, pp. 140–186.

24. Chaiken, "What Is Known," p. 130.

25. Ross, "Interrupted Times Series Studies," p. 93.

26. Cook, "Research in Criminal Deterrence," pp. 226–227; H. Laurence Ross, "Law, Science and Accidents: The British Road Safety Act of 1967," *Journal of Legal Studies* 2 (1973): 1–78; Jan M. Chaiken, Michael W. Lawless, and Keith A. Stevenson, "The Impact of Police Activity on Subway Crime," *Urban Analysis* 3 (1974): 173–205.

27. Thomas E. Cronin, Tania Z. Cronin, and Michael E. Milakovich, *U.S. v. Crime in the Streets* (Bloomington: Indiana University Press, 1981), p. 168.

28. Blumstein et al., eds., *Deterrence and Incapacitation*, p. 7.

29. Ibid., p. 63.

30. Zimring and Hawkins, *Deterrence*, chap. 5, and Gibbs, *Crime, Punishment, and Deterrence*.

31. Blumstein et al., eds., *Deterrence and Incapacitation*, pp. 19–90.

32. Hagan, ed., *Deterrence Reconsidered*, pp. 7–13.

33. Gibbs, *Crime, Punishment, and Deterrence*, pp. 40–55.

34. David Lewis Smith and Charles Wicker Warren, "Use of Victimization Data to Measure Deterrence," in Cramer, ed., *Preventing Crime*, pp. 47–74.

35. David Nagin, "General Deterrence: A Review of the Empirical Evidence," in Blumstein et al., eds., *Deterrence and Incapacitation*, pp. 112–114.

36. Gibbs, *Crime, Punishment and Deterrence*, pp. 157–159, originally described this regression effect.

37. Blumstein et al., eds., *Deterrence and Incapacitation*, placed much emphasis on the problems of simultaneity.

38. Ross, "Interrupted Time Series Studies," has a discussion of these problems in drunk driving research and suggests methodological strategies.

39. See, for example, Walter B. Miller, "Lower Class Culture as a Generating Milieu of Gang Delinquency," *Journal of Social Issues* 14 (November 1958): 5–19.

40. See, for example, Richard Quinney, *Class, State and Crime* (New York: David McKay, 1977).

41. Charles R. Tittle, "Sanction, Fear and the Maintenance of Social Order," *Social Forces* 55 (March 1977): 579–96.

42. Christie, *Limits to Pain*, pp. 27–36.

43. Ernest van den Haag, *Punishing Criminals* (New York: Basic Books, 1975), pp. 157–158.

44. These costs vary widely by jurisdiction and type of construction; $50,000 is a conservative figure.

45. James Coleman, Safeco Lecture, Seattle, Washington, 1984.

46. Jeffery, *Crime Prevention*, p. 207.

47. Jeffery's book was published in 1971. Ignition locks were mandated by federal legislation in the late 1960s. David Barry, Jared Collard, Eugene Perchonok, Walter Preysnar, and Harold Steinberg, *Preliminary Study of the Effectiveness of Auto Anti-Theft Devices* (Washington, D.C.: U.S. Government Printing Office, 1975).

48. The National Crime Prevention Institute, *The Practice of Crime Prevention*, Vol. 1, pp. 4–2 through 4–8.

49. Charles A. Murray, "The Physical Environment and Community Control of Crime," in James Q. Wilson, ed., *Crime and Public Policy* (San Francisco: ICS Press, 1983), p. 109.

50. Michael R. Geerken and Walter R. Gove, "Deterrence, Overload, and Incapacitation: An Empirical Evaluation," *Social Forces* 56 (December 1977): 424–447. These authors make this point in relationship to deterrence. James A. Cramer, "Introduction" in Cramer, ed., *Preventing Crime*, pp. 13–14.

51. Jeffery, *Crime Prevention*, p. 207.

52. Lawrence W. Sherman, "Patrol Strategies for Police," in Wilson, ed., *Crime and Public Policy*, p. 149.

53. Sally Engle Merry, *Urban Danger: Life in a Neighborhood of Strangers* (Philadelphia: Temple University Press, 1981), pp. 167–172.

54. G. F. Pyle, *The Spatial Dynamics of Crime* (Chicago: University of Chicago, Department of Geography, 1974).

55. P. L. Brantingham and P. J. Brantingham, "Residential Burglary and Urban Form," *Urban Studies* 12 (October 1975): 273–285.

56. *The Cost of Negligence: Losses from Preventable Household Burglaries: A Natural Crime Survey Report* (Washington, D.C.: U.S. Government Printing Office, 1979).

57. Carl E. Pope, *Crime-Specific Analysis: An Empirical Examination of Burglary Offense and Offender Characteristics* (Washington, D.C.: U.S. Government Printing Office, 1977), p. 45.

58. Eleanor Chelimsky, Frank C. Jordan, Jr., Linda Sue Russell, and John R. Strack, *Security and the Small Business Retailer* (Washington, D.C.: U.S. Government Printing Office, 1978), pp. 5–6, 9–11.

59. Merry, *Urban Danger*, pp. 167–168.

60. Ibid., p. 142.

61. Ibid., p. 151.

62. This typology is an extension of that suggested by the Lexington Crime Institute staff in *The Practice of Crime Prevention*, p. 5–1.

63. Oscar Newman, *Defensible Space* (New York: Macmillan Publishing Co., 1972).

64. Wesley G. Skogan and Michael G. Maxfield, *Coping with Crime: Individual and Neighborhood Reactions* (Beverly Hills, Calif.: Sage Publications, 1981), p. 207.

65. Merry, *Urban Danger*, p. 142.

66. Information about Business Watch is available from the Crime Prevention Division, Seattle Police Department.

67. Cook, "Research in Criminal Deterrence," p. 258.

68. Murray, *The Physical Environment*, pp. 113–116.

69. Barry et al., *Auto Anti-Theft Devices*, pp. 12–17.

70. Pope, *Crime-Specific Analysis*, p. 45.

71. Compare International Training, Research and Evaluation Council, *Crime Prevention Security Surveys* (Washington, D.C.: U.S. Government Printing Office, 1977),

p. 18, and Allan Wallis and Daniel Ford, eds., *Crime Prevention Through Environmental Design: The Commercial Demonstration in Portland, Oregon: Executive Summary* (Washington, D.C.: National Institute of Justice, 1980), p. 6.

72. Douglas W. Frisbie, *Crime in Minneapolis: Proposals for Prevention*, Governor's Commission on Crime Prevention and Control, St. Paul, Minnesota, May 1977, p. 275.

73. James Q. Wilson and George L. Kelling, "Broken Windows," *Atlantic Monthly* 249 (March 1982): 29–38.

74. Ibid.

BIBLIOGRAPHY

Blumstein, Alfred; Jacqueline Cohen; and Daniel Nagin, eds. *Deterrence and Incapacitation: Estimating the Effects of Criminal Sanctions on Crime Rates*. Washington, D.C.: National Academy of Sciences, 1978.

    This report reviews previous work on general deterrence and argues that current evidence is insufficient to accept or reject its effect. A series of methodological problems are identified, and future research topics are suggested.

Christie, Nils. *Limits of Pain*, Oslo: Universitetsforlaget, 1981.

    This book is a reaction to deterrence. The author raises numerous criticisms of its harshness and suggests alternative social mechanisms.

Cook, Philip J. "Research in Criminal Deterrence: Laying the Groundwork for the Second Decade." In Norval Morris and Michael Tonry, eds., *Crime and Justice: An Annual Review of Research*. Chicago: University of Chicago Press, 1980, pp. 211–268.

    This author examines the criticisms that have been directed at deterrence theory and reviews the last decade of research, placing particular emphasis on the studies of policy innovations.

Duncan, J. T. Skip. *Citizen Crime Prevention Tactics: A Literature Review and Selected Bibliography*. Washington, D.C.: U.S. Government Printing Office, April 1980.

    Duncan summarizes the various forms of crime prevention and provides an annotated bibliography.

Feins, Judith D. *Partnerships for Neighborhood Crime Prevention*. Washington, D.C.: National Institute for Justice, June 1983.

    This report on neighborhood crime prevention not only describes numerous programs, but also provides a coherent strategy for their development. It offers a clear assessment of the difficulties for these programs, both from the community and from the police perspective.

Gabor, Thomas. "Crime Displacement: An Empirical Investigation." *Crime and Delinquency* 27 (July 1981): 390–404.

    Using an evaluation of Operation ID program, the author looks at three types of displacement: to nonparticipants, to businesses, and to unmarked items in the residence. Only the first occurred at a statistically significant level.

Hagan, John, ed. *Deterrence Reconsidered: Methodological Innovations*. Beverly Hills, Calif.: Sage Publications, 1982.

    This author responds to the numerous methodological problems raised earlier and proposes more sophisticated techniques for addressing deterrence questions.

Liska, Allen E., Mitchell B. Chamlin, and Mark D. Reed. "Testing the Economic Production and Conflict Models of Crime Control." *Social Forces* 64 (September

1985): 119–138.

   A large sample of Federal Bureau of Investigation arrest data is employed to compare the applicability of two theoretical perspectives for explaining the relationships between certainty of arrest and reported serious crimes.

Lundman, Richard J. "Beyond Probation: Assessing the Generalizability of the Delinquency Suppression Effect Measures Reported by Murray and Cox." *Crime and Delinquency* 32 (January 1986): 134–147.

   In *Beyond Probation: Juvenile Corrections and the Chronic Delinquent* (1979), C. A. Murray and L. A. Cox, Jr., reported that Illinois data showed that juvenile institutions were more effective than community programs in suppressing further delinquency. Using two other studies, Lundman questions whether or not the case has been established.

Merry, Sally Engle. *Urban Danger: Life in a Neighborhood of Strangers*. Philadelphia: Temple University Press, 1981.

   This ethnographic study examines both victims and offenders from a housing project in an Eastern city. The author relates offender behavior to victim methods of crime prevention.

Sherman, Laurence W. "Patrol Strategies for Police." In James Q. Wilson, ed., *Crime and Public Policy*. San Francisco: ICS Press, 1983, pp. 145–163.

   This chapter reviews the various studies of police and private surveillance and proposes future policy questions.

Whisenand, Paul M. *Crime Prevention*. Boston: Holbrook Press, 1977.

   A chapter on hardware is included in this textbook. The most useful section describes the crime data necessary for planning a burglary reduction program.

White, W. Thomas, Katryna J. Regan, John D. Waller, and Joseph S. Wholey. *Police Burglary Prevention Programs*. Washington, D.C.: U.S. Government Printing Office, 1975.

   Police department and community efforts to control burglary are discussed.

Zimring, Franklin E., and Gordon J. Hawkins. *Deterrence: The Legal Threat in Crime Control*. Chicago: University of Chicago Press, 1973.

   This book organizes a wide array of earlier theoretical and research work which impinges on the issues of deterrence.

3

Environmental Design as a Rationale for Prevention

JAMES L. LEBEAU

Three frequently asked questions illustrate that the spatial patterning of crime has a most personal impact that gives individuals reasons to be concerned about the prevention of delinquency and crime. How close in geographical space is the threat of crime to me? What should I do in my daily activities to avoid those environments where I am most vulnerable to victimization? What is there about the environment of my home that increases the chances that I will be victimized?

The questions imply that, since some environments are especially conducive to crime, it is possible to reduce the probability of victimization by identifying the features of the high-risk environments and subsequently by manipulating these features. Recognition of the possibility is not new, as witnessed by Chapter Five of the Statute of Winchester issued by Edward I in 1285.

It is likewise commanded that the highways from market towns to other market towns be widened where there are woods or hedges or ditches, so that there may be no ditch, underwood or bushes where one could hide with evil intent within two hundred feet of the road on one side or the other, provided that this statute extends not to oaks or to large trees so long as it is clear underneath. And if by the default of a lord, who will not fill up a ditch or level underwood or bushes in the manner aforesaid, robberies are committed, the lord shall be answerable: and if murder is committed, the lord shall be condemned to make fine at the king's pleasure. And if the lord is unable to cut down the underwood, the district shall help him to do it. And the king is willing for the roads in his demeane lands and woods, within forest and without, to be widened as aforesaid. And if perchance there is a park near the highway, it will beehove the lord of the park to reduce his park until there is a verge two hundred foot wide at the side of the highway as aforesaid, or to make a wall, ditch or hedge that malefactors cannot get over or get back over to do evil.[1]

It is instructive to note the similarities between the Statute of Winchester, issued over 700 years ago, and the recent recommendations of an expert in crime prevention, Robert L. O'Block:

Landscaping should be given particular attention when the grounds are checked for security. Large bushy plants or shrubs should be avoided as much as possible, particularly near entryways. Although attractive, removing them will eliminate ideal hiding places for potential intruders, rapists, or voyeurs. Large trees or plants that obstruct viewing of the structure from the street should also be avoided if feasible. Tall shrubbery and trees can provide camouflage for an intruder and, in many cases, it is best to eliminate or significantly reduce large amounts of foliage located near a structure. Landscaping can also be used advantageously in that dense, thorny hedges and bushes serve natural barriers and can add privacy if planted close to basement or ground-floor windows.[2]

Regardless of the span of 700 years, both Edward I and O'Block call for manipulation of the immediate environs, but the Statute of Winchester addressed the safety of travelers and O'Block is concerned about the risk of victimization for residents when landscaping around residences screens the activities of intruders.

ROOTS OF ENVIRONMENTAL DESIGN

As shown above, contemporary people are not unique in their awareness that the physical environment has much to do with the risk of crime. The scientific concern about manipulating the environment has a shorter history but also extends back at least to the nineteenth century in the work of Adolphe Quetelet of Belgium and A. M. Guerry of France in what has been called the geographical, or cartographic, school of criminology. Human ecology, as a branch of sociology, shares the interest of human geography in the influence of habitat on men and women. The implications have been investigated by sociologists such as Robert E. Park, Ernest W. Burgess, Henry D. McKay, and Clifford Shaw.

The early 1970s lent unprecedented impetus to the empirical and theoretical interests in the possibilities of manipulating the environment as a means of preventing delinquency and crime. Two works were particularly influential.[3] Oscar Newman's *Defensible Space* was oriented mainly to the design problems of multifamily dwelling units in general and urban public housing projects in particular. In his *Crime Prevention Through Environmental Design* (CPTED), C. Ray Jeffery followed a more general conceptualization in emphasizing the organism and the environment.

Those works have been given special credit to stimulating the recent burgeoning of environmental criminology which sets out to examine the place or location of crime.[4] Those specialists have an obligation to the discipline of geography which has place as its raison d'etre. Although crime is not a primary research topic of geography, many of the techniques, methods, and concepts utilized by environmental criminologists were developed by geographers in their studies of other human phenomena.[5]

The thoughts and labors of architects and urban planners also have major influence. The terms "environmental security" and "built environment" illustrate a more specific focus than the earlier attempts to relate crime to the general physical environment through variables such as climate, weather, geologic structure, or the physical landscape. In the latter sense, the physical environment was conceived to include everything that is not part of the social environment.

Environmental security has been defined as an "urban planning and design process which integrates crime prevention with neighborhood design and urban development."[6] The unit of analysis is larger than a housing project, but emphasis on the neighborhood defines a specific spatial-social entity, as opposed to a more general reference to the environment. The phrase "crime and the built environment" (C/BE) also has a more specific focus in its use by the American Institutes for Research in a review of numerous crime and environment studies.[7] The "built environment" refers to the physical constructions of human beings in which they live, work, learn, and play.

To advance the ultimate purposes of the *Handbook on Crime and Delinquency Prevention*, this chapter will enunciate and criticize environmental design as one of the fundamental rationales for prevention. The uniqueness of the rationale lies in its emphasis on the characteristics of the built environment that can stimulate delinquency and crime but that can also be manipulated to encourage actions by potential victims to curb antisocial actions. The work of Oscar Newman will be the foundation for this chapter because it has received major attention and because its concepts lend themselves to this necessarily succinct analysis.[8]

THE DEFENSIBLE SPACE APPROACH

R. I. Mawby offers two explanations for the remarkable acclaim with which Newman's defensible space model was received. First, the focus on high-rise public housing complexes appealed to the critics of those massive housing developments. Second, Newman insists that his model has been verified through careful research.[9] Newman provides a summary statement:

[It is] a model for residential environments which inhibits crime by creating the physical expression of a social fabric that defends itself. All the different elements which combine to make a defensible space have a common goal—an environment in which latent territoriality and sense of community in the inhabitants can be translated into responsibility for ensuring a safe, productive, and well-maintained living space. The potential criminal perceives such space as controlled by its residents, leaving him an intruder easily recognized and dealt with. A defensible space is a living residential environment which can be employed by inhabitants for the enhancement of their lives, while providing security for their families, neighbors, and friends.[10]

Target Hardening But More

Newman's statement frees the term "defensible space" from misinterpretation of his model as a mere listing of specific procedures for the individual to follow in protecting himself or herself from the ravages of criminals by expressing a "fortress mentality." The standard fortifying or target-hardening procedures— such as the use of locks, alarms, fences, and the like—are not the core of the environmental design theory. Instead, Thomas A. Reppetto reports, Newman's model avoids the intellectual sterility and the deeply segregated community implied by the standard fortifying procedures.[11] This urban fortress scenario envisions the residents routinely retreating to their habitats and hiding behind a configuration of security hardware and giving control of the streets, neighborhood, and the external environment, by default, to the criminals. Thus, there is less probability of creating a neighborhood where the residents use, control, and develop a sense of responsibility for it.[12]

In her seminal work, *The Death and Life of Great American Cities* (1961), Jane Jacobs addressed the relationships between crime and residential neighborhoods,[13] but, unlike the work of Newman, her conclusions and generalizations were derived from personal observations, hearsay, and glib anecdotes.[14] Her worthy contribution was bringing to light three very important ideas.

First, there must be a clear demarcation between public space and private space. Public and private spaces cannot ooze into each other as they do typically in suburban settings or in projects.

Second, there must be eyes on the street, eyes belonging to those we might call natural proprietors of the street. The buildings on a street equipped to handle strangers and to insure the safety of both residents and strangers must be oriented to the street. They cannot turn their backs or blank sides on it and leave it blind.

And third, the sidewalk must have users on it fairly continuously, both to add to the number of effective eyes on the street and to induce the people in buildings along the street to watch the sidewalks in sufficient numbers. Nobody enjoys sitting on a stoop or looking out a window at an empty street. Large numbers of people entertain themselves, off and on, by watching street activity.[15]

Essentially, Jacobs is advocating an environmental design that attempts to maximize the conspicuousness of activities. Moreover, this environment would contain a variety of land uses and activities so as to insure a constant circulation of residents and patrons whose presence would deter crime because these people would report all suspicious activities. In short, Jacobs' underlying theme appears to be safety in numbers and diversity.

Crime and Characteristics of Public Housing

In trying to verify his defensible space model, Newman uses two general sources of information. First, he uses records of crimes committed during 1969 in 100 housing projects under the control of the New York City Housing Authority. The second set of information emanates from a comparison of two housing projects which are alleged to be relatively identical in the number and density of tenants. Moreover, the tenants of each project have similar socioeconomic characteristics. Finally, the two projects are located in the same type of geographic area. The main difference between the two projects, according to Newman, is that the one with a lower crime rate also has more defensible space characteristics in its design and layout.

Newman claims that there are several physical characteristics of housing developments for low- and middle-income occupancy that reinforce criminal behavior. The housing projects are very large and accommodate over a thousand families in high-rise apartment towers exceeding seven stories in height. The buildings occupy a space that was previously built-up four to six city blocks. Now the structures are located in a free compositional fashion on a superblock that is closed to city traffic.

Finally, this design provides an open continuous space which enhances free unobstructed movement and access to the buildings and the surrounding streets.[16] The extreme size of the housing project makes it very difficult for a resident to determine who is a resident of the development; thus, open access and unobstructed movement aggravate this situation.[17] Newman addresses these design defects and resulting problems in four areas of discussion: the three concepts of territoriality, natural surveillance, and image and milieu; and, fourth, his efforts to test those concepts with data on crime, fear of crime, and perceptions of community instability.

TERRITORIALITY AS A DIMENSION

According to the geographer Yi Fu Tuan, "every dwelling is a fortress built to defend its human occupants against the elements."[18] Of course, "elements" refers to a variety of behaviors, phenomena, and events real and imaginary. Therefore, a universal and persistent function of the dwelling unit of the home has been to satisfy the psychological need for security.[19] Consequently, the dwelling or home fulfills a territorial instinct in the sense that it provides an identity and a place for its occupants.[20] These needs and instincts are part of the concept of territoriality, which for humans emphasizes physical possession, actual and potential, and defense.[21] An important assumption in the defensible space model is that humans are concerned with the demarcation and defense of their territory.[22]

Identity and Place for Residents

Newman does not succinctly convey an operational definition of territoriality. Yet, he presents the ideal type of dwelling unit which somehow is supposed to represent the optimum example of territoriality in the Western world. Namely, this ideal type is the single-family detached dwelling unit, because it is situated on a separate piece of land and buffered from its neighbors and the public street by intervening grounds.[23]

Newman's first research hypothesis pertains to providing a design that maximizes territoriality in multifamily dwelling units. More explicitly, he defines territoriality as follows:

The capacity of the physical environment to create perceived zones of territorial influence: mechanisms for the subdivision and articulation of areas of the residential environment intended to reinforce inhabitants in their ability to assume territorial attitudes and prerogatives.[24]

Therefore, following this prescription, the design of the housing project will convey a real or symbolic expression of which places or spaces belong to private individuals; of which spaces people may have to seek some sort of permission to use or restrict their range of behaviors; and of which spaces are open or accessible to all. Furthermore, this design will release the latent territorial instincts of its residents.

Promising But Speculative Proposition

Newman offers scant empirical evidence in support of the territoriality hypothesis. It consists mainly of two tables. The first implies a positive association between the rate of crime in hallways and the number of apartments per hallway. The second implies the same relationship between crime rate and the number of units in a housing project. Specifically, projects with more than 1,000 units have higher crime rates than those with fewer than 1,000 units.[25]

Newman's assertion that physical design can release latent territorial instincts in a project's tenants is a rather provocative proposition. Yet, he does not explain why or how physical design should promote territoriality. In other words, the process between physical design and territorial behavior is not illuminated. This oversight or omission has attracted considerable criticism.[26]

Newman's conceptualization of territoriality and the mechanisms for invoking territorial behavior may be too simplistic for many social-behavioral scientists. However, Newman may have confused territoriality with the concept of accessibility. He presents convincing proof that public housing projects are too large and too open. Thus, the design of the developments produces a situation where the adjective "public" is more descriptive of a type of access than a form of trusteeship. Nevertheless, territoriality and accessibility have been the subjects of many subsequent studies in environmental design.

NATURAL SURVEILLANCE AS A DIMENSION

To enhance the concept of territoriality, Newman offers his hypothesis on natural surveillance. He defines it as follows: The capacity of physical design to provide surveillance opportunities for residents and their agents: mechanisms for improving the capacity of residents to casually and continually survey the nonprivate areas of their living environment, indoors and out.[27]

This is a contingent proposition because, if it is to be operative, residents must practice their territorial instincts and possess a high degree of social responsibility. Easy and unobstructed visibility of all portions of the housing development for crime prevention would be a design parameter important for crime prevention.

Newman contends that some traditional designs for public housing projects inadvertently create blind spots or simply handicap observation and surveillance. Particularly hazardous in the interiors of buildings are the lobbies, halls, elevators, and fire stairs. These features are likely to have those defects, Newman explains, because they are public rather than private space. Yet, unlike other public spaces, these features are not routinely patrolled, observed, or used by police officers, residents, or bystanders.[28] Furthermore, these traditional designs have made the exterior areas of a housing project very hazardous. Newman explains that one of the tenets of early planning theory called for housing designs that looked inward on themselves.[29] Thus, the windows and entrances of such projects focused on the development's grounds, leaving the bordering streets and connecting footpaths unobserved and seemingly perilous.

Newman proposes a design that would ameliorate both problems by locating potential blind spots in places easily observed from the street and sidewalks by police officers, residents, and passersby. This notion vaguely reflects the "eyes of the street" prescription of Jane Jacobs. Likewise, Newman claims that the apartments in a building can be designed so as to enhance the surveillance of footpaths, entries, and play and seating areas of the project.[30]

To generate data in support of the natural surveillance hypothesis, Newman assigned the New York City housing projects to one of three categories: (1) those with buildings facing and within 50 feet of the street; (2) those with buildings facing and within 50 feet of the street and with good lobby visibility (large window area); and (3) those with less than 30 percent of the buildings facing and within 50 feet of the street.[31] The second category appeared to have a lower crime rate, but Newman's descriptive statistics are not convincing.[32]

In reality, the null hypothesis should be labeled the Kitty Genovese hypothesis. On an April night in 1964, in Queens, New York, Catherine Genovese was returning from work during the early morning hours. She was attacked and stabbed repeatedly over an extended period of time. Her plight was witnessed by at least thirty-eight residents of an until-then respectable New York neighborhood—but no one went to her aid or at least summoned help until it was too late.[33] Newman joins many other social critics in using the Kitty Genovese tragedy as an example of a breakdown in our sense of social responsibility.

NEGATIVE DISTINCTIVE IMAGE AND THE MILIEU

The design of government-subsidized public housing projects, Newman argues, is distinctive in that its buildings and grounds do not blend in with the surrounding urban landscape. Thus, he is concerned that a negative distinctive image will lead to the stigmatization of the project and maltreatment of its residents.[34]

The defensible space model carries the premise that building design has the capacity to counter the negative effects on residents that stem from a distinctively negative image of public housing. Instead of presenting worthy empirical evidence to support the image hypothesis, Newman relies on a limited number of interviews of tenants, existing public housing design practices, and some previous research. The projects usually were several high-rise buildings that inevitably stand out from other buildings in the area. The interior finishes and furnishings present the uniformity of prisons and hospitals that leaves one with the impression that the residents are being institutionalized and locked into restricted and limited lifestyles. In many instances, residents react by neglecting upkeep of the dwelling unit.[35]

Closely related to the concept of image, the concept of milieu turns attention to the relationship of the housing project to its immediate environment. Ideally, the housing project will be compatible with its neighborhood or immediate environment. Newman advocates the scattered placement of public housing projects within "safe areas" or areas with a safe reputation. Furthermore, these safe areas contain a variety of different land uses that generate a persistent circulation of patrons, employees, and residents, thus returning to the safety in numbers and diversity idea of Jacobs. As for the image hypothesis, Newman does not present any quantitive measurements or empirical evidence to support the milieu hypothesis.

TESTING CORRELATES OF CRIME

As an expression of his continuing involvement in defensible space theory, Newman in collaboration with Karen Franck tested the concepts with a sample of sixty-three low- and moderate-income housing projects in three cities. The purpose of this research was to ascertain the strongest correlates of crime, fear, and instability. Four variables were found to be strongly correlated with the independent variables. Two of the variables pertained to physical design features (building size and accessibility); the remainder were two social variables (percentage of low-income/AFDC residents and the ratio of teenagers to adults).[36]

Unlike the original conceptualization of defensible space, the authors assessed the intermediate effects of intervening effects and localized three intervening effects: (1) control of space: perception of residents that their neighbors would intervene in the event criminal or suspicious activities occurred outside their apartments; (2) use of space: extent to which residents used private areas and outdoor spaces; and (3) social interaction: nature and frequency of contact with residents and the feeling of belonging.[37]

Building size was the strongest physical design determinant of the control of space. In other words, the larger the building the lower the perceived control of space. A decline in the residents' perception of their control of space was accompanied by a greater incidence of personal crime, fear, and instability.[38] This finding should be expected because Newman has consistently nominated size of the housing project as one of the greatest predictors of crime.

The tenets of defensible space theory were also supported by data on the use of space. Building size has an inverse relationship with use of space. Greater utilization of private and outdoor spaces by residents was associated with a lower rate of crime and fear of crime.[39]

The social interaction variable produced some bewildering results. First, the design features of building size and accessibility held an inverse relationship that tended to generate project stability. Thus, the smaller the building the more restricted the access; the more social interaction the less the turnover rate of residents. This linkage is rather logical and expected. However, social interaction tends to increase the amount of personal crime.[40] This finding runs counter to defensible space theory and has been labeled a "methodological quirk" by others.[41]

DEFENSIBLE SPACE REDEFINED

The Newman-Franck research study was partially a reflection of a theme in defensible space theory that surfaced in the mid–1970s. That theme was a greater emphasis on the possibility that changes in defensible space could facilitate greater social cohesion among residents and thereby lead to increased influence of informal control over possible criminal behavior in the residential area. Herb Rubenstein and his colleagues detected two distinctive rationales in the literature on the linkages between the environment and crime. The rationales are social surveillance and community building.[42]

Theme of Social Surveillance

Similar to Newman's concept of natural surveillance, social surveillance rests on the premise that, if residents observe suspicious behavior, they will report the behavior and, if necessary, will intervene. The premise has implications for the community building rationale, but social surveillance concentrates on the argument that modifications in the exterior environment for improving the visibility of behaviors will produce decreased fear, fewer attempted and successful crimes, and increased perceptions by potential criminals that they face a real risk of apprehension.[43] Thus, environmental modification and reduction of crime are believed to be directly related. One strategy is to increase lighting in order to allow the observation of night-time predators. Tuan expresses the argument:

Dark nights curtail human vision. People lose their ability to manipulate the environment and feel vulnerable. As daylight withdraws, so does their world. Nefarious powers take over. Witches and ghosts figure prominently in the lore of the Western world. . . . All evil beings, ghosts included, are denizens of the dark. Countryfolk in the South used to say roving at night was a sin; respectable people stayed indoors.[44]

As the sole environmental design modification, improved lighting does not have a clear effect on the level of crime. An evaluation of lighting projects by J. M. Tien et al. does not support the theory that improved lighting increases the reporting of crime, but improved lighting does appear to reduce citizens' fears or apprehensions.[45] Perhaps fear of the dark stems from childhood when adults discipline children with threats of being put at the mercy of creatures for whom the dark is their habitat.[46] A review of the research indicates that "environmental features that afford concealment increase vulnerability to crime."[47] Moreover, citizens are more fearful of features in and around buildings that provide concealment opportunities for the offender. Like lighting, it has yet to be determined if changes in concealment opportunities are effective in reducing crime.[48]

In Newman's defensible space theory, the accessibility of public housing structures referred to such features as the number and positioning of exits and entrances and the number of windows on the ground floor, whereas circulation usually referred to the pathways and corridors in and around the housing project. The only type of land use discussed was the housing project. However, at the geographic scales of the city block, census tract, residential neighborhood or the community, these concepts have new or expanded meanings.

Accessibility in the environmental design research refers to the street network whereas circulation is both pedestrian and vehicular movement. The basic hypothesis guiding accessibility research is that "locations most accessible to outside traffic are the most vulnerable to crime."[49] Many studies have supported this hypothesis. In their comparison of high- and low-crime neighborhoods in Atlanta, S. W. Greenberg, William J. Rohe, and Jay R. Williams found that the low-crime neighborhoods were characterized by "homogeneous residential land use, small streets, and few major thoroughfares."[50] Another study examined the relationship between burglary and the accessibility afforded by different forms of street intersections. The resulted indicated a positive association between burglary rates and street intersection accessibility.[51] Furthermore, Paul Brantingham and Patricia Brantingham found that blocks forming the border of residential neighborhoods had higher burglary rates than blocks composing the interior or core of homogeneous residential neighborhoods.[52]

Previous works have reported a positive association between the transportation infrastructure and crime. However, after their review of investigations of the relationship between pedestrian and vehicular circulation and crime, Herb Rubenstein and his associates concluded "that crime is associated with both low and high volumes of traffic."[53] The factor common to the two extreme conditions is isolation. Those crimes related to low circulation appear to occur in areas that are isolated from surveillance or lack the "eyes on the street" condition of Jane Jacobs.[54] Higher circulation areas appear to generate crime because of the emotional isolation and withdrawal or noninvolvement of pedestrians and residents. The relationship between higher circulation areas and crime reflects personal adaptation to an overloaded social environment where one becomes involved only when it is relevant to personal needs.[55]

The quantity of movement of people from place to place may produce varying levels of crime, but, in addition, the types of land uses may bring a qualitative dimension to the process. Fairly homogeneous land uses, such as single-family detached-dwelling residential areas, may attract only small and local flows of people who basically belong to that area. Other research, however, has indicated that certain types of land uses, as well as conflicting or incompatible land uses, may be arenas for a variety of crimes. "In a broad sense, land use 'generates' crime in a manner analogous to the way in which it generates traffic."[56] Because varying quantities and qualities of accessibility, circulation, and land use may affect the levels of certain types of crime, the relationship is not ubiquitous in its intensity. Crime is not a static phenomenon but involves movement and interaction between different areas of a community or city. Finally, the environmental design approach to crime prevention implies that crime exhibits a geometric rather than an arithemetic progression.

Community-Building Rationale

The social surveillance rationale rests on the central idea that modification of the built environment will directly limit or restrict opportunities for crime. In advancing that idea, Newman rejects the pessimism that crime is so embedded in the basic social and economic condition of urban society that little can be done to overcome it. He argues that physical design changes in themselves would "release latent attitudes in tenants which allow them to assume behavior necessary for the protection of their rights and property."[57] In his later study in collaboration with Karen Franck, Newman included social variables as well as physical design variables in a test of the concepts of defensible space.[58] Thus, he recognized a trend in defensible space research that Charles Murray has summarized as follows: "By 1975 or 1976 changes in design were no longer expected to reduce crime in and of themselves, but they could, it was believed, be one important component in a package of crime reduction measures."[59]

The community-building rationale thus emphasizes the contribution of modifications of the built environment to a broader effort to instill a sense of living in a common community by residents of a neighborhood. The broad effort would also include the creation of groups dedicated to crime prevention among residents, better policing, and better relationships between the police. In other words, "physical characteristics affect social interaction and cohesion, which in turn affect crime and the fear of crime."[60]

In Hartford, Connecticut, a neighborhood crime prevention project was implemented in Asylum Hill, an older urban residential neighborhood on the verge of deterioration. As controls to compare outcomes, two other inner-city neighborhoods (Clay Hill and South Arsenal) were selected because they, too, were experiencing increases in fear of crime and crime rates. The project was designed to test whether or not motivations for crime are stimulated by crime opportunities provided by the residents and environmental features of the neighborhood. The opportunities were to be reduced, first, by altering the physical features of buildings and streets to increase surveillance to reduce the vulnerability of victims, to enhance the neighborhood's attractiveness to residents, and to decrease the fear-producing features; second, by increasing the concerns and involvement of citizens in crime prevention; and, third, by using the police in support of those purposes.[61]

Three primary changes in physical design in Asylum Hill were implemented: creation of street cul-de-sacs to interdict exterior traffic; diversion of exterior vehicular traffic similarly to define subneighborhoods; and encouragement of private property fencing. A sense of residential ownership and residents' control of their neighborhood was to be produced by increasing the use of immediate physical space and by discouraging outside pedestrian activity. To supplement the effects of physical design changes, the Asylum Hill program also included decentralized team policing, active relationships between the police and residents, and creation of viable organizations of residents to change traditional attitudes and behavior patterns.[62]

Evaluation of the experiment, compared with the two control neighborhoods, "indicated a substantial reduction in burglary and fear of burglary while a pattern of increasing robbery/pursesnatch was halted and may have undergone a reduction."[63] Floyd J. Fowler and his associates argue that three components of the experiment—changes in physical design, police operations, and community responses to crime—are essential to crime prevention, but the physical design changes made possible the contributions of the other two components. "A physical environment which encouraged informal efforts of individual residents (such as using neighborhood spaces and watching one another's homes)," they say, "appears to have been the key to the reduction that occurred."[64]

LINGERING QUESTIONS FOR THE MODEL

Environmental design as a rationale for crime prevention capitalizes on the common sense observation that the physical environment does have some relationship to the risk and fear of crime. The rationale has brought architects and urban planners into the dialogue on what can be done to reduce crime and raise the quality of life. However, there are lingering questions on precisely how environmental design variables influence citizen behavior.

The initial version of Newman's defensible space model ignored social phenomena either as predictor or mediating variables.[65] The community-building rationale has an important contribution to make but raises serious methodological problems for the researcher. In his later work, Newman has given greater attention to social variables.[66] Rubenstein and his associates point out that environmental design research has not given proper respect to the methodological difficulties of rigorously testing their speculations:

As a class, they have been overly ambitious. They have tried to show too much. They have traded precision for grandeur. They have oversimplified rather than dug. We find it neither surprising nor damning that the theory has not been supported. The problems of testing these subtle dynamics demand a more humble approach.[67]

An excellent example of overly ambitious research is the Westinghouse CPTED projects of the late 1970s. This research consisted of three demonstration projects: a commercial corridor, a school, and a residential setting. This type of environmental design effort was to be more comprehensive in the sense that environmental design changes would be accompanied by supporting citizen management programs, and special law enforcement strategies.[68] The major problem with the projects was the simultaneous implementation of various environmental design strategies. To isolate and localize cause-and-effect relationships was a cumbersome enterprise.[69] An optimal research strategy may be to concentrate on fewer variables while exerting greater control over exogenous circumstances and intervening variables.

The future of the environmental design research appears to lie in illuminating the process by which people will come together to form a protective alliance.[70] Then, the place and function of the model in crime prevention can be determined more precisely.

NOTES

1. Harry Rothwell, ed., *English Historical Documents 1189–1327* (New York: Oxford University Press, 1975), p. 461. Also refer to Yi Fu Tuan, *Landscapes of Fear* (Minneapolis: University of Minnesota Press, 1979), p. 133.

2. Robert L. O'Block, *Security and Crime Prevention* (St. Louis, Mo.: C.V. Mosby Co., 1981), p. 310.

3. Oscar Newman, *Defensible Space: Crime Prevention Through Urban Design* (New York: Collier Books, 1973) and C. Ray Jeffery, *Crime Prevention Through Environmental Design* (Beverly Hills, Calif.: Sage Publications, 1977).

4. Paul J. Brantingham and Patricia L. Brantingham, eds., *Environmental Criminology* (Beverly Hills, Calif.: Sage Publications, 1981), p. 8.

5. Two major contributions by geographers are Keith D. Harries, *The Geography of Crime and Justice* (New York: McGraw-Hill, 1974) and Gerald F. Pyle et al., *The Spatial Dynamics of Crime* (Chicago: University of Chicago, Department of Geography, 1974).

6. Richard A. Gardiner, *Design for Safe Neighborhoods: The Environmental Security Planning and Design Process* (Washington, D.C.: American Institutes for Research, 1980).

7. See H. Rubenstein et al., *The Link Between Crime and the Built Environment— The Current State of Knowledge*, Vol. 1 (Washington, D.C.: American Institutes for Research, 1980).

8. For a discussion of why criminology initially ignored design or the defensible

82   James L. LeBeau

space model, see Thomas A. Reppetto, "Crime Prevention Through Environmental Policy: A Critique," *American Behavioral Scientist* 20 (November-December 1976):275–288.

9. R. I. Mawby, "Defensible Space: A Theoretical and Empirical Appraisal," *Urban Studies* 14 (1977):169.

10. Newman, *Defensible Space*, p. 3.

11. Reppetto, "Crime Prevention Through Environmental Policy," p. 283.

12. Gardiner, *Design for Safe Neighborhoods*, p. 14, 31.

13. Jane Jacobs, *The Death and Life of Great American Cities* (New York: Vintage Books, 1961).

14. Mawby, "Defensible Space," p. 169.

15. Jacobs, *The Death and Life of Great American Cities*, p. 35.

16. Newman, *Defensible Space*, p. 22.

17. Ibid., p. 22.

18. Tuan, *Landscapes of Fear*, p. 6.

19. Amos Rapoport, *House Form and Culture* (Englewood Cliffs, N.J.: Prentice-Hall, 1969), p. 79.

20. Ibid.

21. F. D. Becker and C. Mayo, "Delineating Personal Distance and Territoriality," *Environment and Behavior* (December 1971): 377. Citing R. Sommer, "Man's Proximate Environment," *Journal of Social Issues* 22 (1960): 59–60.

22. Becker and Mayo, "Delineating Personal Distance and Territoriality," pp. 376–377.

23. Newman, *Defensible Space*, p. 51.

24. Ibid., p. 50.

25. Ibid., pp. 69, 71.

26. See Ralph B. Taylor et al., "The Defensibility of Defensible Space: A Critical Review and a Synthetic Framework for Future Research," in Travis Hirschi and Michael Gottfredson, eds., *Understanding Crime* (Beverly Hills, Calif.: Sage Publications, 1980), pp. 54–55.

27. Newman, *Defensible Space*, p. 50.

28. Ibid., p. 86.

29. Ibid., p. 80.

30. Ibid., p. 91.

31. Ibid., p. 83.

32. Herb Rubenstein, Charles A. Murray, Tetsuro Motoyuma, and W. V. Rouse, *The Link Between Crime and the Built Environment*, Vol. 2 (Washington, D.C.: American Institutes for Research, July 1980), p. C–153.

33. Stanley Milgram, "Living in Cities," in Mihajlo D. Mesarovic and Arnold Reisman, eds., *Systems Approach and the City* (New York: Elsevier Publishing Co., 1972), pp. 393–394.

34. Newman, *Defensible Space*, p. 102.

35. Ibid., pp. 102–106.

36. Oscar Newman and Karen Franck, *Factors Influencing Crime and Instability in Urban Housing Developments: Executive Summary* (Washington, D.C.: U.S. Department of Justice, 1980), p. 32.

37. Ibid., p. 79.

38. Ibid.

39. Ibid.

40. Ibid.

41. Rubenstein et al., *Link Between Crime and Built Environment*, Vol. 1, p. 50.

42. Ibid., pp. 23, 42.

43. Ibid., p. 23.

44. Tuan, *Landscapes of Fear*, pp. 107, 129.

45. J. M. Tien et al., *Street Lighting Projects* (Washington, D.C.: U.S. Department of Justice, 1979).

46. Tuan, *Landscapes of Fear*, p. 15.

47. Rubenstein et al., *Link Between Crime and Built Environment*, Vol. 1, p. 40.

48. Fred Heinzelmann, "Crime Prevention and the Physical Environment," in D. A. Lewis, ed., *Reactions to Crime* (Beverly Hills, Calif.: Sage Publications, 1981), p. 91.

49. Rubenstein et al., *Link Between Crime and Built Environment*, Vol. 1, p. 25.

50. S. W. Greenberg, William M. Rohe, and Jay R. Williams, *Safe and Secure Neighborhoods: Physical Characteristics and Informal Territorial Control in High and Low Crime Neighborhoods* (Washington, D.C.: U.S. Department of Justice, 1982), p. 122.

51. C. Davis and J. Nutter, *Changing Street Layouts to Reduce Residential Burglary* (St. Paul: Minnesota Governor's Commission on Crime Prevention and Control, 1977).

52. P. L. Brantingham and P. J. Brantingham, "Residential Burglary and Urban Force," *Urban Studies* 12 (1975): 273–285.

53. Rubenstein et al., *Link Between Crime and Built Environment*, Vol. 1, p. 34.

54. Ibid.

55. Milgram, "Living in Cities," p. 393.

56. Keith D. Harries, *Crime and the Environment* (Springfield, Ill.: Charles C Thomas, 1980), p. 93.

57. Oscar Newman, *Architectural Design for Crime Prevention* (Washington, D.C.: U.S. Government Printing Office, 1973), p. xii.

58. Newman and Franck, *Factors Influencing Crime and Instability in Urban Housing Developments*, p. 3.

59. Charles A. Murray, "The Physical Environment and Community Control of Crime," in James Q. Wilson, ed., *Crime and Public Policy* (San Francisco: ICS Press, 1983), p. 113.

60. Rubenstein et al., *Link Between Crime and Built Environment*, p. 11.

61. Floyd J. Fowler, Jr., with Mary Ellen McCalla and Thomas W. Manglone, *Reducing Residential Crime and Fear: The Hartford Neighborhood Crime Prevention Program—Executive Summary* (Washington, D.C.: National Institute of Law Enforcement and Criminal Justice, December 1979), pp. 2–4.

62. Ibid., p. 10–13.

63. Ibid., p. vii.

64. Ibid., pp. 56–57.

65. Taylor et al., "The Defensibility of Defensible Space," p. 53.

66. See Oscar Newman, *Design Guidelines for Creating Defensible Space* (Washington, D.C.: National Institute of Law Enforcement and Criminal Justice, 1976).

67. Rubenstein et al., *Link Between Crime and Built Environment*, Vol. 1, p. 68.

68. See Edward J. Pesce et al., "Creating Safe Environments: Crime Prevention Through Environmental Design," in B. Galaway and J. Hudson, eds., *Perspectives on Crime Victims* (St. Louis: C.V. Mosbay Co., 1981), pp. 347–362.

69. Taylor et al., "Defensibility of Defensible Space," p. 61.

70. See Sally E. Merry, "Defensible Space Undefended: Social Factors in Crime Control Through Environmental Design," *Urban Affairs Quarterly* 16 (June 1981): 397–422.

BIBLIOGRAPHY

Booth, Alan. "The Built Environment as a Crime Deterrent: A Reexamination of Defensible Space." *Criminology* 18 (February 1981): 557–570.

  Matched samples of victimized and nonvictimized households are compared. Booth reports that defensible space has slight impact on feelings of responsibility for public space. Crime is deterred in indoor areas but not in outdoor areas.

Brantingham, Paul J., and Patricia L. Brantingham, eds. *Environmental Criminology.* Beverly Hills, Calif.: Sage Publications, 1981.

  This collection of essays by criminologists, geographers, and planners probes the essence of environmental criminology.

Gillis, A. R., and John Hogan. "Density, Delinquency, and Design: Formal and Informal Control and the Built Environment." *Criminology* 19 (February 1982): 514–529.

  The literature review on the impact of the physical environment focuses on two perspectives: the impairment of informal control and the attraction of the police as formal control agents.

Greenberg, S. W., William M. Rohe, and Jay R. Williams. *Safe and Secure Neighborhoods: Physical Characteristics and Informal Territorial Control in High and Low Crime Neighborhoods.* Washington, D.C.: U.S. Department of Justice, 1982.

  The spatial-social distinctions between high- and low-crime neighborhoods and accessibility of the neighborhood are posited as being positively associated with crime. Interviews of residents indicated that accurate assessments of local crime levels did not translate into protective action; rather, meshing local contacts into a network may lead to collective prevention behavior.

Heinzelmann, Fred. "Crime Prevention and the Physical Environment." In Dan A. Lewis, ed., *Reactions to Crime.* Beverly Hills, Calif.: Sage Publications, 1981, pp. 87–101.

  The literature on crime prevention and environmental design with respect to structures, residential blocks, and neighborhoods is reviewed. The author indicates that design must relate to more specific features of the environment, but changes in the built environment can reduce crime and most certainly the fear of crime.

Merry, Sally E. "Defensible Space Undefended: Social Factors in Crime Control Through Environmental Design." *Urban Affairs Quarterly* 16 (June 1981): 397–422.

  This work is an anthropological participant observation study of a small inner-city housing project. The author feels that environmental design can influence crime, but any design modifications are limited in a socially fragmented setting.

Murray, Charles A. "The Physical Environment and Community Control of Crime." In James Q. Wilson, ed. *Crime and Public Policy.* San Francisco: ICS Press, 1983, pp. 107–122.

  In his critique, Murray argues that the effectiveness of defensible space theory depends crucially on the preexisting social environment and that the theory is least relevant to areas where crime rates are highest.

Pesce, Edward J., et al. "Creating Safe Environments: Crime Prevention Through Environmental Design." In Burt Galaway and Joe Hudson, eds., *Perspectives on Crime Victims*. St. Louis, Mo.: C.V. Mosby Co., 1981, pp. 347–361.

This work is basically a description of the Westinghouse Crime Prevention Through Environmental Design Projects. The work is informative but not too analytical.

Rubenstein, H., et al. *The Link Between Crime and the Built Environment—The Current State of Knowledge*, Vol. 2. Washington, D.C.: American Institutes for Research, 1980.

The authors examine a number of environmental design studies and offer thorough and concise criticisms of each study's design, methodology, conclusions, and contribution to understanding the linkage between crime and the environment.

Taylor, Ralph B., Stephen D. Gottfredson, and Sidney Brower. "The Defensibility of Defensible Space: A Critical Review and a Synthetic Framework for Future Research." In Travis Hirschi and Michael Gottfredson, eds., *Understanding Crime: Current Theory and Research*. Beverly Hills, Calif.: Sage Publications, 1980, pp. 53–71.

The authors chronicle the development of defensible space theory, offer criticisms, and propose a new generation of theory based on territoriality.

4

Treatment and Behavior Change in Juvenile Delinquents

GERALD E. DAVIDSON

The treatment of juveniles had undergone a radical cycle of change over the last twenty years. Through the 1960s, juvenile delinquents and neglected youngsters were regularly taken into the custody of juvenile courts, acting *in loco parentis*. Under the paternalistic supervision of a judge, the juvenile could be taken from his home, confined to long periods in detention homes, and have major life decisions put in the hands of the judicial authorities.

All this changed overnight with the Supreme Court decision, *Gault vs. United States (1967)*, which extended due process rights of juvenile courts. Juvenile justice is now handled with the full legal paraphernalia that burdens the adult court system. Legal-aid attorneys available to all offenders almost automatically throw the proceedings into an adversarial mode. While older judges and attorneys often acted ''in the best interest of the child,'' juvenile-justice defense counselors now think only in terms of ''civil rights'' and ignore the obvious conclusions that some adolescents need help—both for their own protection and for the sake of society.

TREATMENT AND PREVENTION

Meeting the need for help is the core of the therapeutic rationale for the prevention of deliquency and crime; the means are diagnoses and treatment of the sources of the client's difficulties. Competent help is indispensable when the individual's nature or nurture is defective, either preventing or aborting normal personality growth. The individual may exhibit an incapacity to control impulsive

The author acknowledges the helpful suggestions of Father Robert C. Allanach, OMI, Director of Psychological and Counseling Services at Elan, in preparation of the chapter.

behavior, to sustain mutual relationships with others, to be consistent in life acitivities, and to nurture the sense of life goals. The result is an incompetent, existentially frightened young person, terrified of the demand to grow up and productively earn a place in the world. His or her behavior may or may not become defined as delinquent or criminal, but the focus of therapeutic intervention is to provide help to the troubled individual. That focus distinguishes the therapeutic rationale from the legalistic, rights-oriented approach and its concentration on the deviant act.

Effects of Change on Treatment

In the new atmosphere characterizing the juvenile justice system, the bringing of that help to disturbed individuals has suffered. The legal professionals set out to curb indiscriminate incarceration and other adverse consequences of paternalistic legal intervention. Their reform efforts, however, have carelessly identified those faults with all forms of treatment. Enthusiastic lawyers and child advocates have gone to the extreme of regarding liberty and escape from social responsibility as the only desideratum. It is as if ten year olds were given the "right" to refuse appendectomies because the advocates cannot imagine that a frightened child would make the decision on the bases that it might hurt.

This attitude among advocates of treatment has made them vulnerable to the claims of "excessive leniency" advanced in support of the legalistic, rights-oriented approach. Many contemporary modes of thought about delinquency are the conscious, unconscious, or just inadvertent tendencies of therapists to blame society or to blame parents. Another tendency is to pity or to patronize adolescents by viewing them as materially or psychologically deprived and then trying to "make up for" the "deprivation."

This chapter will critique three typical approaches to delinquency prevention, each of which has played a part in the radical changes in conceptions of what the therapeutic rationale implies. Those approaches are : (1) the legalistic, rights-oriented approach, (2) the sociological approach, and (3) the purely psychoanalytic and psychodynamic approach.

Relevance of Elan One

As a more promising alternative to those approaches, I will present a model for a therapeutic facility that, unlike the sociological approach, focuses on individuals, that, unlike the legalistic approach, avoids the "adversarial game," and that, unlike the psychoanalytic approach, insists that adolescents grow into adults by becoming responsible for their own behavior. In presenting that alternative and testing its effectiveness, this chapter will draw on the practices and experiences of Elan One, a school for troubled boys and girls in Maine.

Elan One has been able to avoid most of these legal tangles and at the same time make progress in treating troubled teenagers. Its experience may serve as a guide to other efforts. The school's success rate now ranges between 80 and 90 percent in taking youths that have been judged unmanageable and returning them to "normal society."

These results have not been tested against control groups, but considering that this is an institution of last resort and that youngsters often come to Elan only after everything else has failed, its track record speaks for itself. A two-year followup of the "Class of 1984," for example, shows that of twenty-two Elan residents who finished high school that year, twenty (91 percent) are now in postsecondary settings that require a high school diploma. Of the "Class of 1983," 89 percent are still pursuing their education. No hospital adolescent program, no other residential treatment school, indeed even few public high schools, can even think about claiming such a record.

Elan in located in Poland Spring, Maine, 140 miles north of Boston. The founders were myself and Joseph Ricci, who serves as executive director. My own experience in psychiatric institutions in Boston had led me to believe that something different was necessary. Ricci, himself a graduate of a self-help community which was a crude precursor of Elan, was anxious to work with troubled adolescents.

From the first, we handled both middle-class and lower-class delinquents; the latter frequently came from "delinquent environments." After some experience, however, we found that the mix was troublesome. The upper-middle-class youngsters tended to idolize the "street kids" as more "macho" and tried to emulate their "strength." The lower-class youngsters found this extremely demoralizing. They had the American ethos of upward mobility and both looked up to and envied the educated and affluent youngsters. The affluent youngsters' discarding of their society's cultural and moral values destroyed the less advantaged students' social ideals and left them without a sense of reasonable social goals. It took work and time to bring about a consensus that moral values are universal, the property and obligation of each individual regardless of social origin. We found that moral values are extremely important and that moral neutrality is an affectation, a copout by professionals uncertain about themselves. We insist that adolescents grow into adults by becoming personally responsible for their own behavior. So, we have reverted to what might be labeled an older and more authoritative approach.

Implications for Prevention

From the perspective of the therapeutic rationale, prevention cannot be directed only to legally prohibited acts but must go beyond even status offenses to include antisocial attitudes and general lifestyle. The susceptibility of predelinquents makes Elan One relevant to secondary prevention; the institution is dedicated to bringing therapeutic help to adolescents who have not violated legal prescriptions.

For secondary prevention, potential delinquents and criminals have been variously identified as school dropouts, vocationally inept, victims of poverty or racism, members of disorganized families, and so on. This chapter is directed toward the individuals who suffer inner conflicts, low self-esteem, and other psychological effects of being included in one or more of such groups with major social and personal problems.

Tertiary prevention refers to intervention undertaken in the lives of persons who have become subject to criminal justice processing. The objective is prevention in the sense of forestalling further offenses. The distinction between secondary and tertiary prevention has little relevance to the functions of Elan One. However, if the reader insists on that distinction, the functions and methods of Elan One are instructive for private or public programs directed toward reducing the risk of further offenses by seriously disturbed adolescents.

CRITIQUE OF THREE USUAL APPROACHES

The more contemporary frameworks for implementing the therapeutic rationale are flawed. These approaches are : (1) the legalistic, rights-oriented approach; (2) the sociological approach; and (3) the purely psychoanalytic and psychodynamic approach.

The Legalistic, Rights-Oriented Approach

The old juvenile justice system was not as defective as indicated by the controversy culminating in the *Gault* decision. Although it may have violated the niceties of due process, it avoided the adversarial, confrontational mode that now dominates procedures.

Legal punishment alone—the obedience/conformity model—works least well. When the courts think only in terms of punishment or incarceration, there can only be one dimension of variability, from cruelty to kindness. Paradoxically, the more kindly or "civilized" we try to make incarceration, the more we destroy the authority of the caretakers and the more brutal and brutalizing our institutions become as the inmate criminal subculture takes over. Equally paradoxically, length of sentence reform destroys any impulse for constructive change. The delinquent's desideratum becomes to "do time," to get it over with, rather than to develop mature character.

This single variable does not offer society too many options, but we must still recognize that punishment is often necessary. The Juvenile Justice Standards Project of the American Bar Association sabotaged everything by their proposed (1981) standards whereby a maximum sentence of eighteen months was set for first-degree murder. It must be recognized that for anyone to get away with murder is profoundly demoralizing both to the society and to individual criminals.

The legalistic approach falls short in another way. "Crusader-Rabbit-type" defense attorneys do everything they can to get their clients off, no matter what the consequences. All this does not help juveniles who are not yet responsible adults and who need serious help in trying to pull their lives together.

The Sociological Approach

The sociological approach reached its apogee in the 1963 publication of a small book entitled *Delinquency and Opportunity* by criminologists Lloyd Ohlin and Richard Cloward.[1] They held that juvenile delinquency was basically social in origin and had little to do with individual personalities or individual responsibility. Instead, delinquency was described as the legitimate desire of material and monetary goals as expressed by lower-class youths for whom all social pathways were blocked and were forced to turn to illegitimate channels. As their mentor, Robert K. Merton, expressed it, delinquency was a "symptom of dissociation between culturally prescribed aspirations and socially structured avenues for realizing these aspirations."[2] Thus, the sociological approach casts much of the blame on an abstract "society," which supposedly encourages lower-class youngsters to want material things, but "denies" them the means of achieving them. In a very subtle way, Cloward, Ohlin, and Merton, were providing a rationale for delinquents that delinquents might not even feel the need of putting forth themselves.

In our experience, this model has proved very unhelpful. First, it is almost meaningless for upper-class delinquent youths who are often deluged with material goods. But neither does the Cloward and Ohlin model seem to have much relevance for the very lower-class youth it is supposed to be describing. Their notion is that monetary rewards—licit or illicit—lie at the core of delinquent behavior. There is much talk about "providing jobs" but little recognition that these youngsters are incapable of holding jobs—and that the same personal disorganization that makes them unable to do useful work is also what drives them to exhibit antisocial behavior and commit crimes. They have not done the psychological "work of adolescence," and they remain incompetent children.

In addition, many empirical studies have shown that it is not the "legitimate" desire for monetary reward that drives many delinquents. Many people grow up poor. Few ever become criminals. Marvin Wolfgang's longitudinal study of 9,000 Philadelphia age cohorts showed that only 6 percent of the entire population accounted for over half the delinquent acts and for two-thirds of the violent crime.[3] "There is accumulating evidence that failure, particularly anticipated failure to achieve long-range educational and occupational goals, in not a highly significant factor in delinquent behavior," concluded Delbert S. Elliott and Harmon Z. Voss in another study.[4]

The Psychoanalytic Model

The psychoanalytic approach is in some ways successful in that it provides clinically proven insight into what actually occurs. However, techniques for delivering limit-setting confrontation, insight, positive identification, and positive relating ability are only now being developed. Fundamentally, these techniques are the subject of this chapter. In particular, reliance on insight therapy alone, or on Skinneresque behavior-modification programs (such as token economies) alone, produced superficial results and left plenty of leeway in the residential setting where peer-dominated delinquent behavior could thrive.

It is now more than twenty years since Howard Polsky published *Cottage Six*. Polsky described how intensive psychotherapeutic efforts were entirely negated by a criminal subculture that thrived in the institution and really controlled the patients' lives. His book is the classic statement about how good institutions can indeed become "schools for crime." "If the goal of therapy is reintegration of the individual into a rational cooperative of human being," Polsky concluded, "then we must concentrate on the social relationship in which the resident is integrated as well as individual psychotherapy."[5]

Polsky probably had a major influence on treatment models that take into account the residential milieu and seek to turn peer pressures toward rehabilitation, rather than letting it work as an undertow pulling the residents away from personal growth. Yet on the whole there has been very little improvement over the past twenty years. Programs still tend to be fragmented, with administrators, therapists, and paid staff operating in isolation. All too frequently, the patients find themselves in a peer subculture where hostile and antisocial behavior becomes either a status model or a tool of survival.

Above all, we still find that too many therapists of whatever discipline work too much from the heart and too little from the head. They equate treatment with kindness or indulgence and end up trying to bribe delinquents to be good. Or they try to make up for previous deprivation and foster infantilization which infuriates the adolescent and makes the criminal and subculture more attractive, since, in reality, it is more mature, albeit evil.

NOSOLOGY: SERIOUSLY TROUBLED YOUTH

What kind of youngsters are "delinquent," then, and how do we see their problems? Instead of covering the full spectrum of psychological pathologies, this chapter concentrates on the seriously disturbed individuals who pose the challenge for treatment.

In our experience, the young people sent to Elan One generally fall into four categories: (1) children with attention-deficit disorder (ADD); (2) oppositional children; (3) children who are victims of abuse or psychodynamic conflict within the family; and (4) children with antisocial or sociopathic personalities. Let me describe each of these:

Attention-Deficit Disorder

While still not completely understood, ADD is estimated to affect between 5 to 15 percent of all school children, with a male/female ratio of about 4:1. One recent study showed that 23 percent of a group of children diagnosed as having ADD in their early years were later diagnosed as having antisocial personalities in early adulthood.[6] Crudely extrapolated, this means 2 percent of the total adult population! About 50 percent of the adolescents who come to Elan have a history of ADD, with or without hyperactivity.

A child with ADD has difficulty paying attention or sitting still at any task for very long. Such children have a very short attention span. This not only limits cognitive intake, but also makes it difficult to achieve any affectual communication with others, except momentarily and superficially, and makes impulsive reactions too easy.

The child, of course, soon becomes aware that something is terribly wrong in communication and impulse control. In order to get attention, (s)he resorts to provocative or avoidant behavior. There are also a loss of self-esteem, a tendency to project blame onto others, and, above all, determined efforts to get attention at any cost, whether others are manipulated into anger or into feeling sorry for and delivering what James Masterson terms a "rewarding unit fantasy."[7]

With the onset of puberty, matters become much more complicated. Now the need for contact with others is dramatically increased, but the ADD child has less "money" in his or her emotional bank than the normal peer, who has been learning to relate and integrate for years. The normal child now has a fund of experience and friends on which to draw when moving into adolescence. The ADD child has no such saving or investment.

Adolescent communication is enormously overladen with affect. Consider how long they talk on the telephone as an exchange of information, checking back and forth on observations about motivation, personalities, and the character of others. From peers the adolescent also learns an ethos—exactly how far one can go in self-assertiveness with parents and teachers, what clothes are mandatory, what's "cool" in music and movies, and how to approach the opposite sex.

Much of this is beyond the reach of the adolescent with ADD. If his or her behavior has not been provocative in latency, (s)sh has more inducement as the loneliness becomes utterly poignant in adolescence. But outrageousness and provocativeness only serve to alienate others. The vicious cycle becomes tighter, and the loneliness worse and worse.

The adolescent does try to attack the problem. Some friends are made but naturally among similarly disabled peers. A group of "cool" friends is sought out. The "gang" is not just a phenomenon of the inner city where sociological factors like ethnicity make it more obvious and well organized. The network of troublesome kids is well known in every high school and every community.

To this group adhere the adolescents who sense themselves as being defective and incompetent, who are angry about this injustice, or who have given up in the face of it. Some have explosive tempers, and some are more passive. Inasmuch as society, they feel, has rejected them, they in turn reject it. What is "cool" is any activity that gives the illusion of power, of control and adult status. Limitative pseudo-adult, authority-defying behaviors are "cool." Smoking, alcohol, drugs, vandalism, rudeness, assertive violence, manipulating others, "getting over on" parents and school authorities—all are "cool." Depending on personal experience and psychopathology, inflicting pain or hurt on others may be rationalized as a privilege of pseudo-adulthood.

How does the delinquent bond to this subculture? Because of isolation, (s)he is not just receptive, but also exquisitely vulnerable to negative peers. Consequently, the fear of rejection by peers, always a problem for normal adolescents, is an absolute terror for the defective adolscent who has fewer peers from whom to choose. (S)he will do anything which the negative network demands or only suggests.

All groups have initiation rites, and the negative delinquent group will formally or informally demand proof of adherence to pseudo-adulthood by actions. These will vary with sociological factors, from Amerindian adolescent torture rites to the Mafia or Hells' Angels, to "I dare you to stay out after your parents' curfews (the old fogies have no right to tell me what to do)," or steal liquor from your house, or even help to break into your home and rob it. Whatever the demand, the defective adolescent simply cannot resist. These tasks provide *identity building blocks* of which (s)he is so empty.

The Oppositional Child

These adolescents usually have a personal history of reacting with what Phillipe Pinel called "instinctive and abstract fury" to any parental request or demand.[8] In such cases, the child or adolescent may form relationships and find significant others. But the usual story is that the friends are manipulated objects in the nonstop war. Personality development suffers because most of the energy is devoted to "getting over" and there is little time for getting ahead. Besides, success would please the parents and redound to their credit. This cannot be allowed. The intensity of this passion seems similar to the stubbornness of autism.

Inasmuch as the "psychological working space" is largely occupied by the talionic passions of getting even instead of getting ahead, these children, like the ADD adolescent, do not have room to do the developmental work of adolescence. They, too, are incompetent, and they, too, join the negative delinquent group. This adherence to the negative group is the final common behavioral pathway for each of the four crude ad hoc diagnostic categories. They all become incompetent, band together, and reinforce one another.

Psychodynamics and Family Pathology

Other "parent killers" have started this activity later, usually at the onset of puberty. They have psychodynamic conflict. In one case, a ten-year-old boy, the apple of his father's eye, found his mother *in flagrante* with his father's best friend. The mother started a conspiracy with the son and bribed him not to tell.

As the father continued in his enthusiastic affection for the boy—mutual athletics, fishing, help with school work—the guilt became unbearable. The psychological solution was to attack and disappoint the father in order to drive him away. Six years of this resulted in quite a record of delinquency.

Cases in which the parent has been physically or psychologically abusive or neglectful provoke a psychology of identification with the malign aggressor, which in turn is a source of shame, self-rejection and low self-esteem. To this is added the guilt, realistic or irrational, for having participated. Peers cannot be trusted with this information, so abreactive relief is not available. Since openness is not possible, peer relations do not develop. Instead, a hostile dependency on the parents grows and occupies the adolescent's psychological space.

Sometimes the shame and guilt are great enough to produce an indiscriminate lashing out at everyone and a refusal to enter into any relationship. These syndromes of self-destruction in order to avenge oneself on the parent or to "solve" an internal conflict produce the same incompetency and hostile dependency as does ADD.

Overprotectiveness or overindulgence by the parent can often produce the hostile dependency. An infantilized baby-doll girl is unprepared for adolescence and unprepared to correctly interpret a father's love as parental. Instead, at puberty, she sees both his interest and hers as sexual. The guilty pseudo-conflict, usually unconscious, leads to violence directed at the mother, sexual promiscuity, eating disorders, and substance abuse.

Children of sociopathic parents get subtle, unconscious instructions to act out their parents' secret pathologies. As S. A. Szurek pointed out, "The most overt symptom of a parental personality disorder is the behavior of the child."[9] Adelaide Johnson continued along these lines and found many cases in which "the parent's forbidden impulse is acted out vicariously by the unfortunate child. But this very acting out, in a way so foreign to the conscious wishes of the parent, served often as a channel for hostile destructive impulses that the parent felt toward the child."[10] She goes on to discuss the adolescent's justified rage and depression over the betrayal, emphasizing that both the parents and child are unconscious of what is behind the escalating destruction.

Finally, there are adolescents whose psychodynamic conflicts are oedipal or involve sibling rivalry or have to do with being adopted. All suffer arrested development and resultant incompetence.

The Antisocial Personality

This group seems to excite the most interest and for some authors, like Stanton Samenow, constitutes the whole of delinquency. Actually, it would seem that there are two populations. Howard Wishnie and George E. Valliant speak more of individuals with poor impulse control. But Samenow's group positively enjoys doing harm to or despoiling everyone else with malice aforethought. This latter group seems to be the oppositional child grown up. Alternative terms such as "sociopath," "psychopath," "impulse disorder," and "character disorder" are often used interchangeably. The phenomenon is a very old one. The Bible describes it as follows:

If a man has a stubborn and rebellious son, which will not obey the voice of his father or the voice of his mother and though they have chastened him, will not harken unto them, then shall his father and his mother lay hold on him and bring him out unto the elders of the city and unto the gate of his place. And they shall say unto the elders of the city, "This our son is stubborn and rebellious, he will not obey our voice, a glutton and a drunkard." And all the men of his city shall stone him with stones, that he die: So shalt thou put away the evil from the midst of thee. And all Isreal shall hear and fear.—Deuteronomy XXI

Post-canonical Jewish jurisprudence made extreme efforts to avoid capital punishment; hence, these verses always posed a difficult problem. Rashi (1040–1105), the French exegete and most authoritative biblical commentator, related "stubborn" and "rebellious" conduct to individuals without impulse control. He believed that such persons wreaked so much destruction in society that the capital sentence was a legitimate preventive.

The late Samuel Yochelson and his associate, Stanton Samenow, worked successfully in an original fashion with what they called the "criminal personality." Yochelson decided after much experience that psychoanalysis did not work; instead, he concentrated on cognitive psychology and a confrontational system that emphasized responsibility and changes in both behavior and mental habits.

Recently, Samenow published a popular book reviewing their viewpoint and treatment methods.[11] He repeatedly emphasizes the real personal agenda to destroy and despoil, which is sometimes hidden but is often quite open. Samenow blames the failure of psychoanalytic therapies on the "rational agenda" of the therapists, which is usually irrelevant to character change. He also rejects the newer cognitive therapies for the antisocial personality: notably, Glasser's Rational Therapy, the Cognitive Therapy of Beck and Mechenbaum, Ellis' Rational-Emotive Therapy, and Maultsbie's Rational Behavior Therapy. Quoting Glasser's remark, "children want to become responsible," Samenow rejoins, "in most instance, he is right. The criminal is an exception."

Our experience at Elan has confirmed this observation many times. For example, here are the comments of a mother who was also a trained clinical observer:

At age two, Tom first began showing difficult, unyielding behavior. He was seldom satisfied, always required attention of others who were supposed to amuse him and give him everything he wanted. In school, beginning in first grade, he showed impulsive behavior, poor concentration and self-control, baiting other children and stealing lunches, etc.

I first noted these difficulties at age two and in nursery school at ages three to four. All teachers, relatives and friends had the same difficulties with him as I had at home. He was never satisfied or happy with available toys or work or play at school. Always looking for something he was not to have, something not his, readily lying and stealing to have it.

He was asked to leave the last two schools he attended. School "A" was for disruptive behavior, stealing and pot and liquor abuse. No warnings, punishments or *interested* counseling or psychotherapy made any difference. After he was expelled from School "B," we tried having him at home working full time. he spent all his money on consumables—mostly pot and candy, until we finally impounded his earnings to pay some of his own expenses. Despite our dire warnings about the use of pot in the house, he continues—with many lies and denials. All our money and that of visitors must be locked up. He seeks company of younger boys when possible, largely to supply them with pot. However, he has *no* friends or outside activities that we can approve of and is extremely unhappy with himself for his restricted life. Unless a qualitative change can occur in his outlook and behavior, he will be in deep trouble as soon as he is on his own and we have no control.

It should be noted that Tom, although described as impulsive and having poor concentration, did not suffer from ADD. This was not distractibility nor a war against parents, but an aggressive fixation on short-term and narcissistic objectives. In childhood, Tom's diagnosis would have been a conduct disorder, unsocialized aggressive type. His may be a congenital disorder. In adulthood the label becomes an "antisocial personality."

The word "unsocialized" is the key because it refers again to our final common-pathway hypothesis. Tom did not relate to others even superficially. He had neither friends nor real relationships. Hence, there was little hope of containing his behavior for the sake of others, or their regard or good opinion. Psychotherapy, a relationship procedure, did not touch him. Parenthetically, Tom did complete the Elan program and then a second-tier Ivy League college. However, he still maintains an air of impulsivity which makes others uneasy.

There have been many attempts to describe the antisocial personality. Francis C. Carney, for example, characterizes aggressive patients as having the following four problems:

Inability to trust others or form objective relationships. There is usually a pervasive distortion of all interpersonal relationships, with no willingness to believe other human beings can be sincere. The patient has no true sense of self. (S)he creates a new role with each new person or situation, and has an amazing capacity to sense even the secret needs of others and respond accordingly. Carney states:

Therapists, too, become fooled by patients . . . who develop astounding insights . . . (the therapists) never realizing that over a period of months they themselves have provided the patients with all the cues they need to work the successful coup.

Inability to feel emotions, with a callous freedom from anxiety and depression. "It is not that these patients cannot feel," states Carney.

They will not feel because the pain is too great. To defend against feeling, they have a number of maneuvers, two of which are particularly predominant. The first is acting out ... Action relieves tension and so long as one is doing one doesn't have to think, feel or introspect ... [Second,] when the patient has a feeling he doesn't care to experience, he elicits the same feeling from someone else in his environment; in this way, the other experiences the emotion and the patient doesn't have to ... We almost always find that while the relatives are terribly concerned, the patients aren't ... The empathetic therapist does become aware of the intense pain his therapy will uncover, and too often he responds to the patient's plea to spare him. The caring therapist can be too willing to accept the sham feelings ... too hesitant to let the patient hurt ... Most therapists don't like to see their patients hurt, yet there are times when the absence of pain perpetuates the disease.[12]

Valliant makes the same point: the sociopath avoids feeling depression or anxiety.[13] Like Valliant, we do not see an inability to feel, but rather an avoidance of feeling depression or anxiety *at all costs.*

Other authors also describe the explosive rage that occurs when these patients are confronted. Howard Wishine points out that the extreme fear of feeling leads to panic, which is immediately translated into blame and rage at others.[14] The panic, rage, and blame are discharged by impulsive behavior which he practically equates with delinquency. Hence, in-the-heat therapeutic confrontation—the only effective kind—must take place in a safe setting with real limits. Many therapists are genuinely frightened by this—particularly in an outpatient setting—and will back off. As a result, these patients' sense of danger about their own feelings are confirmed, their power of intimidation is reinforced, and the therapy makes them worse.

Inability to fantasize. This characteristic results in acting out—doing rather than thnking. The normal person can often emulate Walter Mitty and delay the pain, which provides enough time to anticipate problems and to work out solutions. The character-disordered individual cannot do this. As a result, he or she appears to be impulsive, with poor judgment and an inability to plan.

Carney also links this defect with an inability to empathize. "As patients relate their crimes," he notes, "especially some particular act of violence, one is struck by the fact that they really don't comprehend the pain they were inflicting, and they are often genuinely surprised the victim has experienced injury or death ... They truly do not understand why the victim is angry." Carney infers two corollaries from the inability to empathize: a heightened ability to rationalize and a callous disregard for the rights of others.

Inability to profit from experience. Unable to fantasize, antisocial personalities become incapable of transferring experience from one situation to another. Since there is no real identity and each new encounter calls for a new personality role, the fantasy function is inadequate to imagine plans for new contingencies. It is as though the person were fixed in time with no awareness of past experience and no expectation for the future. Such a state requires satisfaction of the here and now. Carney points out that this inability to learn makes the crude behavior modification therapies such as token economies ineffectual. Such efforts focus on disruptive behavior, which really is the problem of the caretaker. The real problem, the inability to transfer learning from one experience to another, is ignored. All this reminds us that learning is not purely cognitive, but affect-laden as well.

The descriptions offered by Carney, Wishnie, and Samenow have converged with other efforts. Millon, for example, describes the "essence of antisocial individuals" through the following characteristics:

1. *Hostile affectivity.* Irascible temper that flares quickly into argument and attack, as evidenced in frequent verbally abusive and physically cruel behaviors.

2. *Social rebelliousness.* Contempt toward authority, tradition, sentimentality, and humanistic concerns.

3. *Hyperthymic fearlessness.* Impulsive accelerated and forceful responding, attracted to and undaunted by danger and punishment.

4. *Malevolent projection.* Justifying one's mistrustful, hostile, and vengeful attitudes by acribing them to others.[15]

Other descriptions of antisocial personalities rely more on sociological explanations: in the theoretical model proposed by Delbert S. Elliott and his colleagues, for example, defective bonding to normal peers and bonding to a delinquent peer group.[16] Edwin H. Sutherland's model posits the notion that delinquents have learned criminal behavior through interaction with others in small personal groups.[17] Travis Hirschi argues that delinquents lack strong attachments to conforming members of society.[18] Albert K. Cohen[19] and Walter B. Miller[20] suggest that delinquency is essentially normal behavior in the lower class subculture. In our view, all these mechanisms describe the attempts of incompetent adolescents to defend their precarious status and to obtain human relationships on their own level.

We have already mentioned that these sociological explanations leave little room for psychological intervention, and instead suggest macrosocial solutions like creating new jobs or reordering society. Whether such large-scale solutions can affect delinquency—and whether they are even possible—is a question we will not undertake here. Our experience has been, however, that *individuals* are treatable.

CONCEPTUALIZING DELINQUENCY

Delinquency is an attitude, a lifestyle, a tenaciously held psychology that keeps the individual at odds with human society. Most criminal acts occur when there is opportunity to relieve the tension by pretending adulthood, acting out a conflict or impulsive acts fueled by panic.

Duane: An Empirical Illustration

In opposition to those premises, the criminal justice system operates in a legalistic fashion that focuses on the offense without serious consideration of the qualities of the offender and his or her background. The implications and consequences can be seen more readily by examining the reactions to one individual.

Duane, a sixteen year old, is caught while driving drunk. He was sent to Elan shortly after his arrest, but later the court referred him to a diversionary program. Under the threat of a $300 fine, he was instructed to attend classes and pass an examination on the dangers of drunk driving.

The court acted as though the drunk driving episode was a discrete aberration, but Duane was aberrant long before his arrest. He had an extensive history of serious incivility at home and in school. He had been involved in alcohol and marijuana abuse, petty theft, school failure, and truancy. The diversionary program did not take this history into account. The diversionary personnel did not take a history or form a diagnosis. All they had was a charge of drunk driving on a specific date.

Without some attempt at a comprehensive approach, the diversionary program may do more harm than good because it ignores the following factors: (1) Duane is an isolated, alienated adolescent without sources of legitimate satisfaction from academics, achievement, personal friendship, athletics, or a steady girlfriend. He truly suffers but overcomes this feeling by "exporting" it to those about him, particularly his family. Duane derives too much status at home and school by being a bad-ass. (2) Inasmuch as few discrete offenses ever come to the attention of the police, Duane's major regret was that this once he had been caught and he felt it was unfair because most others had not.

Implications of Legalistic Reaction

Perhaps Duane's actions were an unconscious attempt to get caught. Freud noted this phenomenon in "Criminality from a Sense of Guilt" (1915) when he wrote that many offenders are motivated to expiate prior guilt by deliberately courting punishment. Most clinicians recognize that guilt is often a powerful inducement to misbehavior, which is really a depressive "giving up" to "get it over with." If this is true of Duane and he cannot get help, the behavior will recur and progressively escalate.

Also complicating the situation today is the question of whether Duane will be punished at all through courtroom procedures. Young attorneys, especially those specializing in juvenile advocacy, seem to have abandoned the professional role of doing what is best—within moral limits—for the client. Instead, they become legal technicians and try to get only what a frightened, inexperienced adolescent with proven bad judgment thinks (s)he wants. For many of these advocates, getting clients off the hook has become a game to be played to hone one's skills, at the expense of both the family and society.

STUDENTS AND MISSION OF ELAN ONE

In the past sixteen years, more than 2,000 severely acting-out adolescents—"obnoxious, but not crazy"—have been brought to Elan, usually after other efforts at treatment have failed. Despite the varied etiologies, Elan's approach has proved comprehensive in most cases. The failing of these youngsters, as we express it, is that they have not been able to do the "work of adolescence."

Backgrounds and Qualities of Students

These youngsters have come from all socioeconomic strata of American society, as well as from different parts of the world. They represent many cultures but have had similar psychological development. They may retain differing class views about vocations, goals, and opportunities, but almost all come to share the same feelings about personal responsibility, respect for other people's psyches and property, and the need for self-esteem and affiliation to the group.

Prior to Elan, each of these adolescents was trapped in his or her own predisposing situation which produced the psychology of Carney's "inability to trust" and Millon's "hostile affectivity." From the patient with ADD to the adopted child obsessed with fear of another rejection, none had been able to relate to others or to organize a network of supporting people around themselves. Feeling no empathy, they have magical expectations and expect perfection in others. They project blame and deny or repress painful feelings. All have turned instead to "acting out"—some in order to pretend an adult identity, some out of rage, and still others out of fear of affect or the despair of Samson.

The longer and more severe these conditions, the less time there is to do the "work of adolescence"—building a strong and secure sense of identity. Instead, there is incompetence, low self-esteem, guilt, despair, rage, and hatefulness—the final common pathway.

Mission of Elan One

Elan's here and now treatment philosophy bespeaks a program with a sense of mission, not a hospital attending physician model. The mission is:

1. to develop the capacity to control impulsive behavior, particularly in the face of the inevitable injustices of human life and relationships;

2. to create the capacity for mutual relationships with others, particularly with the opposite sex;

3. to create the capacity to maintain consistency in work and study;

4. to develop the ability to obtain help from others when hard hit either by outrageous fortune or by the vicissitudes of anxiety and depression; and

5. to nurture a sense of life goals and personal destiny, such as a secure identity.

With relatively explicit goals, it is possible to monitor progress and assess special needs as required. Explicit goals enable us to work within a time frame appreciated by all. Elan's program lasts approximately eighteen months. We know where the individual should be at each time interval, and (s)he knows it, too. Another successful program, the New Mexico State Adolescent Program, is geared to a twenty-four month cycle. Generally, it seems to take eighteen to twenty-four months for a youngster to put his or her life together. The most important concern of the program is not the heinousness of a specific act or the vagaries of sentencing and parole, but the need to accomplish necessary psychosocial personal development.

Implications of Program Goals

The mission differs from the legal goals of getting off or doing time; from the behavioral/sociologic goals of no offenses for a period of time with the hope that the habit becomes permanent or that the deterrent remains strong enough; or from the medical psychodynamic/social work goals of resolving internal conflicts and feeling better and releasing growth to start again spontaneously.

Another implication of program goals is to concentrate on specifics, to take things seriously and transmit that sense to the students. In this context, limit setting and confrontation make more sense and are not easily taken personally. Serious business becomes an ethos, and then only does the community so aptly described by Gerald Caplan become possible.

The characteristic attribute of those social aggregates that act as a buffer against disease is that in such relationships the person is dealt with as an unique individual. The other people are interested in him in a personalized way. They speak his language. They tell him what is expected of him and guide him in what to do. They watch what he does and they judge his performance. They let him know how well he has done. They reward him for success and punish or support and comfort him if he fails. Above all, they are sensitive to his personal needs, which they deem worthy of respect and satisfaction.[21]

LIMIT SETTING, ETHOS CONFRONTATION, AFFECTS

The first aspect of serious business, of course, is setting limits. If a juvenile institution has any vandalism whatever, any violence or intimidation, any subculture in which clients titillate or congratulate each other about their "war stories," any jailhouse lawyering, alcohol, drugs, or sexual misconduct, its program will probably fail. Only when the clients live in a lawful, law-abiding society—often for the first time in their lives—will it become possible for change to occur.

Limit Setting by Students

This does not imply a punitive or adversarial format. On the contrary, self-government can be more effective. At Elan, the American tradition in which government is the creature of the people holds sway. Democracy does not mean running for a student council, but rather each holding community offices, which are actually important. The principle of voluntary organization—so praised by de Tocqueville—is Elan's foundation stone. If a society is to be lawful, the governed must exercise authority. Only in this framework does a mutuality in human relationships become possible.

At Elan, the limits and rules are made explicit from the first moment of entry, when the newcomer is searched for drugs by other students. It becomes immediately clear that the individual is entering a situation in which peer pressure—not just the authority of older, wiser, but better people (Saki)—is the standard for the society. Often youngsters do not believe this. One newcomer offered to share his supply of grass with the strip-searcher and was promptly reported. "He ratted on me," was his amazed reaction. It was his first introduction to a moral code in which allowing drug use by a buddy—for whom one is personally responsible—is regarded as destructive both to the individual and to the community.

Ethos Confrontation

After entry, the new patient undergoes many "data sessions," which are exercises in cognitive information about rules, right and wrong, and the reasons therefore. At first, the cardinal rules are given—no violence, no sex, no drugs. Reasons are given, but it is not important whether the student accepts the rationale. Rules are rules and must be obeyed. Infractions will bring consequences.

Infractions are not offenses so much as actions that represent an attitude. These attitudes—carelessness (i.e., lack of self-esteem), anger, aggrievement, guilt—are the material for concern. All offenses ("attitudes") are regarded as serious and require a "cleanup." The cleanup varies according to the "mess" it created. It involves both acknowledgment of wrong doing and repair of the damage.

Offenses against the self—like "copping out" in confronting a peer, in giving directions (orders) to someone bigger or older, or in an anxiety-producing situation like a special event—are discussed in individual or group therapy. A consensus is reached with others about what should be an adequate punishment—real or symbolic—and what actions undertaken by the individual and the peers together can help the person overcome the problem.

Punishments are called "learning experiences" to give them other than a talionic meaning. They must include practice, with the help of significant others and peers, in overcoming the area of weakness. They include discussing the meaning of the matter at length with at least two other peers.

Building Affectual Contacts

An offense against another person or against the community calls for public apology, and then the learning experience includes mutual expression of aggrieved feelings in a ritualized confrontative group. However, the important factor is the resolution of these feelings by developing insight into their antecedents. "I always get angry when I feel that others are . . . " "When I'm scared of rejection, I tend to . . . "

These procedures set limits, make feelings and the antecedent experiences that evoke them manifest, provide affectual empathetic contact with peers to build relationships, give psychological distance and insight, provide cognitive understanding, provide extinguishing and reinforcing experiences and a reality base.

Above all, feelings are legitimized, and the difference between thinking and doing is made clear. So, too, the difference between needs and desires is clarified. Everyone learns to recognize anger, fear, resentment, sexual attraction, and guilt and learns what to do about them. These are psychodynamic, behavioral, cognitive, and social control therapies. There is nothing new in any of this except doing it better, not because anyone is smarter or works that much harder, but because of ethos and organization.

Functions of the Staff

The staff at Elan has an ethos; they believe their mission is to do the best for the students by being fair to them, not to love them, not to be frightened of their aggression, not to feel good by being giving, not to pander. They know that the rationalizations of liberation, due process, psychodynamic objectivity, and bribes for "good behavior" are copouts and are wrong.

They know that if they cop out by being vengeful, avoiding their own feelings, being too giving, expecting too much or demanding too little—that is, not paying responsible attention—that students will not get identity-building units and not learn responsibility, no matter how much exhortation, how much psychodynamic exploration, how many token economy units, and how much punishment. If the staff knows right and wrong and acts on that knowledge, then the students will identify with them.

When Jerome Miller became Youth Commissioner in Massachusetts, he found himself, to his horror, in charge of concentration camps. But the solution was not to replicate *Lord of the Flies* via "patient's rights" or to send frightened and dangerous adolescents onto the street without support. "Onto the street without support" refers not only to Miller's impulsive use of college dormitories already occupied by legitimate students, but to many group homes as well.

PARTICULARS, SERIOUSNESS, AND SERIOUS FEELINGS

"He who would do good to another must do it in Minute Particulars," William Blake said. "General good is the plea of the scoundrel, hypocrite and flatterer.

For Art and Science cannot exist but in minutely organized Particulars. And not in generalizing Demonstrations of the rational Power.''[22]

Bad institutions—Cottage Six, Massachusetts Training Schools, hospitals, and group homes—are not designed to be bad. They become contratherapeutic or pseudotherapeutic or, at best, marginally harmful because they are not organized to attend to minute particulars.

Particulars: Means of Understanding

A system designed for psychological growth must develop the adolescent's capacity to recognize feelings in self or others, to contain the resultant anxiety, and to release the tension by appropriate action. Unless the dose is small enough, related to a munute particular, powerful emotions will be overwhelming and will result in violence or repression and then further psychological retreat. Good limit setting ensures that offenses will be minute, a sneer or unpleasant word rather than a broken jaw or a rape. The resolution of such interpersonal events builds relationships, and this builds identity. Development of the observant ego, and the sense of self-control and self-destiny, requires an awareness that all acts are meaningful and serious.

Particulars must be observed with the purpose of understanding the attitude each represents and using this to confront the student immediately. If a verbal reprimand is indicated, it is delivered by others who have a relationship of affection/respect with the individual so that the reprimand is understood to be responsible concern, not punishment. Inasmuch as we are dealing with a chronic state, like heart failure, not an acute infection, our medication is like digitalis— small doses every day, not just one shot of penicillin to cure pneumonia.

Staff Again and Who Does the Work

A purposeful observer must be omnipresent. Only if the observer has time to see and act purposefully can (s)he function therapeutically. If there is no time to understand and to resolve, then the observers become angry, vindictive, depressed and withdrawn, or panderers for peace at any price. When the staff deteriorates in such a way, they will become punitive or, if they withdraw, aggressive persons in the student population will take over. In either case, a concentration camp is the result.

In order to avoid this outcome, there is a need for sufficient trained personnel with sufficient time to fulfill the purposeful observer role. This *quantity* is difficult to achieve with a paid staff. Our model utilizes the students themselves, who thus are not only purposeful observers but participant observers as well. Each incident becomes a therapeutic experience for two or more instead of one.

PROGRESS BEYOND BEHAVIORAL LIMIT SETTING

Our terminology focuses on attitude change rather than behavior change. Behavior is actually a legal term, whereas attitude bespeaks the feeling and thinking that results in behavior. Part of the legal fallacy is the assumption that delinquents can control their behavior by an act of will. Unless there is attitude change, the fatigue of controlling impulse inexorably overcomes the best intentions.

Manipulation, Then Affectual Openness

After the student finds that direct behavioral limits are firm, s(he) will resort next to manipulation. During a visit by the surveyor from a state agency, a student went into the bathroom and cut his arm, carefully, in a "suicidal gesture." He was very surprised when he had to clean up the floor and washbasin before being taken to the doctor. That episode became a legend at Elan. Hence, we do not have to contend with the manipulative suicidal gestures that often bring mental hospital wards to a standstill.

Next follow direct demands for risking open psychological work. In one case a student did not allow himself to show emotion or relate to others. After this problem was worked on in group therapy without result, the other students told him how his attitude deprived and offended them; as a consequence, he was assigned to scrubbing kitchen pans for a day. While at this task, he was observed to be crying. He was promptly brought back to his fellow students who reprimanded him for pretending to be without feelings and for lying and for cowardice about expressing feelings. The consequence was yet another day at the dishpans.

Developing Responsible Concern

Progressively, then, the limits are related to fundamental attitudes and then even to responsibility for poor judgment calls, such as carelessly enabling another student to run away. Being a loner and not asking for help from others in one's job, albeit well done, merits reprimand. Wearing sexually provocative clothing is related to feelings of self-doubt about being attractive as a person. There are consequences, possibly a sandwich board which says, "Please confront me about why I think I'm not good enough without indecent clothes." After group sessions in which the issue is explored and the student works through some of the self-esteem problems, status is restored.

If a student has a depressed or dysphoric day, there are consequences for the others in his or her immediate group. Those who noticed are commended, while those who did not notice or did nothing to help are reprimanded. Insensitivity to another and failure to extend a helping hand to a peer in need becomes a negative attitude, a lack of "responsible concern." Lack of responsible concern requires examination of one's personal feelings about the other student in a group session, for it is serious business.

The reader will note the repeated use of the word "serious." Once a visitor remarked to an Elan student that there seemed to be comparatively little playfulness and laughter. The reply caught him up short, "Man, this is serious business." We realized then that our student put his finger on an essential factor. The limit setting is for real, serious. So is the ethos, so are the group meetings, so is the confrontation, however minute the particular, so is every minute of the day, so are all the peer relationships.

As the program progresses, the student faces the demand to "give back what you got." As others take responsibility for a person, so must that person later take it for others.

Psychotherapy and Relating

Formal group psychotherapy sessions are held three times weekly and are either aberative-emotional (encounter groups) or exploratory-psychodynamic (static groups). Gestalt and role-playing techniques are utilized when necessary. There are constant meetings and consultations, beginning with a morning meeting of the whole house and continuing throughout the day: department meetings, administrative meetings of the director and the coordinators, coordinators' meetings, department head meetings, daily staff meetings, verbal reprimands delivered by three or four students to an offender, constant personal discussion between staff and student and student to student. One observer described the whole scene as twenty-four hours of continuous therapy. In addition, special attention is given to the PIT—"people in trouble"—list who may be sought out for brief discussion, be relieved of duties, and be at the "relating table" to talk themselves out.

Organization: Praxis to Competence

One important aspect of developing identity and competence is to be provided with genuine experiences in life tasks. This is not found in patronizing makework activities such as occupational therapy or student councils. Elan's student population of 160 is divided into forty member units. Twenty-five of every forty members are in administrative positions, which means there are more chiefs than Indians. The rationale for this seeming imbalance is that those adolescents who rebel against authority to achieve pseudo-adult identity are precisely those who must learn about authority by exercising it.

The Business Office is responsible for recordkeeping, supplies, and sundries. A population record is made daily, along with records of group therapy, special group meetings, and visitors. A diary of daily occurrences every twenty minutes is kept on a twenty-four hour basis. Cleaning supplies, paper towels and tissues, office supplies, toothpaste, shaving cream and cigarettes are all ordered, recorded, and distributed daily. Consumption charts are maintained to check waste. Laundry is dispatched, dry cleaning is received and delivered, and towels and sheets are kept in inventory. A sixteen-or seventeen year-old "coordinator" heads a staff of six, and being in charge of the business of a community of forty people, (s)he has a real job, equivalent to actual responsible employment.

Other departments are "gurus"—primary care peer counselors—and the "expiditors," who are essentially police, the kitchen, communications, and maintenance.

This deliberately widespread dissemination of responsibility is a self-correcting mechanism designed to ensure that students are involved in authority and decision making. In practice, students are constantly being shifted around, promoted and demoted. Close supervision is beyond the capacity of the five paid staff members, so once again we must rely on students, both to perform supervisory functions and to train other students in their tasks. Students are not always expected to function well; in fact, they are often deliberately placed in jobs they are not expected to perform. Both the inevitable failings and the eventual successes are regarded as important parts of their maturing experience.

LAWFUL SOCIETY, HARD NOSES, AND TIGHT SHIP

Before coming to Elan, many students solved (or tried to solve) their interpersonal anxieties by overt violence, intimidation, and aggressiveness. It is exceedingly important—serious—to recognize that a bloody nose is barely the tip of the iceberg. Violence is 99 percent intimidation; the occasional scuffle is only to establish the pecking order. The daily degradation of intimidation is the real violence and the essence of the concentration camp. In almost every adolescent institution, the staff is content if no overt fights take place. Thus, they become accomplices to the criminal culture.

Managing Interpersonal Conflict

At Elan we recognize that interpersonal conflict is always arising and must always be resolved. Angry and hurt feelings are vociferously expressed with the aid and encouragement of peers; resolution of the immediate issue and exploration of the ambivalent (transference) feelings follow. These resolution procedures produce affectual bonding and understanding much as a fist fight or hair pulling does among children. From this base, the student progressively learns to resolve feelings and issues by communicating and negotiating.

There is a hierarchy of consequences or sanctions for acting out behavior. These range from an individual talking, to loud vociferous verbal reprimands, to sign boards, to reprimand in front of the entire student body, and even to a ritualized boxing match for repeated violence.

Students are expected to function effectively and to build relationships, to deal with their fears of opposite sex relationships, to discuss feelings, to evaluate their previous difficulties, and to develop long-term life plans. The goal is to help them acquire confidence, build a personal identity, and learn to accept the vicissitudes of their own passions.

In this environment of unremitting cooperation and confrontation, students come to know one another intimately. There are no secrets about anyone's character. The awareness that others are struggling with the same problems removes the enormous burden of secretly feeling differnt from others. Knowing that one's competence or incompetence is about the same as another's can be enormously helpful. In this kind of fishbowl situation, the staff not only conducts psychotherapy around immediate issues but also organizes therapy groups around issues they know the individuals will confront as they progress. For perhaps the first time in their lives, these former incompetents may be able to start thinking constructively about their future.

Key Elements of the Elan Program

In summary, then, six key elements make up the Elan program.

1. Students perceive treatment as their own effort to change, and that effort leads to the respect and affection of others and to self-respect. At Elan, about 80 percent of the patients "graduate" in a ceremony in which they receive a brass and gold leaf diploma mounted on walnut and red velvet. The students take it seriously.

2. Limit setting must be done in a way that mobilizes the support of the entire population, through both fear and respect for authority.

3. Cognitive therapy must provide explanations of what went wrong before, what values must be reinforced, and what to do in trouble.

4. Insights and feelings of interpersonal competence must be developed. The experience of understanding that feelings are due to recoverable antecedents is very liberating. One no longer feels at the mercy of irrational feelings, and emotional competence does wonders for self-esteem.

5. Rebels without causes come to see peers in authority as persons with whom they can identify. Promotion through the ranks gradually achieves this aim. The genuinely frightening problem of giving direction to others begins an identification with the entire hierarchical structure itself. Eventually, there is a transmission of authority in which the individual plays a fully responsible, constructive role equivalent to real employment in the society at large.

6. Finally, to have a lawful society, an ethos is necessary. This moral philosophy, the basis of both confrontation and indoctrination, engenders a sense of self-esteem and of personal long-range goals or destiny in life.

The organization of these possibilities into a cohesive program for change is what we feel we have accomplished at Elan. To quote Polsky once more, "If the goal of therapy is reintegration of the individual into a rational, cooperative human community, then we must concentrate on the social relationships in which the resident is integrated as well as (on) individual psychotherapy."

NOTES

1. Richard A. Cloward and Lloyd E. Ohlin, *Delinquency and Opportunity: A Theory of Delinquent Gangs* (Glencoe, Ill.: Free Press, 1960), pp. 150–159.

2. Robert K. Merton, *Social Theory and Social Structure* (Glencoe, Ill.: Free Press, 1957), p. 128.

3. Marvin Wolfgang, Robert M. Figlio, and Thorsten Sellin, *Delinquency in a Birth Cohort* (Chicago: University of Chicago Press, 1972), pp. 88–89.

4. Delbert S. Elliott and Harmon L. Voss, *Delinquency and Dropout* (Cambridge, Mass.: Lexington Books, 1974).

5. Howard W. Polsky, *Cottage Six: The Social System of Delinquent Bosy in Residential Treatment* (New York: John Wiley and Sons, 1965), p. 174.

6. G. Weiss et al., "Psychiatric Status of Hyperactives as Adults," *Journal of the American Academy of Child Psychiatry* 24 (1985):211.

7. James Masterson, personal communication.

8. Phillipe Pinel, *Traite Medico-Philosophique sure l'Alienation Mentale* (Paris: Richard, Caille et Ravier, 1801).

9. S. A. Szurek, "Some Impressions from Clinical Experience with Delinquents," in K. R. Eissler, ed., *Searchlights on Delinquency* (New York: International University Press, 1949), pp. 115–127.

10. Adelaide M. Johnson, "Sanctions for Superego Lucanae in Adolescents," in Eissler, ed., *Searchlights on Delinquency* pp. 225–245.

11. Stanton Samenow, *Inside the Criminal Mind* (New York: Times Books, 1984).

12. Francis C. Carney, "Treatment of the Aggressive Patient," in Denis J. Madden and John R. Lion, eds., *Rage, Hate, Assault and Other Forms of Violence* (New York: Spectrum, 1976), pp. 229, 231–232.

13. George E. Valliant, "Sociopathy as a Human Process," *Archives of General Psychiatry* 32 (February, 1975): 178–181.

14. Howard Wishnie, *The Impulsive Personality* (New York: Plenum, 1977), pp. 81–82.

15. Theodore Millon, *Disorders of Personality, DSM III: Axis II* (New York: John Wiley and Sons, 1981), p. 198.

16. Delbert S. Elliott, Suzanne S. Ageton, and Rachelle J. Canter, "An Integrated Theoretical Perspective on Delinquent Behavior," *Journal of Research in Crime and Delinquency* 16 (January 1979): 3–27.

17. Edwin H. Sutherland and Donald R. Cressey, *Principles of Criminology*, 10th ed. (Philadelphia: Lippincott and Co., 1978), pp. 80–81.

18. Travis Hirschi, *Causes of Delinquency* (Berkeley: University of California Press, 1969), pp. 16–19.

19. Albert K. Cohen and James F. Short, "Research in Delinquency Subcultures," *Journal of Social Issues* 14, no. 3 (1958): 20–37.

20. Walter B. Miller, "Lower Class Culture as a Generating Milieu of Gang Delinquency," *Journal of Social Issues* 14, no. 3 (1958): 5–19.

21. Gerald Caplan, *Support Systems and Community Mental Health* (New York: Behavioral Publications, 1974), pp. 5–6.

22. The author is indebted to Alfred Stanton, M.D., for bringing this statement of William Blake and its import to my attention. Coauthored with Morris S. Schwartz,

Stanton's *The Mental Hospital* (New York: Basic Books, 1954) was among the first to suggest the crucial role of staff affect in treatment.

BIBLIOGRAPHY

Albee, George W., and Justin M. Joffe, eds. *Primary Prevention of Psychopathology*, Vol. 1, *The Issues*. Hanover, N.H.: University Press of New England, 1977.

    In the report on the First Vermont Conference on the Primary Prevention of Psychopathology, a team of experts explores the far-ranging parameters of this broadly defined research area. Among the topics considered are the identification of "high-risk" children and adolescents and intervention in such cases.

Cohen, Murray L., A. Nicholas Groth, and Richard Siegel. "The Clinical Prediction of Dangerousness." *Crime and Delinquency* 24 (January 1976): 28–39.

    The authors cite two studies in support of their claim that dangerousness can be predicted clinically and to a degree superior to statistical prediction. Furthermore, they draw on their clinical experience to argue that a total treatment effort had profound effect on 60 percent of 160 offenders managed by the Massachusetts Treatment Center.

Grant, J. Douglas. "Delinquency Treatment in an Institutional Setting." In Herbert C. Quay, ed., *Juvenile Delinquency*. New York: D. Van Nostrand Co., 1965, pp. 236–297.

    Arguing that "we have the beginning of a delinquency-treatment science," Grant describes a number of experimental approaches.

Hampson, Sarah E., and Paul Kline. "Personality Dimensions Differentiating Certain Groups of Abnormal Offenders from Nonoffenders." *British Journal of Criminology* 17 (October 1977): 310–331.

    Hampson and Kline make a factor analysis of personality data from a sample of offenders defined by the courts requiring treatment as "abnormals" and three nonoffender groups. They report that personality characteristics alone differentiated "social inadequacy and authoritarianism" and "insecurity and aggression" subgroups from comparison subjects and the rest of the offender sample.

Herrnstein, Richard. "Some Criminogenic Traits of Offenders." In James Q. Wilson, ed., *Crime and Public Policy*. San Francisco: ICS Press, 1983, pp. 31–49.

    Personality traits are included in this brief review of individual traits "that, under given circumstances predispose people to less internalization of standards of conduct, to greater resentment for inequality, to shorter time horizons, to frustration in the competition for good jobs or satisfying companionship, or to diminished sensitivity to criminal penalties."

Karoly, Paul, and John J. Steffen, eds. *Adolescent Behavior Disorders: Foundations and Contemporary Concerns*. Lexington, Mass.: Lexington Books, 1984.

    Seeing individualistic patterns in the evaluation of adolescent behavior problems, experts explore the process of maturation from three perspectives: attitudes and values, emotional and maturational processes, and cognitive behavior.

Mawson, A. R. "Aggression, Attachment Behavior, and Crimes of Violence." In Travis Hirschi and Michael Gottfredson, eds. *Understanding Crime: Current Theory and Research*. Beverly Hills, Calif: Sage Publications, 1980, pp. 103–116.

    Mawson postulates that many interpersonal acts involving lethal or minor injury are a fortuitous result of the perpetrator's attempt to achieve intensive physical contact with the victim.

Monahan, John. *Predicting Violent Behavior: An Assessment of Criminal Techniques.* Beverly Hills, Calif.: Sage Publications, 1981.

The premises of prevention include the belief that future antisocial behavior can be predicted. Monahan summarizes the core concepts and ethical issues in the prediction of violent behavior and supplies guidelines for clinical examinations.

Redl, Fritz, and Hans Toch. "The Psychoanalytic Perspective." In Hans Toch, ed., *Psychology of Crime and Criminal Justice.* New York: Holt, Rinehart and Winston, 1979, p. 183.

This "theory of personality" is briefly reviewed, and its relevance to delinquency is outlined.

Sandersen, Hilary. "Dependency on Mother in Boys Who Steal." *British Journal of Criminology* 17 (April 1977): 180–184.

Recidivist thieves, referred to child guidance clinics, were compared according to scores on a dependency instrument, with boy referrals who had not been thieves and nondisturbed referrals. The thieves had lower scores for dependency on mothers and higher antisocial scores.

Schoenfeld, C. G. "A Psychoanalytic Theory of Juvenile Delinquency." *Crime and Delinquency* 17 (October 1971): 469–480.

Emphasis is placed on the need for better inner controls, as well as better outer or societal controls, in order to curb the growing incidence of delinquency.

5

The Community and Prevention

ROBERT P. WEISS

Community prevention of crime and delinquency has been a popular ideological notion since the early 1930s, and it has experienced a strong renewal in the last two decades. Today, advocates of "community prevention" include those of every ideological persuasion. Whether one's political belief system is left, right, or center, everyone should favor something so human as "community," at least in the abstract. There must be a great deal of ambiguity, however, in a social policy proposal that is positively valued by so many. Indeed, there are few concepts in social science as nebulous as "community."

CONTRASTING VIEWS OF COMMUNITY

"Community prevention" is used in the criminological literature as if the meaning of the term were self-evident. Few attempts are made to specify the parameters of that which is called "community." One result of neglecting to fashion explicit, careful, and precise definitions has been a crime prevention literature characterized by two extremely different—though equally unsatisfactory—treatments.

Latent Assumptions About Community

At one extreme, there are unimaginative and very limited proposals that see preventive programs merely as civilian adjuncts to the formal criminal justice system. Community is understood in the most limited sense, as a "locality" in which neighborhood crime watch, opportunity reduction, and target-hardening programs are promoted. For instance, in *Community Based Crime Prevention* (Pacific Palisades, Calif.: Goodyear Publishing Co., 1975), Robert C. Trojanowicz et al., devote only a small portion of their last chapter to the topic of citizen involvement. That suggestion is circumscribed by a warning against local activism; their conception of community prevention excludes "empowerment." Furthermore, they warn against programs that would provoke "traditional bureaucratic resistance." In this extreme, community (urban neighborhood) is merely a vehicle for preventive effort and is conservative in its implications.

The other extreme in the literature is characterized by very abstract and vague discussions alluding to a radically different alternative. The idea of community *as* prevention is presented; that is, that certain root causes of crime are within the scope of community to thwart. But these authors are very short on specifications. Rather than positive programs, these discussions center largely on what community prevention supposedly is *not*: it is not bureaucratic, and it is non-stigmatic; it is distinct from (or opposed to) the formal justice system; it is a model based on persuasion, not coercion.

Instead of attempting to describe in empirical terms the nature of community prevention programs, most "radical" discussions so far have been cavalier and polemical in their assessment—either *celebrating* "community" (as opposed to "state" forms of social control), or *denouncing* "community control" as camouflage, delusion, or ideology, in that such programs actually function as an extension of state power into the private sphere.[1] The result of this "either/or" approach is a failure to move beyond moralism.

Properties of Community as Concept

Raymond Plant attributes much of the vagueness of "community" to the concept's dual properties: its evaluative meaning and its empirically descriptive meaning.[2] David W. Minar and Scott Greer also observe this point: "Community is both empirically descriptive of the social structure and normatively toned. It refers to a unit of society as it is and to aspects of that society that are valued if they exist and are desired in their absence."[3] Plant reviews numerous attempts to fashion a descriptive meaning of community devoid of normative connotation, but these are so formal and abstract as to be useless for social explanation. He maintains that there is no value-neutral definition of community possible that would at the same time be meaningful or useful.

Plant's essay works with the core descriptive meaning of community suggested by David B. Clark: "A social structure is a community if and only if it embodies a sense of solidarity and significance."[4] A sense of solidarity is a "we-feeling" sentiment involving togetherness and a sense of belonging. A sense of significance involves a feeling of achievement and fulfillment derived largely from the performance of roles that contribute to group functioning. Solidarity and significance are inseparable, according to Clark. However, Plant points out that the kind of institutional structures and social relationships that might promote these communal elements, and even how to recognize "solidarity and significance," are matters of interpretation.

Figure 5.1

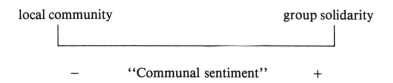

The meanings of "community action," "community prevention," and "community development" are not simply empirical questions; the various notions are embedded in differing political and philosophical assumptions. One can discern, then, conservative, liberal, and radical meanings of community, each reflecting a different notion of what would characterize an ideal community, and hence the preferred way of approaching the prevention of crime and deviance through community resources.

What does community have to do with prevention? Various dimensions of community have been selected to construct a typology of community crime prevention programs and their rationales. The value of our scheme lies in its comprehensiveness and internal exclusiveness, bringing together the entire array of preventive programs into three distinct categories that allow systematic comparison and contrast on important dimensions of community. In this way, a typology can help formulate hypotheses and help guide research.

COMMUNITY AS A CONTINUUM

Although the meaning of community is elusive, one must begin somewhere, and theorists have identified the following dimensions, which we borrow from Minar and Greer: (1) patterned social interaction, (2) culture or shared perspective, (3) place, and (4) human bonds, as sense of interdependence and loyalty.

Dimensions of Community

Two basic dimensions of community are especially useful in a preliminary categorization of preventive programs. One meaning refers to a geographic area, "a physical concentration of individuals in one place." Another dimension of community refers to "the social organization among a concentration of individuals." Community as merely a *geographic area*, and community as *group solidarity*, the highest expression of social organization, can serve as anchors for the construction of a continuum (see Figure 5.1)

At one end, there is community as merely locality, a piece of geography, characterized by locally based relationships that require minimal social interaction and little group sentiment. In social policy literature, this dimension most often refers to residents of towns, cities, and neighborhoods, as though their common living in a particular place on earth is the only important element in "community." At the other end of the continuum we find community in its ideal form—as solidarity. According to Robert Nisbet, this notion of community extends far beyond local community and encompasses "a high degree of personal intimacy, emotional depth, moral commitment, social cohesion, and continuity in time."[5] As we move from one end of the continuum to the other, then, we can observe variability in communal sentiment: more or less loyalty, greater or lesser interdependence, stronger or weaker bonds, more or less shared perspective. At one extreme, community is little more than locale; as one moves toward the other end, the processive dimension of community becomes more important. Community as process involves persons in social interaction, community as institutional network, but it also implies communal forces, persons expressing group solidarity.

At the most basic level, the problem of community is the problem of how human relationships are transformed into regularities. How is social interaction structured or patterned? Conrad Arensberg rejects the view that community is based exclusively on harmony and willing solidarity, or that there is automatic acceptance of cultural traditions and norms. Societies are dynamic; people, "in their lives together, alternate between strife and accommodation, solidarity and antagonism."[6] Kenneth E. Boulding has identified three sets of social control processes that are employed to help ensure community as a unit of social organization: threat, exchange, and integrative processes.[7]

The threat process is based on a conscious power relationship and says, "You do something nice to me or I'll do something nasty to you." This contrasts with the promise of mutual benefit, one of the basic ordering principles of social systems. Exchange relationships work in a market of any kind; for instance, the politician bidding for votes. Integrative relationships, on the other hand, work in consensual systems and are based on status recognition, love, trust, and legitimacy, the bond of consensus.

By placing Boulding's three processes on our continuum of sentiment, threat, exchange, and integrative processes can each denote a different community crime prevention emphasis or approach. So, rather than treating community prevention as a bi-polar concept, a dichotomy wherein we either have prevention or we do not, the various prevention programs and their rationales can be arranged along our continuum. (See Figure 5.2)

Typology of Preventive Approaches

In the introductory chapter to this handbook, Elmer H. Johnson has suggested that community can be considered from three points of view: the community as a unit of social organization, community as a social service delivery system,

Figure 5.2
Three Approaches to Prevention

Prevention Programs:	Situational (1)	"Stake in Conformity" (2)	Informal Control (3)

$$- \xrightarrow{\hspace{6cm}} +$$

"Communal Sentiment"

Community as:	*Locale* for "Walling, Watching, Wariness"	*Mediating Instrument* in Social Service Delivery	*Cultural Symbolic Unit* of Collective Identity—Group Solidarity
Social Processes: (Boulding)	Threat	Exchange	Integrative
Type of Power: (Etzioni)	Coercive	Remunerative	Normative
Type of Subordinate Ideological Involvement:	Alienative	Calculative	Moral

and community as informal control.[8] As a unit of social organization, community is identified with a particular locality. Community as a social service delivery system refers to the use of community as an intermediary between the family and large state bureaucratic structures in the delivery of social welfare services, such as education, health care, child care, and employment opportunities. These services are thought to provide potential deviants with a "stake in conformity."[9] Finally, informal controls are generated by a sense of solidarity derived from a common culture and common social experience, Johnson notes, and involve personal commitment as well as loyalty, personal dedication, and willing obedience.[10]

These three dimensions can be thought of as requiring more or less group sentiment. When placed on our continuum, we find community as a unit of social organization (locality) at the left pole, community as a social service delivery system in the middle, and community as informal control at the right pole. We have called the three types of community crime prevention programs and their respective rationales: (1) Situational, (2) "Stake in Conformity," and (3) Informal Control (see Figure 5.2).

Situational programs involve community (usually urban neighborhood) as a locale for "walling," "watching," and "wariness" programs, and draw mostly on threat processes. Lawrence W. Sherman describes these basic and age-old strategies to prevent crime:

"Walling" includes the use of locks, bars, fences, and similar obstructions to deny criminal access to person and property. "Wariness" includes all the adjustments in personal behavior that people make in order to avoid criminal attack . . . "Watching," in contrast, refers to the various methods of observing people and places that criminals might attack, as well as apprehending the criminal in the act if an attack does occur.[11]

In contrast to the basically negative and alienating strategies of the situational approach, "stake in conformity" preventive programs use community as a social service delivery system and as a socioeconomic opportunity structure, and depend on exchange processes. In this approach, the quest for private purposes is harnessed to social purposes through the recognition of the individual that performance of socially structured roles will maximize the probability of satisfactions and will minimize the penalization. The assumption behind this approach is that those who are provided with health, education, and other services will be more likely to obtain meaningful roles in society, thereby developing a sense of competence and usefulness that will translate into greater allegiance to the established order.

The third preventive type, Informal Control, relies on integrative processes; these programs promote solidarity and normative compliance through moral suasion. Here social involvement is based on status relations such as closely knit reference groups that involve communal forces and emotional identification.

Amitai Etzioni set out a typology of social control and development based on three different (social) patterns of application of social power, and these correspond to the threat, exchange, and integrative processes outlined by Boulding. Etzioni's theoretical perspective permits the comparative analysis of organizations on the basis of the nature of the compliance of the "lower participants" in the organizational hierarchy. "Compliance" refers to the willingness of these participants to allow organizational authority to exercise power. His "compliance theory" postulates that there is a relationship between the type of power employed for control (coercive, remunerative, or normative), and the subordinate's type of ideological involvement in the compliance relationship (alienative, calculative, or moral).[12] For instance, high coerciveness by power-wielders is the source of totalitarianism. Etzioni places the three different types of power and subordinate involvement on an "involvement continuum" applicable not only to complex organizations but also to orientations in general. The following section discusses our three ideal-types of community crime prevention programs in relation to the kinds of human relationships they utilize and promote.

THREE APPROACHES TO COMMUNITY CRIME PREVENTION

In this section we will identify (1) the dimension of community on which each draws, (2) the purpose of the program, (3) its theoretical rationale, and (4) the strategy used to achieve prevention. Finally, we will (5) discuss the empirical assessments of specific programs that have taken various approaches and critique the rationales.

The reader should keep in mind that these approaches to community prevention are ideal types constructed from observation of the characteristics of subjects under study and are not intended to correspond to any single case. In empirical reality, there is some overlap between our three types of community prevention possibilities, and some programs have attempted to encompass all three approaches.

SITUATIONAL CRIME PREVENTION

Here prevention is based on the geographic dimension of community, community "as a functional spatial unit"[13] in which to conduct

measures directed at specific forms of crime that involve the management, design, or manipulation of the immediate environment in as systematic and permanent a way as possible so as to reduce the opportunity for crime and increase its risks as perceived by a wide range of offenders[14]

Prevention draws on community as a unit of social organization, but one that requires little communal sentiment.

Reliance on Deterrent Philosophy

Taken by itself, the purpose of situational crime prevention is merely to mobilize neighborhood residents in discouraging or deflecting potential deviants from dwellings, business establishments, or large areas of property. This approach involves an "us" and "them" mentality, and threatens force to deal with the danger of crime.

When used as a primary method of prevention, the theoretical rationale behind the situational approach is basically one of deterrence. The root causes of crime play no part in the situational measures; rather, the intent is to create a "vigilant and efficient system of social control."[15] Prevention is achieved through the "defended neighborhood," in the words of Gerald D. Suttles,[16] and includes a number of strategies. Efforts to create "defensible space" through "watching," for instance, include surveillance by (a) street gangs and vigilante groups such as the Guardian Angels, (b) citizen patrols, and (c) private security firms. Other opportunity reduction strategies include target hardening (making objects of crime less vulnerable) and environmental schemes like defensible space architecture.

Have these programs provided "a vigilant and efficient system of social control"? Research so far suggests not.[17] Studies of citizen patrols fail to provide rigorous evidence of their effectiveness, but most such studies are flawed because they neglect to provide controls and rely instead on impressionistic and anecdotal measures.[18] However, studies conducted by the Police Foundation indicate that neither concentrated policing in automobiles nor foot patrols decrease the incidence of serious crime.[19]

Displacement and Fear of Crime

Research findings on the variety of situational preventive strategies are mixed. The Minneapolis Community Crime Prevention Demonstration was one of the nation's most ambitious community crime prevention projects, covering three carefully selected demonstration neighborhoods, and recording crime between 1975 and 1978 not only for the demonstration neighborhoods, but also for "displacement control areas" surrounding demonstration neighborhoods, and for noncontiguous control tracts. Designed to limit criminal opportunity, the objectives of the program included resident involvement; target hardening, with cash subsidies for hardware; opportunity reduction through environmental design; and increased awareness and cooperation. The careful and extensive evaluation of the program's process and impact had the advantage of pre-project data on attitudes, opinions, and behavior. Post-test comparisons were conducted. The data did not indicate that the programs had any effect on crime.[20] However, a 1977 report of Seattle's Community Crime Prevention Program reported a significant decrease in burglary. But, generally, programs report little or no effect.[21]

Criticisms of the Approach

Features of the situational crime prevention approach receiving the greatest criticism are summarized in a paper on the future of community prevention prepared for the Minnesota Crime Prevention Center, Inc.[22] The Center's paper criticizes past programs which adopted the situational model because they merely displace crime to targets of greater vulnerability. And the situational prevention approach benefits the middle and upper classes at the expense of poor people.

Although most working-class urbanites must rely solely on municipal policing, the wealthy and those of the middle strata who reside in collectively financed security dwellings enjoy elaborate private security services. According to a recent panel of major city police chiefs, the rapid growth of private security forces is draining the resources for municipal public services, with those in the poor neighborhoods suffering most.[23]

Those who reside in deteriorated urban areas cannot depend on external protection in any form, whether public or private security. Instead, these slum dwellers must rely on "street corner gangs, open bigotry, and physical abuse as a first line of defense against people from other ethnic or racial groups.[24] In Boston, a group of twenty Guardian Angels on a crime patrol was rescued from 400 irate area residents by police and escorted through the predominantly black, middle-class Mattapan neighborhood where the Angels were perceived as dangerous "outsiders."[25] This incident illustrates how racial and ethnic tensions can be exacerbated—and community forces undermined—when there exists neither adequate public policing nor genuine community self-defense. Finally, some are too poor to have the capacity to defend their neighborhoods *at all*, living in what Suttles terms "defeated neighborhoods."

The situational crime prevention approach also has been criticized for its conservative bias, often making people *more* fearful of crime. As the evaluators of the Minneapolis Community Crime Prevention Demonstration observed, fear of crime is an important indirect cost of crime:

The changes, which fear of crime can induce, can range from curtailing evening activities and avoiding specific areas to, in some cases, moving out of the neighborhood. Besides the social loss of decreased involvement in the community, an economic problem may develop from the subsequent loss of revenue by area businesses.[26]

Yet, the findings of their study indicated that, in addition to the failure of the programs to have any effect on crime, residents "still fear crime more than the recorded level of crime should be. There was little change in the level of fear expressed."[27] Analysis of the results of another important Minneapolis neighborhood crime prevention project, undertaken by the Whittier Alliance, indicated an increase in residents' fear of crime at the end of the program.[28]

In some forms, the situational approach also creates a siege mentality, isolating individuals and families. For those who cannot afford to pay for "walling" and professional "watching," city blocks, housing areas, and entire neighborhoods have become their stockades. For these residents, the "target population" must appear as a hostile encampment of the "dangerous class." Community forces are undermined, not enhanced, by such measures. This is particularly distressing in those urban areas that are experiencing "gentrification." Many cities are in the midst of profound demographic changes, a "reverse-migration" of young middle-class professionals who possess the resources to help sustain public mindedness. But instead of building communities, these migrants from suburban strongholds are merely replacing their former geographic isolation with environmentally designed barriers. To them, life outside their compound is alien.

Richard Sennett argues that the very diversity of human backgrounds and interests provides the best basis of community life. But only when individuals are forced to confront each other in urban life ("so the individual has to deal with those around him, in a milieu of diversity") do they develop the tolerance and learn the social skills with which to develop communal life in a pluralistic society.[29]

In the following sections, we move our discussion from an approach that merely uses community as a locale for deterrent efforts, to a consideration of two approaches based on the rationale of community as process: the first approach ("stake in conformity") is predicated largely on rational forces, and the other (informal control) on communal forces. Both approaches seek compliance to norms by self-policing and stress greater direct involvement of the family, the school and various community agencies in prevention. But, as Stanley Cohen argues:

This implies something more profound than simply using more volunteers or increasing reporting rates. It implies some sort of reversal of the presumption in positivist criminology that the delinquent is a different and alien being. Deviance, rather, is with us, woven into the fabric of social life and it must be "brought back home."[30]

THE "STAKE IN CONFORMITY" APPROACH

The "stake in conformity" approach to the prevention of crime and delinquency stresses community as process, as an institutional network. The purpose is to help gain voluntary compliance to norms or laws. In this model human nature is viewed as rational and self-seeking; inner motivational controls derive from an elective contract based on utility and rational motivation. Rephrased in terms of Etzioni's compliance theory, whereas the previous model used external controls and was coercive, this approach employs remunerative power and is calculative in the type of subordinate ideological involvement.

The theoretical rationale of the "stake in conformity" model is that the quest for private ends is thereby harnessed to community purposes. LaMar T. Empey expresses this view succinctly:

A legitimate identity among young people is most likely to occur if they have a stake in conformity; if, in other words, they develop a sense of competence, a sense of usefulness, a sense of belonging, and a sense that they have the power to affect their own destinies through conventional means.[31]

This requires, Empey continues, "socially acceptable, responsible, and personally gratifying roles." The dimension of community important here is community as a "social service delivery system" and as a socioeconomic opportunity structure. The urban neighborhood could serve as a mediating instrument to help provide employment, welfare services, and political power as a *quid pro quo* for normative allegiance. Expanding the range of legitimate roles must involve institutional change. Historically, there have been two basic approaches to the provision of meaningful roles: the empowerment of local citizens to enable them to exert stronger control of community affairs, and the enhancement of social services proper.

Empowerment of Citizens

The Chicago Area Project (CAP), one of the first community organizational efforts, was the outgrowth of the sociological studies of the 1930s and early 1940s by Clifford R. Shaw and Henry D. McKay at the University of Chicago. The aim of CAP was to promote community organization and to stimulate the latent potential for community control through the use, as much as possible, of "indigenous leaders." Field workers were to offer guidance but avoid manipulation and control; the responsibility for planning and management was to rest with area residents, creating a local participatory democracy. Shaw and McKay never forced direct conflict with Chicago's political and business leaders, however. According to Shaw, specific youth activities conducted by CAP were in most respects the same as those of the YMCA. The goals and strategy of CAP contrasted sharply with those espoused by one-time CAP worker, Saul Alinsky who, almost forty years after being fired by Shaw, quipped:

Finally, I quit Joliet and took a job with the Institute for Juvenile Research, one of those outfits that were always studying the causes of juvenile delinquency, making surveys of all the kids in coldwater tenements—with rats nibbling their toes and nothing to eat—and then discovering the solution: camping trips and some shit they called character building.[32]

In Alinsky's Back of the Yard's Project of the 1940s, confrontation with city leaders replaced accommodation as a strategy to obtain counseling and jobs. While Alinsky's Back-of-the-Yard's Council met with apparent success in lowering delinquency rates,[33] CAP has been judged largely a failure.[34]

Jon Snodgrass argues that CAP should have attempted broader types of social action to counter the forces destroying the community; namely, the continual expansion of industry. At bottom, Shaw and McKay wanted to "restore village life and tradition to city folk."[35] They had hoped to restore the "natural" social controls of traditional communal life. In that belief, they showed the anti-urban bias and romanticism about traditional society that marked the reaction of early sociologists to industrialization.

Social Welfare Bureaucracy

After World War II, the emphasis of delinquency prevention efforts moved from community empowerment toward the provision of social services proper by large public and private agencies. Then, by the early 1960s, the massive bureaucratization of social services came under attack—at first, by business leaders—as inefficient. The Ford Foundation, through its Grey Area Projects, funded research and planning to increase public agency coordination and improve educational opportunities. One of the resultant programs, the Mobilization for Youth (MFY), begun in New York City in 1962, is particularly noteworthy.

The Mobilization project was drawn from the theoretical perspective of Richard

Cloward and Lloyd Ohlin expressing the liberal vision of the American social structure as an "open order," given the existence of a rough equality of opportunity, and the notion that the "legitimate opportunity structure" could be enhanced by the welfare activities of the state.[36] Poverty and unemployment were linked with delinquency; they saw youths choosing crime as a rational alternative in the face of blocked legitimate alternatives. The project was aimed at a large area of New York's Lower East Side, and attempted to provide employment opportunities and work training in combination with community organization and improved social services. The core of the program, however, was to organize residents to assume "the power resources of the community by creating channels through which consumers of social welfare services can define their problems and goals and negotiate on their own behalf."[37]

MFY did not have much of a chance in its fight over the redistribution of city power and resources. After mass protests against the welfare bureaucracy by residents, in which agency workers participated, the organization's handsome funding (approximately $2 million per year) was cut and its programs limited. "Maximum feasible participation" became *Maximum Feasible Misunderstanding*, in the words of one critic.[38] After the 1964 presidential election, MFY returned to "normal." Delinquency prevention and welfare services were back in the hands of state bureaucrats.

Community development activists hoped for governmentally funded programs run for, by, and with local community members. More often, however, this has resulted in programs run by professional workers and reformers on behalf of the poor population, with local citizens not involved in key decisions. In the end, Irving Spergel observes, "Delinquents or pre-delinquents, however defined, may become targets for community attention and agency services that contribute more to the growth and status of organizations than to the solution of problems of individual and collective delinquency."[39]

The welfare system has done much to erode the authority of communal relations, resulting in just another control structure with which the poor must cope. Harry C. Boyte concurs: "The emergence of the modern welfare state has meant the rise of professions that reduce laymen to incompetence and to dependence on experts.[40] Under the welfare system, bureaucrats at the federal, state, and local levels, allied with members of the medical and psychiatric establishment, have penetrated nearly every aspect of individual and family life of the poor. One only has to be reminded of the intrusion of the state into the family by the juvenile court, and the power that is exerted by social workers, psychiatrists, and psychologists over children and their parents. This has been a familiar subject for radical critique, and, of course, the state's intrusiveness has been a favorite conservative complaint as well.

Mediating Structures

"Neoconservatives" have been influential in the shaping of recent public policy, and they have presented their own version of the "stake in conformity" approach.[41] Unlike traditional conservatives, proponents of this approach do not espouse a *laissez-faire* public policy, although they advocate private sector involvement whenever possible. Neoconservatives do not deny the existence of social problems, and they acknowledge the need for social welfare provision, but it "does not follow that the state is the only, or the most effective, or the cheapest, or the most sensitive social agency," Michael Novak claims.[42] The totalitarian tendencies of government can be avoided by diverting some of its traditional responsibilities to other social structures. Conceptualizing community in terms of an axis of influence and power can be helpful in understanding this approach.

Roland L. Warren distinguishes between the vertical and horizontal axes of community.[43] The horizontal axis involves relationships of individual to individual or group to group within a given locality, and the vertical axis links the local community with the regional and national levels of social and political organization. As we have seen, since the New Deal the vertical axis has become the most influential method of delivering social services and in this way has extended the power of centralized policy makers. Neoconservatives stress the horizontal axis.

"The principle," according to Novak, "is to empower individuals through local agencies to achieve their own independence.[44] Novak says he recognizes that in many cases the government must do the empowering, but it is possible to use the vertical axis without "statism" through the use of "mediating institutions," such as churches, schools, unions, fraternals, neighborhood organizations, and "other voluntary associations of every sort."[45] The idea is to help "empower" these institutions through tax incentives, low interest loans, reduction of "onerous paperwork," and a lower minimun wage scale. For instance, private associations or networks, already in place, to feed the elderly or develop supervised activities for teenagers could receive governmental subsidies. Small businesses and the service sector could receive tax credits or deductions to hire minority youths.

These "mitigating" institutions would provide a link between the solitary individual and the state; the government would serve only as a "catalyst." The government could, according to Novak, "through positive actions release the manifold energies of the private sector," thereby helping those in need of assistance while avoiding the problem of "the welfare state."[46]

Neoconservatism denies both the New Deal liberal emphasis on a "great national community" facilitated by megastructures such as big government and professional bureaucracies, and traditional conservatism's reliance on the solitary individual. Is this a nostalgic invocation of traditional community? Novak argues that it is not. His ideal model of human community is not one drawn from premodern experience, the agricultural village. Rather, Novak sees communal relations as involving "an elective contract or covenant." This is not to overstress the rationalism and voluntarism of the American character, he continues. Historically, the American has been a "communitarian individual," stressing cooperation and teamwork as virtues, while at the same time shunning allegiance to one single overarching institution:

Between individualism and collectivism, there is in America a third way. Between the individualist and the collectivist there is the communitarian individual—the individual whose life is given substance by the many communities and associations in which he or she participates. The American way of overcoming individualism is not an all-consuming attachment to the state or any other collective, but through the building up of many diverse associations and communities.[47]

The "notable" American capacity for free association is at the heart of his notion of the "associative community." Robert L. Woodson, chairman of the National Center for Neighborhood Enterprise, points to Philadelphia's House of Umoja as an example of a successful mediating structure that reaches young black gang members by instilling racial pride and democratic participation in their family-like residential facility.[48] Proposals to revitalize local community structures have received support from radicals as well.[49] However, public policy that emphasizes voluntary associations and the private (profit) sector to the exclusion of broader initiatives has been criticized by others as myopic and as encouraging individual isolation and competition.

Critique of Neoconservatism

In seeing threats to mediating structures from only big government's intrusiveness and bureaucratic unresponsiveness in the delivery of social services, neoconservatives overlook other pressures exerted outside of local community, including "economic forces like inflation and unemployment; cultural influences like TV; drugs," urban renewal, and especially corporations that, through their "vast sums of money, communications systems, and huge political resources, come to dominate our society."[50] When corporations come to exert so much influence, fear of the growth of the state seems overdrawn. Christopher Lasch reminds us that the human relations movement of industrial management had extended "managerial control from the factory into every other area of worker's life.[51]" Other cultural influences also undermine primary relations.

Claude Brown, returning to the Harlem of his youth, sees a connection between the unprecedented violence among young blacks, where "killing a mugging or robbery victim is now fashionable," and a society "severely afflicted with matierialism" and rife with violence.[52] Brown compares the black, urban manchild of thirty years ago to the manchild growing up today, and finds today's youth considerably more sophisticated, "more knowledgeable, more sensitive, more amicable—and more likely to commit murder." The neoconservatives claim that crime is a matter of values and that this is solely the responsibility of schools, churches, and family.[53] However, Brown implies that that interpretation is based on an unreasonably narrow conception of value-acquisition.

Professional and laypersons who work as traditional providers of social welfare (for example, those funded by the United Way) help perpetuate conservative values in their communities, but neoconservatives fault them for not being responsive to market conditions. The real focus of neoconservative ideology is the "privatization" of social welfare services. Unlike traditional conservatives, neoconservatives do not hold to the doctrine of the separation of government and business; they advocate their "coordination."

The marketing of social welfare, which socializes its costs during a time of fiscal crisis, has already occurred in the areas of social work, mental health (community institutional care), corrections (private halfway houses), and emergency services for children.[54] So, in a complete reversal, government programs that were once considered a drain on business because the tax money could have been better used for capital investment are now valued as a new market where entrepreneurs can turn administrative costs into big profits.

The privatization of social welfare should in no sense be considered an expression of community, critics argue.[55] The marketing of social welfare depoliticizes and individualizes social problems, leaving atomized recipients as individual "consumers" in the marketplace. Besides favoring middle-class clients, as we witness in private policing, this policy shifts the mission of traditional social welfare away from social and economic justice.

The welfare state, observes Michael Waltzer, "expresses a certain civil spirit, a sense of mutuality, a commitment to justice. Without that sense, no society can survive for long as a decent place to live—not for the needy, and not for anyone else."[56]

INFORMAL CONTROL AND COMMUNITY

"A sense of community cannot be yielded as a consequence of a strategy undertaken for self-interested rather than fraternal reasons," argues Plant.[57] From that perspective, relationships are communal only when they are based on subjective feeling, when there is a sense of belonging, when individuals are implicated in each other's total existence. Community is based on wholeness rather than people acting in their individual roles. We turn now to crime and delinquency prevention programs that draw heavily on communal sentiment, a model we call "informal control."

In terms of Etzioni's compliance theory, the informal control approach stresses normative power and uses moral involvement in the compliance relationship. In horizontal relationships—those that involve actors of equal rank—this is "the power of an 'informal' or primary group over its members."[58] Based on "social commitment," this kind of power employs manipulation of acceptance and positive response rather than the threat of force or the promise of remuneration. Whereas actors are means to each other in alienative and calculative relations, "they are ends to each other in 'social' relationships," Etzioni observes.[59]

At the local level, tightly knit primary groups help instill conscience so that individuals become self-policing. School and peer groups are important in promoting adherence to norms through socialization. Besides pressures of primary groups and members, political and religious organizations and "core" organizations of social movements are typical examples of normative compliance. In such organizations, participants display a high commitment to the organization's leaders and rituals. In this section we will focus on this as a crime preventive potential.

Racial Solidarity

Blacks and Hispanics have developed their own organizations. Malcolm X and the Muslim organization of twenty years ago gave meaning and collective identity to debased street people, drug addicts, prostitutes, and thieves as well as less neglected blacks.

Urban America of two decades ago was abundantly populated with genuine, deeply devout Muslims. And they were an extremely constructive presence, despite the espousal of a few absurd doctrines. They were consistently neatly attired, well-mannered and industrious, and comported themselves in an exemplary manner that demanded respect and admiration.[60]

Both religious and political, the 1960s civil rights movement inspired by Martin Luther King, Jr., promoted community among blacks and, according to Harry C. Boyte, it "was not only directed at transformation of unjust structures; it was also a 'school for citizenship' through which ordinary men and women would acquire a 'new sense of somebodyness'," and develop "a new sense of dignity and destiny."[61]

The involvement of poor blacks in civil rights struggles has a demonstrated crime prevention potential as well. Harlem experienced a dramatic drop in the crime rate on August 18, 1963, the day thousands went to Washington to demonstrate for "jobs and freedom." And in Washington, police reported a 63 percent drop in major crime.

Intrigued by these events, members of the Center for Youth and Community at Howard University initiated a study to measure the impact of the civil rights movement—which involved sit-ins, economic boycotts, desegregation campaigns in cities and rural communities of the Deep South—on the crime rate. In one city, assaults by blacks against blacks dropped 30 percent; in a rural community major crime dropped 33 percent the first summer of the civil rights activity, even though unemployment exceeded 30 percent. Apparently, blacks found political channels for the expression of aggression. The Center's researchers concluded:

It is the pooling of resources, the setting up and certifying of goals, priorities and methods in a community effort to produce social change that draws neighbors together in an organization whose very existence would tend to discourage crime . . . A spirit of common concern pervades the community and serves to discourage crime.[62]

But there is a profound irony here: the pursuit of justice can militate against small-scale community.

Roland L. Warren selects three widely used community values or desiderata of community and examines their interrelationships.[63] If considered as dimensions rather than as states, these values—community autonomy, community viability, and decision-making power—are inversely related. When considering community autonomy as one extreme of a dimension whose opposite is dependence, particularly on institutions outside of local community such as the federal government or national corporations, we find that as a community's autonomy increases, it becomes less viable, that is, less able to confront and solve local problems. And as autonomy increases, the distribution of power becomes more concentrated. In other words, community and justice are in tension. Within any given locality, various groups or classes have their own values and goals, which conflict, so a community's viability is a matter of definition: "community viability cannot be considered an objective concept in the sense of being value-free," Warren tells us. When considering informal control, one must ask: who is controlling whom?

Local community involvement holds out the promise of solidarity on the one hand and the probability of parochial intolerance on the other. Herein is the danger of so-called "decentralization" of social control lauded by many liberals, radicals, and conservatives alike. As Richard Sennett observes, the removal of central authority "all too often means the passing of central authority to a few private individuals who cannot be touched by the public at large. What is needed in order to create cities where people are forced to confront each other is a reconstituting of public power, not a destruction of it."[64]

Labor Solidarity

There are other exemplary normative organizations that could have relevance for crime prevention besides those that support racial community. Etzioni mentions ideological unions in democratic societies as an example of normative compliance, and one nineteenth-century American union can perhaps offer inspiration to the fragmented and declining contemporary labor movement. The Knights of Labor was a movement opposing big corporations and great fortunes, banks, railroads, and large landholders. To combat these giants, the Knights formed a loose organization around dozens of autonomous groups, called District Assemblies. "The one great sentiment embodied in the Knights of Labor was the idea of solidarity among all workers, whether white or black, skilled or unskilled, men or women," Jeremy Brecher observes.[65]

The loosely collected local associations were "designed partly to re-create and partly to protect a sense of community among its members," according to

Robert H. Wiebe.[66] "The community core—the District Assembly—would develop according to its own social logic. It did not have exact physical boundaries, for no lines could define a community; and it excluded only those who manipulated money and corrupted morals, for all honorable men, laborers 'of the land or the brain,' properly belonged to the healthy community." A moral movement, the Knights attempted to provide a substitute for the prevailing climate of competition and egoism in their promotion of producer and consumer cooperatives. The Knights constituted a moral brotherhood based on obligations to fellow members; like other ideological unions of the time, member compliance was based on normative power.

The District Assemblies had their own courts with which to discipline union members, and expulsion was the ultimate sanction. Members could be expelled for three types of offenses: (1) offenses against the order, such as dishonesty or contempt of court; (2) violations of statute law, such as embezzlement and family abuse, and (3) offenses against class solidarity, such as "scabbing." According to the constitution of the first local of the Knights, officers included a judge, a judge advocate, and a clerk of court, forming a "grievance committee for the settlement of disputes among members or to act as a court, if friendly settlement were impossible."[67] Thus, the Knights of Labor courts were intended to serve as an alternative or informal justice system, a substitute for what was widely perceived as a class-biased legal system. In the process, their organization provided an opportunity to learn the principles of democracy in a highly stratified society.

According to some investigators, the experience of democracy at the workplace has an important influence on family compliance patterns, which in turn bears on delinquent conduct.[68] Mark Colvin and John Pauly have developed an analysis that borrows from Kohn and Etzioni.[69]

According to this perspective, the social control structure at the workplace greatly influences the family control structure, and "the coerciveness of family control structures, conditioned by parents' work experiences, contributes at least indirectly to the production of delinquency"[70] because children who experience alienative bonds at home are more likely to be placed in more coercive school control structures, which reinforce and attenuate initial bonds.[71] In turn, these alienated bonds lead to greater association with alienated peers, who form peer group control structures. On the other hand, Colvin and Pauly's theory holds that parents who experience normative control as opposed to punitive and authoritarian forms of workplace discipline are more likely to socialize their children to be receptive to informal controls in peer, school, and neighborhood relationships.

Normative workplace control patterns are encouraged in industries that are worker-owned and managed, and there has been a recent surge in one form, called "employee stock ownership plans" (ESOP). ESOPs are especially promising in promoting normative compliance when they involve a high degree of employee participation in management. Weirton Steel Corporation promises to be one such example. Its 7,700 workers purchased the aged and nearly bankrupt subsidiary in January 1984, and in the first year they managed an astonishing economic rebound in an otherwise moribund domestic industry.[72]

So, in addition to fostering normative patterns, worker ownership of Weirton has aided the community's crime prevention effort by enhancing the area's economic viability. Low unemployment helps keep families intact and provides positive role models for local youth. In addition, local social and communal networks are sustained in stable communities.

SUMMARY AND CONCLUSION

Criminologists are far from agreement on the meaning of community crime prevention, largely because the meaning of community is problematical. Various dimensions of "community" have been given emphasis in preventive theory and program application, and based on these we constructed a typology delineating three basic approaches which we termed situational, "stake in conformity," and informal control. Taken by themselves, the first two approaches are defective. The first is undesirable because it is based on an ideological involvement that is alienative. Moreover, with segments of the urban population organizing mainly or exclusively for the prevention of crime, situational prevention strategies foster a siege mentality inimical to social solidarity. Community prevention must be integrative, not exclusionary.

While it attempts to elicit voluntary compliance, the "stake in conformity" approach in the form of a welfare state bureaucracy may be criticized for its impersonality and intrusiveness. The neoconservative version of this approach emphasizes mediating structures and the private provision of social welfare. Intermediary institutions, however, are besieged by forces largely beyond the control of local communities alone. And the policy of privatizing social welfare has the effect of fragmenting and isolating the poor. Social solidarity involves mutual dependence and collective responsibility; thus, rational calculation of self-interest cannot sustain community.

Finally, we considered preventive activities based on informal control rooted in moral involvement and social commitment. Although there are normative vertical organizations, those most useful for crime prevention are horizontal. Here, prevention *as* community assumes that there are not great power differentials between actors; the power of the informal group works only with actors of equal rank. Etzioni's theory recognizes that the creation of conflict by lower level norm senders is the source of democracy, and the solution to social problems in this view must involve upward and lateral processes.

Short of achieving important social structural changes, there are medium-range goals to pursue in creating safer communities. Effective community crime prevention programs should strive to integrate situational strategies such as neighborhood watches with broader strategies of locally based economic development. But the promotion of economic equality and social justice cannot be neglected.

Without the latter goals, "community" crime prevention too easily degenerates into paranoia and vigilante justice.

NOTES

1. Stanley Cohen, a critic of correctional ideology who *does* explore meaning carefully, cautions against quick celebration over the "decentralization" of social control. See Cohen, "Social Control Talk: Telling Stories About Correctional Change," in D. Garland and P. Young, eds., *The Power to Punish* (London: Heinemann, 1983), p. 119. See also Cohen, "The Punitive City: Notes on the Dispersal of Social Control," *Contemporary Crises* 3 (October 1979): 339–363, and Dario Melossi, "Institutions of Social Control and Capitalist Organization of Work," in Bob Fine et al., eds., *Capitalism and the Rule of Law* (London: Hutchinson, 1983) .

2. Raymond Plant, "Community: Concept, Conception, and Ideology," *Politics and Society* 8, no. 1 (1978): 81.

3. David W. Minar and Scott Greer, *The Concept of Community: Readings with Interpretations* (Chicago: Aldine, 1969), p. 9.

4. David B. Clark, "The Concept of Community: A Re-examination," *Sociological Review* 21 (August 1973): 404.

5. Robert Nisbet, *The Quest for Community* (New York: Oxford University Press, 1969), p. 47.

6. Conrad Arensberg, "The Community as Object and as Sample," *American Anthropologist* 63 (April 1961): 259.

7. Kenneth E. Boulding, *A Primer on Social Dynamics: History as Dialectics and Development* (New York: Free Press, 1970), pp. 23–29.

8. See Elmer H. Johnson, "Introduction," in this handbook.

9. LaMar T. Empey, "Crime Prevention: The Fugitive Utopia," in Daniel Glaser, ed., *Handbook of Criminology* (Chicago: Rand McNally, 1974).

10. Johnson, "Introduction."

11. Lawrence W. Sherman, "Patrol Strategies for Police," in James Q. Wilson, ed., *Crime and Public Policy* (San Francisco: ICS Press, 1983), p. 146.

12. Amitai Etzioni, "Compliance Theory," in O. Grusky and G. A. Miller, eds., *The Sociology of Organizations* (New York: Free Press, 1970), pp. 103–126.

13. Albert Hunter, "The Loss of Community: An Empirical Test Through Replication," *American Sociological Review* 40 (October 1975): 537–552.

14. "Crime Prevention and Control Strategies," *Criminal Justice Abstracts* 5 (September 1983): 362.

15. Empey, "Crime Prevention: Fugitive Utopia," p. 1095.

16. Gerald D. Suttles, *The Social Construction of Communities* (Chicago: University of Chicago, 1972), pp. 21–23.

17. Anne M. Newton, "Prevention of Crime and Delinquency," *Criminal Justice Abstracts* 10, no. 2 (1978): 245–266; Ronald J. Troyer, "Community Response to Crime: Two Middle-Class Anti-Crime Patrols," *Journal of Criminal Justice* 13, no. 3 (1985): 227–241.

18. Ibid.; Robert K. Yin et al., *Patrolling the Neighborhood Beat: Residents and Residential Security* (Santa Monica, Calif.: Rand Corporation, 1976), *passim*.

19. George L. Kelling et al., *The Kansas City Preventive Patrol Experiment* (Wash-

ington, D.C.: Police Foundation, 1976), and "Hiring More Police Does Not Cut Crime—Report," *Houston Chronicle*, February 29, 1984.

20. Marcy Rasmussen et al., *Evaluation of the Minneapolis Crime Prevention Demonstration* (St. Paul Minnesota: Crime Control Planning Board, 1979).

21. Newton, "Prevention of Crime and Delinquency," p. 245.

22. Marlys McPherson, *The Future of Community Crime Prevention: A Retrospective Examination* (Minneapolis: Minnesota Crime Prevention Center, 1982), *passim*.

23. "Private Guard Forces are Feared as Drain on Money for the Police," *New York Times*, February 5, 1984.

24. Suttles, *The Social Control of Communities*, p. 238.

25. "Guardian Angels Halt Boston Patrols in a Dispute," *New York Times*, September 2, 1984.

26. Rasmussen et al., *Evaluation of the Minneapolis Crime Prevention Demonstration*, p. 2.

27. Ibid., p. 221.

28. Rebecca L. Smith and Thomas L. Anding, *Community Involvement in the Whittier Neighborhood: An Analysis of Neighborhood Conditions and Neighborhood Change* (Minneapolis: Center for Urban and Regional Affairs, University of Minnesota, 1979), p. 21. The survey found that only 10 percent of those queried perceived any decrease in residential burglaries or in crime generally.

29. Richard Sennett, *The Uses of Disorder: Personal Identity and City Life* (New York: Vintage, 1970), p. 164.

30. Cohen, "The Punitive City: Notes on the Dispersal of Social Control," p. 356.

31. Empey, "Crime Prevention: The Fugitive Utopia," p. 1107.

32. Saul Alinsky, "Interview," *Playboy* 19 (March 1972): 68.

33. Peter W. Born, *Street Gangs and Youth Unrest* (Chicago: Chicago Tribune Education Service Department, 1971), p. 5. However, others have suggested that Alinsky's organization is effective as long as it involves middle-class persons who are trying to combat serious lower class social problems.

34. Irving A. Spergel, "Community-based Delinquency-Prevention Programs: An Overview," *Social Service Review* 47 (1973): 25.

35. Jon Snodgrass, "Clifford R. Shaw and Henry D. McKay: Chicago Criminologists," *British Journal of Criminology* 16, no.1 (1976): 1–19.

36. Richard A. Cloward and Lloyd E. Ohlin, *Delinquency and Opportunity* (New York: Free Press, 1960), pp. 208–209.

37. George A. Brager and Francis Purcell, *Community Action Against Poverty* (New Haven, Conn.: College and University Press, 1967), p. 71.

38. Daniel Moynihan, *Maximum Feasible Misunderstanding* (New York: Free Press, 1969), pp. 167–203.

39. Spergel, "Community-based Delinquency-Prevention Programs," p. 19.

40. Harry C. Boyte, *Community Is Possible* (New York: Harper, 1984), p. 33.

41. On neo-conservatism, the reader is referred to P. Steinfels, *The Neo-conservatives* (New York: Simon and Schuster, 1979); Michael Waltzer, *Radical Principles* (New York: Basic, 1980); and Irving Kristol, *Reflections of a Neo-conservative* (New York: Basic, 1983).

42. Michael Novak, "Mediating Institutions: The Communitarian Individual in America," *The Public Interest*, no. 68 (Summer 1982): 12.

43. Roland L. Warren, *Perspectives on the American Community* (Chicago: Rand McNally, 1966), pp. 12–13.

44. Novak, "Mediating Institutions," p. 9.

45. Normally, most voluntary associations would belong to our third type, "Informal Control," as these organizations are classified by Etzioni as normative. But Novak emphasizes the rational and calculative in these relationships.

46. Ibid., p. 5.

47. Ibid., p. 8.

48. Robert L. Woodson, *A Summons to Life: Mediating Structures and the Prevention of Youth Crime* (Cambridge, Mass.; Ballinger Publishing Co., 1981), pp. 45–88.

49. Elliot Currie, "Crime and Ideology," *Working Papers* 9, nos. 3 and 4 (1982): 23–25.

50. Boyte, *Community Is Possible*, pp. 137–138.

51. Christopher Lasch, "Liberalism in Retreat," in Douglas MacLean and Claudia Mills, eds., *Liberalism Reconsidered* (Totowa, N.J.: Rowan and Allanheld, 1983), p. 117.

52. Claude Brown, "Manchild in Harlem," *The New York Times Magazine*, September 16, 1984, p. 36.

53. James Q. Wilson, *Thinking About Crime* (New York: Basic Books, 1983), p. 45.

54. Donald Fisk et al., *Private Provision of Public Services* (Washington, D.C.: Urban Institute, 1978).

55. Others would not even consider the proprietary provision of social services as true social welfare. See H. Wilensky and C. Lebeaux in *Industrial Society and Social Welfare* (New York: Free Press, 1965), p. 142.

56. Quoted in Theda Skocpol, "Legacies of New Deal Liberalism," *Dissent* (Winter 1983): 33–43.

57. Pland, "Community," p. 105.

58. Etzioni, "Compliance Theory," p. 104.

59. Ibid., p. 107.

60. Brown, "Manchild," p. 38.

61. Boyte, *Community Is Possible*, p. 217.

62. Quoted in Frank Browning, "Nobody's Soft on Crime Anymore," *Mother Jones* 7, no. 25 (1982), p. 41.

63. Warren, *Perspectives on the American Community*, p. 223.

64. Sennett, *The Uses of Disorder*, p. 141.

65. Jeremy Brecher, *Strike!* (Boston: South End Press, 1977), p. 28.

66. Robert H. Wiebe, *The Search for Order 1877–1920* (New York: Hill and Wang, 1967), p. 67.

67. Norman J. Ware, *The Labor Movement in the United States 1860–1895, A Study in Democracy* (New York: Vintage, 1964); see Appendix. Also see J. Garlock, "The Knights of Labor Courts: A Case Study of Popular Justice," in Richard L. Abel, ed., *The Politics of Informal Justice, Vol. I: The American Experience* (New York: Academic Press, 1982), pp. 17–34.

68. Melvin L. Kohn, *Class and Conformity* (Chicago: University of Chicago Press, 1977); "Social Class and Parental Values: Another Confirmation of the Relationship," *American Sociological Review* 41 (June 1976): 538–545.

69. Mark Colvin and John Pauly, "A Critique of Criminology: Toward an Integrated Structural-Marxist Theory of Delinquent Production," *American Journal of Sociology* 89 (November 1983): 513–551.

70. Ibid., p. 537.

71. For research support, see Samuel Bowles and Herbert Gintis, *Schooling in Capitalist America* (New York: Basic, 1976); Martin Carnoy and Henry M. Levin, eds., *The Limits of Educational Reform* (New York: David McKay, 1976); David Noble, *America by Design* (New York: Oxford University Press, 1977); and Joel H. Spring, *Education and the Rise of the Corporate State* (Boston: Beacon, 1972).

72. See "Employees Make a Go of Weirton," *New York Times*, January 6, 1985, p, 4-F.

BIBLIOGRAPHY

Abel, Richard L., ed. *The Politics of Informal Justice*, Vol. 1: *The American Experience*, Vol. 2: *Comparative Studies*. New York: Academic Press, 1982.

"Informal justice" is said to be an unofficial, noncoercive, decentralized, and nonbureaucratic method of dispute resolution. Informal justice processes can promote community crime prevention insofar as they protect rights, promote equality, and increase community solidarity. However, the twenty historical and comparative essays gathered in the two volumes present a skeptical view; most of the contributors argue that informal legal institutions are, on closer inspection, coercive in nature and function so as to expand rather than diminish state control.

Conklin, John E. "Dimensions of Community Response to the Crime Problem." *Social Problems* 18 (Winter 1976): 373–383.

Conklin compares samples of a high-crime rate urban area with samples of a low-crime rate suburban area. Those in the urban area perceive a higher crime rate, feel less safe, are less trustful, and show a less positive feeling for the community itself.

Greenberg, Martin. *Auxiliary Police: The Citizen's Approach to Public Safety*. Westport, Conn.: Greenwood Press, 1984.

The author promotes the notion of semiformal control in the form of "citizens in uniform," and he envisions volunteer or auxiliary police as a model for crime prevention nationally.

Herting, Jerald, and Avery M. Guest. "Components of Satisfaction with Local Areas in the Metropolis." *Sociological Quarterly* 26, no. 1 (1985): 99–115.

The evaluation of the physical/social environment, characteristics of the homes, and the social character of the local environment are among the strongest correlates of residents' satisfaction with local areas.

Lewis, Dan A., and Greta Salem. "Community Crime Prevention: An Analysis of a Developing Strategy." *Crime and Delinquency* 27 (July 1981): 405–421.

Instead of the usual direction of preventive efforts toward motivations and predispositions of offenders, the authors would emphasize potential victims and their environment to reduce the opportunities for victimization.

Oliver, Pamela. " 'If You Don't Do It, Nobody Else Will': Active and Token Contributions to Local Collective Action." *American Sociological Review* 49 (October 1984): 601–610.

Persons in a Detroit sample who were most active in efforts to improve the neighborhood had less respect for their neighbors and more of a belief that, if something was to be done, they would have to do it themselves. Thus, a real tension exists between community activists and their communities.

Podolefsky, Aaron, and Fredric Dubow. *Strategies for Community Crime Prevention: Collective Responses to Crime in Urban America.* Springfield, Ill.: Charles C Thomas, 1981.

Analyzing the results of an extensive field research and telephone survey of residents in ten urban locales, the authors were able to classify in two broad categories collective responses to crime: a social problems approach aimed at the root causes of crime, and a victimization or target-hardening approach. These behaviors are viewed as lying on a continuum and are discussed in terms of the "world views" and philosophies that underlie them.

Skogan, W. G., and M. G. Maxfield. *Coping with Crime: Individual and Neighborhood Responses.* Beverly Hills, Calif.: Sage Publications, 1981.

This book discusses crime, victimization, and fear in a community context, and the neighborhood as a locus for action. Their research indicates what many other investigations have found: that in communities with a high level of social integration there is larger commitment to crime prevention activity and greater cooperation with local police than in less established (lower income) neighborhoods.

Sorrentino, Anthony, ed. *Organizing Against Crime: Redeveloping the Neighborhood.* New York: Behavioral Publications, 1977.

Based on an analysis of one of the Chicago area projects, the book demonstrates how neighborhood residents can help change social situations that contribute to delinquency.

U.S. National Criminal Justice Reference Service. *Citizen Crime Prevention Tactics: A Literature Review and Selected Bibliography*, by J. T. Duncan. Washington, D.C.: U.S. Government Printing Office, 1980.

This work presents an annotated bibliography and literature review of community, individual, and collective crime prevention initiatives.

6

Police and Crime Prevention: A Political Approach

ROBERT A. LORINSKAS

When attempting to relate the concept of crime prevention to the institutionalized police bureaucracy, one faces a serious disjuncture between the hypothesized and actual relationships of the two phenomena.[1] In analyses of the crime prevention activities of the police, the range of often-conflicting ideas is likely to be supplemented by the tendency of theoretical discussions to exceed the span of reality.[2] For these and other reasons, police administrators should approach the topic of crime prevention with caution.[3]

This chapter will take a political approach to the analysis of the prevention function of the police as suggested by Robert I. Mendelsohn[4] and James Q. Wilson.[5] The police department is an element in the institutional network of the community. Specifically, it is charged with administering legal norms that have been enacted politically by legislators to preserve domestic tranquility and the social order.

Order maintenance is only one of the responsibilities assigned to law enforcement as an element of the political system. Law observance, rather than only law enforcement in and of itself, is the ultimate objective. Thus, crime prevention becomes either the direct or indirect function of policing. That function is carried out in several ways, and its place within the context of the police department as a political institution is the focus of attention in this chapter.

POLITICAL CONTEXT AND POLICE PREVENTION

Although the police department is a vital participant in crime prevention activities, its participation is colored by the incentives for and course of development of American police bureaucracies.

Crime Control and Prevention

That history has been marked by public concerns about perceptions of general disorder under the conditions of urbanization and industrialization at a time when societies have been undergoing remarkable socioeconomic transition. The ideas underlying the crime control rationale, as considered previously in this book, lent impetus to the development of policing as a political institution.

The crime control ideology presents officers in a role similar to that of military sentinels manning "the walls" against aggressive and violent criminals. The faults of that ideology have been emphasized by critics, including some observers within police circles as well as some members of the academic community, who follow Herbert L. Packer's "crime control," sociolegalistic mode.[6] From that perspective, the role expectations of the "crime fighter" conflict with the role expectations of the police officers engaged in prevention activities.[7] However, that perspective overlooks the legitimacy of law enforcement, drawn from the public demand for order maintenance and community protection that historically has marked the development of the contemporary police organization as a political entity.

As we will see, the American situation that imposed an initial demand that the police be an instrument of moral coercion, later enabled the police to develop the more neutral stance of professionalism, subjected departments to the interference of machine politicians, and pressed departments to emphasize "crime fighting" over other functions in obtaining public and financial support. These political factors justify the habitual emphasis on crime control measures when police executives speak of prevention.

In that situation, the deterrent effects of law enforcement and target-hardening strategies are prominent in police activities for crime prevention. The usual prescription is to correct shortages of hardware and personnel to increase chances that the active criminals will be caught and that potential offenders realize that the risk of apprehension and punishment is excessive. Crime reporting by citizens may be encouraged in some form of convergence between the crime control and community rationales for prevention. Citizen participation may be further encouraged through auxiliary police, neighborhood watch, vacation premise inspections, and school liaison programs. Target-hardening strategies for family and commercial self-protection can utilize better locks and other security devices.[8] Under the crime control rationale, the need to revise police policy and practices would be essentially ignored in efforts to generate public support of the immediate purposes of the police department.

Community-Oriented Prevention

In the highly dynamic American society, police departments have been pressed to develop closer ties with other elements of the community. That pressure is not universal among communities, and the response of a given department cannot be predicted with confidence. However, broadly speaking, those pressures operate in some degree within a political context. "Police work is carried out under the influence of a *political culture* though not necessarily under day-to-day political direction," Wilson says. "By political culture is meant those widely shared expectations as to how issues will be raised, governmental objectives determined, and power for their attainment assembled; it is an understanding of what makes a government legitimate."[9]

The constant presence of the police in the community, police discretion, and their service functions place police departments in a strategic position for lending support to the community rationale for prevention. Whereas most community agencies operate during regular office hours, the police carry out their work around the clock. As we will see, the employment of police discretion is controversial, but it is crucial to programs of referral and diversion to other community agencies. The involvement in services to citizens, beyond law enforcement per se, will be described below to document the fact that a great portion of ordinary police work and budgets is diverted to routine regulatory and emergency services.[10]

The strategies for community involvement of the police are manifold. The term "police-community relations" encompasses a variety of departmental efforts to gain public acceptance of constructive relationships with the police. Team policing has been conceived as decentralized professional patrol that generates the officer's understanding of the parameters of a neighborhood and the residents' acceptance of their functions. Neighborhood watch, operation identification, and crisis intervention lend themselves to more profound involvement of the police in more spontaneous interaction with citizens. Criminal justice planning is the most sophisticated and demanding sector for police involvement in prevention. The planning process entails relationships with other agencies in rational development of ultimate goals, mobilization of resources, and implementation of a coordinated scheme for improving prevention activities.

AMERICAN POLICING—A DEVELOPMENTAL OVERVIEW

The crime prevention function may be traced back to the establishment of the London Metropolitan Police as a prototype from which emerged the contemporary organization of the police, including that in the United States. However, as for all political institutions, the typical police agency has been shaped by historical antecedents and the social conditions of the time.

The Contemporary American Police Organization

In spite of the English heritage, American policing has developed its own characteristics which profoundly affect its involvement in crime prevention. In a federated system, such as the United States, and in state systems, one has to differentiate between state power and local control. There are several sources of legitimacy and power. Stated simply, federal law enforcement agencies tend to have limited specific authority and jurisdictions, for example, Customs and the Internal Revenue Service. The only agency that might seem to have broad powers is the Federal Bureau of Investigation, but again, although broader than other federal agencies, they are limited by their charter. In general, most federal agencies are concerned with controlling and protecting public revenue and other functions rebated to the federal government. Their function is therefore very much related to the federal criminal justice system and the administrative law system.

The second group of agencies exists at the state level and is generally comprised of three types. One classification is the state police, which may have both law enforcement and peace officer powers. The second type of agency is a state patrol, which is primarily for traffic control. Third, a criminal investigation division may exist at the state level, as well as various assorted regulatory agencies. These regulatory agencies have very narrow functions, such as the collection of revenues and licensing.

At the local level there are sheriffs' departments as well as municipal police; there is a tremendous range of size and ability(s) among these departments, depending on the rural or urban nature of the community served. It is important to clarify the function of police in terms of the local agencies because they are the most numerous and handle the vast bulk of police and law enforcement duties. Thus, one should focus not on the FBI, the State Revenue Department, or the State Police, but on the municipal police. These officers and administrators have a very broad mandate for action, and the greatest volume of action, both individually and as organizations, occurs at the municipal level of government. One needs to understand the stated functions of the police in order to understand the importance of this "mandate for action."

Qualities of the English Experience

At the onset, it is appropriate to observe that urban policing as an organized and comprehensive function of society is a relatively recent social innovation in America, with clear roots in Western Europe. The London Metropolitan Police Force was formed in 1829, with American departments coming into existence shortly thereafter.

Prior to this time, the police function probably rested on a reasonably high degree of public moral consensus in England, Europe, and America and crime prevention and repression were perceived as being well within the province of citizen responsibility. The establishment of police organizations in England was impeded by the traditional English distrust of any potentially absolutist force. The distrust raises the question of whether a centralized and powerful civil force, such as the London police, would have been organized at all had it not been for an English repugnance and fear of the urban excesses of the French Revolution, and a need to reinforce property rights against the unruly lower class elements flooding the urban-industrial areas of nineteenth-century England.

At that time, the stratified nature of English society, coupled with a rather high national moral consensus, made resolution of the conflict between preservation of property rights and the mandates of liberation premises somewhat easier for the counterpart American experience. The position of the English officer was articulated in terms of an unarmed citizen-policeman, joining with the community for mutual protection of life and property, and also providing it with an idealized male role model. The responsibility for police behavior was given to top-level police administrators, who held high social class positions. Various techniques, such as a mixture of civilian and police positions within law enforcement, were instituted in order to preserve the actual as well as the publicly perceived democratic tone of the organizations, while administrative and line operations were treated as separate and distinct career tracks.[11]

Differences of the American Experience

The keystone of English and European policing has been a public consensus about the moral order, a consensus that was maintained by organized law enforcement and one that was seldom if ever applied by the police as an alien normative system against targeted segments of the community. The American policing experience is in rather sharp contrast to this development and mode of operation.

To fully appreciate this contrast, it is important to consider the nature of the earliest social experiences of the Republic, as well as the events culminating in the organizing of policing. Colonial writings, in general, provide salient proof of the moral homogeneity of the original settlers, and early political writings provide the social justification for insisting that new immigrants conform to existing social and political forms.[12] Although the *Federalist Papers* and political writings ranging from Adams to Jefferson form the boundaries of proper political power and action, all may be viewed as providing the context for what has been characterized as a ''conservative'' revolution.[13]

The American Revolution may be viewed not as a radical social and political transformation, but more in terms of the perfecting of social and political ideas transported out of English history and culture. Thus, it is possible that nativists even into the early nineteenth century perceived themselves as possessing special virtue; then later immigrants from other ethnic origins would be seen as ''nonbelievers'' who would threaten the social stability by their ''alien'' ways. Unless the newcomers accepted the colonial heritage, they were likely to be seen as deviants and their ''pathological'' behavior as the key source of social disorder. With the immigration of great masses of the Irish, most of whom were Catholic, the defenders of the colonial heritage were likely to perceive them as a danger to the moral climate and social organizations of the nation. Thus, the social disorganizations powered by urbanization of that time—effects stimulated by sources other than the ethnic or religious origins of city inhabitants—aroused calls for actions against crime and other symptoms of public disorder.

Emphasis on the Crime Control Rationale

It cannot be realistically maintained that organized policing came into being merely to stabilize a moral consensus, since there is scant evidence that such a consensus existed. Nevertheless, American urban policing assumed major functional responsibility for the creation, conditioning, or coercion of conformity to the moral and behavioral code of nativist Protestants.

In that sense, the rhetoric of the police activities for crime prevention became heavily charged with the crime control rationale. Although general progress has been achieved in the professionalization of law enforcement, that linkage continues to be present. Certainly, the focus of this responsibility has shifted through time—from the "old immigrants" from Western Europe, to the "new immigrants" from Southern and Eastern Europe, to blacks, to various types of activists. American urban policing came into being at a time when serious normative disjunctures already existed in the quickly transforming national social structure.

Thus, serious problems of acceptability have always existed in regard to a substantial segment of the population being policed and the proper role of the police. In short, the normative conflict inherent in a nation of immigrants, coupled with an actual nativist intolerance of pluralism, provides the point of greatest departure from English and much of European policing.

CORRELATES OF NORMATIVE CONFLICT

Nor has this difficulty been resolved as a function of time. Conflict pluralism underlies what the police say they do, what they actually do, how their function is legitimated, and the techniques used to gain public acceptance. The period from 1850 to 1950 witnessed the development of such a wide-ranging series of events that only major dynamics can be considered in this chapter.

Linkages with Machine Politics

Of first note is the fact that policing quickly devolved from any semblance of social neutrality and became an integral element in the machine politics which characterized most urban centers prior to the reform era. Second, it soon became apparent that the achievement of moral coercion was easier said than done. Policing units were staffed with members of the very same socioeconomic (and often ethnic) background as the targeted population. In addition, the normative conflict that existed provided viable grounds for the establishment of a social/political/economic *quid pro quo* that at once reflected the existence of particular normative input demands to policing as well as a popular public perception that the police were corruptible and corrupted.[14]

The period from the late 1800s past the turn of the century saw many states actualizing the mandates of the reform movement by assuming prerogatives in police appointments and tenure. The development of civil service protections and standards during this same era introduced some degree of objectivity into policing. The same can be said of the concurrent movement in organizational design, efficiency-oriented management models, legal-rational modes of conceptualizing function and product, and the specification of quantifiable standards of police service. None of these developments can be necessarily assumed to have had the effect of either making urban policing a particularly rational activity or of providing police organizations with the adaptablility so often called for in a dynamic urban environment.

Consequences for Professionalism

These developments, singly or in combination, may have provided law enforcement with all the necessary mechanisms for survival as an organization, while providing a concurrent shield against public debate as to police goals and actions and derogating against an urban police policy which reflects the greatest possible consensus in individual and group needs. Civil service, for example, has done noticeably little to increase the relative occupational standing of the police, and probably serves best to protect a demonstrable lower and lower-middle-class occupational pyramid.

In spite of the appeal of police professionalism, lateral movement below the top administrative positions, for example, remains almost as rare today as it was fifty years ago. In addition, preemployment residency requirements are still the norm, not the exception, although this practice may be of questionable constitutionality to some.[15]

Shield against Public Debate

The impact of reformism and legal-rational models of organizational action—as reflected, for instance, in centralized departments with city-wide policies and operational priorities—may have the net effect of systematically alienating particular citizen populations or treating the conditions necessary to destabilize community equilibrium. On the other hand, the emphasis on quantification of function can lead to a false legitimation of function, concurrent with distorted actual police fiscal needs in relation to other city services by merely a minor change in operational emphasis.[16]

When organizational efficiency is given high priority, police departments tend to be closed systems that oppose public input in departmental affairs. The tendency jeopardizes the creditability of police activities that is especially important for enlisting public participation in crime prevention. The usual awe accorded laws in general, a valuable asset for eliciting public support, is undermined.

"Keep politics out of policing," a cliche frequently expressed in movements to reform law enforcement agencies, may also serve to neutralize any citizen output.

FUNCTIONAL EMPHASIS OF AGENCIES

The cumulative impact of prevention on the development of American policing is best viewed in terms of its evolving emphasis among law enforcement functions. Broadly speaking, the functions of law enforcement departments are crime repression by apprehending and investigating criminal events; regulation of non-criminal conduct in traffic, crowds, and so on; provision of public services such as information, advice, licensing, registration, and other general assistance; protection of citizens in domestic or other disputes and in disasters; and crime prevention.

The various functions involve differing role expectations for the officers performing the particular tasks. The role expectations are usually distinctive for the given function, but the evolution of American policing has produced three major roles: (1) the maintenance of civil stability through the provision of routine regulatory and emergency services, including crowd and riot control; (2) the creation or maintenance of a preferred moral state, as, for example, the passive or aggressive enforcement of moral laws, especially in the area of "victimless" crimes; and (3) the detection, prevention, and repression of serious felony deviance—in short, "crime fighting."

All police departments engage in each type of behavior. The actual role as contrasted with the advertised role of the agency in question constitutes the most salient comparison in analyzing police policy positions. Each role area presents certain constraints and opportunities in policy development and articulation.

Priority for "Crime Fighting"

The provision of routine services usually elicits a positive public response, and the maintenance of civil stability through the service functions consumes much of police time and resources. The service role is particularly congenial to the prevention of criminal incidents because the emphasis is on meeting "client" needs instead of enforcing laws per se. Nevertheless, in practice the police's first priority is given to crime fighting. When prevention is the stated policy, the deterrent effect of crime fighting is likely to be the chief justification. The crime fighting function provides the greatest payoff to organizational survival, police prestige, and citizen acceptance of the police. The term "crime fighting" seldom fails to elicit public and fiscal support, for "wars on crime" have a way of arousing the American taxpayer.

Crime fighting provides a blanket organizational legitimation. Moreover, because unreported crime is so widespread, mere attention to it will increase its officially noted occurrence. The simplest administrative techniques are often sufficient either to raise or to lower the "crime rate" as the need arises. Lastly, even a failure to repress or to maintain crime at a level approximate to a national increase can often be rationalized in terms of inadequate "hardware" such as helicopter patrols, new rolling stock, and inadequate communications, thus forming the basis for drastic upward revisions in budget needs.

Thus, the policy of contemporary urban police has evolved from primary emphasis on a value-control stance to one of crime fighting, but, in actuality, the majority of their resources have involved expenditures in the area of public services. Police have compensated for the alienated perceptions of many citizens by publicly promoting their major function as crime fighting, even though this area involves far less than half of the total police resources, and is essentially reactive, in sharp contrast to the oft-presumed proactive stance.[17]

Maintenance of the Moral State

Historically, the enforcement of morals has given the police their largest headache, not only because of the damage to functional integrity from corruption and from alienated citizen perceptions, but also because of uneven and casual legal judgments in these areas. Citizens are often convinced that the police do not act out of the public interest, but rather are indulging in their own moral persuasions.

In their research on a morals detail, Jerome R. Skolnick and J. Richard Woodworth report that morals detectives uniformly disliked their responsibilities in this area, considering it not "real police work" in contrast to search, chase, and capture responsibilities.

Morals detectives express frustration that their activities produce little appreciation from the victim and no beneficial results. They are skeptical of the benefits of prosecution, for the statutory rapist is difficult to interpret as a danger to the community.[18]

Little actual police effort is usually expended in the area of morals enforcement, although the media coverage of periodic forays may greatly increase the public perception of actual resource expenditures. Conversely, a majority of police effort is expended in the provision of routine services—traffic control, patrol, emergency services, domestic disputes, the public order—areas that may account for over 80 percent of total police resources.[19] The problem for the police organization is that these routine services provide little of the visceral impact necessary to justify or maintain organizational needs. This role is not nearly as competitive in the yearly fight for scarce fiscal resources as is the need to deal with the occurrence of, for example, a series of rape-murders, a bank robbery, or a "crime wave," even though the ability of the police to repress such acts is questionable.

To recap, the vast majority of police work involves the provision of services, a role that is seldom preeminent in police policy. Morals enforcement constitutes a minor, but volatile, aspect of police work; normative conflict, however, dictates against the articulation of policy in other than the most amorphous terms.

It may be speculated that the police moral guardian stance is intitiated in response to cues from urban power centers; "tacit understandings" about the desired state of community morals; police biases; or a combination of all three. These lead to the concept of discretion.

POLICE DISCRETION: THE UNBALANCED EQUATION

Crime prevention involves the police in mediation, referral, and diversion—all of which entail discretion in the sense of deciding whether the power of arrest should be employed. Mediation includes conflict management, crisis intervention, and violence prevention; it implies that alternatives to arrest may be the superior action. Referral and diversion relate to removing individuals from criminal justice processing and sending them for services to other community agencies. All of those strategies imply that the police officer is substituting either the therapeutic or the community rationale for the more common crime control rationale for law enforcement work. In that instance, the officer lends support to the first two rationales—not his or her own active participation—by employing discretion to bring other community agencies into relation to the individual.

The topic of police discretion is controversial and complicated. For the purposes of this discussion, it may be sufficient to note that police discretion is subject to an "unbalanced equation." An analogy would be our studies of local elections. One knows that personal contact by the candidate has an impact; one also knows that his or her media presentation has an impact and that local political organizational support is a factor, but it is impossible to isolate the most important and the most efficient factors for any given election.

The Relative Visibility of Police Discretion

Consideration of police discretion involves at least four parameters that heighten its visibility: public concern about possible injustice; the involvement of police in order maintenance; police services intended to assist individuals, a function that is not necessarily consistent with order maintenance; and the conflict between the patrol officers' freedom to make decisions on the street and organizational control of their official conduct.

Compared with other components of the criminal justice system, the police are subject to particular public attention when discretion is practiced. The other institutions within the criminal justice process have at least "definable" parameters and to some extent are effectively shielded from public input. For example, prosecutors, defense counsel, and judges have the "law" to fall back on; probation and parole officers and wardens, excluding the most blatant exceptional cases, have the luxury of low visibility decisions.

Historically, police discretion has always been a concern. Specifically, it was a concern of accountability and control by the public and by the police administrative officer or the patrol officer. This concern began with what many consider the model of policing. The reform movement of the early 1900s constantly called for controlling and limiting police discretion.[20] Only recently, however, has anyone taken a serious look at the task and need for an effective police operation. Only in the past fifteen years has it been recognized that discretion does occur and, perhaps more importantly, needs to occur. Before then, a legalistic orientation was taken, with any deviation from the "rule of law" being considered an abuse or corruption of police power.

In one view, police administrators are reluctant to acknowledge police discretion for fear of adverse public reactions.[21] Some authors imply that the police are the protectors of the status quo and are, among other things, intellectually and psychologically inferior. Police policies, they say, are formulated to make up for this sense of inadequacy.[22] Other authors maintain that police administrations that fear admitting to discretion will violate their oath of office and will soon confront problems with citizen disagreements over how police were carrying out their functions. In addition, it has been suggested that allowing discretion will lead to corruption.[23]

Multifaceted Police Work

The second parameter of police discretion is the multifacted nature of police work. One needs to define what we mean by "police" before police discretion can be intelligently considered. In the United States, there are large city departments, small city departments, state police, sheriffs, and federal agencies. In the context of crime prevention, discretion is most relevant at the local level of law enforcement. That point may be clarified by relating the level of law enforcement to three basic functions of policing: law enforcement, order maintenance, and social integration.

As previously noted, the first function, law enforcement, also exists at other levels of government. This is simply the enforcement of criminal statutory law.

The second function, which distinguishes local police from other law enforcement agencies, is the nature of its order maintenance function. Through this function, the police strive to maintain a stable society by controlling or reducing conflict situations, for example, settling a dispute between neighbors or moving juveniles off a street corner into more "acceptable" activities. This is a particularly relevant context for the aforementioned mediation as a tool for prevention.

The third function, social integration, can be defined as providing and enhancing the society's police powers to sustain individuals in their daily lives.[24] It can also be described as the social welfare function in its broadest sense. Here police discretion holds possibilities for referral and diversion as tools for prevention.

With regard to the second and third functions, resistance to police discretion becomes a stumbling block to recognizing its legitimate use to the benefit of crime prevention. Initially, researchers adopted a legalistic orientation, focusing on police failures to follow the "rules of law" or interpreting statutes according to their preferences. In their view police officers were "lower level ministers" of the court, and their crime fighting and prevention functions should be proscribed by the criminal justice system. One could determine crime policy and its correct application by making the police aware of the law and criminal procedures. For example, some of the earlier suggestions were that police officers should get more training in criminal law during their recruit periods. But when empirically tested, one finds that the typical police recruit gets more criminal law than lawyers do in law school.

The problem for those still beholden to legal solutions is how to structure and control police activities because state statutes are written in ambiguous terms. Furthermore, the courts have only a limited function in controlling police behavior, since the police can control the flow of cases in and out of the court docket. Finally, policy officers may view legal ramifications as not having legitimacy and may respond to other forces.

Administrators who enforce the legal perspective may or may not have the support of operational personnel. Historically, police administrators have conflicted with line personnel. There has been limited movement in this area because only recently have professional police administrators been upgraded. Surprisingly, there has probably been a more effective control of police policy from the legal field, although not via the criminal justice system or cases, but in the civil courts. These are the vicarious liability suits brought against police departments, in which the individual citizen sues not only the police officer, who in most cases is judgment proof, but also the police supervisor, the chief, and the city council.

Although still in the developmental stages, these suits are forcing some police departments to expand crime prevention functions—although departments follow a contrary trend—as an example of outside forces on crime prevention policy.

Several Types of Police Intervention

The third parameter of the discretion issue is the type of police intervention which influences whether or not the police administrator can monitor the officer's decision for its consistency with departmental policy. Administrative control is promoted when the decision situation lends itself to the application of enunciated standards and when the officer is the sole decision maker on the street. Wilson has postulated a set of four types of police intervention.[25]

The first is police-involved law enforcement, involving Uniform Crime Reports Part One crimes: traffic, vice control, and the targeting of certain crimes for special attention. In those situations, the crime prevention activities are under the police administrator's direct control. One can measure field activity, that is, the increase in arrests of prostitutes and burglars, increased traffic citations, driving under the influence of alcohol, and so on. In addition, the quality of these arrests, that is, conviction rate, can be reviewed.

The second type of intervention is the citizen-invoked law enforcement wherein the police officer has the least amount of discretion because both the administrator and citizen are making judgments on the quality of the officer's actions. It is at this point that community values and anticipated reactions come into play and that the goals of the police organization and community/citizen may come into conflict.

The third type of intervention is police-invoked order maintenance, in which the police officer views some activity in the community as being disruptive to the values and tranquility of the community. This observation gives the department or officer the widest latitude in discretion and implementation of crime prevention programming, because the problem can be defined in terms of law enforcement and, of course, powers.

The fourth and last intervention is citizen-invoked order maintenance. Demands are made on the police organization or individual officer to take action on a nonlaw enforcement problem. Although citizen activity and input discretion are somewhat limited, a number of discretionary alternatives remain, depending on who is involved, or whether the community as a whole views the situation as threatening, and on what level the police response will take, formal or informal.

GENERAL POLICY IMPLICATIONS

The state of the art for police policy making in prevention may be traced to the historic development of American policing; the changing substance of demand input; reactions to the changing political culture of policing, especially during the turmoil of the 1960s; and the heterogeneity of citizen audiences. The great diversity of policy making can be explained by the existence of more than 40,000 police organizations in the United States.

Special Developmental Parameters

American policing presents an interesting case study in the functional development of an organization and its impact on policy content and articulation. This is especially true in view of the following social dynamics: unique historical antecedents; the interaction of the police in a complex American urban development; and law enforcement's ambiguous functional realities at present. Although such developmental consideration may continue the process and content of policy in almost any organization, American policing presents some special developmental parameters that alter the traditional models of observing policy making, whether systemic, normative, or behavioral in design.[26] Few functional areas of American urban life occupy positions that are so critical to the social stability and public well-being as the police role. Conversely, in the urban policing area policy is often poorly articulated, seldom discussed publicly beyond the level of polemics, and often finds its most explicit form in terms of nonpolicy. One form of nonpolicy, police crime prevention, may be understood by the review of the definition and parameters of police discretion. One makes the assumption that the police are a communal institution and then notes the activities of this institution in relationship to the broad approaches of crime prevention. The police do not always fit into categories or operations that one would expect. One also needs to include reviews of politics, normative or moral decision making, and general risk application in order to explain the crime prevention process and policy development.

Four general police policy tendencies—maximizing legitimation, emphasis on crime fighting, crime specific orientation, and quantification of product—may be discerned, but they must be reviewed in the context of their deviation from traditional definitions of crime prevention.[27] First, crime prevention can be defined as the process whereby social institutions function to eliminate the motivation and opportunity for crime. The development of specific crime prevention measures has been repeatedly prescribed in this handbook. As Wilson notes, both motivation and opportunity have empirical and normative problems in definition and measurement.[28] These models indicate that social institutions such as the police develop into bureaucracies and carry out well-defined crime prevention functions. The police will prevent future crime through arrest rates, along with general deterrence, such as high visibility, community watch, operation identification, and consumer arrest in vice enforcement.

It is argued that the input on the police's proactive functions by external groups who try to carry out their role as social institutions in order to eliminate the motivation and opportunity is a misguided one. The police are a reactive institution, and the output has very little congruence with the input demand. The real output described in this chapter puts the police function in proper context in the environment of crime prevention. The intervening variable of the bureaucratic process and police "professionalism" explains why this needs to be understood.

Maximizing Legitimation

Policy formulation that maximizes legitimation strives to convince political decision makers and the public that police operations are credible. This policy trend tends to drain the efficiency of organizational models, that is, a policy emphasis which demonstrates that policing has its administrative and organizational "house in order." The typical bureaucratic response to external pressures which steer the organization onto a path other than its traditional mode is to symbolically process this demand.[29]

When police agencies are pressured to enter into crime prevention, typically nonessential resources are reassigned, with the intention of giving the appearance of doing crime prevention. The realignment of nonessential resources has usually included beefing up the public relations staff, or a crime prevention staff might be created composed of officers who are not considered necessary or adequate for routine operational work. In addition, research or statistical bureaus may be assigned to provide community groups with statistical information on crime trends. The public relations staff may actively or reactively contact local business groups and refer them to other public or private sources that specialize in security or crime prevention efforts as desired by external pressure groups. As will be discussed below, this may, in fact, be desirable.

Emphasis on Crime Fighting

An emphasis on crime fighting, far out of proportion to actual services rendered, is the second policy tendency. Casting the police in the crime prevention role leads to a stronger emphasis within the police organization on their crime fighting mission.[30]

From the police point of view, the most efficient approach to crime prevention is to fight crime by using the traditional tough approaches. Hence, the police position that increased arrest rates will lead to fewer criminals on the street and thereby advertise a healthy deterrent to others contemplating crime is iterated as a normal police organizational response to demands for crime control.

Greater crime control efforts will be manifested by an increase in aggressive police patrol practices, that is, providing more deterrent visibility, "sting" programs, efforts in crime solving, such as providing more training to recruits in the area of bureaucratic processing of crime scenes, and efforts to increase communication with the prosecutor's office—all with the purpose of increasing arrest and clearance rates. From the police point of view, the increase in arrest and clearance rates will be evidence of successful crime prevention programming.

Crime-Specific Orientation

The third policy tendency avoids any substantive or specific content in regard to morals enforcement, concurrent with the police stance in opposition to the reform of morals laws, especially victimless crimes.

In keeping with the spirit of crime prevention, police organizations will pursue activities to enhance their arrest and clearance function in those areas of greatest concern to those promoting crime prevention, for example, burglaries, shoplifting, crimes of violence, and crime affecting business commerce. Victimless crimes will be ignored as long as they don't overlap those categories, or are useful to beef up arrest and clearance statistics. In other words, the pursuit of favorable and acceptable statistics will focus police activity on arrests and clearances in those crimes that will gain them favorable visibility in their crime prevention efforts.

Although the manifest attitude of police toward victimless crimes may encourage some to call for the decriminalization of these crimes, police bureaucracies will vociferously oppose decriminalization. Such opposition will be on moral grounds but will consider the social control and crime prevention value to the bureaucracy.

Quantification of Product

The fourth policy tendency is the increased quantification of product in crime fighting terms, with an organizational emphasis on those activities that are of the greatest statistical interest to city administrators and public. Therefore, similar to all public bureaucracies, police organizations can redefine crime prevention inputs to fit their traditions, values, and operational preferences.

These traditions, values, and operational performances cause a "mobilization of bias" to redefine crime prevention inputs, and allow the police to develop statistical reports that are considered to be a legitimate output by their crime prevention constituents. One of the skills of a developed bureaucracy is adeptness at providing statistical reports, summaries, descriptions, and so on, as a viable organization output. This skill, along with crime fighting, will be seen as acceptable by political leaders and the public.

CONCLUSION

American policing has historically generated police work values which, in turn, are heavy handed in determining decision making at the policy level, as well as street-level discretion. Inputs demanding philosophical or operational change will be subjected to modification to conform to well-established traditions and practices.

As has been argued, the press for increased forms of proactive crime prevention on the part of police organizations will be instinctively modified to conform to the police view of reality. The modification of crime prevention input will create outputs and social consequences other than those intended and may be politically undesirable.

But, even considering all of the foregoing, it should become apparent that the police are one manifestation of social control developed into a complex political bureaucracy. One has to ask whether we want the police to define crime, or whether it's a political question, with the police being only one part and function of the total equation. The fact may be that the police are ipso facto performing their proper crime prevention role in a democratic society.

NOTES

1. Kevin Krajick, "Crime Prevention: The Unfulfilled Promise," *Police Magazine* 2 (November 1979): 6–17; James K. Stewart, "Public Safety and Private Police," *Public Administration Review* 45, special issue (November 1985): 758–765.

2. Robert A. Lorinskas, David Kalinich, and Dennis Banas, "Symbolism and Rhet-

oric: The Guardians of Status Quo in the Criminal Justice System,'' *Criminal Justice Review* 10 (Spring 1985): 41–46.

3. Charles H. Levine, "Police Management in the 1980s: From Decrementalism to Strategic Thinking," *Public Administration Review* 45, special issue (November 1985): 691–699.

4. James R. Klonoski and Robert I. Mendelsohn, "The Allocation of Justice: A Political Approach," in James R. Klonoski and Robert I. Mendelsohn, eds., *The Politics of Local Justice* (Boston: Little, Brown, and Co., 1970), pp. 3–19.

5. James Q. Wilson and Richard J. Herrnstein, *Crime and Human Nature* (New York: Simon and Schuster, 1985), pp. 13–40, 289–311.

6. Klonoski and Mendelsohn, "The Allocation of Justice," pp. 7–8.

7. Frank A. Schubert, "Police Discretion: Enforcing the Drinking-Age Law," presented at Midwest Association of Criminal Justice Educators, Chicago, October 23, 1980.

8. Stewart, "Public Safety and Private Police," p. 758.

9. James Q. Wilson, *Varieties of Police Behavior* (Cambridge, Mass.: Harvard University Press, 1967), p. 233.

10. Stephen Goldsmith, "A Practitioner's Approach to Selective Incapacitation," *Public Administration Review* 45, special issue (November 1985): 801–804.

11. The need to institute such techniques in American policing, toward a normative reintegration of police and the policed, is the focus of the classic book by Geroge E. Berkley, *The Democratic Policeman* (Boston: Beacon Press, 1969). For a current applied version, see Robert C. Trojanowicz and Paul R. Smyth, *A Manual for the Establishment and Operation of a Foot Patrol Program* (East Lansing: National Neighborhood Foot Patrol Center, School of Criminal Justice, Michigan State University, 1984). While appearing to be "operational," the analysis has political ramifications for the police organization.

12. See especially Edmund S. Morgan, ed., *Puritan Political Ideas* (New York: Bobbs-Merrill Co., 1965); Bernard Bailyn, *The Ideological Origins of the American Revolution* (Cambridge, Mass.: Harvard University Press, 1967).

13. Alan Grimes, "Conservative Revolution, Liberal Rhetoric: The Declaration of Independence," *Journal of Politics* 38 (August 1938): 1–20.

14. James F. Richardson, *Urban Police in the United States* (Port Washington, N.Y.: Kennikat Press, 1974), p. 70, has observed that many top-level police administrators are merely "fifty-five-year-old patrolmen," and to this day the policing remains a highly inbred occupation. The working-class and particular ethnic background of police officers, as a group, has been empirically demonstrated.

15. The courts to date have still upheld this as a valid community concern.

16. As an example, "crime waves" may be rapidly created, even in the area of minor drug abuse, by the creation of proactive narcotics units and the production of arrest statistics.

17. Donald T. Black and Albert J. Reiss, Jr., *Field Survey III: Studies in Crime and Law Enforcement in Major Metropolitan Areas, Volume I*, A report of a research study submitted to the President's Commission on Law Enforcement and Administration of Justice, Washington, D.C.: U.S. Government Printing Office, undated.

18. Jerome K. Skolnick and J. Richard Woodworth, "Bureaucracy, Information, and Social Control: A Study of a Morals Detail," in David J. Bordua, ed., *The Police: Six Sociological Essays* (New York: John Wiley, 1967), p. 233.

19. George Antunes and Eric J. Scott, "Calling the Cops: Police Telephone Oper-

ations and Citizen Calls for Service,'' *Journal of Criminal Justice* 9, no. 2 (1981): 165–179 and Victor G. Strecher, *Environment of Law Enforcement: A Community Relations Guide*, (Englewood Cliffs, N.J.: Prentice-Hall, 1971), pp. 96–97. There is a general consensus that the service role accounts for the majority of police resource expenditures, a role that often leads to serious relationship problems among officers socialized to a crime fighting image of police work.

20. See, for example, Robert M. Fogelson, *Big City Police* (Cambridge, Mass.: Harvard University Press, 1977); and Thomas A. Reppetto, *The Blue Parade* (New York: Free Press, 1978).

21. Rodney Stark, *Police Riots* (Belmont, Calif.: Focus Book, 1972).

22. See the radical view on the police in Center for Research on Criminal Justice, *The Iron Fist and Velvet Glove: An Analysis of the U.S. Police* (Berkeley, Calif.: 1975), pp. 138–142.

23. Ibid.

24. Paul G. Shane, *Police and People: A Comparison of Five Countries* (St. Louis: C. V. Mosby, 1980), p. 53.

25. Wilson, *Varieties of Police Behavior*, pp. 85–89.

26. Here, reference is primarily to the link between public opinion and policy, in contrast to information processing or particular decision models. See Norman R. Luttbeg, *Public Opinion and Public Policy: Models of Political Linkage*, 3d ed. (Itasca, Ill.: F. E. Peacock Publishers, 1981), for an excellent presentation of the various linkage models.

27. David C. Perrier and Herbert W. Chapman, "Law Enforcement or Crime Prevention: Problems of Evaluating Police Officers in a Rapidly Changing Role," presented at the Midwestern Association of Criminal Justice Educators, Chicago, October 23, 1980.

28. Wilson and Herrnstein, *Crime and Human Nature*, pp. 374–403.

29. Donald Schneller et al., "The Police Officer as a Determining Factor in the Dispostion of Juvenile-Police Contacts," presented at the Midwestern Association of Criminal Justice Educators, St. Louis, October 23, 1981.

30. Gary W. Cordner, " Routine Patrol: An Analysis of Police Use of Uncommitted Patrol Time," presented at the Academy of Criminal Justice Sciences, Cincinnati, March 14–16, 1979.

BIBLIOGRAPHY

Bittner, Egon. *The Functions of Police in Modern Society*. Cambridge Mass.: Oelge-schlager, Gunn and Hain, 1980.

    In this classic work, the police, according to the author, are a "mechanism for the distribution of situationally justified force in society." He also notes that the ability to arrest is incidental to the use of force by the police. Bittner argues that neither the courts nor the legal process control the actions of the police. The control is imposed by the community and its acceptance of police actions and behavior.

Brown, Michael K. *Working the Street: Police Discretion and the Dilemmas of Reform*. New York: Russell Sage Foundation, 1981.

    Observation, police statistics, and interviews provide data in three departments for this study of the social and organizational forces shaping officer decisions and the input of professionalism on police work.

Johnson, David R. *American Law Enforcement: A History*. Arlington Heights, Ill.: Forum

Press, 1981.

Crime trends and the evolution of American policing from the colonial era are interpreted within the influential political framework.

Levine, Charles H. ''Police Management in the 1980s: From Decrementalism to Strategic Thinking.'' *Public Administration Review* 45, special issue (November 1985): 691–699.

Many police departments face problems caused by fiscal stress, and the author calls for strategic management and a reevaluation of mission and structure. This change of scope will involve political as well as resource and technical considerations.

Lorinskas, Robert A., David Kalinich, and Dennis Banas. ''Symbolism and Rhetoric: The Guardians of Status Quo in the Criminal Justice System.'' *Criminal Justice Reveiw* 10 (Spring 1985): 41–46.

This study argues that criminial justice bureaucracies depend on symbolism and rhetoric as a major component of organizational stability. Because pressures by the public are reactive rather than sustaining, they can be placated through symbolic rather then substantive responses.

Luttbeg, Norman R. *Public Opinion and Public Policy: Models of Political Linkage.* Itasca, Ill.: F. E. Peacock Publishers, 1981.

This work presents a systematic conceptualization of the various models to explain political linkage and policy articulation in a democratic society. Five models are presented, and the history, strengths and weaknesses of each are noted.

Nagel, Stuart, Erika Fairchild, and Anthony Champagne, eds. *The Political Science of Criminal Justice.* Springfield, Ill.: Charles C Thomas, 1983.

Political dynamics, constitutional constraints, discretion in decision making, administrative efficiency, and policy evaluation are emphasized in an analysis of criminal justice. The police and crime reduction incentives receive attention in the course of the analysis.

Schneller, Donald, et al., ''The Police Officer as a Determining Factor in the Disposition of Juvenile-Police Contacts.'' Presented at the Midwestern Association of Criminal Justice Educators, St. Louis, October 23, 1981.

This study reveals that the police officer's role in the disposition to refer a case to a new social work agency is based not on personal values and background but on organizational needs as communicated by the supervisors.

Terry, W. Clinton, III. ''Police Stress as a Professional Self-Image.'' *Journal of Criminal Justice* 13, no. 6 (1985): 501–513.

Police stress, combining the image of danger and responsibility for public order, would seem to enhance the public's acceptance of the police claim to professional status, but Terry argues that social and political conditions underlying police work inhibit such acceptance.

Wilson, James Q., Richard J. Hernstein. *Crime and Human Nature.* New York: Simon and Schuster, 1985.

A political scientist and psychologist review the literature on the definitions of crime and criminal behavior and reject, for the most part, social-structural variables. They approach it from a new perspective which puts the responsibility on the individual. If accurate, it will have added implications for the traditional definitions of crime prevention and programs derived from these concepts.

7

Preventive Function of the Courts

NANCY TRAVIS WOLFE

In a sense, all activities of courts can be seen as having a crime preventive aspect. Even when the court is adjudicating civil and public law cases, the degree to which the decision is perceived as just may affect public evaluation of the judicial system. Public perception is a critical factor in the court's ability to deter criminal behavior and thereby be an agent of prevention.[1] In considering the court's preventive role in criminal matters, it is useful to distinguish between punitive prevention (threat of prosecution and punishment) and corrective prevention (actions that diminish criminogenic factors through provision of treatment and services).

TWO CONCEPTIONS: COURTS AND PREVENTION

From the perspective of prevention, the court is charged primarily with the responsibility of protecting the community from the effects of criminality and of sustaining the public order by deterring crime. Vis-à-vis the defendant in a criminal case, the court's preventive goal can be specific deterrence (to affect the individual charged in the case) or pure deterrence (to affect potential criminal activity by other persons). To perform their deterrent function effectively, courts must adhere to the principles of due process, and they must accomplish their mission with dispatch and celerity. The celerity concept raises a number of issues (for example, provision of treatment and services, and fairness and efficiency) when crime prevention is seen as a means of sustaining the public order by deterring crime.

From the perspective of corrective prevention, the court is an element in the larger system of community institutions intended to mimimize the impact of criminogenic influences in society. We will use the term "social role of courts" to refer to their functions within that institutional matrix. Thus, the court becomes involved in diversion and social service delivery, which entails relationships with social agencies of the community.

Examination of these crime preventive activities of courts, which often involve their social role, brings up the controversy about the appropriate judicial function. The federal courts, according to Article III of the U.S. Constitution, are to decide cases and controversies, and state courts are similarly empowered. They are, then, passive bodies; only when an issue is properly presented to a court with jurisdiction over it can action be taken. Can courts, therefore, legally take measures that are truly preventive? The tendency of courts to do so, to function in a social capacity, is sharply criticized.[2] The cry goes up that judges are going beyond their constitutional or legal mandate, and that they are usurping executive or legislative power. Cogent as these legal arguments may be, the fact is that courts inevitably formulate and enact social policy.[3]

Clearly, the two preventive modes of deterrence and service provision are not mutually exclusive; a single decision by a judge could be directed toward both punitive and corrective prevention. As mentioned, the primary emphasis in criminal courts has, by the very nature of the judicial mission, been largely reactive. The focus of the discussion in this chapter, however, will be on the active role of the courts.

DECISION-MAKING POINTS

In all of the decision points discussed in this section, a judge must seek a balance between conflicting principles: protection of public safety and minimization of criminogenic influence on the offender brought into court. Neither principle can be upheld without infringing on the other, nor can either be sacrificed to the other. Emphasis on deterrence is evident in judicial policies and practices in regard to pretrial detention, diversion, and sentencing, but at the same time more judicial attention is not being given to provision of services which can forestall criminal activity, particularly, programs designed to render assistance to victims and to children who, because of abuse or neglect, may resort to criminal remedies. In addition, courts are involving themselves to a great extent in the community through utilization of community resources and through informational programs.

Pretrial Detention

Judges face a dilemma when deciding whether or not to allow an accused person to remain at large pending trial. Many arguments, based on crime prevention theory, support detention as a deterrent factor. Concern for public safety can prompt a judge to incarcerate a person he or she believes to be dangerous. Research studies indicate that a small number of offenders commit a large percentage of crimes. If an arrested person who has a criminal record constitutes a statistically greater danger to the public, it is reasonable to allow preventive pretrial detention. This prevention rationale prompted passage of the District of Columbia Court Reform and Procedures Act of 1970 which provided for the detention of dangerous suspects, without allowing financial bail. Because of U.S. Supreme Court interpretations of the bail clause of the Eighth Ammendment, the law specified extensive rules for the courts to follow.

Such "preventive detention" has been attacked on two grounds. When a judge jails a person who *might* commit a crime, he or she is violating the fundamental principle of "innocent until proven guilty." The U.S. Supreme Court has ruled that federal law requires that a person arrested on a noncapital offense shall be admitted to bail.[4] Thus, a judge who orders an accused person detained prior to trial is "punishing" an innocent person; violation of such a cardinal value breeds disrespect of law and may alienate the misjudged suspect. More concretely, preventive detention is castigated as an unsubstantiated concept; research has not proven that there is, in fact, the ability to gauge "dangerousness" reliably. Judges, therefore, face a hard choice in the initial hearing—whether to detain suspects (and possibly increase criminal tendencies) or to release them (and possibly allow them to endanger the public).

Equally persuasive arguments, stressing rehabilitation potential, support a decision to release a suspect pending trial in the interest of reducing criminal tendencies. Detention in jail prior to trial is demonstrably detrimental to a suspect, not only because it interferes with the suspect's social and occupation relationships, but also because it immerses him or her in an environment that often exposes the suspect to criminal influences. Being held in custody pending trial in the same institution where convicted prisoners are housed results in "labeling," can be demoralizing, and may interfere with educational opportunity. The Federal Bail Reform Act of 1966 created a presumption favoring pretrial release.[5]

In making the critical decision regarding bail, a judge is hampered by paucity of information about the accused; only general statistics are usually available. A national evaluation analysis of 6,000 defendants in eight jurisdictions found that 87 percent of the released defendants appeared for all trial dates and that 84 percent of the released defendants remained arrest free prior to the trial.[6] Even were judges to be fully knowledgeable about research regarding flight propensity during bail periods, they would still not be in a position to make informed decisions in most cases; personal details in the files available at initial hearings or preliminary hearings are not sufficient. Some jurisdictions are experimenting with programs whereby police officers or volunteers assemble pertinent data prior to the bail hearing in order to give the judge a better basis for his or her decision.

Diversion by Courts

It is difficult to separate deterrent from rehabilitative functions in the use of diversion by courts. The term "diversion" can be used in two senses: first, avoiding involvement of the suspect in the formal criminal justice system (e.g., discretion at the police level) or, second, avoiding formal adjudication. It is in the second sense that the courts can play a preventive role.

Many states now have highly structured programs of diversion; in return for suspension of prosecution, the suspect "contracts" to adhere to certain conditions (working, going to school, participating in treatment or training programs, etc.). Successful completion of the diversion agreement results in dismissal of the case. Joan Potter has identified more than two hundred such programs in operation, approximately half of which were judicially administered.[7] Although a person who agrees to diversion is to some extent labeled by his or her interaction with the criminal justice system, the degree of stigma is less than if he or she were brought to trial and convicted, and there is also an element of deterrence in the requirement for fulfillment of certain conditions as a quid pro quo for a dismissal of the case.

Recently, juvenile courts have also proven amenable to utilization of similar types of contractual arrangements. A sudden new hope for reaching predelinquents burst on the American scene in 1976 with the project "Scared Straight." By now a staple topic in reviews of possible deterrence methodology, the Juvenile Awareness project which was initiated by life-sentence convicts of the Rahway State Prison in New Jersey then represented an unusual approach. The "Lifers" believed that exposure to the harsh realities of prison could deter. In Juvenile Judge George Nicola they found an enthusiastic supporter; he ordered youths appearing for the fourth time in his juvenile court to participate in the "Scared Straight" program.[8] By virtue of spectacular television exposure, the tactics of the Lifers have become familiar to the American public. Inmates, confronting the youths, in a constricted setting, deliberately traumatize them through verbal abuse, homosexual advances, and dramatic descriptions of the harsh life in prison.

The hope of a miracle cure (panacea) through such "shock confrontation" led quickly to replications in other jurisdictions. In New Jersey the major referral source was the juvenile courts.[9] In some states, this type of "treatment" was made a part of pretrial diversion agreements. Although the Rahway program was limited to juveniles, the method has been extended to include "youthful offenders" as well as adults. The critical question, whether recidivism rates are reduced, is still hotly debated, and it is uncertain whether courts will continue to support prison encounter programs.[10]

Rationales for Sentencing

Three of the four classical rationales evident in sentencing are clearly directed toward crime prevention: deterrence (both specific and general), rehabilitation, and isolation. American judges, unlike their counterparts in Europe, are not required to write a substantiation of their sentences in individual cases. It is not, therefore, always clear exactly why a judge chose a particular sentence from within the available legislative frame. Analyses of sentencing practices by judges themselves and researchers indicate that the purposes envisaged by the judges run the gamut from *lex talionis* to adaptation of punishment to the individual characteristics of the convictee and the offense in an effort to foster rehabilitation.

Even when the goal of a sentence is specific deterrence, adjustment of the legislatively determined frame of punishment to the individual being sentenced is requisite in order to achieve this goal. For example, for a fine to operate as a deterrent, it must be attuned to the specific economic position of the convictee. Such adaptation by the judge can occur effectively only when he or she has full knowledge about the convicted person. Although this ideal is obviously impossible to achieve, preparation and utilization of presentence reports can facilitate judicial decision making at the point of sentencing. Some states have laws requiring presentence reports for all serious crimes.[11]

Serious questions arise pertaining to the writing and use of presentence reports. Whether they are prepared in all required instances, and whether they are sufficiently complete, their queries point to dangers inherent in presentence report practices. Significantly, severe limitations to rehabilitative effect can be engendered by inclusion of false information, possibly gained through heresay evidence. Furthermore, it is far from certain how judges react to the reports. On the one hand, it is argued that not all judges actually read them.[12] Conversely, it has been asserted that the judges are overly dependent on them.

Proper utilization of presentence reports may well have positive rehabilitative effects on the offender. Concern about a potentially negative effect has nevertheless often been expressed as well. Information disclosed in confidence by relatives, psychologists, and so on, could be psychologically damaging to the defendant. Federal judges, under Federal Rule of Criminal Procedure 32c 3 (B), have discretion; if disclosure of information in the presentence investigation, in the court's view, would be harmful to the defendant, the judge may instead provide a summary of the background information.

In an effort to enhance rehabilitation, juvenile courts are experimenting with judgment and sentencing by peers. New York has led the way with courts in which juveniles play key roles.[13] The most usual type of peer involvement is in the form of a jury. Although the U.S. Supreme Court has not held a jury constitutionally necessary in juvenile court, the American Bar Association and the Institute of Judicial Administration recommend that juveniles be given the right to a jury trial.[14] The hope is that young offenders, who so often demonstrate a resistance to authority per se, will more readily accept the judgment by their peers, and evidence suggests that the rationale is valid. One jurisdiction, where all participants were juveniles, including the judge, reported a recidivism rate of less than 10 percent.[15]

Typically, the authority of such youth courts is restricted to status offenses or minor criminal acts, but in Denver a juvenile jury was granted jurisdiction over some felonies.[16] Methods of referral can vary. In Horseheads, New York, the arresting officer may offer the option of a hearing in youth court or may decide to send the juvenile to the Family Court. Elsewhere, discretion lies in the office of the prosecutor[17] or the intake officer.[18] Utilization of young volunteers can provide the personnel necessary to adjudicate more cases with less delay. It is also customary to stipulate that the arrested youth or the parents make the decision whether to have the hearing in a youth court and that at least one parent be present. Agreement to appear entails assent to the sanctions established by the court, a form of binding arbitration. Initially, it was feared that the involvement of peers would lead to greater stigmatization through revelations by court members, but the pledge of confidentiality appears to be honored. Open exchange between the charged youth and his or her peers is often encouraged by having part of the session closed to adults.[19]

Commentary of the function of the youth courts stresses the point that the existence of these tribunals increases the likelihood that a juvenile who commits an offense will be brought before a court, strengthening the deterrent effect and allowing the court a chance to provide valuable services. Traditional juvenile courts are overburdened and tend to dismiss minor offenses, a practice that fosters disrespect for the law and a feeling that one can transgress norms with impunity.

Sanctioning authority of the youth tribunals extends to sentencing to an institution. More usual, however, is a disposition that incorporates performance agreements: a number of hours of work, school attendance, writing essays, participation in counseling sessions, observation of court, and so on. Adult advisors in the youth courts find that peers can sometimes devise appropriate sentences that might not occur to professionals.

Service on a jury can itself have a crime preventive effect in that juveniles who as members of a court impose sanctions personally experience the application of principles of justice to instances of norm violation. Furthermore, they gain knowledge about organizations to which they can turn for help. On the suggestion of student participants, it has become the practice in Denver to allow persons who have been adjudicated by a youth court to become members of it subsequent to successful completion of the imposed dispostion.[20]

Feedback from juveniles who appeared before youth tribunals indicates a positive response. Fears of the organizers that the embarrassment that a charged youth would feel in front of his or her peers would offset the advantages to be gained from a discussion in an atmosphere of shared values proved to be unfounded. Nor have the young judges and juries demonstrated excessive leniency or stringency. Their decisions fall well within the norms of those made by juvenile court judges. Estimation of success can be measured in two ways: whether the sanctioned youths fulfill their sentences or "contracts" and whether they recidivate. On both points, the indications are positive, especially if followup counseling is provided, as in the Youth Forum in Horseheads.[21]

Strategies for Deinstitutionalization

The courts have long practiced deinstitutionalization in the interest of rehabilitation through suspension of sentence or probation. In both instances, the courts retain control over the convictee for the period of the sentence, and failure to adhere to the conditions set can mean incarceration. Focus on the preventive role of probation can be noted in the jurisdictions that follow a program of intensified probation supervision. Heightened scrutiny can be a deterrence in that it both reduces the opportunity to commit crime and increases the likelihood that the offending probationer would be caught. If special counseling is part of the intensive probation program, rehabilitation potential is greater.

Whereas research suggests that for some offenders minimal supervision during the probationary period is sufficent (and therefore preferable) for others the alternative to incarceration must be in the form of extensive intervention. Robert M. Carter and Leslie T. Wilkins distinguish between probation and intensive intervention, maintaining that intervention goes beyond mere supervision and constitutes an attempt to "achieve a considerable modification of values, attitudes, and behaviors which may extend beyond the prevention of specific violations of the law.[22] The authors identify three types of intensive intervention programs: specialized probation and parole, nonresidential intensive treatment, and residential programs and out-of-home placements.

The process is complicated by definitional difficulties. What degree of intervention is needed to warrant the label "intensive special probations" (ISP)? Are recidivism measures to apply only to the period during which the person is under ISP? Studies concerning caseload reduction detected no significant differences in recidivism rates among adult parolees but did find some increased success with juveniles.[23]

Responding to the call for deinstitutionalization, California passed a law in 1977 which included an article on home supervision. Rather than being sent to a detention home, youths were to be allowed to remain in their homes during court disposition, and probation officers were to make daily checks. A report written by a probation officer in the program argued that constant supervision prevents the youths from committing further crimes, inasmuch as they are limited in their opportunities.[24] Significantly, school attendance is a requirement.

In innovative ways, too, courts are endeavoring to avoid the criminogenic aspect of incarceration by utilizing a variety of experimental sentencing. Greater use is being made of a judicial alternative which has been part of the British scene since 1972: community service.[25] Most often utilized as an alternative to imprisonment, a judicial order for public service can also be made a part of pretrial diversion and probation agreements, or it can be in lieu of payment of court costs. The particulars of a community service order or sentence are as myriad as the number of jurisdictions that follow this practice. As a general definition, that of James L. Hurd and Kenneth D. Miller will serve: nonsalaried service, for a predetermined period, for nonprofit organizations, needs groups, and individual citizens.[26] While not legally a form of restitution, such service functions in a similar manner and may be considered as "symbolic restitution."

Benedict S. Alper and Lawrence T. Nichols[27] describe a number of community service programs in the United States and Great Britain, and a list of those extant in 1979 can be found in a manual for community service establishment.[28] Normally, this alternative is offered only to minor or first-time offenders,[29] that is, to persons for whom there is strong potential for rehabilitation. The preventive effect is necessarily related to willing cooperation on the part of the accused person. For this reason, most judges restrict the orders to volunteers, a decision that may be seen by the defendant or convict as a "Hobson's choice." Evaluation of the impact of these orders is just beginning, but the slight information available on the rate of completion suggests that community service orders are generally complied with.[30]

Judicial designation of public service instead of trial or imprisonment can contribute to crime prevention in several ways. First, there is less drastic interruption of the individual's normal lifestyle. Usually, the arrangements are such that the service can be performed at times that do not conflict with the client's regular occupation or schooling, thereby maintaining his or her status. Nor is the relationship with family and friends disturbed as it would otherwise be by further court action or incarceration.

Some analysts assert that institutionalization of community service in lieu of incarceration for minor offenders represents a democratization of the judicial system, inasmuch as judges have long been prone to find alternatives for white-collar criminals. Though not the intended purpose, development of specialized skills sometimes occurs, and, in some instances, the required "volunteer" service has led to the offer of a job with the agency. Regular and responsible performance of a task can provide valuable experience which may increase the chance that the person will retain a future job. It could also be contended that pretrial community service orders, especially if the person serves along with regular volunteers, avoid labeling in that they forestall adjudication, conviction, and incarceration. This may often be so, but on the other hand, there is a possibility, especially in a small town, that the person will be recognized and that his or her known involvement with the court will therefore result in a certain degree of stigmatization.

Difficult to evaluate, but nevertheless significant, are the potential psychological benefits. The classic principle of penance can be realized if the persons feel that they are, in fact, doing something positive to atone for antisocial behavior. The offender can gain greater understanding of the impact of crime, can develop a sense of responsibility for the community, and can experience a sense of pride in performing a service.

Judicial use of community service sentencing is hampered by uncertainties. Statutes are not always clear in regard to the authority of a judge to sentence a person to community service; nor is it always easy to find significant work for the sentenced person to perform. The possibility of lawsuits arising from the work situation has a dampening effect, too, as does unfavorable feedback from persons who feel endangered by having convictees working in the community. Resistance from the executive branch sometimes arises from the fact that the court must rely on it to carry out the sentence, a process that can cost more in supervisory and transportation time than the labor is worth. The author of a

British report on community service programs stated that "community service has yet to prove that . . . it is more effective . . . but as an alternative to custody it is at least more humane as well as cheaper."[31]

A proposal that might overcome some of these difficulties was made by Steven Balkin in 1980.[32] He suggested a nonresidential work facility. On a voluntary basis convictees could be sentenced to work in such state-run business, to be paid at the prevailing rate. The facility would provide a means of supervision over the persons sentenced, and a portion of their wages could be withheld for retribution to the victim.

Intermittent sentencing, a practice in America from the colonial period, has become more frequently utilized and has proliferated into a variety of forms. Nicolette Parisi found that thirty states have some type of periodic confinement sentencing statutes and noted that the remaining states and the federal government do not prohibit it.[33] As in some European countries, American jurisdictions are experimenting with weekend sentences for those convicted of misdemeanors and for first offenders. A similar, though more stringent, sentence is one that requires the person to return to jail each night. Theoretically, a convictee can then retain his or her job and normal contact with family and friends, factors that are crucial for rehabilitation.

As intermittent sentencing becomes more prevalent, negative aspects come to light. In addition to the additional workload that intermittent incarceration imposes on jail administrators, there is a significantly low rate of cooperation on the part of those sentenced. Either through inadvertence or through willful disregard of their responsibilities, prisoners frequently fail to sign into the jail for the required weekends. Failure to abide by the sentence constitutes contempt of court, and the judge can then sentence the delinquent prisoner to "straight service" in jail. Because of overworked staff, however, courts do not always follow through to ensure that the sentence is served as ordered or take action against a defaulter. Allowing convictees to flaunt the courts in this manner could, in the long run, promote rather than prevent criminal tendencies.

Also significant in regard to rehabilitation is the manner in which this type of sentence is perceived. Is it felt to be more severe, because it means that the offender remains under the court's authority for a longer period of time? Would the perceived severity differ according to the type of offense? These are questions that must be investigated to provide insight into the preventive aspects of weekend sentencing.

In recent years, the trend toward use of alternative corrective measures rather than incarceration or institutionalization has been evident in juvenile courts as well. When considering these programs from the point of view of rehabilitation, it is important to note whether the particular alternative is one that is offered to persons on a voluntary basis. Too often, they are given a choice of acquiescing or of going into incarceration, and psychologists argue that participation under this type of "threat" can reduce the rehabilitative effect intended.

Analysts of alternative sentencing raise the question as to whether the person given this type of sentence is one who would not have been incarcerated anyway. Under such circumstances, the alternative sentence can be interpreted as a harsher one than could have been expected. Attempts to evaluate the programs empirically have failed to produce data that definitively demonstrate success.[34] A measure of the effectiveness of alternative sentencing would be a change in the rate of recidivism. H. Ted Rubin states, however, that there is little empirical evidence to substantiate claims of success.[35]

SERVICE DELIVERY AND COURTS

Even though judges do not provide services directly to persons under their jurisdiction, they frequently function as the medium through which need and the proper agency of aid are identified. In order to function effectively, courts require a close working relationship with other agencies, public and private. Achievement of this goal is hindered by the differing views of court and social agency personnel, a divergence that can result in friction. All are concerned with favorable outcomes for the accused person within the jurisdiction of the court but have contrasting perspectives deriving from the type of interaction between the judicial or social agency personnel and the client. The result can be lack of cooperation or actual resistance.

Consonant with the principle that the child is a ward of the state, juvenile courts are perceived as paternal agencies, and children removed by court order from their family environment are held to have a right to treatment.[36] In juvenile court, the judge is to act as a nurturing parent, and because of the intricate nexus of the family situation of a delinquent, the help proferred by the court is often extended to the whole family under the concept of "family with service needs petition." Despite the efforts of courts to provide adequate service, H. Ted Rubin found in his survey of 1,223 judges of juvenile jurisdiction that, among the fourteen areas of concern tested, the fourth highest ranked was inadequacy or insufficiency of detention or shelter care, foster placement facilities, correctional institutions, and probation or social service staff.[37]

Victim Assistance As a Service

Without the cooperation of victims and other witnesses, criminal courts are hampered in their crime prevention efforts; yet before the 1970s little research had been done concerning the role of these crucial participants in the judicial process. Within the last decade, however, programs that provide assistance to victims and witnesses have been established; President Ronald Reagan has appointed a Task Force on Victims of Crime, and Congress passed the Victim and Witness Protection Act in 1982.[38]

Being the victim of a crime can be a devastating experience, both in terms of psychological shock and its practical effect on lifestyle. As victimization studies appear, evidence mounts that even a minor property crime can be a traumatic experience, and in the event of violence the effect is exacerbated. Insofar as the victim reacts with anger and an urge for revenge, the offense can be a precipitant of further crime. The manner in which the judicial system reacts, then, is critical. Unmet needs of victims have led to the establishment of associations such as the National Organization of Victim Assistance. Should the victims feel that their cases have not been effectively and justly handled, the potential remains that they will despair of legal remedies and turn to vigilante action.

Surprisingly high on the list of complaints by victims is simple lack of information. In the early stages of legal development of criminal procedure, the role of the victims was primary and direct; they carried the responsibility for accusation, prosecution, and determination of sentence. Gradually, the state assumed these functions, and the victim has been relegated to a position of an outsider, often finding it difficult even to gain information about the progress of the case. In 1981 Roberta C. Cronin and Blair B. Boruque investigated 280 local victim/witness programs and found that they generally served a positive function, but they were not able to document changes in dismissal or conviction rates.[39]

A new actor is appearing on the judicial scene: a legally qualified ombudsman. As in Sweden where the concept originated in the early twentieth century, the American ombudsman is to serve as an advocate for persons coming into contact with the courts. In the International Symposium of Victimology in Jerusalem in 1973, John Dussich suggested the creation of a legal ombudsman for victims.[40] The primary function of this official would be to act as intermediary between the victim and community agencies and organizations. Dussich particularly stressed the provision of information and counseling in regard to available services as a means of aiding the victim in overcoming the trauma and practical problems engendered by the crime. The ombudsman could also affect the rehabilitation of the offender by supplying critical information to the court through a presentence report or through testimony in the sentencing phase of the process.

In 1978 an Oregon jurisdiction created the office of legal ombudsman in the Lane County District Attorney's Office.[41] The mission is that of factfinder and assistant to victims and witnesses. In addition to the reactive role, the ombudsman is to function proactively. For example, in regard to the crimes of rape, drunk driving, burglary, and domestic relations, the official can help develop and administer programs to identify criminogenic factors and to devise solutions. Robert P. Davidow, who has proposed a national office of ombudsman for the protection of the constitutional rights of police officers in exclusionary cases, suggests that the ombudsman be chosen by the U.S. Supreme Court.[42] This power would derive from the constitutional clause enabling Congress to vest appointment of inferior officers in courts of law.

A high rate of conviction is essential if criminal courts are to have a deterrent effect, but statistical analyses indicate that many cases are dismissed because of lack of witnesses or because identified witnesses fail to cooperate.[43] While researchers seek to determine the reasons for noncooperation, states are beginning to allocate resources to overcome this weakness in the judicial process.

At a second point, that of testimony in court, victim/witness assistance programs can be crucial in overcoming unwillingness to appear in court, whether it be through explanation of judicial procedure or practical help such as provision of transportation or babysitters. Trained assistants also are alert to the legal significance of information given them by the victim or witness and can in turn inform the appropriate attorneys, so that testimony is more complete. Positive and negative aspects of victim participation at various phases of the criminal justice system have been reported by Donald J. Hall; he concluded that officials at all stages should know and consider the attitudes of victims.[44] Although most discussion of victim/witness assistance focuses on humanitarian aspects, the preventive effect of these programs is far from negligible. In the first place, their existence can help overcome the reluctance of victims or other witnesses to notify authorities of the occurrence of a crime, particularly in cases of rape and domestic assault, thereby contributing to certainty of conviction and sentencing.

Another aspect of the judicial involvement of victims in crime prevention is receiving increasing attention: the blameworthiness of the victim either through provocation or facilitation. Basically this is, of course, a matter of legal definition; nevertheless, the extent to which the prosecutor or judge is fully informed clearly has a bearing on the accuracy of the charge and on the justness of the sentence. Judicial awareness of criminogenic factors in the dyadic relationship of the offender and victim can offer opportunity for remedial action in the form of judicial orders or sentences and through counseling of the victim. As more attention is given to victim behavior which encourages commission of a crime ("passive" provocation), court statistics are proving useful in developing "vulnerability profiles." This in turn leads to valuable suggestions to the public as to ways in which the individual can reduce opportunity for crimes, a significant factor in crime prevention.

An experimental, and extremely controversial, practice is that of jurisdictions where the victim and offender confront each other directly in a noncourt setting.[45] Patterned on the Victim Offender Program (VORP) which originated in Canada, this approach has been instigated by Prisoners and Community Together, Inc. and the Mennonite Church. VORP projects, staffed largely by volunteers, operate in conjunction with courts but remain administratively independent of them. The technique is utilized at pretrial and postconviction levels.

It is hoped that face-to-face confrontations will be conducive to rehabilitation of the offenders who are forced to recognize the psychological and practical impact of the criminal act. They can then no longer take refuge in rationalizations that depersonalize the victim and must acknowledge responsibility in human, not merely legal, terms. The emphasis is on reconciliation, and a second hope is that the victim can also achieve greater understanding and a reduction in feelings of hostility and vengeance. Victim-offender confrontation also occurs in a court setting when victims are directly involved in the sentencing procedure.

In one research project, it was found that victims, when asked about appropriate punishment, tended to request incarceration, especially if they were questioned within a short period of the event.[46] The authors found, however, that when they informed victims of alternate types of sentences, victims were inclined to agree to a lesser punishment.

With increasing frequency, the criminological literature presents statements concerning the link between the physical or psychological abuse of a child and the child's later delinquent behavior. For example, a federal manual for judges in child abuse and neglect litigation states, "It is often said that parents who were abused as children tend to be child abusers."[47] Usually, no statistics or reference to research accompany such assertions. It is, of course, impossible to separate the criminogenic factors that result from the abuse and those that stem from the general environment of the child.

Testing of this theory has begun, however, and the findings confirm the hypothetical connection. Joan McCord carried out a longitudinal analysis of the effects of abuse, neglect, and rejection.[48] Using case records from the period 1939 through 1945, she differentiated between children who were mistreated and those who were loved. Able to trace 98 percent of the cohort between 1975 and 1979, she found significantly higher rates of juvenile delinquency among those who had been mistreated as children. Nearly half of the abused or neglected boys were later convicted of serious crimes, became alcoholic or mentally ill, or died when unusually young. A brief review of the literature and examples of careful research on this point are to be found in Elizabeth Elmer.[49] One specific form of crime appears to be associated with physical mistreatment of children; such children tend to become abusive parents themselves.[50] Another form of maltreatment of children, neglect, also has implications for crime prevention programs. Thomas J. Reidy included a control group of children of "non-nurturant" parents in his study on the effect of abuse. His findings indicated that neglected children, while differing in some respects, were prone to react aggressively to provocation and frustration.[51]

Judicial concern about the criminogenic potential abuse and neglect of children is evident in the family courts. Although they technically have no jurisdiction over crime per se, the decisions made there and the judicial orders pertaining to treatment and provision of services clearly constitute a critical part of the crime prevention network. The role of the court in such cases can be discussed in regard to five categories of activity: identification of abuse, determination of abuse or neglect, investigation of the alleged incident and environment, adjudication, ordering treatment, or services, and subsequent review.

An initial problem concerns identification of abuse or neglect. Despite the establishment of supportive organizations such as Parents Anonymous, abusers are understandably reluctant to seek judicial aid in regard to what is, after all, a criminal act. Often there are no witnesses on whom the court can rely, inasmuch as family members may "cover" for each other, either as a move of solidarity or because of fear of retaliation by the abuser. Most states now have laws requiring persons in certain occupations, such as physicians and teachers, to report suspected abuse or neglect to governmental agencies, which in turn make preliminary investigations before deciding to file a petition with the family court. The way in which a given court responds to a petition obviously has an effect on decision making by agency personnel.[52]

During investigation following the filing of a petition, judges must call on other personnel to elicit details of the alleged incidents and to explore legal implications. Often the persons on whom the court must rely are professionals—social workers, lawyers, doctors, teachers—all of whom have urgent demands on their time. The consequence has been that, even though most fulfilled their responsibilities, they tended to do so without consulting one another. Formerly, state and federal law requiring that the child have a guardian *ad litem* had been satisfied through appointment of a lawyer. Pressed for time, the attorney guardian rarely had an opportunity to make full inquiries prior to the hearing, thereby depriving the abused child of proper representation. To provide more investigatory aid for the judge and to provide a link among the various professionals in a case, states have begun involving volunteers in the role of guardian *ad litem*.[53] In addition, the use of volunteers represents a substantial savings in costs.

In regard to crime prevention, the manner in which the court adjudicates may be as significant as the actual decision itself. Proceedings in family court are civil and therefore remedial in nature. Not only does the judge have to evaluate the harm caused to the child, but he or she must also be cognizant of the effect of the abusive behavior and of the court proceedings on the parents. Although physical abuse is a criminal act and charges could be brought before a criminal court, the family court judge, in the interest of a favorable living environment for the child, may rule that the child remain with the parents. By avoiding an accusatorial manner of address to the parents, the judge could be a critical factor in precluding further abuse. On the other hand, the parent could perceive the action of the court as toleration of the past criminal behavior, and this could be a criminogenic factor.

Similarly, the effect of the hearing on the child (whether or not he or she is present in the courtroom) is crucial, not only because of the impact on the child's relations with the parents, but also because it affects the child's attitude toward the judicial system. An exploratory study of the reactions of children to their court experiences was made by Janet K. Wiig.[54] Should the court decision leave the child vulnerable, perhaps in an effort to maintain an intact family, the child may conclude either that the court failed to provide protection or, far worse from the perspective of crime prevention, that the judicial system is an unjust one.

DRAWING ON COMMUNITY RESOURCES

Critics, who decry the tendency of courts to extend their function into a social role within the institutional matrix of the community, urge that greater use be made of local resources to handle some of the problems that have been brought within the purview of judicial authority. One suggestion is extension of judicial evaluation of the need for commitment to mental institutions at the point at which a suspect is first brought to the police station. This early action would obviate further processing in the criminal justice system of those who are mentally incompetent. Judges could make greater use of available alcohol and drug treatment agreement. Referral to community services is particularly evident in family courts, where judges can inform persons appearing in the court about counseling and make participation a part of the court order.

Concept of Community Courts

Courts may contribute to crime prevention by divesting themselves of authority. In line with the recommendations of the National Advisory Commission on Criminal Justice Standards and Goals for greater use of nonjudicial procedures, courts in some districts have begun yielding some of their authority over minor disputes to community arbitration or mediation panels. In his review of the development of "community courts" in the United States, Paul Wahrhaftig stressed an aspect that has particular relevance to the effort to forestall crime— an emphasis on future behavior.[55] Rather than polarizing the parties, as in civil courts, or embittering the accused person, as often occurs in criminal courts, the informal tribunals seek to delineate a solution that is acceptable to all concerned. Empirical research provides evidence of user satisfaction.

Because the hearings typically are private and the setting is informal, the "degradation effect" of adjudication is reduced. Furthermore, by seeking to resolve underlying conflict, community courts could obviate violence or illegal methods of dispute resolution. Arbitration-mediation panels can have preventive impact in both the "pure" and "rehabilitative" sense. Although jurisdiction of the panels is limited to small amounts of money in civil matters and to minor criminal charges, speedy consideration and the search for a mutually satisfactory solution can ease the situations that might otherwise "erupt in violent 'self-help' or other antisocial conduct."[56] The model of a neighborhood justice system developed by Richard Danzig suggests a general deterrent effect through decentralized responsibility for behavior control and dissemination of control mechanisms.[57] In addition, unlike formal courts, community tribunals can evaluate civil and criminal aspects simultaneously. This alleviates a frequent cause of frustration for victims in criminal courts: since a finding of guilty does not automatically provide compensation, the victim must bring a civil suit.

The rehabilitative potential of community courts may be extensive. If classical theory is valid, rapid identification of guilt and immediate punishment should constitute a strong specific deterrent. To achieve this goal, the tribunal must not only function as a conciliator; its authority to impose sanctions must be recognized by the community as well as the offender.[58] Some critics of community courts are quick to point out, however, that the "rule of law" principle would preclude adjudication of guilt by a nongovernmental tribunal. Proponents respond by noting that the accused still retains access to formal law through the option of a trial. An interim report on the operation of three Neighborhood Justice Centers, prepared by the Institute for Social Analysis for the Department of Justice, found that in Kansas City the project was well integrated into the local criminal justice system. The significance of neighborhood panels was recognized during the administration of President Jimmy Carter with the passage of the Federal Dispute Resolution Act, providing federal funding for development of resolution centers.[59]

Educational Role of the Judiciary

Recognizing that knowledge of the law can sometimes forestall criminal activity or litigation, judges are taking an active role in informing the public. For example, a judge in Hammond, Indiana, participates in a weekly radio talk show which has generated considerable public enthusiasm; Judge James J. Richards was prompted to do this by the 1978 Yankelovich survey of public attitudes toward and knowledge of courts.[60] Judges from all levels of the Indiana court system appear on the program to answer questions about civil and criminal substantive and procedural law. Other judges urge a still more activist role: instigation by judges of public opinion polls.[61] Judge Nat H. Hentel, asserting that the low esteem in which the courts are held results from a "woeful lack" of public understanding of court operations, called on his fellow judges to conduct polls of jurors and members of the community.

The efforts discussed in this section are directed primarily toward building respect for the judicial system through increasing understanding. More precisely focused on this need are programs that explain the law and alert students of the consequences of illegal activity. Courts are begining to develop programs similar to the police-school liaison effort that is basically informational. The hope is that the incipient delinquent will be amenable to help if there is not an adversarial relationship with the court, and if possible remedial elements are emphasized. The court is given an opportunity to suggest aid for children before they commit a delinquent offense. Court-school linkages generate the cooperation of teachers and supervisors in identifying children likely to become delinquent and foster reporting of delinquent occurrences in the school to the courts.

Community perception of judicial contributions to crime prevention is enhanced by the increase in participation of volunteers in court-related service. The types of volunteer involvement mentioned above by no means exhaust the list; the movement has become so significant that there is now a National Information Center on Volunteers in Courts.

CONCLUSION

The very nature of the judicial mission of courts as conservators of law predisposes them to maintenance of the status quo. Change is thus more likely to come about by an incremental process rather than by innovations. It is, nevertheless, manifest that courts are becoming more active in responding to high crime rates by undertaking prevention of crime through punishment or provision of treatment and services. Whether or not the courts are able to realize this goal depends on the perception of their function by the defendant and by the general public.

Little research has been done on the reactions of defendants to the judicial process. From the point of view of rehabilitation, it is crucial that they perceive their treatment by the court as fair. Aside from the pioneering work of Jonathan Casper, however, this element remains unexplored.[62] Nor is there an accurate method of measuring recidivism or the lack thereof. Even if a person previously handled by the courts reappears on a criminal charge, this cannot, with certainty, be considered a failure by the judicial system. Defendants may, for instance, have been "partially deterred"—that is, they may have committed a lesser crime than they would have otherwise; or there may have been a longer interval between crimes.

Courts do not make up a single administrative hierarchy, as found in business or military organizations; courts cannot be viewed as part of a system in regard to policy making and implementation, yet courts are a component of the criminal justice "system." Our discussion of their "social role" in prevention indicates that courts cannot be viewed merely as adjudicators. They are necessarily interconnected with the other two branches in the efforts directed toward crime prevention through deterrence and rehabilitation. Courts always operate under constraints; the persons mentioned above and collateral court personnel must work within a "social given." Even if they believe that a major restructuring of society is a necessary prerequisite to prevent crime, they must, on a daily basis, use the currently available legal and administrative means to ameliorate problems. It remains to be seen whether this preventive function of courts will continue to expand or whether it will be curtailed by efforts to assign some of these responsibilities to the police or other governmental agencies.

NOTES

1. Even civil litigation, while minor in monetary terms, can have a high emotional charge.

2. To a certain extent, the controversy over the social role of courts can be bypassed by distinguishing between the judicial function of applying the law and the social function of other court personnel, such as probation officers or pretrial diversion directors.

3. Gary L. Albrecht, "Subcontracting of Youth Services: An Organizational Strategy," in H. Ted Rubin, ed., *Juveniles in Justice: A Book of Readings* (Santa Monica, Calif.: Goodyear, 1980), pp. 317–331; Nathan Glazer, "Should Judges Administer Social Services?" *Public Interest* 50 (Winter 1978): 64–80.

4. *Stack v. Boyle*, 342 U.S. 1 (1951).

5. 18 U.S.C.A. Article 3146.

6. M. A. Toborg, *Pretrial Release: A National Evaluation of Practices and Outcomes* (Washington, D.C.: National Institute of Justice, 1981).

7. Joan Potter, "The Pitfalls of Pretrial Diversion," *Corrections Magazine* 7 (February 1981):5–7, 10–11, 36.

8. James O. Finckenauer, *Scared Straight and the Panacea Phenomenon* (Englewood Cliffs, N.J.: Prentice-Hall, 1982), p. 82.

9. Ibid., p. 114.

10. Gray Cavender, " 'Scared Straight': Ideology and the Media," *Journal of Criminal Justice* 9, no. 6 (1981): 431–439; James O. Finckenauer and J. Storti, *Juvenile Awareness Project Help: Evaluation Report No. 1* (Newark, N.J: School of Criminal Justice, Rutgers University, 1978): Finckenauer, *Scared Straight and the Panacea Phenomenon*; Sidney Langer, *The Rahway State Prison Lifers' Group: A Critical Analysis* (Newark, N.J.: Kean College, Department of Sociology, October 1979); Douglas G. Dean, "The Impact of a Juvenile Awareness Program on Select Personality Traits of Male Clients," *Journal of Offender Counseling and Services and Rehabilitation* 6 (Spring 1982): 73–85.

11. Howard Abadinsky, *Probation and Parole: Theory and Practice* (Englewood Cliffs, N.J.: Prentice-Hall, 1982); p. 75.

12. Abraham S. Blumberg, *Criminal Justice: Issues and Ironies* (New York: Franklin Watts, 1979), p. 70.

13. Suzanne Charle, "Young Offenders Face Their Peers," *Corrections Magazine* 6 (December 1980): 18–41.

14. *McKeiver v. Pennsylvania*, 403 U.S. 528 (1971).

15. Jesse Swackhammer and Curtis Roberts, "Youth Court: One Way of Dealing with Delinquents," *FBI Law Enforcement Bulletin* 49 (March 1980): 17–21.

16. Charle, "Young Offenders Face Their Peers," p. 39.

17. Ibid., p. 40.

18. Philip L. Reichel and Caroll Seyfrit, "A Description and Evaluation of a Peer Jury in the Juvenile Court," paper delivered at annual meeting of American Society of Criminology, Denver, November 1983, p. 7.

19. Ibid., p. 8.

20. Charle, "Young Offenders Face Their Peers," p. 41.

21. "Horseheads Youth Forum Background Information" (Mimeographed), 1980.

22. Robert M. Carter and Leslie T. Wilkins, eds., *Probation, Parole, and Community Corrections* (New York: John Wiley, 1976), p. 251.

23. J. Banks, A. L. Porter, R. L. Rardin, T. R. Siler, and V. E. Unger, "Evaluations of Intensive Special Probation," in Robert M. Carter, Daniel Glaser, and Leslie T. Wilkins, eds., *Probation, Parole, and Community Corrections* (New York: John Wiley, 1984), p. 250.

24. William G. Swank, "Home Supervision: Probation Really Works," *Federal Probation* 43 (December 1979):51.

25. M. Kay Harris, *Community Service by Offenders* (Washington, D.C.: U.S. Government Printing Office, January 1979), p. 28; P. Ralphs, "Community Service: A Growing Concern But Where to?" *International Journal of Offender Therapy and Comparative Criminology* 24, no. 3 (1980): 234.

26. James L. Hurd and Kenneth D. Miller, "Community Service: What, Why, and How," *Federal Probation* 45 (December 1981): 39.

27. Benedict S. Alper and Lawrence T. Nichols, *Beyond the Courtroom: Programs*

in Community Justice and Conflict Resolution (Lexington, Mass.: D. C. Heath and Co., 1981).

28. Harris, *Community Service by Offenders*, pp. 49–58.

29. Mark W. Umbreit, "Community Service Sentencing: Jail Alternative or Added Sanction?" *Federal Probation* 45 (September 1981): 3.

30. Ibid., p. 4.

31. Quoted by Harris, *Community Service by Offenders*, p. vi.

32. Steven Balkin, "Prisoners by Day: A Proposal to Sentence Non-violent Offenders to Non-residential Work Facilities," *Judicature* 64 (October 1980): 254–264.

33. Nicolette Parisi, "Part-time Imprisonment: The Legal and Practical Issues of Periodic Confinement," *Judicature* 63 (March 1980): 385.

34. James Austin and Barry Krisberg, "The Unmet Promise of Alternatives to Incarceration," *Crime and Delinquency* 28 (July 1982): 374–409.

35. Rubin, *Juveniles in Justice*, p. 299.

36. Samuel M. Davis, *Rights of Juveniles: The Juvenile Justice System* (New York: Clark Boardman Co., 1980), pp. 6–20: Justine Wise Polier, "Professional Abuse of Children: Responsibility for Delivery of Services," *American Journal of Orthopsychiatry* 45 (April 1975): 357–362.

37. H. Ted Rubin, *Juvenile Justice: Policy, Practice, and the Law* (Santa Monica, Calif: Goodyear Publishing Co., 1979), p. 137.

38. U.S. Department of Justice, Bureau of Justice Statistics, *Victim and Witness Assistance* (Washington, D.C.: U.S. Department of Justice, May 1983), p. 1.

39. Roberta C. Cronin and Blair B. Bourgue, *Assessment of Victim/Witness Projects* (Washington, D.C.: U.S. Government Printing Office, May 1981), p. 39, 43.

40. John Dussich, "The Victim Ombudsman: A Proposal," in Israel Drapkin and Emilo Viano, eds., *Society's Reaction to Victimization*, vol. 2, *Victimology: A New Focus* (Lexington, Mass.: D.C. Heath, 1974), pp. 11–15.

41. Geoffrey P. Alpert, "Legal Ombudsman: New Role for an Old Office," *Victimology: An International Journal* 4, no. 2 (1979): 271.

42. Robert P. Davidow, "Criminal Procedure Ombudsman Revisited," *Journal of Criminal Law and Criminology* 73, no. 3 (1982): 953.

43. Frank J. Cannavale, Jr., and William D. Falcon, eds., *Improving Witness Cooperation* (Washington, D.C.: U.S. Government Printing Office, August 1976).

44. Donald J. Hall, "The Role of the Victim in the Prosecution and Disposition of a Criminal Case," *Vanderbilt Law Review* 28 (October 1975): 982.

45. Howard Zehr and Mark Umbreit, "Victim/Offender Reconciliation: An Incarceration Substitute?" *Federal Probation* 46 (December 1982): 63–68.

46. Joel Henderson and G. Thomas Gitchoff, "Using Experts and Victims in the Sentencing Process," *Criminal Law Bulletin* 17 (May-June 1981): 1.

47. U.S. Department of Health and Human Services, *Child Abuse and Neglect Litigation: A Manual for Judges* (Washington, D.C.: U.S. Government Printing Office, March 1981), p. 1.

48. Joan McCord, "A Forty Year Perspective on Effects of Child Abuse and Neglect," *Child Abuse and Neglect* 7, no. 3 (1983):270.

49. Elizabeth Elmer, "A Follow-up Study of Traumatized Children," *Pediatrics* 59 (February 1977): 273–279. Also see Norman A. Polansky, Mary Ann Chalmers, Paul Buttenweiser, and David P. Williams, *Damaged Parents: An Anatomy of Child Neglect* (Chicago: University of Chicago Press, 1981); Thomas J. Reidy, "The Aggressive Char-

acteristics of Abused and Neglected Children,'' in Joannes Cook and Roy Tyler Bowles, eds., *Child Abuse: Commission and Omission* (Toronto: Butterworths, 1980), pp. 471–477.

50. Larry D. Silver, Christina C. Dublin, and Reginald S. Lourie, "Does Violence Breed Violence? Contributions from a Study of Child Abuse Syndrome," *American Journal of Psychiatry* 126 (September 1969): 404–407.

51. Reidy, "The Aggressive Characteristics of Abused and Neglected Children," pp. 471–477.

52. Sally T. Owen and Herbert H. Hershfang, "An Overview of the Legal System: Protecting Children from Abuse and Neglect," in Nancy B. Ebeling and Deborah A. Hill, eds., *Child Abuse and Neglect: A Guide with Case Studies for Treating the Child and Family* (Boston: John Wieght, 1983), p. 299.

53. Carmen Ray-Bettineski, "Court Appointed Special Advocate: The Guardian ad Litem for Abused and Neglected Child," *Juvenile and Family Court Journal* 29 (1918): 65–70.

54. Janet K. Wiig, "Toward a Focus on Children in the Court Process," in Hortense R. Landau, ed., *The Abused and Neglected Child: 1982* (New York: Practicing Law Institute, 1982), pp. 57–72.

55. Paul Wahrhaftig, "Dispute Resolution Retrospective," *Crime and Delinquency* 27 (January 1980): 99–105.

56. Michael Bridenbach, Kenneth R. Palmer, and Jack B. Planchard, "Citizen Dispute Settlement: The Florida Experience," *American Bar Association Journal* (April 1979): 570.

57. Richard Danzig, "Toward the Creation of a Complementary System of Justice," *Stanford Law Review* 2, no. 26 (1973): 1–54.

58. Eric Fisher, "Community Courts: An Alternative to Conventional Criminal Adjudication," *American University Law Review* 24 (1975): 1253–1291.

59. James Podgers, "Dispute Resolution Act: Dying Budgetary Death?" *American Bar Association Journal* 66 (August 1980): 954.

60. James J. Richards, "Radio Justice: How One Judge Teaches Hundreds of People About Our Courts," *Judges Journal* 21 (Spring 1982): 21.

61. Nat H. Hentel, "For Whom the Polls Toll: Insights of a Judge with a Passion for Probing the Mind of the Public," *Judges Journal* 21 (Spring 1982): 16–19.

62. Jonathan D. Casper, *American Criminal Justice: The Defendant's Perspective* (Englewood Cliffs, N.J.: Prentice-Hall, 1972), p. 18.

BIBLIOGRAPHY

Abel, Charles F., and Frank H. Marsh. *Punishment and Restitution: A Restitutionary Approach to Crime and the Criminal.* Westport, Conn.: Greenwood Press, 1984.
    Rather than being agents of retribution, deterrence, or reformation, the courts would become, in the author's view, a day-to-day arbiter among interests promoting the smooth functioning of society and the pursuit of public policy.

Blomberg, Thomas G. *Juvenile Court and Community Corrections.* Lanham, Md.: University Press of America, 1984.
    In his assessment of community corrections of a California juvenile court, Blomberg concludes unanticipated consequences, including widening the reach of the court's control.

Bortner, M. A. "Traditional Rhetoric, Organizational Realities: Remand of Juveniles to Adult Courts." *Crime and Delinqency* 32 (January 1986): 53–73.

Case histories of juveniles remanded to adult courts and interviews with key decision makers, Bortner says, offered little evidence that those juveniles were singularly dangerous or intractable. He sees the strategy as a symbolic gesture for public safety.

Fisher, Eric A. "Community Courts: An Alternative to Conventional Criminal Ajudication." *American University Law Review* 24 (Summer 1975): 1253–1291.

Informal courts in American universities, labor unions, prisons, and other settings, Fisher says, are lay bodies that perform adjudicatory and conciliatory functions relevant to prevention.

Hillsman, Sally T. "Pretrial Diversion of Youthful Adults: A Decade of Reform and Research." *Justice System Journal* 7, no. 3 (Winter 1982): 361–387.

After outlining the history of the pretrial diversion movement, the author summarizes the results of research evaluation diversion programs and the problems encountered when attempting to do empirical research within the criminal justice system. She concludes that the findings of a decade of research have not demonstrated a positive effect by diversion programs on the behavior of defendants.

Hofrichter, Richard. "Neighborhood Justice and the Social Control Problems of American Capitalism: A Perspective." In Richard L. Abel, ed., *The Politics of Informal Justice*, vol. 1, *The American Experience*. New York: Academic Press, 1982.

From a leftist viewpoint, the author reviews the development of community mediation centers. He argues that neighborhood mediation programs reflect the reproductive system of capital and that they serve the interests of corporate planners and public officials.

Kelley, Thomas M. "Status Offenders Can Be Different: A Comparative Study of Delinquent Careers." *Crime and Delinquency* 29 (July 1983): 365–380.

Analysis of records of Wayne County, Michigan, Juvenile Court indicates that status offenders are less likely to recidivate than other types of first offenders, that they are unique in offense careers, and that those status offenders who recidivate do so because they had been stigmatized as delinquents.

Klein, Andrew R. "Custom-tailored Sentencing: Alternatives to Traditional Punishment." *Judges Journal* 21, no.1 (Winter 1982): 37–43, 59–60.

In this examination of the theory and practice of restitution sentencing, the author stresses ways in which the process of making amends can postitively influence an offender.

Kobrin, Solomon, and Malcolm W. Klein. *National Evaluation of the Deinstitutionalization of Status Offender Programs: Executive Summary*. Washington, D.C.: U.S. Government Printing Office, June 1982.

Following an outline of the goals and the development of the federal program to aid states in deinstitutionalization projects, the report is a summary of the problems encountered in implementation of the principle. Particularly significant is the section discussing evaluation measures.

Logan, Charles H., and Sharla P. Rausch. "Why Deinstitutionalizing Status Offenders Is Pointless." *Crime and Delinquency* 31 (October 1985): 501–517.

Programs to remove status offenders from juvenile institutions are found to rest on conflicting assumptions that are pointless without decriminalization and divestiture of court authority.

Osgood, D. Wayne, and Hart F. Weichselbaum. "Juvenile Diversion: When Practice Matches Theory." *Journal of Research in Crime and Delinquency* 21 (February 1984): 33–56.

The opinions of both clients and service providers were collected for nine diversion programs. Compared with service providers, clients had less favorable views of the programs in terms of coercion, social control, and serving needs, but service providers described their clients more negatively than the clients thought they would.

Palmer, Ted B., and Roy V. Lewis. "Differentiated Approach to Juvenile Diversion." *Journal of Research in Crime and Delinquency* 17 (July 1980 : 209–227.

Evaluation of California diversion projects leads to the recommendation that several diversion alternatives be used in a given geographical area to match the heterogeneity of youths as a proper balance between five valid but often conflicting goals.

Schneider, Peter R., William R. Griffith, and Anne L. Schneider. "Juvenile Restitution as a Sole Sanction or Condition of Probation: An Empirical Analysis." *Journal of Research in Crime and Delinquency* 19 (January 1982): 47–65.

The analysis of 10,000 juvenile cases involving restitution indicates a greater chance of successful termination of cases and less likelihood of recidivism.

Statsky, William P. "Community Courts—Decentralizing Juvenile Jurisprudence." *Capital University Law Review* 3, no.1 (1974): 1–3.

A Mediation Forum was established in the Bronx in 1971 in an effort to deal with juvenile antisocial behavior outside the formal judicial system. Using lay volunteers from the community, the Forum hears cases referred from the probation department and endeavors to identify needs and possible services.

8

Schooling and Delinquency

J. DAVID HAWKINS and
DENISE M. LISHNER

In recent years there has been an increasing emphasis on excellence in education.[1] Improvements in schools have been advocated in order to increase their effectiveness as institutions of socialization and education. A primary goal has been to increase the quality of education to enable students to achieve greater competence in mathematics, science, language arts, and other core subjects.

A large body of research links various aspects of schooling with student misbehavior and delinquency. The evidence regarding schools in the etiology of delinquent behavior suggests that the creation of more effective schools might have an ameliorating effect on delinquent behavior.[2] There is some evidence that the practices of effective schools may inhibit school misbehavior and discipline problems.[3] This chapter reviews the existing evidence regarding delinquency and schooling. The relationship between delinquency and student attributes such as ability, academic performance and commitment to education is explored, as is evidence regarding the characteristics of schools as organizations that may affect delinquent behavior. Finally, the chapter reviews a range of school-based prevention programs to assess their impact on student misbehavior and delinquency.

DO SCHOOLS FOSTER DELINQUENCY?

It has been argued that for certain youths, schooling itself may foster antisocial behavior[4] since juvenile offense rates decrease after the age of school leaving,[5] decline during weekends and summer months,[6] and decrease subsequent to dropping out of high school.[7] The evidence regarding schooling and delinquency suggests several linkages.

Academic Ability

Studies using self-report data and officially recorded delinquency have shown a modest but consistent inverse relationship between academic ability, including IQ, and delinquent behavior.[8] D. J. West and D. P. Farrington found that low intelligence at age eight to ten was one of the better independent predictors of juvenile convictions and was highly related to other measures of early school failure.[9]

The correlation between ability and delinquency is not purely spurious and does not disappear when controlling for factors such as socioeconomic status or race.[10] However, the link between ability and delinquency may be indirect, operating through performance in and attitudes toward school. Alternately, it has been suggested that high rates of delinquency among low achievers may reflect the ability of bright delinquents to avoid detection.[11] Gary D. Gottfredson concluded that a consistent correlation between ability and delinquency exists, particularly for serious juvenile crime, despite controversy concerning the construct of ability, questions regarding the cultural bias of ability tests, and problems of differential detection of delinquency.[12]

Learning Disabilities

Learning disabilities are impairments of perceptual thinking and communicative processes manifested by a significant discrepancy between expected achievement (based on intelligence test scores) and actual achievement.[13] While learning disabilities are related to ability, they have been studied as distinct contributors to delinquency. The preponderance of available evidence indicates a higher level of official delinquency among youths who are learning disabled than among nonlearning disabled youths.[14]

This apparent link has been explained by alternative hypotheses which propose that learning disabled youths experience academic failure and frustration leading to low self-esteem and behavior problems, that cognitive and personality characteristics associated with learning disabilities contribute directly to delinquency, that there are differential criminal justice system responses to learning disabled as compared to nonlearning disabled youths, and that learning disabled delinquents lack the ability to avoid detection for illegal acts they have committed. Research by J. Zimmerman found that, while learning disabled youths engaged in the same amount of delinquent behavior as nonlearning disabled youth, they were often treated differently by the juvenile justice system.[15]

Self-report data from a sample of 1,617 boys classified as to presence or absence of learning disabilities indicated that youths characterized as learning disabled committed more offenses than normal population youths.[16] In a study of 973 nonadjudicated high school boys and 970 officially adjudicated boys in correctional schools, 19 percent of the high school sample as compared to 34 percent of the delinquent sample were found to be learning disabled.[17] When the two samples were combined, learning disabilities appeared to be related to the total number of self-reported delinquent acts, though no relationship was found between learning disabilities and serious self-report delinquency. It should be noted that the relationship between delinquency and negative attitudes toward school was much stronger than was the relationship between delinquency and learning disabilities in this study. However, when the adjudicated and nonadjudicated samples were combined and when data were analyzed so that learning disabilities entered into a path analysis equation before school attitudes, modest direct and indirect effects were found for learning disabilities on general self-reported delinquency.[18]

Academic Performance

There is considerable evidence that, whether measured by self-report or by official police data, male delinquency is related to academic performance at school.[19] Similar results have been found for females.[20] A. Lewis Rhodes and Albert Reiss found that grades were strongly related to apathy, truancy, and delinquency when social class was held constant.[21] Anthony Meade showed that school failure was one of the best independent predictors of recidivism among first offenders appearing before juvenile court.[22]

Although the magnitude of the association was probably exaggerated in early reports a moderate negative association between academic performance and delinquency has repeatedly been demonstrated.[23] Low academic attainment at age eight to ten has been shown to discriminate between convicted and unconvicted persons and between chronic and nonchronic offenders.[24] Self-reported delinquency is negatively related to grade point average[25] and self-evaluations of school performance.[26]

The relationship between academic performance and delinquency is stronger than the association between ability and delinquency.[27] Moreover, the relationship appears to hold regardless of social class. While youths from low socioeconomic and minority backgrounds are more likely to experience academic failure than are white middle-class students, the experience of academic failure or success itself appears to be related to delinquency.[28] Kenneth Polk and associates found that controlling for social class did not alter this relationship among boys.[29] E. B. Palmore and P. E. Hammond[30] replicated this finding for black and white boys and girls, and George W. Noblit found that grade point average was associated with delinquency within socioeconomic classes.[31] Youths who experience academic success are less likely to be delinquent[32] while those who fail in school are more likely to engage in disruptive classroom behavior and delinquency.[33]

Several studies have concluded that the relationship between school performance and delinquency is mediated by peer influence. Martin Gold found that boys with low grade point averages and delinquent friends had higher rates of self-reported offenses than those with low grade point averages (GPAs) and no delinquent friends.[34] This finding was not replicated among girls in this study. Noblit found that friends' delinquency made no difference for boys' official delinquency *except* among those with high GPAs.[35] Those with high GPAs and friends in trouble were just as delinquent as those with low GPAs, which suggests that successful school performance may not inoculate youths against the influence of delinquent friends.

FAILURE AND MISCONDUCT: CAUSE OR EFFECT?

It is not clear whether school failure causes delinquency, whether school misconduct causes school failure, or whether both school failure and misbehavior are manifestations of an underlying deviance syndrome.[36] John E. Phillips and Delos H. Kelly argue that school failure precedes delinquency in a causal process;[37] they note evidence of a sharp decline in delinquency rates after school dropout and a decline in delinquency at the school-leaving age.[38] J. G. Bachman and associates, in a longitudinal self-report study, conclude that school failure produces both delinquency and dropping out.[39] While early school experiences appear to predict later delinquency, delinquent involvement, once in process, also appears to inhibit future educational attainment.

Early School Misconduct

The question of causality in the relationships between ability, achievement, and delinquency has been informed by longitudinal studies of early school misbehavior, early achievement, and later behavior. Generally, an association has been documented between student misbehavior in early grades, and both subsequent academic and behavior problems.

In early research by Maude Craig and Selma Glick, teacher ratings of students' behavior in grades one through three improved prediction of later problem behaviors by 66.3 percent.[40] John Feldhusen and associates found that aggressive and disruptive children achieved at significantly lower levels than their peers.[41] G. Spivack found that kindergarten and first grade signs of acting out, overinvolvement in socially disturbing behaviors, impatience, impulsivity, and defiance predicted conduct disturbances ten years later.[42] S. G. Kellam and associates found that first grade aggressiveness and aggressiveness combined with shyness, as rated by teachers, predicted later adolescent delinquency in males.[43]

In contrast, the relationship between indicators of achievement and ability in early elementary grades and subsequent delinquency is not well established.[44] Spivack, in a twelve-year panel study of 660 randomly selected inner-city youths,[45] found that initial signs of academic achievement in the first grade were not predictive of subsequent conduct disorders or delinquency. However, academic failure in grade 5 did predict subsequent community delinquency among males. Academic performance appears to emerge as a predictor of misconduct and delinquent behavior in the late elementary grades.[46] Low achievement, poor vocabulary, and poor verbal reasoning at the *end* of elementary school are predictors of delinquency.[47] Early school misbehavior and adjustment problems increase the risks for both later academic problems and delinquency in males. The combination of serious misbehavior in early elementary grades and academic problems in late elementary grades increases the risk of later delinquency in males. G. Spivack and J. Marcus suggest that problems in early adaptation to the classroom environment and school are involved in a cycle of events that continue through early adolescence and adulthood.[48] M. Rutter and H. Giller propose that cognitive deficits and conduct disturbances may share a common etiology.[49]

Attachment to Teachers and School

Travis Hirschi[50] and Michael Hindelang[51] found inverse relationships between delinquency and both liking school and caring about teachers' opinions. Delos Kelly and Robert Balch found that males who disliked school were more delinquent than those who liked school.[52] Youths admitting to involvement in delinquent activities scored higher on a school normlessness scale than those who did not report offenses.[53] J. Sederstrom and J. Weis found that delinquents tend not to like their school or teachers and to experience alienation from school.[54] As with school performance, peer variables have been shown to interact with attitudinal variables, and peer influence may operate independently of the effects of low attachment to school.[55]

R. Lawrence found that lack of participation in school activities was associated with a greater likelihood of involvement in self-reported delinquent behavior as were lower grades, more rule violations, and truancy.[56] Number of school rule violations, attachment to school, and truancy were the most important school performance variables, while ''adventurous, bold'' and ''disregards rules'' were the most important personality variables explaining delinquent behavior. These five variables together accounted for 50 percent of the variance in delinquent behavior in Lawrence's study.

Attachment to school appeared to be the most effective restraint to involvement in minor delinquency for both males and females in a study of two schools, and certain characteristics of the school context itself appeared to produce different levels of school attachment.[57]

Commitment to Educational Pursuits

Students who are not committed to educational pursuits are more likely to engage in delinquent behavior.[58] Time spent on homework and perception of the relevance of coursework are also related to delinquency.[59] William Glasser found that students who exhibit discipline problems generally have no stake in school and rarely participate in school activities.[60]

Hirschi found an inverse relationship between an achievement orientation and delinquency, as well as a negative relationship between educational aspirations and self-reported delinquency.[61] Edgar Epps[62] and Gerald J. Pine[63] found similar negative relationships between educational aspirations and self-reported delinquency. Kenneth Polk and David Halferty found an inverse relationship between official delinquency and a scale including measures of educational aspirations.[64]

The same trend is revealed in studies of expectations of going to college. Polk,[65] Elliott,[66] and Hirschi[67] found that boys who expected to go to college were less delinquent.

School Dropout and Delinquency

Several investigators have examined the relationship between school dropout and delinquency. Sederstrom and Weis[68] note the similarity between correlates of dropping out and correlates of delinquency—including low grade point average,[69] noncollege bound track,[70] dislike of school,[71] and low aspirations.[72] Those who eventually drop out have higher rates of police contact and self-reported delinquency than those who complete school.[73] However, dropping out of school does not lead to increased involvement in delinquent activity. J. G. Bachman and associates found that male high school dropouts reported less delinquency after leaving school,[74] and this finding was replicated for both males and females by Delbert Elliott and Harwin Voss.[75] Bachman et al. found that misbehavior in school precedes dropout, but that rates of delinquency stabilize or decline subsequent to dropping out.[76]

In summary, the available evidence suggests a link between certain individual attributes related to school and delinquency, especially among males. That evidence is summarized in Figure 8.1. Developmentally, poor adjustment to school in the early elementary grades characterized by aggressive and disruptive behaviors is the first school-related factor that appears to increase the risk of later delinquent behavior. Early school misconduct has both direct and indirect effects on later delinquency. Early school misconduct appears to increase the risk of poor academic performance in later elementary grades which is, itself, associated with delinquency.

Low cognitive ability, measured by IQ, and the presence of learning disabilities which appear to inhibit academic achievement regardless of IQ also increase the risks of delinquent behavior. While ability appears to have some modest direct effect on delinquency, most of the effect of low ability and learning disabilities is probably indirect. Like early school misconduct, low ability and learning disabilities contribute to poor academic performance in school, which is more strongly associated with delinquency than is ability itself.

Poor academic performance in school beginning in late elementary grades and continuing on into junior high grades also appears to increase the risk of delinquent behavior both directly and indirectly. Poor academic performance is associated with reduced levels of attachment to school and teachers, and with lowered levels of commitment to educational pursuits and aspirations for edu-

Figure 8.1
School-Related Risk Factors for Individual Delinquency in Males

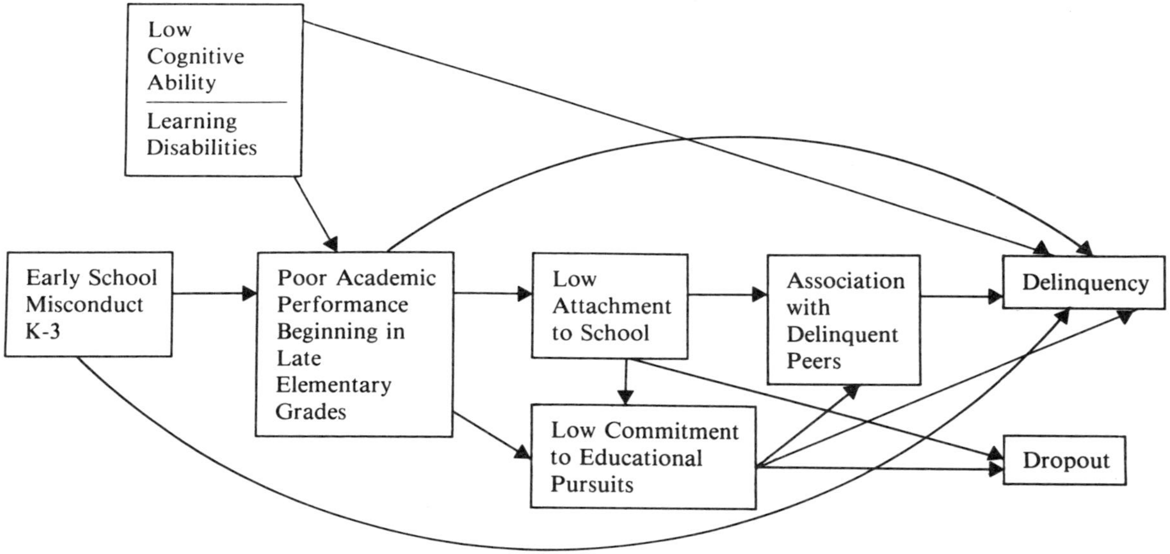

cation. Both these elements of a low degree of social bonding to school appear to increase the risk of delinquent behavior. Note that the relationship between poor academic performance and delinquency appears to be reciprocal. Poor academic performance in late elementary grades increases the risk of delinquency. However, involvement in delinquent behavior appears to contribute to further deterioration in academic performance.

The school-related factors reviewed above appear to increase the risks of both school dropout and delinquency. However, dropping out of school does not appear to increase delinquent behavior, but rather to be followed by lower rates of delinquent behavior. This finding is consistent with the contention that school experiences themselves are factors in delinquent behavior, which, when removed, no longer contribute to delinquent behavior.

This review does not discuss genetic, family socialization, and other factors that appear to be implicated in the etiology of delinquent behaviors. Figure 8.1 is not a comprehensive model of delinquency etiology, but rather a representation of how school-related factors appear to be implicated in delinquency. In this regard, it should be noted that Elliott et al. did not find direct effects of school-related factors on delinquency, but rather that school experiences and school bonding are mediated by peer associations.[77] They found that social bonds to school decreased the likelihood of involvement with delinquent peers. Association with delinquent peers is highly correlated with delinquent behavior, and such association increases the risks of delinquent behavior even when school-related risk factors such as poor academic performance are not present.

CHARACTERISTICS OF SCHOOLS

The findings regarding dropout and delinquency suggest that, for some youngsters, school experiences themselves may promote delinquent behavior. Several studies have focused on the school as the unit of analysis and have attempted to explain variance in school delinquency rates by isolating the institutional characteristics of schools which may promote or inhibit delinquent behavior.

Examining High-Delinquency Schools

There is considerable evidence that school organizational factors cause differences in levels of achievement and rates of school misbehavior.[78] Schoolwide structural arrangements and practices appear to be associated with rates of school failure,[79] alienation,[80] dropout,[81] isolation from prosocial peers,[82] and delinquency.[83] Researchers have found that variations in school delinquency rates are not sufficiently explained by catchment area served[84] or differences in student attributes at intake.[85] West and Farrington found that, while high-delinquency schools accepted more boys already involved in problem behaviors, boys were more likely to become involved in delinquent behavior when attending a high-delinquency school.[86] These findings lend support to the contention that certain school features are associated with high rates of delinquency.

Rutter found that high crime schools generally are characterized by ability tracking, high rates of corporal punishment, high staff turnover, and a custodial or authoritarian climate.[87] An in-depth case study of eight secondary schools in London to assess the characteristics of schools that were conducive to crime replicated these results.[88] Rutter and associates conducted an extensive ecological study of twelve secondary schools in London, and concluded that children's attitude and behavior were shaped by their experiences in school and by certain qualities of the school.[89]

The investigators found that academic success and positive classroom behavior were generally associated with good classroom management, active student involvement in productive activities, teacher praise, infrequent disciplinary interventions, high teacher expectations of students, relative stability of pupil groups, and immediate and direct feedback regarding performance and behavior. School factors had a negligible impact on the extent of individual variation in behavior or academic attainment when compared with family variables. However, school variables had considerable impact on the overall level of behavioral disturbance or school performance.[90] The authors conclude that the general tendency for the student body of a particular school to be well behaved or disruptive is shaped by school characteristics. J. S. Coleman et al. report similar findings in a study of U.S. high schools.[91] Thus, differences between schools in delinquency outcomes appear to be systematically related to their characteristics as social institutions and are not due solely to intake factors, though Farrington notes that intake factors may have been inadequately measured and considered in these studies.[92]

Safe Schools Study

The Safe Schools Study examined over 600 junior and senior high schools, utilizing a variety of data collection instruments and procedures, including principal and teacher questionnaires, student surveys, and victimization reports.[93] (No self-report delinquency data were collected.) Case studies were also conducted in ten schools. Some of the characteristics that were found to be negatively correlated with school violence included low crime rate in the surrounding area, effective classroom management, students' perceptions of the fairness of rules and enforcement, frequent student-teacher interaction, and small to moderate school size. Outcomes regarding student characteristics and attitudes did not fall into clear patterns. For example, reported college aspirations were inversely related to violence but positively related to property loss, a finding that may reflect the greater value of equipment, materials, and facilities of schools with high proportions of college-bound students.

All of the case study schools were located in deteriorating neighborhoods and were varied in their responses to common problems. In general, the more successful schools tended to have energetic reformist administrators, a reduced atmosphere of anonymity, parent participation, clear rules, latitude for nonserious misconduct, grievance procedures for students, little tracking, and expanded educational opportunities for noncollege-bound students.

A reanalysis of the Safe Schools data regressed rates of student and teacher victimization on community and school characteristics.[94] The investigators tested the hypothesis that the school social organization contributes to the level of disruption. They concluded that the variation in school victimization rates is largely explained by external variables, such as community poverty, educational disadvantage, urban location, and community crime levels. However, even after statistical controls for community characteristics and demographic composition of students were applied, a number of school characteristics were moderately associated with victimization rates. These included the way rules were administered and the degree of cooperation between administrators and teachers.

D. C. Gottfredson suggests that schools with high rates of disorder can be classified on two dimensions: urban social disorganization and lack of soundness of the school's administration.[95] This latter construct is indicated by poor teacher/administrator cooperation, teacher emphasis on control in classes rather than instructional objectives, ambiguous sanctions, and student perceptions that rules are not clear or fair. These school characteristics appear to be amenable to alteration.

The Safe Schools Study and the Gottfredson and Daiger reanalysis reached similar conclusions regarding school administration, governance, and educational practices. Recommendations for reducing discipline problems in schools include moderate school size, reducing the impersonality of teacher-student relationships, strong coordination and cooperation between faculty and administrators, strong and effective governance that is firm, fair, and consistent, clear and well-publicized rules that are consistently enforced, relevant curricula, provision of adequate resources, and rewards for academic accomplishment including individual improvement.

Tracking and School Organization

Tracking or ability grouping in schools has been widely studied in relationship to delinquency. D. H. Hargreaves suggested that tracking and an absence of rewards for students with low academic standing generate a delinquent subculture in the low academic tracks.[96] Delos H. Kelly found that low track students in high school reported more delinquent acts.[97] In a longitudinal study of 661 inner-city children, George Spivack and Lois Rapsher reported a significant relationship between being left back, assignment to special classes, and subsequent police contact.[98] In contrast, in a longitudinal study of 1,600 high school boys, Michael D. Wiatrowski and associates concluded that high school tracking was an important determinant of subsequent educational outcomes, but did not change the probability of delinquent behavior when prior levels of delinquency were controlled.[99] However, the authors hypothesized that tracking prior to high school may be more likely to affect delinquency.

Although aggregate level studies relating school characteristics to delinquency are relatively rare, numerous authors have studied the impact of school organization on variables associated with delinquency including academic achievement and peer interactions. In a study of twenty high schools, Edward L. McDill and associates found that where intellectualism, achievement, and competition are stressed, the environment is conducive to higher achievement.[100] Ronald R. Edmonds reported that achievement levels are influenced by instructional leadership, instructional emphasis, school climate, and teacher expectation.[101] Wilbur B. Brookover et al. concluded that achievement is related to expectations and school climate.[102] In a study of 1,000 classrooms in thirty-eight schools, John I. Goodlad found that lower track students were exposed to the least effective teaching methods, curricula, and interactions.[103]

Michael Cohen identified strong principal leadership, school climate conducive to learning, emphasis on basic skills instruction, teacher expectations that students can reach high levels of achievement, and a system for monitoring and assessing student performance as school characteristics related to achievement.[104] Thomas L. Good reported that higher expectations for student achievement characterize teachers and schools which maximize student learning gains.[105] He suggested that patterns of instructional behavior associated with student achievement include active teaching, classroom management, and high teacher expectations for student learning.

Peer Group Interactions

Other researchers have examined the relationship of peer group interactions in schools to student behaviors. It has been suggested that cooperative rather than competitive learning structures reinforce positive peer interactions, liking of school, feelings of peer acceptance, mutual helping, interethnic relations, self-esteem, and, possibly, achievement.[106] Since delinquent peer association is among the strongest predictors of delinquency apart from prior delinquent behavior, the structuring of peer groups within classrooms may have implications for promoting positive peer influences and preventing antisocial behavior.[107]

J. L. Epstein and N. Karweit content that friendship choices are influenced by the way in which classrooms are organized.[108] Tracking and homogeneous grouping promotes subgroups of students which may develop counternorms that insulate them from the influence of the dominant value climate.[109] The school environment can be changed to alter patterns of contact and interaction among students so as to encourage positive peer interaction.[110]

In summary, there is evidence that school organizational arrangements and practices affect levels of school crime, misbehavior, and victimization, and that this effect remains when effects of family, neighborhood, and characteristics of the student body are controlled. Moreover, school practices and arrangements also affect school-related factors, including achievement and peer associations which are implicated in delinquency. However, school factors appear to have considerably greater effects on behavior in school than on delinquent behavior outside of school.[111] This suggests that school-focused delinquency prevention strategies may have limited potential to prevent delinquency in the absence of intervention in other key areas of socialization which affect delinquent behavior.

SCHOOL AND DELINQUENCY: THEORETICAL PERSPECTIVES

Data indicating a link between schooling and delinquency have been variously interpreted by delinquency theorists. W. C. Kvaraceus,[112] A. K. Cohen,[113] and A. C. Stinchcombe[114] argued that delinquency is a result of rebellion against school or an adaptation to frustrating school experiences. Hirschi suggested that academic incompetence and poor school performance lead to dislike of school, which precipitates rejection of school authority and results in an increased likelihood of delinquent behavior.[115] Elliott and Voss theorized that school failure leads to alienation from school and subsequently to dropout and delinquency.[116] They viewed delinquency as an adaptation to school failure, arguing that those who fail in school become frustrated and are rejected and shunned by others, leading to negative attitudes to school and adoption of alternative standards of conduct.

Other theorists explain the relationship between school failure and delinquency by examining student self-esteem.[117] Measures of self-esteem have been positively correlated with grades[118] and reading and math proficiency.[119] Howard B. Kaplan found that more students with low self-esteem reported committing delinquent acts than those with high self-esteem.[120] M. Gold similarly viewed delinquency as a defense against feelings of low self-esteem derived from school failure.[121] He suggested that youths who fail in school seek recognition by engaging in criminal behaviors with delinquent peers. Such students may provide each other with support, rewards, and reinforcements for delinquent behavior that they have not found in a conventional context.[122]

Alternative Sociological Approaches

Most of the major theories of delinquency implicate schooling as a factor contributing to adolescent deviance.[123] Cultural deviance theorists contend that children learn deviant behavior socially, through exposure to others and modeling of others' actions. When imitation is followed by positive consequences, it is more likely to recur than when it is followed by negative or no consequences. Through differential reinforcement, children eventually learn to value some behaviors over others. Social definitions of behaviors derive from consequences provided by peers, parents, teachers, and others who tend to reward behaviors that are consistent with their own values, norms, and attitudes.[124] In this way, children may come to define delinquent behaviors as acceptable as a result of exposure to others whose social definitions of such behavior are positive. School organization reflects the characteristics of the community, and attending schools in high crime areas may increase the likelihood of delinquent associations.[125]

From the perspective of strain theory, certain classes are denied legitimate access to culturally determined goals and opportunities, and the resulting frustration results in involvement in illegitimate means or a rejection of society's goals.[126] From a strain theory perspective, the school may be seen as a middle-class institution in which lower class youths are frequently unable to perform successfully. These youths turn to delinquency to compensate for feelings of status frustration, failure, and low self-esteem.

Labeling theory argues that once individuals become defined as deviant, they adopt a deviant role in response to their lowered status.[127] In schools, labels are attached early on the basis of achievement and behavior, and those labels may influence the subsequent treatment of youths despite their actions. Thus, youths labeled as aggressive, difficult to manage, or slow learners at an early stage in school may be put into a slow track for the remainder of their schooling and treated differentially, thus contributing to delinquent identities and behaviors according to labeling theory.

Social Development Model

Control theory posits that deviance varies according to the strength of an individual's bond to the social order.[128] This bond consists of attachment to conventional others, commitment to and involvement in legitimate pursuits, and belief in the legitimacy of the legal order. The school is one of the major socializing institutions which provides youths with structures, incentives, expectations, and opportunities for bonding. According to control theorists, delinquency is likely to result when a strong bond to school does not develop.

Social control and social learning theories have been integrated in the social development model of delinquency which identifies three general conditions necessary for the formation of a social bond to school and other units of socialization.[129] This bond is viewed as an inhibitor of delinquent behavior. The social development model posits that social bonds are developed to families, schools, and among peers when youths have the opportunity to be involved with others in activities and interactions in these settings, when they have the skills necessary to perform competently in the activities and interactions of the settings, and when they experience consistent positive reinforcement for their involvement in the settings.

Thus, when youths experience opportunities for involvement in school, when they develop the requisite social, cognitive, and behavioral skills to perform as expected in school activities and interactions, and when they are rewarded consistently for adequate performance in the school, they will develop a social bond of attachment and commitment to school according to the social development perspective.

The social development model asserts that the school is one of several important socializing institutions. Experiences in the family, peer group, and community as well as individual characteristics are also implicated in the etiology of delinquency.[130] While intervention in schools to prevent delinquency may be indicated, the social development perspective suggests that such intervention should be made in conjunction with intervention in other important areas of socialization (family, peers, community) to address contributing factors arising within those social settings.[131]

SCHOOL-BASED EXPERIMENTS IN PREVENTION

Over the past several decades, a number of school-based delinquency prevention programs have been implemented, ranging from programs seeking to assist individual students at high risk for delinquency to major alterations in the school environment. This section briefly reviews early school-based prevention efforts and focuses primarily on recent programs in schools which have been evaluated for their effectiveness in preventing delinquency and related outcomes.

Past School-Based Prevention Strategies

Early prevention efforts in the schools focused on altering characteristics of high-risk students rather than on making institutional changes in schools.[132] Commonly utilized approaches included counseling, tutoring, positive role models, and academic remediation.

Most of the early school-based prevention efforts which were well evaluated failed to prevent delinquency. A study of counseling for potentially deviant high school girls in New York found no significant effect for the counseling intervention when compared to a control condition on outcomes of retention in school, suspensions and discharges, attendance, truancy, conduct marks, teacher and counselor ratings, or court records.[133] Similarly, the evaluation of a demonstration project in eight junior high schools in which vulnerable boys were randomly assigned to a control group or to an intervention involving teacher role models, an emphasis on reading improvement and character development, remediation, and parent visits showed little or no differences between the experimental students and controls in school performance, police contact, or self-reported offenses three years later.[134] An experimental study which provided work-study and employment for inner-city high school boys with low achievement records showed no significant effects on police contacts after six years when compared with a randomly assigned control condition.[135]

G. Rose and T. F. Marshall reported some desired effects of a school social worker program.[136] Students referred because of truancy, delinquency, or related behavioral problems were seen for an average of four hours by a school social worker. The research was conducted in four selected secondary schools in high-risk areas. While over 500 students were seen by social workers, the analysis focused on 156 boys and 92 girls seen most frequently. The comparison group consisted of untreated students in two schools without a social worker, who were comparable on test measures and behavioral characteristics, and would have been eligible for services if available. Experimental and comparison subjects were compared on officially reported behavior, attitudinal measures, and social measures (e.g., parental relations and social class). No self-reported delinquency data were collected. Delinquency rates were slightly higher over a two-year period for the untreated group, although the difference was not significant. Success in treatment was generally related to length of contact. Children whose delinquency rates were most likely to improve were those already delinquent but not maladjusted. Slight improvements were found for the treated group on attendance and situational measures. However, design limitations and other methodological weaknesses in the study prevented the evaluators from concluding that changes in experimental subjects could be attributed to the social work intervention.

The Cities in Schools Program integrated the delivery of educational and social services to inner-city students to insure a successful school experience for students who traditionally fail in school.[137] The project provided academic support, counseling, education, and cultural enrichment activities, and arranged for other human services as needed. Each student had a caseworker who monitored the student's well-being. To provide positive support networks, school "families" were established, each of which consisted of forty students and four staff each.

A three-year study in which students were randomly assigned to treatment or a comparison group showed positive effects for the treatment group at one site in increased understanding of options and requirements, increased sense of control over the future, stricter standards of personal control, increased attention and effort in the classroom, increased success in interpersonal relations, increased success in learning situations, and acquisition of basic reading skills and better attendance. However, outcomes at two other demonstration sites were not positive. The number of officially recorded arrests preceding and following entry into the program varied at the three sites. Compared to the arrest rate for ninth graders the preceding year, arrests for program participants dropped at one site, rose less than the expected rate at a second site, and rose at the expected level at a third site. Looking at total number of arrests, the amount of recorded delinquency went up at two schools examined, with a reduction at he third school. Unfortunately, attrition from control groups, lack of equivalent comparison data, and inaccessibility of police files for the control groups limit the study.

Although these early programs focused on school factors related to delinquency, all worked with junior and senior high school youths who were, in many cases, already involved in delinquent behavior. Thus, they sought to remediate, rather than prevent, delinquent behavior.[138]

Current School Prevention Strategies

School-based prevention strategies which have been evaluated more recently for delinquency-related outcomes are summarized below and in Table 8.1.

Early Educational Enrichment Programs

In contrast to the programs reviewed above, early childhood education programs seek to address the childhood predictors of antisocial behavior through education and socialization provided before the traditional age of school entry. There is some evidence that early childhood education for high-risk populations holds promise for preventing delinquency.

A long-term followup of the Perry Preschool Project found positive effects on delinquency of early childhood education.[139] A group of 123 disadvantaged black youths matched on background variables was randomly assigned to experimental and control conditions. Treatment consisted of one to two years of preschool education and weekly teacher home visits. Followup of participants continued through the age of nineteen.

The preschool program was directed at intellectual and social development and was staffed by well-trained teaching teams, with a student-teacher ratio of six to one. Classes were conducted for two and a half hours each morning for five days a week. Teachers in elementary or secondary schools were not informed about the treatment of study participants, so as not to bias outcomes. The premise underlying this project was that preschool education would increase positive adjustment and success in elementary school and, through this link, would produce higher educational attainment in subsequent grades. This attainment was hypothesized to decrease rates of delinquent involvement.

Results to age nineteen indicated lasting benefits in cognitive performance, scholastic placement and achievement, decreased use of welfare assistance and incidence of teenage pregnancy, increased high school graduation rates and enrollment in postsecondary schools and employment, and reductions in official delinquency rates. Fifty-one percent of the control group, as compared to 31 percent of the experimental group, had been arrested or charged at followup. Experimentals had fewer contacts with the criminal justice system, fewer arrests, less frequent offenses, a lower number of self-reported offenses for four offense categories, and lower ratings on a serious delinquency scale than did controls.[140] Although the two groups did not differ significantly on overall number of self-reported delinquent offenses, twice as many of the controls (52 percent compared to 25 percent of experimentals) reported five or more offenses.

Experimental evaluations of other preschool programs have produced similar results to the Perry Pre-School Project in showing positive effects on school-related risk factors for delinquency, though delinquency outcomes have not been assessed in these studies. In a meta-analysis of the long-term effects of eleven rigorously evaluated early preschool programs for low-income minority children, Irving Lazar and Richard Darlington found that, controlling for ability and home

Table 8.1
Evaluations of School-Based Prevention Programs

Authors	Program Description	Research Design	N	Results
Berrueta-Clement et al., 1984	Perry Preschool Project: Preschool program designed to prevent educational failure of high-risk youths. Intervention included morning preschool 5 days a week and weekly home visits by the teacher.	Longitudinal, experimental design with random assignment to conditions	123 youths	Followup of preschool participants to age 19 demonstrated positive outcomes for the experimental group, including improved scholastic performance and placement, decreased use of welfare assistance, lower incidence of teen pregnancy, higher rates of high school graduation and enrollment in postsecondary schools and employment, and reduction in official delinquency and crime rates. Significant differences were reported in three individual offense categories, with the number of events reported lower for the experimental than the control group.
Lazar & Darlington, 1982	11 preschool intervention projects	Cross-study meta-analysis of studies with random assignment to experimental and	3,593 in original sample, 2,008 in followup	Early education significantly reduced placement in special education classes or being left back a grade, improved

Table 8.1 (*continued*)

Authors	Program Description	Research Design	N	Results
		control conditions; per/ post 3 wave followup	sample	academic performance in the short term, and demonstrated some improvement in attitudes and achievement orientation. No differences were found between experimental and control students on educational aspirations. Delinquency was not measured.
Kellam et al., 1982	Woodlawn Project: a group process and problem-solving approach for disadvantaged, minority first grade students.	Longitudinal experimental design (random assignment to experimental and control schools)	4 cohorts of 1,242 first graders in 12 schools (followup of 705 cohort members.	Results of first-year evaluation indicated worsening of social adaptation status among experimental group (e). Followup of half of the participants at third grade revealed no differences in ratings of experimental and control students. When addressing mid- and end-year effects, e's showed significant improvement on social adaptation status scores and math, and longer term benefits in reading and/or languages. No differences were found between

Authors	Program Description	Research Design	N	Results
				experimental and control subjects by third grade.
Filipczak & Wodarski, 1979	PREP Project: a behavioral model with classroom curriculum offering individual academic training, interpersonal skills training, individual paced instruction, teacher reinforcement of appropriate behaviors, and clear rules.	Experimental design Treatment and control classrooms at two of three sites.	About 700 students in 3 school settings	Significant increases found initially for experimentals in academic skills, but these were not maintained over time. Highly favorable outcomes found for social behavior ratings, including suspensions and citizenship. Delinquency outcomes were not reported.
Social Science Education Consortium and Center for Action Research, 1981	Law-Related Education (LRE) Project to provide students with an understanding of law and legal processes and knowledge of rights and responsibilities.	Pre/post-outcome study.	323 students in 12 LRE and control classes	Results indicated a gain in knowledge of the legal system among LRE students compared to control students, but mixed results for predictive variables (e.g., school isolation). Knowledge gain was correlated significantly with reduced infractions of school rules, property offenses at school, violence against students, public

Table 8.1 (*continued*)

Authors	Program Description	Research Design	N	Results
				disorder and drinking, and was slightly correlated with five of six other offense categories. Reductions in delinquency were found in four LRE classrooms, but more delinquency was found in three classrooms, with no change in the remaining classrooms.
Shure & Spivack, 1980	Interpersonal Cognitive Problem Solving (CIPS): a social skills training curriculum implemented with nursery and kindergarten students.	Experimental design (treatment and control classrooms at multiple sites)	113 experimentals and 106 controls in daycare nursery, 35 experimentals and 27 controls in kindergarten	Youngsters trained in ICPS improved in consequential thinking skills more than untrained controls, as well as in behaviors characteristic of impulsivity and inhibition.
Gold & Mann, 1983	Evaluation of three alternative schools promoting opportunities for success through flexible and supportive	Short-term longitudinal experimental/control group design	3 alternative schools serving 240 students	Significant reductions demonstrated in disruptive behavior in the schools, and improved school performance shown for subset of students

Authors	Program Description	Research Design	N	Results
	environments, individualized curricula, high-interest learning material, self-paced instruction, evaluation of individual progress, and warm student/teacher relations.			with no prior symptoms of anxiety or depression. Delinquent behavior in the community was not affected.
Gottfredson et al., 1983	School Action Effectiveness Study: study of effects of Alternative Education Project involving alterations in the organization of schools to promote learning, bonding, and prosocial behaviors.	Experimental and quasi-experimental designs. Looked at personal outcomes as well as school-level slimate measures	17 alternative education projects directly targeted 6,548 youth, indirectly targeted 23,934 youth	Positive trends in project schools after one year included greater safety, less teacher victimization, less delinquency on 9 of 10 measures (3 significant), improved attendance (not significant), increased teacher commitment and morale, less student alienation and rebellious autonomy, improved self-concept, and slight improvements on 5 correlates of delinquency. Negative results were found on perception of fairness of rules and reports of individualized instruction.

199

Table 8.1 (*continued*)

Authors	Program Description	Research Design	N	Results
				Outcomes varied for the individual projects.
Murray et al., 1980	Cities in School Program: integrated delivery of educational and social services to inner-city students to promote success experiences.	Longitudinal experimental design	Served about 2,500 students ages 14-19 in 18 school	Positive results were found for treatment group at one site in understanding of options and requirements, increased sense of control over the future, stricter standards of personal control, increased attention and effort in the classroom, increased success in interpersonal relations and in learning situations, acquisition of basic reading skills, and higher attendance. Outcomes of two other demonstration sites were mostly negative.
Grant & Capell, 1983	School-team approach in 200 schools in 47 cities. Teams design problem-solving action plans to address specific school problems.	Prepost design examined differences between initial student and teacher reports and those of subsequent two years.	Data from 35,000 students and 7,000 teachers	Effective teams are associated with reduced school crime during early months of program; then rate of decrease in crime slows. Greater reductions in disruption were found in middle than in

Authors	Program Description	Research Design	N	Results
				elementary or high schools, and greater success was found in reducing personal victimization, classroom disruption, and fear than in reducing theft and drug use.
Gottfredson, 1985	PATHE Project: a school-based prevention program combining organizational change, strong management, and direct intervention for high-risk youths to improve educational experiences and reduce delinquent behavior.	Longitudinal design, treatment, and comparison schools	7 PATHE schools & 2 comparison schools & services to 100 randomly assigned target students at each school.	Direct services did not reduce delinquent behavior but did increase commitment to education as indicated by rates of dropout, retention, graduation, and standardized achievement scores. Students in program schools grew more attached to school, perceived an increase in fairness of school rules and extent to which their schools were characterized by planning and action, developed more positive self-concepts, reported more belief in rules, fewer suspensions, and lower levels of alienation, and reported school to be safer.

Table 8.1 (*continued*)

Authors	Program Description	Research Design	N	Results
Hawkins et al., 1985a Hawkins et al., 1985b	Social Development Project: a test of the effects of a set of improved instructional practices on the achievement, bonding, and behavior of middle school students.	Longitudinal experimental design; random assignment to experimental and control classrooms in 5 middle schools	1,166 seventh grade students	After 1 year of intervention, use of project teachers' practices was associated with student behavior linked to achievement, greater achievement in math, more positive attitudes toward math class, greater educational aspirations and expectations, and reduced rates of suspension and expulsion. Results for a subset of high-risk, low math achievers showed significantly better outcomes for experimental subjects in attitudes toward math, bonding to school, expectations for continued school, and rates of suspensions and expulsions when compared with low achieving control subjects. Self-reported delinquency did not differ for experimental and control groups at the end of one year of intervention.

factors, early education significantly reduced placement in special education classes.[141] Experimentals were half as likely as controls to be assigned to these classes. Experimental students who received early childhood education also were less likely than controls to be held back a grade. Early education graduates were significantly more likely to meet school requirements for adequate performance, showed improved performance on IQ and Math Achievement Test scores (although such improvements were not permanent), and showed some improvement in attitudes and achievement orientation. Thus, the results were consistent with those of the Perry Pre-School Project in showing positive effects on school-related risk factors for delinquency, though delinquency was not measured in these studies.

Elementary School Programs

Some projects have sought to address school-related delinquency risk factors in the elementary grades, again before the emergence of delinquent behavior. In the Woodlawn project, a group process and problem-solving approach were implemented in a four-year program targeting 1,242 disadvantaged, minority, first grade students.[142] Students in schools randomly assigned to experimental condition were compared periodically to untreated students in classrooms in comparison schools on a variety of measures including teacher ratings of social adaptational status, scores from IQ and achievement tests, and grades. Interventions were designed to address factors that influence the child's adaptation to school, and consisted of weekly group process meetings, introductory meetings to inform parents of the program and to elicit their active support, and parent meetings to discuss parent roles, parent/teacher relations, and the student's adaptation to the school.

Results of the first-year evaluation showed a worsening in social adaptation status of experimental students and no change in psychological well-being, although later results demonstrated a lessening in deterioration of IQ among third grade experimental as compared to control students. Assessment at the end of the first year revealed that experimentals were rated less adapted to school than controls, although initially matched. A long-term followup of 50 percent of the participants who were still in Woodlawn by third grade revealed no differences among ratings of experimental and control students. However, when assessing effects from the middle to the end of the year, the time during which the intervention occurred, students in intervention schools showed significant gains over students in control schools on all social adaptation scales. The intervention program was associated with short-term effects from the middle to the end of first grade, as well as with some positive outcomes on third grade measures. Short-term benefits were demonstrated in math for two of the three experimental cohorts, and long-term benefits were shown on reading or oral language scores. However, effects on achievement test scores were very small.

Initially, the Woodlawn program appeared to benefit boys more than girls, younger more than older children, and less maladapted children, on several scales, but by third grade, all but one instance of differential impact disappeared. The evaluators concluded that the program offered no greater immunity against later maladjustment to children in the intervention group when compared with the control group, and that severely maladapted children were not helped.

Behavior Control and Management

In the 1970s, school-based prevention programs that focused on high-risk individual students increasingly used behavioral management and reinforcement methods rather than counseling or casework approaches. The new programs sought to reinforce appropriate behaviors tied to personal adjustment and academic success, while negatively reinforcing problem behaviors or poor performance in school. As an example, the PREP Project was implemented with junior high school students in three schools.[143] Students identified by school staff as having academic and behavioral problems were assigned to experimental and control groups at two of the three sites. The program offered individual academic training, interpersonal skills training, teacher training, individually paced instruction, teacher reinforcement of appropriate student behaviors, clear classroom rules, and family liaison and skill training for family management. At two schools with comparison groups, early achievement gains were found for experimental subjects, although these were not maintained over time. Experimental subjects had significantly better school attendance than controls across all project years in both schools. Favorable outcomes also were found for experimental subjects in social behavior (suspensions, citizenship ratings, and teacher ratings of outstanding school behavior). No results for self-reported or official delinquency were reported.

Reviews of school-based behavior change approaches have consistently found positive effects on educational attainment and school behavior but more limited effects on delinquency.[144] Nevertheless, the behavioral approach appears to be more promising than counseling and casework approaches in producing short-term changes in delinquent behavior.[145]

Enhancing the Curriculum

Another recent prevention approach seeks to change school curricula to promote prosocial attitudes and behaviors. Curricula that have been implemented in schools to prevent antisocial behaviors include law-related education, social skills training, experience-based career education, and drug-focused prevention courses.

To date, law-related education is the curriculum intervention which has been most thoroughly evaluated for delinquency prevention effects. Law-related education seeks to foster civic competency, responsibility, and an understanding of and commitment to social/legal values, principles and processes.

In 1979 six law-related education projects were funded in senior high classrooms in seventy-five sites. These were evaluated for effects on delinquent behavior and factors associated with delinquency.[146]

Students in twelve LRE classrooms were compared to students in ten control classrooms in a classroom impact evaluation in the second year of the project. Results indicated a substantially greater gain in knowledge of the law and legal system among LRE students compared to control students but mixed results for predictor variables (e.g., isolation from school, delinquent peer influence) and delinquent behavior. Knowledge gain was significantly correlated in a favorable direction, with reduced infractions of school rules, property offenses at school, violence against students, and public disorder and drinking, and was slightly correlated with five of six other offense categories. While five of ten LRE classrooms showed improvement relative to controls in knowledge and predictor variables relative to controls, three sites evidenced deterioration and two sites showed only slight improvement or no change. With respect to eleven offenses examined, reductions in delinquency were found in four LRE classrooms but more delinquency was found in three classes, and there was no change in delinquency in the remaining LRE classrooms.

Social skills training has been added to the curriculum in some schools to improve the social development of students. The goal is for youth to understand themselves and others better, to apply this understanding in everyday situations, and to learn to cope successfully with both predictable and stressful events. A social skills curriculum was an integral component of the Prep Project previously described. A review of seven social skills programs in the schools found limited impact on the internal-emotional area but reduced student discipline problems in four of the studies.[147] However, the authors note serious methodological difficulties in affective education evaluations. Most evaluated skills training programs have been remedial and not preventive.[148]

M. B. Shure and G. Spivack tested the impact of interpersonal cognitive problem-solving skills on the behavioral adjustment of preschool and kindergarten children.[149] The study involved 219 black children in daycare (113 experimentals and 106 controls) and 62 kindergarten children (35 of the 106 year 1 controls exposed to the program during the second year and 27 controls). The intervention involved a script consisting of games and dialogues designed to impart specific skills, and implemented daily in twenty-minute lessons for three months. Nursery-trained youngsters improved in three problem-solving skills, and kindergarten-trained youngsters in two. Both experimental groups increased in consequential thinking, and ability to conceptualize alternative solutions to interpersonal problems was significantly related to behavior adjustment. Training also improved observed behaviors characteristic of impulsivity and inhibition; however, these changes could not be attributed to changes in causal thinking skills. Although delinquency was not measured, early maladaptive behaviors are predictors of subsequent antisocial behavior, and delinquent youngsters display interpersonal skill deficiencies[150] which appear to have been addressed by the Shure and Spivack intervention.

Another addition to many school curricula has been drug abuse prevention. Studies in school environments offer evidence that prevention curricula can reduce cigarette smoking. Drug abuse prevention curricula in schools provide information about the harmful effects of drugs and seek to improve decision-making skills, interpersonal skills, and skills to resist social pressure to use drugs.[151] School programs that teach children to recognize and resist social influences that promote cigarette smoking and drug use have proven most effective.[152] However, programs that address a particular form of substance use may not generalize to other behaviors such as delinquency. A recent study of a smoking prevention curriculum in fifteen fifth and sixth grade classrooms demonstrated reductions in self-reported cigarette smoking, but these results did not generalize to alcohol and marijuana use.[153]

Experience-based career education is another classroom curriculum that has been studied for effects on student attitudes and behavior. D. C. Gottfredson notes that when work experience is carefully coordinated with the school curriculum, it can be expected to decrease school dropout and increase learning and school attendance, if the work is perceived as relevant, useful, and the students are well supervised and rewarded for competence.[154] However, there has been little research on the delinquency prevention effects of this curriculum innovation.

Alternative Education Strategies

The rationale for alternative education as a prevention strategy is that specialized educational programs tailored to the needs of students experiencing failure or behavior problems should increase educational success and favorable attitudes toward school, thereby preventing delinquency.[155] Alternative education programs generally change instructional approaches and school organization in programs away from mainstream schools. They generally target identified high-risk students.[156]

A possible negative consequence of placing high-risk youths in separate alternative education programs is exposure to deviant peer influences and isolation from prosocial peers.[157] Thus, the benefits of an intensive tailored learning environment must be weighed against the potential risks of grouping high-risk youths together.

J. David Hawkins and John S. Wall reviewed alternative education programs and concluded that certain approaches appear promising for preventing delinquent behaviors.[158] These include individualized instruction, rewards that are attainable and clearly contingent on effort and proficiency, a goal-oriented work and learning emphasis, small school population, low student-adult ratio, caring and competent teachers, and strong, supportive administrators. However, these conclusions were not based on experimental studies of the delinquency prevention effects of alternative schools.

Martin Gold and David Mann evaluated three alternative schools offering opportunities for success through a flexible and supportive environment, individualized curricula, high-interest learning material, self-paced instruction, evaluation of individual progress, and warm student/teacher relations.[159] Students assigned to participating alternative schools were compared with those who were referred to the programs but could not attend for reasons other than their own characteristics. A three-wave interview process demonstrated significant reductions in disruptive behavior in school and improved school performance for some students. However, students who exhibited prior symptoms of anxiety and depression were not positively affected, and no effects of alternative school involvement on delinquent behavior in the community were found.

A national evaluation of seventeen alternative education projects targeting youths in sixth through twelfth grades residing in high-crime communities was reported by Gottfredson et al.[160] The premise of the alternative programs was that students fail owing to structural arrangements in schools, and that school failure lessens the likelihood of commitment to conventional values. It was hypothesized that school organization could be altered to prevent delinquency and associated problems including dropout, disruptive classroom conduct, and absenteeism. Evaluation designs ranged from experimental designs using random assignment to quasi-experimental designs using comparison groups.

Interventions varied at the seventeen project sites, and included peer counseling, leadership training, affective education, parent involvement, skills lab classes, token economies, vocational education, and school climate improvement. Some positive trends were demonstrated in project schools, including greater safety in program schools in 1982 than in 1981, less teacher victimization, slightly less delinquency on nine of ten measures (three of these differences reached statistical significance), decreases in student alienation and rebellious autonomy, improved self-concept, and slight improvements on five correlates of delinquency.

The projects varied in the degree of implementation of the interventions, and individual project results varied substantially. An interim summary of quasi-experimental and experimental evaluations of the projects indicated positive results for delinquency and related behavioral outcomes for several of the programs.[161] Positive effects on delinquency were reported for an alternative school which placed high-risk youths in a small, personalized educational environment; an in-school peer counseling intervention; a project that worked cooperatively with school administrators and faculty to assess student academic needs and provided academic and prosocial activities; a project in seven schools that implemented schoolwide change and also directly assisted high-risk youths through intensive services; and a small alternative school that offered a token economy system and a vocational curriculum. Negative results were shown for the counseling services component of an alternative education project, and no improvements were demonstrated for a vocational services alternative education project which counseled and attempted to employ dropout youths.

Change in Mainstream School Arrangements and Classroom Practices

Changes in schoolwide operations and classroom practices in mainstream schools have been advocated to prevent delinquency.[162] It has been suggested that creating effective schools that promote academic achievement and prosocial behavior should reduce school contributions to delinquency. The premise is that improvements in overall school climate and operations will benefit all students, including those at high risk for delinquency.

One example of this approach is the U.S. Office of Education's school team approach. Teams consisting of school administrators, teachers, counselors, parents, students, and youth agency representatives have been trained to design problem-solving action plans to address specific problems in their schools. Activities vary by site and have included time out rooms, student monitors, teacher home visits, and rewards for good behavior. The school team approach was evaluated for impact on crime, disruptive behavior, and fear of crime in schools.[163] Reductions in crime were measured by differences between initial student and teacher reports and those of the subsequent two years. No control or comparison schools were studied.

The evaluation found that teams which continued over time were associated with reduced reports of school crime. Greater reductions in disruption were found in middle schools than in elementary or high schools and greater reductions were found in personal victimization, classroom disruption, and fear than in theft and drug use. The kinds of team activities associated with crime reduction depended on the grade level of the school. High school teams which sought increased communication within the school and between school and community, which involved students and adults in solving school problems, and which promoted the development of knowledge and competencies that aided students in dealing with the world beyond the school were most strongly associated with reductions in disruption. In middle and elementary schools, teams that focused on improved discipline and security procedures as well as improved teacher/parent and teacher/student relationships were associated with reductions in disruption. However, the absence of comparison schools limits the ability to attribute observed reductions to the school team program.

Other school-based delinquency prevention programs have combined organizational change with direct intervention for high-risk youths.[164] Project PATHE was a three-year program implemented in seven schools in Charleston County, South Carolina, as part of the Alternative Education Program.[165] Interventions included:

1. Establishing an organizational structure to facilitate shared decision making and management in schools.

2. The use of curriculum and student concerns specialists.

3. Academic innovations including study skills, reading and test-taking programs, field trips, student team learning, climate innovations, and career exploration.

4. Direct services to targeted high-risk students to increase academic involvement and success. These included individual treatment plans, behavioral objectives, and monthly monitoring by specialists.

High-risk students in participating schools were randomly assigned to treatment and control groups. Surveys of students and teachers were conducted each spring for three years. Alienation, attachment to school, belief in conventional rules, self-reported serious delinquency and drug involvement, educational expectation, negative peer influence, disciplinary infractions, school success, and test scores were measured.

Results indicated that school climate improved and risk factors for delinquency for the school population as a whole decreased in PATHE schools, but that direct services for high-risk youths were less effective.[166] One of the two comparison schools was discontinued after one year, so data for that school are incomplete. At the school level, PATHE schools improved on 75 percent of school climate measures from 1981 to 1983 as compared to an improvement of 36 percent at a comparison school in the same period. Survey data for student self-reports of serious delinquency, drug use, suspensions, and teacher and student reports of victimization and school safety showed favorable results for the experimental schools on about 85 percent of the measures. Comparison schools improved by 60 and 28 percent on these measures. Students in all PATHE schools reported increased attachment to their schools over time, with the difference statistically significant in three of the seven schools, whereas students in the comparison school grew significantly less attached to school. Students in all schools reported increased perceptions of rule fairness, increased self-concept, increased belief in rules, greater safety, and decreased rates of suspension and alienation over time. The changes reached statistical significance in some PATHE schools but not in the comparison school. Statistically significant improvements were observed for PATHE schools on delinquent behavior, drug involvement, alienation, school rewards, self-concept, educational expectations, and belief in rules and safety. Significant decreases in self-reported suspensions were observed for PATHE schools, but not in the comparison school. An increase in serious delinquency was found for the comparison school.

High-risk students receiving individual treatment fared better than control students on serious delinquent behavior, drug involvement, arrests, suspensions, victimization, and disciplinary infractions in only one of the seven PATHE schools. An overall positive effect was found for targeted students on academic achievement, and three PATHE schools were able to retain target students in school at statistically higher rates than control students. Two schools increased the attendance rates of target students. However, an increase in drug involvement was reported by target students. More favorable results were shown on those measures at the one school that implemented the target student services according to program standards, but the differences were not statistically significant. In sum, the program as implemented with high-risk students generally was not effective in reducing delinquent behavior.

The evaluators concluded that schoolwide structural and instructional changes in schools in the PATHE project were effective in reducing delinquency and its risk factors at the school level. Factors deemed by the evaluators as likely to have contributed to program success were involvement of school staff in the change process, improved school management, and intervention at several different points in students' lives.[167] The direct services to high-risk students were somewhat effective in improving academic performance but not in reducing delinquency. The evaluators concluded that altering the school organization can be an effective approach to delinquency prevention.

Hawkins et al. conducted a test of the effects of enhanced methods of classroom instruction in five Seattle middle schools with 1,166 seventh grade students.[168] The project employed experimental and quasi-experimental designs to test the effects of the teaching methods on student academic achievement, bonding to school and peers, and behaviors including delinquency.

The classroom-based instructional practices tested included proactive classroom management, interactive teaching, and cooperative learning.[169] At the end of one academic year, it was found that experimental teachers implemented the project teaching practices significantly more than control teachers, that use of the practices was associated with student behavior linked to achievement, greater achievement in math, more positive student attitudes toward math class, greater educational aspirations and expectations, and reduced rates of suspension and expulsion from school.[170] However, no effects on self-reported delinquency were reported at the end of the first year of intervention.

The effect of these same instructional methods on the achievement, bonding, and behaviors of a subset of 160 low achievers was examined in a separate analysis.[171] Low achievers in experimental classrooms showed more favorable attitudes toward math, more bonding to school, greater expectations for continued schooling, and less school misbehaviors as measured by suspensions and expulsions from school than did their low-achieving control counterparts at the end of one academic year. Among low achievers, significant effects of the teaching practices were not found for achievement test scores, or for self-reported delinquency at the end of one year of intervention.

INTERVENING IN SCHOOLS TO PREVENT DELINQUENCY

Evidence from individual and aggregate level studies shows a correlation between school-related factors and delinquency. Although causality has not been conclusively determined, the evidence points to a link between delinquent behavior and individual student attributes including low ability level, conduct disorders in early elementary school, poor academic performance by late elementary grades, learning disabilities, dropping out, association with delinquent peers, and inadequate bonding to conventional persons and school norms. There is also evidence that school characteristics including large school size, impersonal climate, inadequate reinforcements for learning, and inconsistently enforced rules contribute to delinquency.

On the basis of this evidence, education-focused strategies to prevent juvenile crime appear to be warranted. To be effective, prevention programs should address salient risk factors. For example, the evidence generally indicates that school performance is a predictor of delinquency. This suggests the appropriateness of programs aimed at improving the academic achievement of a broad range of students. However, there is also evidence that school performance does not eliminate the impact of delinquent friends, which suggests that efforts to improve academic achievement should be combined with positive peer influence strategies. Student team learning is one example of a strategy that simultaneously addresses both of these predictors of delinquency.[172]

There is evidence that school-based prevention strategies that enhance the overall school and classroom environment have a positive impact on student achievement, bonding, and behavior. Promising results also have been shown for early education programs that increase the opportunities for success of high-risk youngsters; for alternative education approaches and curriculum improvements that make the educational experience more rewarding; and for organizational and classroom improvements that promote learning, bonding to school and teacher, and prosocial behavior. Behavioral reinforcement strategies have been found to be effective in the short term for modifying discrete problem behaviors.

There remain important gaps in our understanding. School and classroom improvements appear to have positive effects overall, but only marginal effects for the most seriously disturbed or underachieving youths. School misbehaviors have been reduced by school-based prevention efforts, but effects on community delinquency have been small. Short-term effects have been demonstrated for behavioral strategies, but they have not been maintained over time. Further study is needed to advance our knowledge regarding effective prevention strategies in the schools.

NOTES

1. John I. Goodlad, *A Place Called School. Prospects for the Future* (New York: McGraw-Hill Book Co., 1984).

2. Ibid.; Martin Gold and David W. Mann, *Expelled to a Friendlier Place: A Study of Effective Alternative Schools* (Ann Arbor: University of Michigan Press, 1984); D. C. Gottfredson, *An Assessment of a Delinquency Prevention Demonstration with Both Individual and Environmental Interventions* (Baltimore: Johns Hopkins University, Center for Social Organization of Schools, 1985).

3. J. David Hawkins, Howard Doueck, and Denise M. Lishner, "Changing Teaching Practices in Mainstream Classes to Reduce Discipline Problems Among Low Achievers" (Seattle: Center for Social Welfare Research, University of Washington, 1985); J. David Hawkins, Tony C.M. Lam, and Denise M. Lishner, "Instructional Practices and School Misbehavior" (Seattle: Center for Social Welfare Research, University of Washington, 1985).

4. Joseph H. Rankin, "School Factors and Delinquency: Interactions by Age and Sex," *Social Service Review* 64, no. 3 (1978): 420–432.

5. Delbert S. Elliott and Harwin L. Voss, *Delinquency and Dropout* (Lexington, Mass.: D. C. Heath and Co., 1974).

6. Delbert S. Elliott, "Delinquency, School Attendance and Dropout," *Social Problems* 13 (Winter 1966): 307–314; John C. Phillips and Delos H. Kelly, "School Failure and Delinquency: Which Causes Which?" *Criminology* 17 (August 1979): 194–207.

7. Elliott and Voss, *Delinquency and Dropout*.

8. Dean E. Frease, "Schools and Delinquency: Some Intervening Processes," *Pacific Sociological Review* 16 (October 1973): 426–448; Travis Hirschi and Michael J. Hindelang, "Intelligence and Delinquency: A Revisionist Review," *American Sociological Review* 42 (August 1977): 571–587; Frank W. Jerse and M. Efrahim Fakouri, "Juvenile Delinquency and Academic Deficiency," *Contemporary Education* 49 (Winter 1978): 106–109; M. Rutter and H. Giller, *Juvenile Delinquency: Trends and Perspectives* (New York: Guilford Press, 1984); D. P. Farrington, "Self-Reports of Deviant Behavior: Predictive and Stable?" *Journal of Criminal Law and Criminology* 64 (March 1973): 99–110; J. Sederstrom and J. Weis, *The Role of the School in Delinquency Prevention* (Seattle: Center for Law and Justice, University of Washington, 1981).

9. D. J. West and D. P. Farrington, *Who Becomes Delinquent?* (London: Heinemann Educational Books, Limited, 1973).

10. Hirschi and Hindelang, "Intelligence and Delinquency," pp. 571–587.

11. Rutter and Giller, *Juvenile Delinquency: Trends and Perspectives*, p. 165.

12. Gary D. Gottfredson, "Schooling and Delinquency," in Susan E. Martin, Lee B. Sechrest, and Robin Redner, eds., *New Directions in the Rehabilitation of Criminal Offenders* (Washington, D.C.: National Academy Press, 1981).

13. N. Dunivant, *Causal Analysis of the Relationship Between Learning Disabilities and Juvenile Delinquency* (Williamsburg, Va.: National Center for State Courts, 1982).

14. Gary H. Bachara and Joel N. Zaba, "Learning Disabilities and Juvenile Delinquency," *Journal of Learning Disabilities* 11, no. 4 (1978): 58–69; Dunivant, *Causal Analysis of the Relationship Between Learning Disabilities and Juvenile Delinquency*; Bruce A. Lane, "The Relationship of Learning Disabilities to Juvenile Delinquency: Current Status," *Journal of Learning Disabilities* 13, no. 8 (October 1980): 425–434; Barbara A. Zaremba, Claire B. McCullough, and Paul K. Broder, *Learning Disabilities and Juvenile Delinquency: A Handbook for Court Personnel, Judges and Attorneys* (Williamsburg, Va.: National Center for State Courts, 1979).

15. J. Zimmerman, W. D. Rich, I. Keilitz, and P. K. Broder, *Some Observations on the Link Between Learning Disabilities and Juvenile Delinquency* (Williamsburg, Va.: National Center for State Courts, 1980).

16. Dunivant, *Causal Analysis of the Relationship Between Learning Disabilities and Juvenile Delinquency*.

17. Ibid.

18. Ibid.

19. J. G. Bachman, P. M. O'Malley, and J. Johnston, "Adolescence to Adulthood; Change and Stability in the Lives of Young Men," in *Youth in Transition*, Vol. 6 (Ann Arbor: Institute for Social Research, 1978); Elliott and Voss, *Delinquency and Dropout*; Gold and Mann, *Expelled to a Friendlier Place*, pp. 22–24; George W. Noblit, "The Adolescent Experience and Delinquency: School Versus Subcultural Effects," *Youth and Society* 8 (September 1976): 27–44; Kenneth Polk and Walter E. Schafer, *School and Delinquency* (Englewood Cliffs, N.J.: Prentice-Hall, 1972), pp. 165–180; Walter E.

Schafer, "Participation in Interscholastic Athletics and Delinquency: A Preliminary Study," *Social Problems* 17 (Summer 1969): 40–47.

20. Josefina Figueira-McDonough, "Discrimination or Sex Differences? Criteria for Evaluating the Juvenile Justice System's Handling of Minor Offenses," paper prepared for the National Workshop on Female Offenders, St. Paul, Minnesota (Michigan State University and Institute for Social Research, University of Michigan, 1985); Walter L. Slocum and Carol L. Stone, "Family Culture Patterns and Delinquent-type Behavior," *Marriage and Family Living* 25 (May 1963): 202–208.

21. A. Lewis Rhodes and Albert J. Reiss, Jr., "Apathy, Truancy, and Delinquency as Adaptations to School Failure," *Social Forces* 48 (September 1969): 12–22.

22. Anthony Meade, "Seriousness of Delinquency, the Adjudicative Decision and Recidivism: A Conceptual Configuration Analysis," *Journal of Criminal Law and Criminology* 64 (December 1973): 478–485.

23. Gottfredson, "Schooling and Delinquency," pp. 435–436.

24. Alfred Blumstein, David P. Farrington, and Soumyo Moitra, "Delinquency Careers: Innocents, Desisters, and Resisters," in Michael Tonry and Norval Morris, eds., *Crime and Justice*, Vol. 6 (Chicago: University of Chicago Press, 1985).

25. Josefina Figueira-McDonough, "On the Usefulness of Merton's Anomie Theory: Academic Failure and Deviance Among High School Students," *Youth and Society* 14, no. 3 (March 1983): 259–279; Delos H. Kelly and Robert W. Balch, "Social Origins and School Failure: A Re-examination of Cohen's Theory of Working Class Delinquency," *Pacific Sociological Review* 14 (October 1971): 413–430; Kenneth Polk, Dean Frease, and F. Lynn Richard, "Social Class, School Experience, and Delinquency," *Criminology* 12 (May 1974): 84–96; Joseph Senna, Spencer A. Rathus, and Larry Siegel, "Delinquent Behavior and Academic Investment Among Suburban Youth," *Adolescence* 9 (Winter 1974): 481–494.

26. Kelly and Balch, "Social Origins and School Failure," pp. 420–421.

27. Gottfredson, "Schooling and Delinquency," pp. 435–443.

28. D. J. Call, "Delinquency, Frustration and Non-Commitment," Ph.D. diss. (University of Oregon, 1965); Gary F. Jensen, "Race, Achievement, and Delinquency: A Further Look at Delinquency in a Birth Cohort," *American Journal of Sociology* 82, no. 2 (1976): 379–387; J. M. McPartland and E. L. McDill, eds., *Violence in Schools: Perspectives, Programs, and Positions* (Lexington, Mass.: D. C. Heath and Co., 1977); E. B. Palmore and P. E. Hammond, "Interacting Factors in Juvenile Delinquency," *American Sociological Review* 29 (1964): 848–854; Kenneth Polk, "Class, Strain, and Rebellion Among Adolescents," *Social Problems* 17 (Fall 1969): 214–224; Polk, Frease, and Richard, "Social Class, School Experience, and Delinquency," pp. 92–94; A. C. Stinchcombe, *Rebellion in a High School* (Chicago: Quadrangle Books, 1964).

29. Polk, Frease, and Richard, "Social Class, School Experience, and Delinquency," pp. 91–92.

30. Palmore and Hammond, "Interacting Factors in Juvenile Delinquency," pp. 850–851.

31. Noblit, "The Adolescent Experience and Delinquency," pp. 32–33; Kenneth Polk and David S. Halferty, "Adolescence, Commitment and Delinquency," *Journal of Research in Crime and Delinquency* 3 (July 1966): 82–96.

32. Jensen, "Race, Achievement, and Delinquency," p. 384. Polk and Halferty, "Adolescence, Commitment and Delinquency," p. 95.

214   J. David Hawkins and Denise M. Lishner

33. Frease, "Schools and Delinquency," pp. 442–445; Kelly and Balch, "Social Origins and School Failure," pp. 421–424.

34. Martin Gold, *Delinquent Behavior in an American City* (Belmont, Calif.: Brooks/Cole, 1970).

35. Noblit, "The Adolescent Experience and Delinquency." pp. 34–36.

36. D. S. Elliott, D. Huizinga, and S. S. Ageton, "Explaining Delinquency and Drug Use" (Boulder, Colo.: Behavioral Research Institute, Report No. 21, 1982); R. Jessor and S. L. Jessor, *Problem Behavior and Psychosocial Development: A Longitudinal Study of Youth* (New York: Academic Press, 1977).

37. Phillips and Kelly, "School Failure and Delinquency." pp. 199–203.

38. Elliott and Voss, *Delinquency and Dropout.*

39. Bachman, O'Malley, and Johnston, "Adolescence to Adulthood," pp. 175–178.

40. Maude M. Craig and Selma J. Glick, "Ten Years' Experience with the Glueck Social Prediction Table," *Crime and Delinquency* 9 (July 1963): 249–261.

41. John F. Feldhusen, John R. Thurston, and James J. Benning, "A Longitudinal Study of Delinquency and Other Aspects of Children's Behavior," *International Journal of Criminology and Penology* 1 (November 1973): 341–351.

42. G. Spivack, *High Risk Early Behaviors Indicating Vulnerability to Delinquency in the Community and School: A Fifteen-Year Longitudinal Study* (Philadelphia: Hahnemann University, 1983).

43. S. G. Kellam, C. H. Brown, and J. P. Fleming, "The Prevention of Teenage Substance Use: Longitudinal Research and Strategy," in T. J. Coates, A. C. Petersen, and C. Perry, eds., *Promoting Adolescent Health* (New York: Academic Press, 1982).

44. R. Loeber and T. Dishion, "Early Predictors of Male Delinquency: A Review," *Psychological Bulletin* 93 (1983): 68–99.

45. Spivack, *High Risk Early Behaviors Indicating Vulnerability to Delinquency in the Community and School.*

46. J. David Hawkins, Denise M. Lishner, and Richard F. Catalano, "Childhood Predictors and the Prevention of Adolescent Substance Abuse," in C. L. Jones and R. J. Battjes, eds., *Etiology of Drug Abuse: Implications for Prevention* (Washington, D.C.: National Institute on Drug Abuse, ADM85–1385, 1985); George Spivack and Lois Rapsher, *Special Class Placement and Being Left Back in School as Elements in a High Risk Delinquency History* (Philadelphia: Hahnemann Medical College, 1979).

47. D. P. Farrington, "Longitudinal Research on Crime and Delinquency," in Norval Morris and Michael Tonry, eds., *Crime and Justice: An Annual Review of Research,* Vol. I (Chicago: University of Chicago Press, 1979), pp. 289–348; M. Rutter, B. Maughan, P. Mortimore, and J. Ouston, *Fifteen Thousand Hours: Secondary Schools and Their Effects on Children* (Cambridge, Mass.: Harvard University Press, 1979).

48. G. Spivack and J. Marcus, "Early School Performance and Classroom Behavior as Paths to Independence and Employment Among Black Urban Youth" (Philadelphia: Preventive Intervention Research Center, 1984).

49. Rutter and Giller, *Juvenile Delinquency: Trends and Perspectives,* pp. 165–168.

50. Travis Hirschi, *Causes of Delinquency* (Berkeley: University of California Press, 1969).

51. Michael Hindelang, "Causes of Delinquency: A Partial Replication and Extension," *Social Problems* 20 (Spring 1973): 471–487.

52. Kelly and Balch, "Social Origins and School Failure," pp. 420–421.

53. Elliott and Voss, *Delinquency and Dropout.*

54. Sederstrom and Weis, *The Role of the School in Delinquency Prevention*.

55. Ibid.

56. R. Lawrence, "School Performance, Containment Theory, and Delinquent Behavior," *Youth and Society* 17, no. 1 (1985): 69–95.

57. Figueira-McDonough, "Discrimination or Sex Differences?" pp. 268–277.

58. Elliott and Voss, *Delinquency and Dropout*; Hirschi, *Causes of Delinquency*, pp. 191–192.

59. Elliott and Voss, *Delinquency and Dropout*.

60. William Glasser, "Disorders in Our Schools: Causes and Remedies," *Phi Delta Kappan* 59 (January 1978): 331–333.

61. Hirschi, *Causes of Delinquency*, pp. 178–179.

62. Edgar G. Epps, "Socioeconomic Status, Race, Level of Aspiration, and Juvenile Delinquency: A Limited Empirical Test of Merton's Conception of Deviation," *Phylon* 28 (Spring 1967): 16–27.

63. Gerald J. Pine, "Social Class, Social Mobility, and Delinquent Behavior," *Personnel and Guidance Journal* 43 (April 1965): 770–774.

64. Polk and Halferty, "Adolescence, Commitment and Delinquency," pp. 83–96.

65. Polk, "Class, Strain, and Rebellion Among Adolescents," pp. 220–223.

66. Elliott, "Delinquency, School Attendance and Dropout," pp. 312–313.

67. Hirschi, *Causes of Delinquency*, pp. 165, 170–182.

68. Sederstrom and Weis, *The Role of the School in Delinquency Prevention*.

69. J. G. Bachman, P. M. O'Malley, and J. Johnston, *Youth in Transition*, Vol. 3: Dropping Out—Problem or Symptom? (Ann Arbor, Mich.: Institute for Social Research, 1971), pp. 99–104; Elliott and Voss, *Delinquency and Dropout*.

70. W. E. Schafer, C. Olexa, and K. Polk, "Programmed for Social Class: Tracking in High School," in K. Polk and W. Schafer, eds., *Schools and Delinquency* (New York: Prentice-Hall, 1972), pp. 41–45.

71. Elliott and Voss, *Delinquency and Dropout*; Kelly and Balch, "Social Origins and School Failure," pp. 421–422.

72. Bachman, O'Malley, and Johnston, *Youth in Transition*, Vol. 3: Dropping Out—Problem or Symptom? pp. 91–98.

73. Bachman, O'Malley, and Johnston, "Adolescence to Adulthood,"; pp. 176–178; Elliott and Voss, *Delinquency and Dropout*.

74. Bachman, O'Malley, and Johnston, *Youth in Transition*, Vol. 3: Dropping Out—Problem or Symptom? pp. 123–125.

75. Elliott and Voss, *Delinquency and Dropout*.

76. J. G. Bachman, J. D. Johnston, and P. M. O'Malley, *Monitoring the Future: Questionnaire Responses from the Nation's High School Seniors, 1978* (Ann Arbor, Mich.: Survey Research Center, 1981).

77. Elliott, Huizinga, and Ageton, "Explaining Delinquency and Drug Use," pp. 143–145.

78. William T. Pink, "Creating Effective Schools," *The Educational Forum* 49, no. 1 (1984): 91–107.

79. Wilbur B. Brookover, John H. Schweitzer, Jeffrey M. Schneider, Charles H. Beady, Patricia K. Flood, and Joseph M. Wisenbaker, "Elementary School Social Climate and School Achievement," *American Educational Research Journal* 15, no. 2 (Spring 1978): 301–318; Ronald R. Edmonds, "Search for Effective Schools," Paper presented at the Strategies for Urban Schools Improvement Workshop Series, Washington, D.C.,

June 12, 1980; Goodlad, *A Place Called School*; Edward L. McDill, Edmund D. Meyers, Jr., and Leo C. Rigsby, "Institutional Effects on the Academic Behavior of High School Students," *Sociology of Education* 4, no. 3 (Summer 1967): 181–199.

80. Gottfredson, "Schooling and Delinquency," pp. 443–448.

81. Elliott and Voss, *Delinquency and Dropout*.

82. S. Hansel and N. Karweit, "Curriculum Placement, Friendship Networks, and Status Attainment," in Joyce L. Epstein and N. Karweit, eds., *Friends in School: Patterns of Selection and Influence in Secondary Schools* (New York: Academic Press, 1983).

83. Bachman, Johnston, and O'Malley, *Monitoring the Future*; National Institute of Education, "Violent Schools—Safe Schools: The Safe School Study Report, Vol. 1" (Washington, D.C.: U.S. Department of Health, Education, and Welfare, U.S. Government Printing Office, 1978); David Reynolds, Dee Jones, and Selwyn St. Leger, "Schools Do Make a Difference," *New Society* 37 (July 29, 1976): 223–225; Rutter, Maughan, Mortimore, and Ouston, *Fifteen Thousand Hours*.

84. M. J. Power, M. R. Alderson, C. M. Phillipson, E. Schoenberg, and J. N. Morris, "Delinquent Schools?" *New Society* 10 (October 19, 1967): 542–543.

85. Reynolds, Jones, and St. Leger, "Schools Do Make a Difference," pp. 224–225; West and Farrington, *Who Becomes Delinquent?* pp. 123–124.

86. West and Farrington, *Who Becomes Delinquent?* pp. 120–124.

87. M. Rutter, "Why Are London Children So Disturbed?" *Proceedings of the Royal Society of Medicine* 66 (1973): 1221–1225.

88. Reynolds, Jones, and St. Leger, "Schools Do Make a Difference," pp. 223–225.

89. Rutter, Maughan, Mortimore, and Ouston, *Fifteen Thousand Hours*.

90. Ibid.

91. J. S. Coleman, T. Hoffer, and S. Kilgore, *High School Achievement: Public, Catholic, and Private Schools Compared* (New York: Basic Books, 1982).

92. D. P. Farrington, "Delinquency Prevention in the 1980's," *Journal of Adolescence* 8 (1985): 3–16.

93. National Institute of Education, "Violent Schools—Safe Schools."

94. Gary D. Gottfredson and Denise C. Daiger, *Disruption in Six Hundred Schools: The Social Ecology of School Victimization*, Report No. 281 (Baltimore: Johns Hopkins University, Center for Social Organization of Schools, 1979).

95. D. C. Gottfredson, *Environmental Change Strategies to Prevent School Disruption* (Baltimore: Johns Hopkins University, Center for Social Organization of Schools, 1984).

96. D. H. Hargreaves, *Social Relations in a Secondary School* (London: Routledge and Kegan Paul, 1967).

97. Delos H. Kelly, "Track Position, Peer Affiliation, and Youth Crime," *Urban Education* 31, no. 3 (October 1978): 397–406.

98. Spivack and Rapsher, *Special Class Placement and Being Left Back in School as Elements in a High Risk Delinquency History*.

99. Michael D. Wiatrowski, Stephen Hansell, Charles R. Massey, and David L. Wilson, "Curriculum Tracking and Delinquency: Toward an Integration of Educational and Delinquency Research," *American Sociological Review* 47 (February 1982): 151–160.

100. McDill, Meyers, and Rigsby, "Institutional Effects on the Academic Behavior of High School Students."

101. Edmonds, "Search for Effective Schools."

102. Brookover, Schweitzer, Schneider, Beady, Flood, and Wisenbaker, "Elementary School Social Climate and School Achievement."

103. Goodlad, *A Place Called School*, p. 156.

104. Michael Cohen, "Effective Schools: Accumulating Research Findings," *American Education* 18 (January-February 1982): 13–16.

105. Thomas L. Good, "How Teacher's Expectations Affect Results," *American Education* (December 1982): 25–32.

106. D. W. Johnson and R. W. Johnson, "Cooperative Learning: The Power of Positive Goal Interdependence," in V. M. Lyons, eds., *Structuring Cooperative Experiences in the Classroom: The 1980 Handbook* (Minneapolis: A Cooperation Network Publisher, 1980); Nancy L. Karweit, Stephen Hansell, and Margaret Ann Ricks, "The Conditions for Peer Associations in Schools" (Baltimore: Johns Hopkins University, Johns Hopkins University Report No. 282, 1979); Robert E. Slavin, "Cooperative Learning." *Review of Educational Research* 50 (Summer 1980): 315–342.

107. Elliott, Huizinga, and Ageton, "Explaining Delinquency and Drug Use"; Hirschi, *Causes of Delinquency*; Denise B. Kandel and Israel Adler, "Socialization into Marijuana Use Among French Adolescents: A Cross-Cultural Comparison with the United States," *Journal of Health and Social Behavior* 23 (December 1982): 295–309.

108. J. L. Epstein and N. Karweit, *Friends in School: Patterns of Selection and Influence in Secondary Schools* (Baltimore: Center for Social Organization of Schools, 1983).

109. Hansel and Karweit, "Curriculum Placement, Friendship Networks, and Status Attainment," pp. 143–158.

110. J. L. Epstein, "School Environment and Student Friendships: Issues, Implications and Interventions," in J. L. Epstein and N. Karweit, eds., *Friends in School*, pp. 235–253; J. D. Hawkins, "Student Team Learning: Preventing the Flocking and Feathering of Delinquents," *Journal of Primary Prevention* 2, no. 1 (1981): 50–55.

111. Gold and Mann, *Expelled to a Friendlier Place*, p. 135; Hawkins, Lishner, and Catalano, "Childhood Predictors and the Prevention of Adolescent Substance Abuse"; Rutter and Giller, *Juvenile Delinquency*, p. 200.

112. W. C. Kvaraceus, *Juvenile Delinquency and the School* (Yonkers, N.Y.: World Books, 1945).

113. A. K. Cohen, *Delinquent Boys* (Glencoe, Ill.: Free Press, 1955).

114. Stinchcombe, *Rebellion in a High School*.

115. Hirschi, *Causes of Delinquency*, p. 117.

116. Elliott and Voss, *Delinquency and Dropout*.

117. Lawrence, "School Performance, Containment Theory, and Delinquent Behavior," pp. 72–74.

118. J. G. Bachman, *Youth in Transition*, Vol. 2: The Impact of Family Background and Intelligence on Tenth Grade Boys (Ann Arbor, Mich.: Institute for Social Research, 1970).

119. Mary A. Prendergast and Dorothy M. Binder, "Relationships of Selected Self-Concept and Academic Achievement Measures," *Measurement and Evaluation in Guidance* 8 (July 1975): 92–95.

120. Howard B. Kaplan, "Self Attitudes and Deviant Response," *Social Forces* 54 (June 1976): 788–801.

121. M. Gold, "Scholastic Experiences, Self-Esteem, and Delinquent Behavior: A Theory for Alternative Schools," *Crime and Delinquency* 24, no. 3 (1978): 290–308.

122. Albert K. Cohen and James F. Short, Jr., "Crime and Juvenile Delinquency," in Robert K. Merton and Robert Nisbet, eds., *Contemporary Social Problems* (New York: Harcourt Brace Jovanovich, 1976), pp. 45–102.

123. Gottfredson, "Schooling and Delinquency," pp. 448.

124. R. L. Akers, M. D. Krohn, L. Lanza-Kaduce, and M. Radosevich, "Social Learning and Deviant Behavior: A Specific Test of a General Theory," *American Sociological Review* 44, no. 4 (1979): 636–655.

125. Gottfredson and Daiger, *Disruption in Six Hundred Schools*.

126. Richard A. Cloward and Lloyd E. Ohlin, *Delinquency and Opportunity* (Chicago: Free Press, 1960), chapter 5; Cohen, *Delinquent Boys*, pp. 121–137.

127. Howard S. Becker, *Outsiders: Studies in the Sociology of Deviance* (New York: Free Press, 1963); Edwin M. Lemert, *Human Deviance, Social Problems and Social Control*, 2d ed. (Englewood Cliffs, N.J.: Prentice-Hall, 1972).

128. Hirschi, *Causes of Delinquency*, pp. 16–26.

129. Hawkins, Lishner, and Catalano, "Childhood Predictors and the Prevention of Adolescent Substance Abuse"; J. David Hawkins and Joseph G. Weis, "The Social Development Model: An Integrated Approach to Delinquency Prevention," *Journal of Primary Prevention* 6, no. 2 (1985).

130. D. P. Farrington, "Early Precursors of High Rate Offending," Paper presented for Executive Session on Delinquency and the Family, Harvard University, November 10–12, 1985; James Q. Wilson, "Strategic Opportunities for Delinquency Prevention," Paper presented at the OJJDP Harvard Executive Session on Delinquency and the Family (Cambridge, Mass.: Harvard University, 1985); James Q. Wilson and Richard J. Herrnstein, *Crime and Human Nature* (New York: Simon and Schuster, 1985).

131. Hawkins and Weis, "The Social Development Model."

132. D. C. Gottfredson, *An Assessment of a Delinquency Prevention Demonstration with Both Individual and Environmental Interventions* (Baltimore: Johns Hopkins University, Center for Social Organization of Schools, 1984).

133. H. J. Meyer, E. Borgatta, and W. C. Jones, *Girls at Vocational High: An Experiment in Social Work Intervention* (New York: Russell Sage Foundation, 1965).

134. Walter Reckless and Simon Dinitz, *The Prevention of Juvenile Delinquency* (Columbus: Ohio State University Press, 1972).

135. W. M. Ahlstrom and R. J. Havighurst, *Four Hundred Losers: Delinquent Boys in High School* (San Francisco: Jossey-Bass, 1971).

136. G. Rose and T. F. Marshall, *Counseling and School Social Work: An Experimental Study* (London: Wiley, 1974).

137. C. A. Murray, B. B. Bourgue, R. S. Harnar, J. C. Hersey, S. R. Murray, D. D. Overbey, and E. S. Stotsky, "The National Evaluation of the Cities in Schools Program Report No. 3," National Institute of Education, U.S. Department of Health, Education and Welfare, Washington, D.C., 1980.

138. Wilson, "Strategic Opportunities for Delinquency Prevention."

139. J. R. Berrueta-Clement, L. J. Schweinhart, W. S. Barnett, A. S. Epstein, and D. P. Weikart, *Changed Lives* (Ypsilanti, Mich.: High/Scope, 1984).

140. Ibid.

141. Irving Lazar and Richard Darlington, "Lasting Effects of Early Education: A

Report from the Consortium for Longitudinal Studies," *Monographs of the Society for Research in Child Development* 47, no. 2–3 (1982).

142. Kellam, Brown, and Fleming, "The Prevention of Teenage Substance Use."

143. J. Filipczak and J. S. Wodarski, "Behavioral Intervention in Public Schools: Implementing and Evaluating a Model," *Corrective and Social Psychiatry* 25, no. 2 (1979): 104–113.

144. Eve E. Gagne, "Educating Delinquents: A Review of Research," *Journal of Special Education* 11, no. 1 (1977): 13–27; A. P. Goldstein and M. Pentz, "Psychological Skill Training and the Aggressive Adolescent," *School Psychology Review* 13, no. 3 (1984): 311–323; Rutter and Giller, *Juvenile Delinquency: Trends and Perspectives*; David N. Shorr, Donald E. English, and Richard L. Janvier, "An Assessment of Evaluations of School-Based Delinquency Prevention Program" (Seattle: Center for Law and Justice, University of Washington, 1979).

145. Rutter and Giller, *Juvenile Delinquency*, pp. 276–283, 317–318.

146. Social Science Education Consortium and Center for Action Research, *Law-Related Education Evaluation Project Final Report Phase II Year 1*, Prepared under grant no. 79–JN–AX–0036 for the U.S. Department of Justice, National Institute of Juvenile Justice and Delinquency Prevention (Boulder, Colo.: Social Science Education Consortium and Center for Action Research, 1981).

147. E. J. Baskin and R. D. Hess, "Does Affective Education Work? A Review of Seven Programs," *Journal of Social Psychology* 18, no. 4 (1980): 40–50.

148. Goldstein and Pentz, "Psychological Skill Training and the Aggressive Adolescent."

149. M. B. Shure and G. Spivack, "Interpersonal Cognitive Problem Solving and Primary Prevention," *Journal of Clinical and Child Psychology* 8, no. 2 (Summer 1979): 89–94.

150. Goldstein and Pentz, "Psychological Skill Training and the Aggressive Adolescent."

151. J. M. Polich, P. L. Ellickson, P. Reuter, and J. P. Kahan, *Strategies for Controlling Adolescent Drug Use* (Santa Monica, Calif.: Rand Corporation Report No. 4–3076-CHF, 1984).

152. Ibid.

153. NIDA Clinical Research Notes, July 1985.

154. D. C. Gottfredson, "Youth Employment, Crime and Schooling: A Longitudinal Study of a National Sample," *Developmental Psychology* 21, no. 3 (1985): 419–432.

155. J. David Hawkins and John S. Wall, *Alternative Education: Exploring the Delinquency Prevention Potential* (Washington, D.C.: U.S. Government Printing Office [1981 0 341–233–1839], 1980).

156. Edward L. McDill, Gary Natriello, and Aaron M. Pallas, "Raising Standards and Retaining Students: The Impact of the Reform Recommendations on Potential Dropouts" (Baltimore: Johns Hopkins University, Center for Social Organization of Schools, Report No. 358, April 1985).

157. Gold and Mann, *Expelled to a Friendlier Place*; Hawkins, Doueck, and Lishner, "Changing Teaching Practices in Mainstream Classes to Reduce Discipline Problems Among Low Achievers."

158. Hawkins and Wall, *Alternative Education*.

159. Gold and Mann, *Expelled to a Friendlier Place*, pp. 99–150.

160. Gary D. Gottfredson, Denise L. Gottfredson, and Michael S. Cook, *The School*

Action Effectiveness Study: Second Interim Report, Part 1, Report No. 342 (Baltimore: Johns Hopkins University, Center for Social Organization of Schools, June 1983).

161. Gary D. Gottfredson, *The School Action Effectiveness Study: Interim Summary of the Alternative Education Evaluation* (Baltimore: Johns Hopkins University, Center for Social Organization of Schools, 1983).

162. Gottfredson, *An Assessment of a Delinquency Prevention Demonstration with Both Individual and Environmental Interventions.*

163. J. Grant and F. J. Capell, *Reducing School Crime: A Report on the School Team Approach* (Social Action Research Center, 1983), pp. 1–12.

164. Gottfredson, *An Assessment of a Delinquency Prevention Demonstration with Both Individual and Environmental Interventions*, pp. 1–72.

165. D. C. Gottfredson, *Project PATHE: Third Interim Report* (Baltimore: Johns Hopkins University, Center for Social Organization of Schools, 1983).

166. Gottfredson, *An Assessment of a Delinquency Prevention Demonstration with Both Individual and Environmental Interventions*, pp. 1–72.

167. Ibid.

168. Hawkins, Doueck, and Lishner, "Changing Teaching Practices in Mainstream Classes to Reduce Discipline Problems Among Low Achievers"; Hawkins, Lam, and Lishner, "Instructional Practices and School Misbehavior."

169. Ibid.

170. Hawkins, Lam, and Lishner, "Instructional Practices and School Misbehavior."

171. Hawkins, Doueck, and Lishner, "Changing Teaching Practices in Mainstream Classes to Reduce Discipline Problems Among Low Achievers."

172. R. E. Slavin, *Cooperative Learning Groups: What the Research Says to the Teacher* (Washington, D.C.: National Education Association, 1983).

BIBLIOGRAPHY

Berrueta-Clement, John R., L. J. Schweinhart, W. S. Barnett, A. S. Epstein, and D. P. Weikart. *Changed Lives*. Ypsilanti, Mich.: Center for the Study of Public Policies for Young Children, 1984.

    This long-term followup study of 123 disadvantaged youths assigned to a preschool program or a control condition demonstrated that preschool education is linked to increased adjustment and success, and to reduction in official delinquency.

Gold, Martin and David W. Mann. *Expelled to a Friendlier Place: A Study of Effective Alternative Schools*. Ann Arbor: University of Michigan Press, 1984.

    An evaluation of three alternative schools offering opportunities for increased success indicated significant reductions in disruptive behavior and improved school performance for a subset of students. However, students exhibiting prior symptoms of anxiety and depression were not positively affected.

Gottfredson, Gary D. "Schooling and Delinquency." In Susan E. Martin, Lee B. Sechrest, and Robin Redner, eds., *New Directions in the Rehabilitation of Criminal Offenders*. Washington, D.C.: National Academy Press, 1981.

    This comprehensive review of the research on schooling and delinquency includes descriptive data about the distribution of delinquent behavior, data on the key school-related correlates of delinquency, a discussion of the major theories of delinquency as they pertain to schooling, and implications for prevention strategies.

Gottfredson, Gary D., Denise L. Gottfredson, and Michael S. Cook. "The School Action Effectiveness Study: Second Interim Report Part 1." Report No. 342. Baltimore: Johns Hopkins University, Center for Social Organization of Schools (June 1983).

This was a national experimental evaluation of seventeen alternative education projects in high-crime communities. Some positive trends were demonstrated in project schools including slightly less delinquency and decreases in factors associated with delinquency. However, the projects varied in terms of implementation of the interventions, and individual project results varied substantially. Effective programs are described.

Gottfredson, D. C. *An Assessment of a Delinquency Prevention Demonstration with Individual and Environmental Interventions*. Baltimore: Johns Hopkins University, Center for Social Organization of Schools, 1984.

An experimental school-based delinquency prevention program combined schoolwide organizational change, strong management, and direct intervention for high-risk youths to improve educational experiences and reduce delinquent behavior. Evaluation results indicated improvements in school climate and reduced risk factors for the school population as a whole, but less favorable outcomes for high-risk youths exposed to direct services.

Hawkins, J. D., T. C. Lam, and D. M. Lishner. "Instructional Practices and School Misbehavior." Seattle: Center for Social Welfare Research, University of Washington, 1985.

An experimental test of the effects of improved instructional practices in seventh grade classrooms demonstrated that use of these practices was associated with improvements in student academic performance, attitudes toward school, educational commitment, and suspension and expulsion rates.

Lazar, Irving, and Richard Darlington. "Lasting Effects of Early Education: A Report from the Consortium for Longitudinal Studies." *Monographs of the Society for Research in Child Development* 47, no. 2–3 (1982).

The long-range effects of an early preschool intervention on low-income minority children are reported. Early education improved school adjustment and performance as well as attitudes and achievement orientation, although some of the positive effects were not maintained.

9

Social Service and Citizen Involvement

ROBERT B. COATES

Crime and delinquency are community problems; these problems require a response on the part of community leadership through the community's formal social control agencies such as the police and the courts. Efforts to prevent criminal and delinquent acts will also require the involvement of the primary socializing social institutions such as schools and churches, as well as the active participation of local citizens who probably are both victims and perpetrators of crime.[1]

PREVENTION, SOCIAL SERVICE, AND CITIZEN INVOLVEMENT

When the community is considered as the locus of actions directed at delinquency and crime prevention, the focus of attention is on a prevention network comprised of formal criminal justice agencies, public and private social service agencies, primary socializing institutions such as families, schools, and churches, and social networks including peers. The interaction among these groups results in policies and actions directed at prevention. Often the resulting policies and actions are as much products of interest group politics as they are of consensus. The interaction designed to influence policy and actions in many communities is typically fluid and ongoing.[2]

"Service" refers to a benefit other than some tangible product derived from labor. Many services including education, healthcare, public sanitation, transportation, and housing are regarded widely as essential to citizen well-being.

Our discussion of social service must be placed in the larger context of fundamental policy questions facing the nation. The questions are as follows: Is government responsible for providing some modicum of social service, and if so, for whom? An ideological debate often ensues, centering on the question of whether or not government should provide social services to the poor and disadvantaged. The debate is frequently characterized as a struggle among the affluent between, on the one hand, the humanitarian impulse to provide for the basic human needs of those who are unable to do so on their own, and, on the other hand, the belief that the poor and disadvantaged are evading the normative prescriptions of the desired moral order and that social service, rather than building people up, erodes the social fabric.

In this debate social service is cast in the light of public welfare for the poor and disadvantaged. As Alfred J. Kahn and Sheila B. Kammerman point out, such a depiction clouds the place and use of social service in this society:

Society masks realities by distinguishing among what it calls public welfare and social services for the poor and troubled, education and public health protections for everyone, and benefits for the affluent. It fails to recognize that, in a more basic sense, there are really two categories, not three: social services and benefits connected to problems and breakdowns (and these are not limited to the poor), and social services and benefits needed by average people under ordinary circumstances.[3]

Social services related to crime and delinquency prevention come into play when there are "problems and breakdowns" such as provision of assistance to families in coping with drug/alcohol abusing youngsters. And social services with prevention thrusts are available for "average people under ordinary circumstances" such as recreational services and social clubs for youth. Although the role of government in social service provision continues to be subject to legitimate debate, the object of social service is the welfare of the whole.

A guiding premise in this chapter is that crime and delinquency prevention is a responsibility of the whole involving government officials, social service professionals, and local citizens—both potential perpetrators and potential victims of crime. Involving "potential deviants" in prevention efforts provides opportunities for a stake in conformity. Serving others can provide occasions for social approval, pride, respect, and the netting of relationships with law-abiding role models as well as the learning of shared social skills and values.

Instead of concentrating on the clients for services, this chapter will be devoted to exploring how local citizens can and do become involved in the delivery of services for preventing crime and delinquency. We will also explore how communities and social service agencies can increase the involvement of the local citizenry in prevention efforts. We will begin by briefly considering some historical patterns of citizen involvement in crime and delinquency prevention. Then we will look at a variety of opportunities for citizen involvement. Finally, we will consider ways by which citizen involvement can be promoted and enhanced.

A BRIEF HISTORICAL OVERVIEW OF THE PLACE OF CITIZEN INVOLVEMENT IN CRIME PREVENTION

Historically, crime and delinquency prevention was a local matter to be dealt with informally by families, schools, churches, and if necessary the police officer on the beat. There was a sense that each community would take care of its own.

Managing the Deviants in Earlier Age

Depending on the nature of the community—agrarian, small town, or city— different levels of acting out behavior received differential tolerance. In rural America during the nineteenth century, for example, horse thievery was a more serious breach of the social bond than aggravated assault. Prevention efforts involved the parent prescribing and enforcing normative behavior, and to a large extent the value placed on such normative behavior was shared by other parents in the local area as well as by the teacher, the preacher, and the local business-person. Each could play a role in modeling law-abiding behavior and in enforcing the community standards of normative behavior. When young persons strayed too far from the acceptable, parents would be contacted to take appropriate action. During this era many young people had legitimate roles to play in the workforce on the family farm or in small business.

For youth and young adults who either did not or would not fit into the expected range of behavior and would not respond to the efforts of others to induce conforming behavior, several acceptable options were available short of formal processing in the criminal justice system. The police and courts could deal with them informally, and if behavior became acceptable there would be no formal record of criminal justice involvement.

The youths or young adults could decide, or perhaps at times it could be mutually agreed, that the best that could happen would be for them to strike out on their own. Many of yesterday's deviants were able to move to other developing areas of the country to start over where their demonstration of independence became an asset rather than a liability. Apprenticeships were sometimes available in the small towns and cities, and work could possibly be had on the farms and ranches. In that day, running away from home, while no easy undertaking, was not formally defined as a crime or a delinquent act.

"Taking care of our own" probably never worked smoothly and without discomfort. By today's standards, at least, it probably fostered a considerable degree of physical and psychological abuse. In order to escape, some placed themselves in essentially temporary bondage, and the responses of local citizens were unlikely to have been equitable across the board for rich and poor, for white and black, or for Protestant and Catholic. And those youths who remained recalcitrant found themselves in reformatories or houses of refuge—institutional names that do not adequately reflect the deplorable and punitive conditions of the settings.[4]

Difficulties with Social Transition

In the latter part of the nineteenth century and the early part of the twentieth century, "taking care of our own" became even more difficult. Who were "our own?" Cities were teeming with recent immigrants from many lands with different languages, colors, religions, cultures, and standards. There was also a significant migration taking place within America from the farms to the city and from the South to the North. Groups with different histories and values were located in a relatively small space competing for jobs, housing, status, and their own perceptions of the American dream. In-groups and out-groups became more sharply defined with fewer options for escaping to new acceptable frontiers. When families of different cultures experienced crime, when teachers of the dominant culture had difficulties with students from other cultures whose parents could not understand the teacher, these families and teachers turned more and more frequently to the official social control agencies, the police and the courts, for resolution of problems.

This was a period of much progressive legislation to protect young people. Child labor laws were passed to prevent the abuse of young people in sweat shops. These laws were also important to the emerging labor unions for controlling the workforce. Mandatory school attendance ages were raised. And juvenile court acts were passed allowing government to respond to delinquent acts in ways that were not previously available to them short of incarcerating youth in adult jails. Although some of these changes were laudable and progressive for their time, an unintended consequence was reducing legitimate options for youth and families for coping with deviant behavior. And crime and delinquency prevention became much more squarely a responsibility of government.

Preventing crime and delinquency became a primary responsibility of the agents of the court which was rapidly becoming professionalized, with the consequent influence of psychiatry and social work. Not only were local citizens withdrawing from prevention efforts out of frustration and turning to government for help, but an emerging set of professions was prepared to take on the task of crime and delinquency prevention. Providing social service for problem youth and problem families, removing youth from their families in the interest of the child, and correcting their past behavior became the goals. And there was little attention given to the local citizen role. In fact, there was considerable distrust between the professional and the citizen, and between the citizen and government.

More Recent Developments

This tension between the citizen and government regarding crime and delinquency prevention has been long felt. In 1934 the Chicago Area Projects were incorporated under the leadership of Clifford Shaw. These projects represented a community organizing attempt to deal with crime and delinquency prevention.

Local citizens were dissatisfied with government attempts to respond to the problem in a piecemeal manner. The Chicago Area Projects were designed to promote local citizen involvement in responding to delinquency and youth crime as a community problem. Community participation was a cornerstone of the projects. And the projects refused to accept federal monies or monies from other sources which had strings attached. Project staff organized local citizens to document the nature of community problems which in their view contributed to crime. And through persuasion and influence, they would try to alter citywide policies effecting the local community.[5]

Saul Alinsky, formerly on Shaw's staff, took this tension between citizen and government further in the 1940s with the Back of the Yard's Project. Alinsky shared Shaw's view of the importance of community participation, but took it a step further, developing tactical strategies and a philosophy supporting local citizen empowerment. Alinsky brought power politics to bear on crime and delinquency prevention. He moved from focusing specifically on delinquency to empowering families, groups, and communities to take hold, to confront, and to manage their own problems—a strategy which, if successful, would also impact on factors related to delinquency.[6]

By the 1950s and 1960s crime and delinquency prevention had clearly become a national issue. In the 1960s, the federal government became a major catalyst in the delinquency field providing incentives, directives, and at times mandates that would impact on local community ability to cope with delinquency. The federal government in cooperation with the Ford Foundation instituted the Mobilization for Youth Projects in fifteen cities across the country. The theoretical underpinning of this effort was greatly influenced by the work of Richard A. Cloward and Lloyd E. Ohlin in *Delinquency and Opportunity*.[7] Ohlin played a pivotal role as special assistant in the federal Department of Health, Education, and Welfare in coordinating this national effort. A key notion that turned out to be very difficult to implement was that representatives of local community institutions, city fathers, and key figures in the local community would participate in a rational planning phase developing the particular components of the project tailored to the needs of the local community.[8]

Difficulties encountered during the Mobilization for Youth Projects included the problem of outside people trying to identify local power influentials, roadblocks of various kinds by city officials who guarded their prerogatives for distribution of spoils on a patronage basis, and the unwillingness of individuals and groups who had seen themselves as natural enemies to coalesce and coordinate merely because of the existence of federal dollars.[9] Although the Mobilization Projects were a valiant effort at involving the federal government in what was clearly a national problem, they failed to elicit the grass-roots support needed to carry out delinquency prevention at the local level.

Today we see an unsteady balance between approaches similar to Mobilization and the Chicago Area Projects and those modeled after Alinsky's efforts. The federal government is still trying to influence direction by promulgating federal standards, issuing mandates, and setting priority areas for funding. However, the emphasis on revenue sharing and local initiative means that much of what happens at the local community level begins there with or without the help of federal funds. And localities that first believed federal money to be a godsend are now wary of seed money for development of programs that will eventually have to be funded from other sources. The local community, while pushed and pulled by outside forces, remains the front-line battleground where policies affecting crime and delinquency prevention are forged and implemented and their impact, positive or negative, is felt.

Many local social service agencies continue to grapple with how best to tap the resources of the local citizenry. For some community-based groups involvement of local citizens is a survival issue. These groups need active citizen support in order to continue politically. And because of the shrinking social service dollar they need active citizen involvement in order to continue providing a diverse array of services. Attention is being devoted to how best to draw creatively on the resources of citizens. The number of opportunities and roles for lay involvement is expanding.

OPPORTUNITIES FOR CITIZEN INVOLVEMENT

Any list of opportunities for citizen involvement in crime and delinquency prevention will obviously be incomplete. New opportunities emerge as individuals and groups come together to explore community problems and pressures on persons that contribute to crime and delinquency. The following discussion is simply meant to be illustrative, not restrictive.

Traditional Service Roles

Traditionally, citizens become involved in social service responses to the prevention of crime and delinquency by volunteering to provide some kind of service to individuals who are identified as at risk. The services run the gamut from Big Brother and Big Sister arrangements to tutoring, to skill development, and to trained professional counselors volunteering their services for a number of hours a week as direct service counselors or as case supervision consultants.

The use of volunteers as direct service providers in delinquency prevention programs is generally regarded as yielding positive results. Research suggests that volunteers can be as effective in performing many concrete service tasks as professionals. However, existing research is not notably rigorous or sophisticated, making it necessary to use considerable caution when relying on research results.[10]

Advocacy: Individual, Community, or Class

Numerous opportunities exist for citizen involvement in crime and delinquency prevention beyond the traditional direct service roles. Some of these fall under the generic rubric of advocacy. For our purposes here advocacy is defined as actions taken on behalf of individuals. These actions can be collapsed under individual case advocacy, community advocacy, and class advocacy. Rather than providing direct services to prevent crime and delinquency, the emphases in advocacy roles are linking individuals to existing services, generating additional community resources, and changing existing policies and procedures affecting service provision.[11]

Individual case advocates are used in a number of different kinds of settings to augment the work of paid staff. Typically, their task is to link persons to available resources and at times to function as ombudsmen assuring that services are being made available and that individuals are not simply shunted from one system to another. These advocates will need to be trained in the documentation of existing resources, the art of negotiating, and followup.[12]

This form of advocacy is frequently found in police, court diversion programs, and youth service bureaus. Youth and adults who are being diverted are identified to a program. Program staff assign an advocate who will make a contact to determine whether any assistance in receiving services is needed. For example, a youth is diverted by the police. The advocate makes contact with the youth and his or her family to offer assistance regarding available services. The police may have stipulated specific services in lieu of processing, or the family may be concerned about acting out behavior.

The advocate will explore the family and youth-perceived needs and discuss some possible helpful resources. These may range from family services to tutoring assistance. The advocate will work with the family weighing and assessing different opportunities. The family will be encouraged to make direct contact with the social service provider. The advocate, however, will be prepared to make the contact on behalf of the family if need be. He or she will follow up on the case in a week or two to determine whether things are proceeding satisfactorily. If not, the advocate must be prepared to start over.

Generating resources and examining how existing policies and procedures impact on youth and adults are the tasks of community advocates. They will be advocating on behalf of a group of people in the local community. For example, the advocates may attempt to garner support for more recreational resources for youth over fourteen years of age. Citizens become involved in community advocacy through informal groups and through the boards, committees, and task forces of local social service agencies. Their activities include documenting problems and conditions which they believe contribute to crime and delinquency, devising action strategies which they believe will ameliorate those conditions, and engaging the local political process to garner support for new resources or changes in policy or procedures.[13]

An example of citizen involvement in community advocacy was observed in Burlington, Vermont, where, through the assistance of staff at the University of Vermont, high school students and parents concerned about delinquency prevention conducted a survey of youth (those in school and those who had dropped out) to determine youth perceptions of need and problems. The number one concern of youth was the extent to which they believed they were hassled by police. The police were equally concerned by these findings. A task force of youth and parents with University support was established to work with police representatives in order to ease the tension between youth and police. Among the agreed on recommendations were (1) less police intervention unless there was demonstrated cause and (2) an effort by youth, parents, and the city to establish drop-in centers for youth to congregate and associate after school hours. The initial task force remained intact to monitor the progress of implementing these recommendations.

Community advocacy, with its emphasis on linking clients to resources and generating community resources, has been a traditional focus of youth service bureaus.[14] In general, many youth service bureaus have floundered and succumbed for lack of community support and funding. Where useful political relationships have been developed, adequate funding has followed allowing these bureaus to continue functioning as delinquency prevention agencies.[15]

Persons involved in class advocacy act on behalf of a class of individuals across city, state, or national jurisdictions. The primary focus of such efforts is to monitor and bring about changes in policies and procedures that will likely have an effect on crime and delinquency prevention. Activities will include policy analysis, policy development, coalition building, engagement of political processes, and followup.[16]

The efforts by citizen groups to monitor and change school suspension policies across a large city would be an example of class advocacy. The advocacy effort is carried out on behalf of a class of persons rather than forged around an individual case or restricted to a local community.

The League of Women Voters conducts court watching programs in a number of states, including Illinois, with the purpose of assuring that status offenders are handled appropriately and are not institutionalized with delinquent youth. This, too, is a class advocacy undertaking designed to respond to a class of youngsters with a focus on system responsibility. The underlying premise of the program is that intervention, if required, ought to take place outside the formal criminal justice system and that by separating status offenders from delinquents the chances of preventing delinquency are enhanced.

Numerous interest groups become involved in attempting to influence state and national legislation affecting jobs, job training, and programs that divert first-time youth and adult offenders from the formal criminal justice system— all based on the belief that such a program can prevent further delinquency or criminality.

Many class advocacy efforts in crime and delinquency prevention are managed by criminal justice professionals and watchdog groups. Those that draw on lay citizens can demonstrate a broader base of support, enhancing their chances of receiving an attentive hearing in the legislative process and bringing about change. It is especially important to involve minority groups who are so frequently the targets of crime and the recipients of social service policies developed predominately by persons representing the majority.[17] Policies regarding out-of-home placement, intake and assessment procedures of Departments of Children and Family Services, and labeling youth as predelinquent or high risks, to name a few, are among those that are too often developed without an adequate understanding of cultural diversity. For example, it has been shown that many Hispanic youth are mislabeled "retarded" because IQ tests are given in English and reflect norms of white America.[18]

Mediation of Disputes

The involvement of lay citizens in mediating disputes between individuals is a rapidly developing area that at least, in part, is designed to resolve disputes without relying entirely or sometimes explicitly on the formal criminal justice system. The mediation movement is based on the rationale that many disputes can and should be handled without relying solely on the courts and the belief that this early, "informal" intervention can contribute to the prevention of crime and delinquency.

One rubric, among many, which these mediation programs fall under is the Neighborhood Justice Center. While Neighborhood Justice Centers will use a variety of strategies for dispute resolution, mediation is one primary strategy and a fair amount of the mediation is conducted by lay citizens. Research on these programs indicates some of the advantages and disadvantages of such involvement.

Clearly the use of trained members of the community as mediators is consistent and even requisite in a model of neighborhood justice which seeks to involve citizens in the remediation of community problems often inappropriately brought before the court. The use of lay citizens provides a project with mediation staff who have a vested interest in the welfare of the community and the satisfactory reconciliation of disputing parties. Moreover, the opportunity to educate participating citizens regarding the functions and problems of the court may also serve an important function in altering community perceptions of official justice. The primary disadvantages of the use of lay citizens are the monetary costs and process time associated with the management of citizen mediators. The credibility of lay citizens may also be a factor to consider, particularly credibility with the project's major sources of referrals and its clients. Recent experience has shown that lay citizen mediator credibility is generally high.[19]

Another general rubric for these mediation programs is the Victim-Offender Reconciliation Program (VORP).[20] This program model was initially conceived in Kitchner, Ontario, and has been promoted and refined, to a large extent, in this country by the Mennonite Central Committee and by PACT.[21] The VORP approach involves bringing the offender and victim together with a trained mediator, often a trained community volunteer, to work through victim and offender feelings about the offense and to work out an agreement regarding appropriate restitution to the victim.

This approach is now used in many jurisdictions across the country. Depending on the jurisdiction, it interfaces with the formal criminal justice system at different points: in lieu of adjudication, post-adjudication, and postsentencing. Although some proponents of the approach would prefer to see the approach used with adjudicated offenders only as an alternative or partial alternative to jail time, others, including some criminal justice officials, are expanding it into diversion and prevention programs. For our purposes here, the significance of the VORP approach is its attempt to bring citizens (victims, offenders, and trained community mediators) together to work through the consequences and accountability issues of deviant behavior.

Self-Help and Mutual-Help

Self-help and mutual-help groups have mushroomed during the past two decades.[22] A link between some of these groups and social service agencies involved with crime and delinquency prevention has also emerged. Many social service agencies with a mission of prevention have facilitated the setting up of self-help groups wherein persons are brought together to help themselves and each other. Some of these groups use a professional as a facilitator; many groups do not. The range of activities is determined by the group and is often broad in scope ranging from empathetic support to skill development.

Social service agencies can play an important role in identifying persons with common concerns and in providing the impetus needed to set up such groups. An illustration of this kind of development is a local delinquency prevention agency that has operated numerous services for youth referred by courts and schools as well as for youth who ''dropped in.'' As part of a community and youth needs assessment, parents of the youth served were called to solicit their views on how well the program was meeting the needs of their youth and to inquire as to whether the parents had needs or concerns to which the program could respond. A consistent response to these questions was surprise and appreciation that any social service staff would ask parents what their needs were.

A number of developments occurred based on the results of the survey. Some parents became more involved in the operation of the program: helping out with recreational supervision and serving on program committees and on the board of directors. Furthermore, two groups of parents were set up under the self-help model. Parents come together in the evening, with childcare services provided by the agency, to discuss problems and share solutions in raising adolescents. Initially, program staff facilitated the groups, but their roles changed fairly quickly to that of being resource persons. This is an example not only of how a social service agency provided an opportunity for persons to help themselves in an organized way, but also how the agency was able to solidify its own political base and strengthen its program development.

Another example of persons helping themselves and others in delinquency prevention is the peer counseling program which social service agencies sponsor with the cooperation of local schools. Program staff train young people in problem-solving techniques and values clarification. The youth in turn work with other youth (individually or in groups) on school problems, drug and alcohol abuse, and family issues. The peer counselors are supervised by program staff.

These examples of self-help are part of a larger realization that effective service is dependent, in part, on enabling the client and his or her social network to help each other.[23] The paid professional will at some point leave the case; the social network is more likely to endure. Therefore, one of the tasks of social service is to identify and build on the natural strengths of the individual social network.

Public Education

Social service agencies involved in crime and delinquency prevention frequently recognize an important public education responsibility. In many instances, the agency's own staff will not have the needed expertise in specific areas but will draw on lay citizens who volunteer to be available for public education. The social service agency through the lay citizen involvement is providing a public service as well as demonstrating its concern for an involvement in the community. The lay expert provides a needed service and also makes known his or her areas of expertise. Clearly, topics of concern to the public are broad in scope. These may include: how the criminal justice system functions, the costs and benefits to the community of developing alternatives to institutionalization, identification of the extent of drug and alcohol abuse in the community and the range of resources available to concerned persons, parenting skills, and child and adolescent development issues. Lay experts with artistic and media skills can also help social service agencies with packaging public education materials, including spot public service announcements for local radio and television.

As indicated above, this list of opportunities for citizen involvement in social service agencies active in crime and delinquency prevention is by necessity incomplete. It includes some traditional roles and some relatively new roles. The role that an agency and a volunteer can work out is limited only by their own creativity. Issues directly related to enhancing citizen involvement are discussed below.

ENHANCING CITIZEN INVOLVEMENT

Meaningful, effective citizen involvement in social service does not simply happen because one can demonstrate need. Citizens do not generally form voluntary associations with the expressed purpose to combat crime and delinquency. Usually, voluntary associations are formed around other social needs or social problems. These associations, however, can be mobilized for crime and prevention if properly addressed by concerned citizens and social service agencies.[24] Churches, PTAs, and service organizations can represent resources for volunteers as well as allies in local community political struggles for setting social service priorities, allocating dollars for crime and delinquency prevention, and implementing policies that hold promise for positive impact on crime and delinquency.

Agencies involved in crime and delinquency prevention have major responsibilities for identifying the need for citizen involvement and providing a means for meaningful involvement. Social service staff should think through their agency's stake in citizen involvement and the citizens' stake in participating with the agency. Staff must also plan carefully as to whom they can use in volunteer roles, how these persons can be integrated into the crime and delinquency prevention effort, how they will be trained, and how they will be supervised.[25]

Incentives and Stakes

For many professionals, working with lay volunteers is a hassle to be avoided if at all possible. Such involvement can take valuable staff time, lead to problems in casework and with other organizations, and raise the public awareness of what the agency is really doing. Why then would an agency choose to develop citizen involvement? What kinds of stakes and incentives are available to the agency?

Five incentives for the social service agency are readily apparent. First, the kinds of activities needed to mount a crime and delinquency prevention effort outstrip most agency resources. Citizen involvement can increase the amount of person hours available for the prevention effort. Second, and perhaps most difficult for some professionals to appreciate, some services may be more effective if carried out with citizens. Such is the case with self-help groups. And this can be equally true with advocacy and public education efforts. Third, by drawing on a broader base of local citizens, the agency may be in a better position to link up with resources in other community groups such as churches, PTAs, block clubs, service organizations, and businesses. Each volunteer comes with a social network which can be potentially drawn on. Fourth, citizen involvement can broaden the social service options available to the agency, and it can broaden and strengthen the agency's local political base. Agency survival depends not only on adequate funding, but also on sufficient community goodwill and political clout. Fifth, citizen involvement is one step in informing the public about the nature of crime and delinquency and the community's responsibility for prevention. Thus, it is in the interest of the client, the community, and the self-interest of the agency to enhance citizen involvement in crime and delinquency prevention.

What are the incentives for the citizen? As trite as it may sound, many citizens are interested in real opportunities to serve their communities. The motivation to be a useful, contributing member of a community cuts across all ages, races, social classes, and religions. Social service staff make a serious mistake if they accept the common stereotype that citizens are merely apathetic or don't care. While the typical volunteer is reasonably well educated and belongs to the middle class, lower class persons do get involved when they see that something is being done that can positively affect their lives now as well as in the future.[26] With fewer resources to expend, it is difficult to expect the poor to become active in large-scale efforts to improve the "collective good" in the distant future.[27] In the self-help example described above, lower class parents became involved in the delinquency prevention program when they saw that it was meeting some of the needs of their children and that it could offer support to them as parents. The current and future benefits allowed these parents to place some priority on becoming involved in committees, boards and as resource persons to the various program components.

Another incentive for lay involvement is experience. Some persons are looking for volunteer experiences that may enable them to obtain social service employment or admission into educational programs. Others are looking for a volunteer experience that provides diversity in their life experience.

One way in which social service agencies can reward volunteer service is through symbolic expression of appreciation for service rendered. Some agencies will hold annual dinners where volunteers will receive public recognition for their efforts. Some will give out awards such as the Outstanding Community Volunteer of the Year. These expressions of appreciation require little cost and yet can go a long way toward extending goodwill to the community and its representatives as well as providing some good media attention for the program.

Attracting and Screening Volunteers

Waiting for persons to come in off the street to offer their services is not a very effective way of identifying appropriate volunteers. Citizens do need to know that the agency exists and what volunteer opportunities are available. Some agencies have found that local newspaper articles and advertisements generate interest. A key to publicizing the agency and its volunteer opportunities, however, is building strong interinstitutional ties. Linkages with local churches, service organizations, and colleges have proven quite useful. The volunteer opportunities ought to be described in a clear, concise manner similar to any other job description.

Social service agencies can coordinate some elements of identifying and screening of volunteers to diminish duplication of effort. For example, the Blue Gargoyle is a delinquency prevention agency serving predominantly low-income youth and families. In addition to these services, it operates a Volunteer Service Bureau. Students from the University of Chicago and persons from the community at large make themselves known to the Bureau staff. Interested persons are invited in for an interview that documents their skills and interests. Bureau staff maintain and update a list of local community groups that have need for volunteers. An initial screening is done to match the person with one or two appropriate community groups. The prospective volunteer then contacts those groups for an additional interview and possible placement. The Bureau conducts a followup interview with the volunteer and the community group to assess the adequacy of the placement and the volunteer experience.

An operating principle is that the successful volunteer placement must prove to be satisfying and rewarding to the volunteer as well as to the community group or agency. The volunteer pool consists primarily of college students, recent retirees, and mothers of preschool children who desire to maintain and sharpen their skills in preparation for future employment. This systematic approach to selecting and matching volunteers with social service groups has proven to be beneficial for both the volunteers and the social service agencies.

The screening done by an agency can also prevent negative consequences for the agency and for the citizen. Not everyone who volunteers will be appropriate; some, in fact, may be detrimental for both the clients and the agency. Their reasons for becoming involved may be to have an opportunity to exercise their own authoritarian needs or to obtain service for themselves. Too many agencies have been "burned" by the volunteer who is psychologically or sexually unstable. These agencies will often cite past negative experiences as reasons for not continuing to solicit or develop citizen involvement. Yet such experiences are, in part, the results of poor advance screening, poor training, and inadequate supervision.

Training of Volunteers

Although a social service agency seeks citizen involvement because it wants to draw on the perspective and skills of the volunteer, it should not be assumed that no further training is required. The specifics of the training are dependent on the expected tasks. The volunteer will need to know how he or she fits into the agency (this should include a job description), and how the agency fits into the larger social service network of the community and the criminal justice system. Each opportunity for citizen involvement described above has a set of skills attached to it and can be passed on to the volunteer. Training packages can and should be developed for roles as diverse as individual case advocacy and membership on the board of directors.

The training should be set forth in a concise and interesting manner. Where possible, experiential techniques should be used to demonstrate the relevance of theory and practice. One component of training frequently includes staff persons and volunteers working side by side for a short period of time. For example, the training of VORP citizen mediators involves a number of sessions focused on mediation skills, dealing with anger, differing perspectives on justice, and role playing. After these pedagogical sessions are completed, the citizen mediator and a staff person will operate as a team for two or three cases before the volunteer is permitted to do mediation solely.

Social service agencies with good training for volunteers are particularly attractive to volunteers because they know that when they cease working with the agency they will have some concrete skills to take with them to be applied in other settings or in their daily routines.

Supervision: A Vital Function

One of the worst occurrences that can happen for volunteer morale is to be assigned a task without systematic supervision being available.[28] Volunteers usually want to feel that they are part of something. From an agency and client perspective, supervision is equally important. The volunteer will be representing the agency in the community and will be responsible for an important set of tasks.

Volunteers need feedback on how they are doing and need to be held accountable for their work. Depending on the tasks, supervisory sessions may be held weekly, biweekly, or monthly. The key here is to have systematic supervision that provides structure and rewards. Supervision should be at least as carefully designed and systematically implemented as supervision of paid staff. As with staff there ought to be room for volunteer feedback on changes regarding tasks, program, and training needs.

CONCLUSION

The community role in social service directed at crime and delinquency prevention has moved back and forth between the poles of wanting "to take care of our own" to letting the government and social service professionals do it. Today we are witnessing a movement to achieve a better balance between these two poles. Crime and delinquency are seen as community problems. Government and social service professionals cannot handle these problems by themselves.

Prevention of crime and delinquency is a shared community responsibility— shared among government officials, social service professionals, and concerned citizens. Older opportunities for citizen involvement remain, while new opportunities are being forged. Unforeseen opportunities are no doubt present and will emerge as government officials, social service professionals, and concerned citizens work together to tackle the complex underlying causes that lead to crime and delinquency.

Citizen involvement in crime and delinquency prevention at its worst leads to frustration and burned up and turned off resources. Citizen involvement at its best represents a partnership that leads to more effective service, better understanding of community problems, and a broader political base for community problem solving.

There is a growing sense among government officials, social service professionals, and concerned citizens of all races and social classes that active citizen participation and collaboration in crime and delinquency prevention is not simply a matter of choice. The stakes are too high in terms of quality of life in our communities for crime and delinquency prevention to be the domain of any one professional group, political party, or social class.

NOTES

1. Joseph G. Weis and J. David Hawkins, *Preventing Delinquency. Reports of the National Juvenile Justice Assessment Centers* (Washington, D.C.: Office of Juvenile Justice and Delinquency Prevention, U.S. Department of Justice, 1981), pp. 18–22; Robert B. Coates, "Thinking About the Community Delinquency Prevention Arena: Implications for Research," in Allan Borrowski and James Murray, eds., *Juvenile Delinquency in Australia* (North Ryde: Methuen Australia, 1985), pp. 2–3.

2. Coates, "Thinking About the Community Delinquency Prevention Arena," pp. 9–17.

3. Alfred J. Kahn and Sheila B. Kammerman, *Not for the Poor Alone: European Social Services* (Philadelphia: Temple University Press, 1975), p. x (emphases theirs).

4. Paul Lerman, "Delinquency and Social Policy: A Historical Perspective," *Crime and Delinquency* 22 (October 1977): 387–389; Steven L. Schlossman, *Love and the American Delinquent* (Chicago: University of Chicago Press, 1977), pp. 33–54.

5. Clifford R. Shaw and Henry D. McKay, *Juvenile Delinquency and Urban Areas*, Rev. ed. (Chicago: University of Chicago Press, 1969), pp. 322–326; Anthony Sorrentino, *Organizing Against Crime: Redeveloping the Neighborhood* (New York: Human Sciences Press, 1977), pp. 81–103; Steven Schlossman and Michael Sedlak, "The Chicago Area Project Revisited," *Crime and Delinquency* 29 (July 1983): 399–409.

6. Saul Alinsky, *Rules for Radicals* (New York: Random House, 1971), p. 113.

7. Richard A. Cloward and Lloyd E. Ohlin, *Delinquency and Opportunity* (New York: Free Press, 1960).

8. Peter Marris and Martin Rein, *Dilemmas of Social Reform: Poverty and Community Action in the United States* (New York: Atherton Press, 1969), p. 19.

9. Ibid. See especially Chapters 6 and 7.

10. Michael C. Dixon and William E. Wright, *Juvenile Delinquency Prevention Programs* (Washington, D.C.: National Science Foundation, 1974), pp. 5–6; Frank P. Scioli, Jr., and Thomas J. Cook, "How Effective Are Volunteers? Public Participation in the Criminal Justice System," *Crime and Delinquency* 22 (April 1976): 195–196.

11. Robert B. Coates, *Advocacy In Juvenile Justice: Concept and Practice* (Valparaiso, Ind.: PACT Institute of Justice, 1981), pp. 1–8.

12. Ibid., pp. 13–18.

13. Ibid., pp. 22–29.

14. William Underwood, *A National Study of Youth Service Bureaus* (Washington, D.C.: U.S. Department of Health, Education and Welfare, Youth Development and Delinquency Prevention, 1972).

15. H. Ted Rubin, *Juvenile Justice: Policy, Practice, and Law* (Santa Monica: Goodyear Publishing Co., 1979), p. 126.

16. Coates, *Advocacy in Juvenile Justice: Concept and Practice*, pp. 32–40.

17. John F. Longres, "Minority Groups: An Interest-group Perspective," *Social Work* 27 (January 1982): 13; Sandra M. Stehno, "Differential Treatment of Minority Children in Service Systems," *Social Work* 27 (January 1982): 44.

18. Jane Mercer, *Labeling the Mentally Retarded* (Berkeley: University of California, 1973).

19. Daniel McGillis, Joan Mullen, and Mary Ann Beck, *Neighborhood Justice Centers: An Analysis of Potential Models; Executive Summary* (Washington, D.C.: National Institute of Law Enforcement and Criminal Justice, 1977), p. 37.

20. Mark Umbreit, *Crime and Reconciliation: Creative Options for Victims and Offenders* (Nashville, Tenn.: Abingdon Press, 1985), p. 98.

21. Ibid., p. 99.

22. Marie Killilea, "Mutual Help Organization: Interpretations of the Literature," in Gerald Caplan and Marie Killiea, eds., *Support Systems and Mutual Help* (New York: Grune & Stratton, 1976), pp. 37–93.

23. Robert B. Coates, "Community-Based Services for Juvenile Delinquents: Concept and Implications," *Journal of Social Issues* 37 (Summer 1981): 95–96; Dolores Norton, Jose Morales, and Edwina Andrews, *The Neighborhood Self-Help Project*, Occasional Paper No. 9 (Chicago: School of Social Service Administration, University of Chicago, 1980).

24. Paul J. Lavrakas and Elicia J. Herz, "Citizen Participation in Neighborhood Crime Prevention," *Criminology* 20 (November 1982): 493–494.

25. Ira M. Schwartz, Donald R. Jensen, and Michael J. Mahoney, *Volunteers in Juvenile Justice* (Washington, D.C.: National Institute of Law Enforcement and Criminal Justice, 1977).

26. Pamela Oliver, " 'If You Don't Do It, Nobody Else Will': Active and Token Contributors to Collective Action," *American Sociological Review* 49 (October 1984): 608.

27. David J. O'Brien, "Public Goods Dilemma and Apathy of Poor Toward Neighborhood Organization," *Social Service Review* 48 (June 1974): 229.

28. Schwartz, Jensen, and Mahoney, *Volunteers in Juvenile Justice*, pp. 47–48.

BIBLIOGRAPHY

Coates, Robert B. *Advocacy in Juvenile Justice: Concept and Practice*. Valparaiso, Ind.: PACT Institute of Justice, 1981.

   A conceptual framework of advocacy is developed. Types of advocacy include: individual case, community, and class. Practice principles are set forth with illustrations from the field of juvenile justice.

Froland, Charles, Diane L. Pancoast, Nancy J. Chapman, and Priscilla J. Kimboko. *Helping Networks and Human Services*. Beverly Hills, Calif.: Sage Publications, 1981.

   "Helping networks" describe a wide range of informal helping activities. Thirty social service agencies were studied in the search for innovative attempts to bridge those networks and formally delivered services.

Gilbert, Neil. "Policy Issues in Primary Prevention." *Social Work* 27 (July 1982): 293–297.

   The policy issues, Gilbert declares, are identification of clients, the unanticipated consequences of intervention, and the capacity of social work to implement primary prevention.

Lavrakas, Paul J., and Elicia J. Herz. "Citizen Participation in Neighborhood Crime Prevention." *Criminology* 20 (November 1982): 479–498.

Based on a random telephone survey of a major metropolitan area, the authors look at citizen participation in crime prevention. They conclude that such participation is often the result of general tendencies for community-based voluntary action rather than because of fear of crime.

O'Brien, David J. "Public Goods Dilemma and Apathy of Poor Toward Neighborhood Organization." *Social Service Review* 48 (June 1974): 229–244.

O'Brien contends that increased participation of the poor at the neighborhood level requires organizers to develop incentive structures making participation an appropriate rational approach. Appeals to the common good may fall short if one has only minimal resources to spare for a collective effort.

Oliver, Pamela. " 'If You Don't Do It, Nobody Else Will': Active and Token Contributors to Collective Action." *American Sociological Review* 49 (October 1984): 601–610.

Oliver presents findings from a study on local collective action in Detroit. The most active persons often do so because they believe that if they do not nobody else will. The most active participants tended to be better educated, with closer ties to the neighborhoods.

Rueveni, Uri, Ross V. Speck, and Joan L. Speck, eds. *Therapeutic Intervention: Healing Strategies for Human Services*. New York: Human Sciences Press, 1982.

In lieu of one-to-one therapies, the contributors argue that health and mental health delivery must take into account the importance of linking troubled people to family, community, and neighborhoods.

Schlossman, Steven L., and Michael Sedlak. "The Chicago Area Project Revisited." *Crime and Delinquency* 29 (July 1983): 398–462.

The authors analyzed previously unused archival records detailing the early experience of the Chicago Area Project in the Russell Square neighborhood of South Chicago. They point out that more may have been accomplished in this neighborhood participation model than was earlier assumed. Links between community action and diminished delinquency rates are discussed.

Weiss, Joseph G., and J. David Hawkins. *Preventing Delinquency. Reports of the National Juvenile Justice Assessment Centers*. Washington, D.C.: Office of Juvenile Justice and Delinquency Prevention, U.S. Department of Justice, 1981.

A "comprehensive model of delinquency prevention" is based on the integration of control and cultural deviance theories. Key factors explored are family, school, peers, employment, and the community setting.

10

Dealing with Crime on the Streets

JOHN P. CONRAD

For most citizens, crime on the streets refers to the crimes most feared: robbery, forcible rape, assault, and burglary. The other "index crimes" qualify as street crimes in the sense that they are often committed by the same kinds of people—in general, criminal opportunists.[1] They are unskilled men and women with neither the talents, the resources, nor the opportunities to plan and commit the complex and much more remunerative offenses open to the professional thief or the white-collar criminal, or those engaged in organized crime. These latter more "sophisticated" criminals also commit index crimes, but do not contribute significantly to the crimes of physical violence.

The street criminal responds to simple opportunities. An elderly widow living alone in an easily accessible tenement, a well-dressed man walking at night on an apparently deserted street, a young woman waiting for help with a disabled car are all opportunities open to those who have no scruples about the use of physical force. The fear that they engender in American cities has seriously distorted the quality of urban life. For the criminal justice system this kind of criminal has become an overriding preoccupation.

In the review that follows, we will consider three levels of intervention by criminal justice. Primary intervention is the operation of the police in investigating, arresting, and charging offenders. In effectively carrying out these missions, the police do much to deter potential offenders as well as initiating the restraint of those they apprehend. Our consideration of secondary interventions is directed at the requirements and the options for the restraint of offenders convicted of street crimes. No one should expect that their incapacitation by imprisonment will greatly reduce the incidence of violence, but criminologists have given much attention in recent years to the identification of dangerous street criminals and the potentiality of differential sentencing in improving their control.

Tertiary interventions are the controls imposed on offenders returning to the community after imprisonment, or, in some cases, in lieu of a prison sentence.

We contend that the effective administration of these interventions is interdependent. When each level of intervention is fair, empirically sound, and predictable, a maximum control of street crime will be achieved. That does not mean that the complete elimination of urban violence is within the reach of criminal justice. It does mean that criminal justice can approach that goal much more closely than is now the case.

INNOVATIVE SOLUTIONS TO SLIPPING CONTROL

With the publication of the reports of the President's Commission on Law Enforcement and the Administration of Justice in 1967, a campaign against street crime took on a national scope.[2] From the Commission's recommendations there emerged the Law Enforcement Assistance Administration (LEAA) and its program of grants to improve the efficiency of the police, courts, and the correctional apparatus. In 1973 the LEAA reinforced the attack on the nation's street crime problem with the reports of its National Advisory Commission on Criminal Justice Standards and Goals.[3] That commission reaffirmed a federal commitment to the reduction of street crime, intensifying the programs of the LEAA.

Although these reports and many other publications stressed the seriousness of the problem, and despite many notable improvements in the administration of justice, a reduction of the prevalence of these generally dreaded crimes has not rewarded the recommendations of these commissions nor the programs of the LEAA. In 1977 the rate of violent crime was 466.6 per 100,000; in 1982 the rate was 555.3 per 100,000. The latest data on police clearance rates for robbery average 25 percent nationally, 51 percent for forcible rape, and 15 percent for burglary. In 1977 these clearance rates were 27 percent for robbery, 51 percent for forcible rape, and 16 percent for burglary.[4] These percentages have not changed markedly for many years.

In the terminology of criminal justice, a police clearance means no more than the identification and arrest of the offender. Not all arrested offenders are prosecuted, not all prosecuted offenders are convicted, and not all convicted offenders are placed under effective control. It is characteristic of the still primitive condition of criminal justice statistics that precise data on these "shortfalls" have never been collected. Close observers of the system have long known that the flow of offenders from the police booking to the prison gate dwindles at each transaction point, but we still have no regularly maintained information about this flow on an offense-by-offense basis.[5] In dealing with crime on the streets, the criminal justice system is still far from the level of effectiveness desired by the general public. Benchmarks for measuring progress and interpreting the lack of it are virtually nonexistent.

In this chapter we will try to outline measures that can be taken to improve this unsatisfactory situation. Many of the anticrime tactics we will suggest call for substantially larger public expenditures on the agencies of criminal justice. Other programs call for fundamental changes in our traditional control of offenders, perhaps at less cost to the taxpayer. The times require innovation. Fortunately, there is a significant mass of research that points to avenues toward increased effectiveness through purposeful intervention by the various agencies of criminal justice.

It cannot be stressed too often that effectiveness must be measured statistically. Recent years have seen marked strides toward systematic monitoring of criminal justice, but relatively few states and cities have completed data banks that enable their policy makers and administrators to know how well they are accomplishing their goals. No one can be sure of the potential of innovation until progress beyond benchmarks can be gauged.

The social forces that generate crime on the streets are far beyond the reach of criminal justice. In this chapter we will abstain from reference to the conditions that propel young men and women into vicious and predatory behavior. We will limit this discussion to three levels of intervention and to the available information that suggests effective change.

PRIMARY INTERVENTION: POLICE IN THE URBAN ENVIRONMENT

To prevent street crimes from being committed in the first place is basic strategy for the criminal justice system. The presence of the police in the community reduces the chances of an offender making a "score" and getting away with it. Nowhere is deterrence by the police infallibly effective. We believe that the primary intervention by the police can be a much more positive influence in reducing street crime. In this section we will discuss the general principles by which this objective might be reached.

Comparison with Foreign Cities

American travelers are regularly impressed with the relative order and sense of personal safety in foreign cities, although more recent terrorist incidents have been disturbing. Although the traditions affecting the administration of justice in Western Europe and Japan also affect the incidence of crime, the number, organization, and development of the police undoubtedly contribute to the lower rates of street crime in the major cities of the West and Japan.

The Prefecture of Paris employs 35,000 police to enforce the law in a city of 2.3 million. That figure compares with 25,000 police in New York City for a population of 7 million.[6] Paris is not free of crime by any means, and we do not have data that enable us to compare the rates of crime and police clearances. Nevertheless, it is obvious that with much greater personnel for a much smaller population, the Paris police can more nearly approach the appearance of ubiquitousness and clear more crimes than is possible in New York. The American investment in police expenditures is unlikely to reach French levels, but the lesson should not be lost that the success of the police in their crime prevention role depends in part on a realistic provision for personnel.

Travelers' impressions and isolated data are unsatisfactory foundations for policy comparisons. For a more comprehensive contrast we may turn to Japan, where comparable data are more readily available. Again, there are enormous cultural and economic differences that lead to the low rates of crime in Japan, and we do not minimize their importance. Nevertheless, there is some crime, and some of it is serious. Recent Japanese statistics show that in 1980 a total of 1,812,798 crimes were reported to the police, of which 1,357,461 were listed as felonies. Of this total, the lion's share consisted of various forms of thievery—1,107,477 incidents. There were 2,208 robberies and 2,610 rapes nationwide in Japan for the whole year. Tokyo, a city slightly larger than New York, had 505 robbery reports and 374 rape reports; for the same year New York City had 100,550 robbery reports and 3,711 forcible rape reports.[7]

According to William Clifford, from whose authoritative account the following data are taken, the police clearance rate for all crime, excluding traffic offenses, is about 58 percent.[8] Clearances for the major street crimes were 81 percent for robbery, 91 percent for rape, and 51 percent for theft. Conviction rates were over 90 percent. The deterrent effect of this level of clearance and conviction is reflected in a crime rate which for many years has been stable or falling.

Applications to American Patrols

To dismiss these low rates of crime and high rates of clearance as irrelevant to the American situation because of the cultural differences between the United States and Japan is to refuse to consider the potential usefulness of the Japanese model of police organization for adaptation in the improvement of law enforcement in this country. For the purposes of the prevention of street crime, we need only discuss the radically different deployment of the police in the metropolitan centers.

The basic unit of police operations is the "police box," which is a small police station. There are about 16,000 boxes in all, nearly 6,000 of which are located in the major urban centers. In rural districts the box may be manned by one officer; in the large metropolitan centers enough personnel may be assigned to maintain round-the-clock patrols and officers on continuous duty at the box. Much stress is laid on the box officers' responsibility for knowing their neighborhood thoroughly. Each resident is regularly visited, not for surveillance but for service, and police officers are expected to furnish information and advice to their neighbors as well as to arrest criminals and provide public protection. As in industrial management, the criminal justice system in Japan relies for its effectiveness on the development of good personal relations.

Studies have raised many questions about the effectiveness of squad car patrol—the standard element of urban police operations in the United States—in which rapid response time is the goal to be achieved. Nevertheless, the police still rely primarily on development of technology to increase the speed and efficiency of impersonal, professional, and socially detached officers in accomplishing the tasks of patrol, apprehension, arrest, and identification.

Some promising experiments in police precinct organization have been made, notably in New York, Los Angeles, and Dayton, Ohio, but standardization of these innovations has not followed.[9] It is not contended that the improvement of police technology is futile, but it should be accompanied by changes in the relation of personnel to the communities they serve. The Japanese model stresses the close familiarity of the police officer with a neighborhood which he or she is responsible for knowing. It is a model that resembles British policing at its best.[10] It need not be obtrusive, but when carried out with a conscientious commitment to service, it will markedly increase clearance of crimes committed and deter potential criminals from committing them in a neighborhood where citizens have easy access to the police.

This is primary intervention to increase the deterent effect of the police through increased visibility by the public, increased knowledge of the community by patrolling personnel, and increased clearance of the crimes committed. The literal adaptation of Japanese police operations to conditions in New York and Chicago is surely impractical, and could not bring about a reduction of street crime to Japanese levels. But it is reasonable to expect that much urban crime can be prevented by adapting the principles of Japanese police deployment to the conditions in our cities. As principles they should not be thought of as peculiarly Japanese in origin. They represent good applied social psychology, a resource common to advanced societies everywhere.

SECONDARY INTERVENTION: PREDICTION, RESTRAINT, AND TREATMENT

After the apprehension of an offender who has committed a crime of violence, the system must act against that person through the imposition of a sanction. The purposes of punishment are first of all to condemn the criminal act, but in punishing the courts may accomplish other objectives, among them the control of the offender. For the purpose of prevention, incarceration in a correctional facility will assure that the offender cannot commit another crime against the general public for as long as he or she is locked up. For some offenders, particularly those who are novices in crime, a program of strict supervision in the community may sufficiently restrict their activities so that the public is protected from them. In considering these choices, a judge must estimate the risk the offender presents of committing more crimes if the restrictions on his or her movements are insufficient. Recent research offers some empirical guidance to reinforce the intuitive judgments on which decision makers have traditionally relied.

Prediction of High-Rate Offenders

From the early 1920s criminologists and statisticians have collaborated on the creation of actuarial tables by which the performance of a released prisoner on parole could be predicted.[11] Some ingenious models were developed, but relatively little use was made of them by the parole boards for whose benefit they were designed. Nevertheless, a good deal of experience was gained with the use of predictors selected from the criminal histories and personal background variables of the offenders whose future criminality was to be forecast.

The experience with parole prediction was adapted for the prediction of future criminal careers by Peter Greenwood, a criminologist directing a study of habitual criminals for the Rand Corporation. Having completed a series of investigations of criminal careers in California, Michigan, and Texas, he noted that in self-report questionnaires administered to convicts in prisons of these states, some reports showed an extraordinarily high rate of criminal activity.[12] Reviewing his data, he divided his universe into three categories: high-, medium-, and low-rate offenders. Some of the high-rate offenders reported over 200 burglaries a year, as compared with about five burglaries a year for medium-rate offenders. High-rate robbers reported an average of thirty-one muggings a year, compared to about two per year for the low-rate predator.

Greenwood reasoned that if the offenders who were destined to become high-rate burglars or robbers could be identified early in their careers, steps could be taken to place them under firm control, thereby preventing a large volume of crime. Making use of the predictors used by earlier investigators, he found that distinctions could be made among high-, medium-, and low-rate offenders. Seven predictor characteristics could be identified in the personal and criminal histories of any offender, to be scored zero if absent, one if present. When added together, a score of four or more identifies a high-rate offender, two to three is a medium rate offender, and less than two predicts a low rate. The high-rate offender who is identified early, perhaps after his or her first arrest for robbery or burglary, would be given a selectively incapacitating sentence to a longer term of imprisonment than a medium- or low-rate offender would receive.[13] If prudently administered, Greenwood thought, the robbery rate in California might be reduced by as much as 20 percent by increasing the terms for high-rate robbers by 25 percent.

How accurate are Greenwood's predictors in identifying the high-rate offenders and weeding out those whose threat to public safety is less persistent? Their past performance in forecasting serious recidivism of parolees is not encouraging. In a review by John Monahan, the false-positive rate in parole prediction was estimated to be a minimum of 54 percent.[14] Greenwood himself concedes that the false-positive percentage is substantial in his selection incapacitation model, perhaps higher than 40 percent.[15] His Rand colleagues, Jan M. Chaiken and Marcia R. Chaiken, estimate that the "violent predator," a class similar to Greenwood's "high-rate robber," cannot be statistically identified without in-

clusion of about 30 percent false-positives.[16] In a hostile critique, Andrew von
Hirsch estimates the false-positive rate at 56 percent, but does not present the
basis for this figure.[17] Whatever the level of inaccuracy may be, the use of the
Greenwood model of selective incapacitation as the primary criterion for sentencing must allow for the probable restraint of a great many offenders whose
future criminality will be insufficient to justify prolonged incarceration.

But even if Greenwood's predictive model could be substantially improved
and ethically justified, it would still be a probabilistic approach to sentencing.
To many commentators the use of such methods to make decisions is fundamentally objectionable. As Moynihan put the matter,

> . . . [S]ocial science *must* be a quantitative discipline dealing with statistical probabilities.
> Law, by contrast, enters the realm of the merely probable at some risk. For the law,
> even when dealing with the most political of issues, must assert that there are the firmest,
> established grounds in past settlements on which to order future settlements. . . .
>
> "In this circumstance, perhaps the first thing a jurist will wish to know about the social
> sciences is: How good are they? How well do they predict? . . . [I]t is a melancholy fact
> that . . . even the most rigorous efforts in social science come up with devastatingly
> imprecise stuff.[18]

Policy of Incapacitation

To answer Moynihan's question with regard to selective incapacitation, it must
be said that it does not predict well enough. It is improbable that it will ever
predict well enough for the purposes of just sentencing. The usefulness of this
predictive model as an adjunct in the sentencing process may be acceptable as
an item for consideration, along with all the other elements of a convicted
defendant's situation. It should never be the controlling determinant of the action
to be taken by the court.

This is not to say that there is no such thing as a high-rate offender. The
indisputable service rendered by Greenwood and his colleagues at Rand is the
attention they have drawn to this class of criminal. Although the criminal justice
system should never rely on a statistical predictive system alone to identify high-
rate offenders for enhanced incarceration, it should be the responsibility of the
courts to make a determination, *based on all the available information about a
convicted offender's record*, as to the probable course of his or her future criminal
career if he or she is allowed to return to the community without restraint. A
recent review by James Q. Wilson of the application of the high-rate offender
concept enlarges at length on the opportunities for street crime control that have
been opened by Greenwood's imaginative study.[19]

Any search for improvement in the control of street crime through more
stringent policies of incapacitation must take into account serious difficulties in
implementation. In a study of the careers of violent offenders, Stuart Miller,
Simon Dinitz, and John P. Conrad found that recidivism after the second arrest

for any offense approached 80 percent for any crime and about 50 percent for a violent crime.[20] No policy suggests itself for the control of such offenders that will not needlessly draw false-positives into the net. Nevertheless, a class of offenders who are arrested for crimes with such frequency (and who probably commit more crimes for which they are not apprehended) requires special sentencing provisions, even within the most strict construction of the just deserts model of sanctions. For the safe control of many of these men and women, no other course is open than enhanced terms of imprisonment. To incorporate this policy within the just deserts model requires the legal theorist to modify his or her insistence that offenders must be sentenced to equal terms for equal crimes regardless of their records or their prospects for committing more.

That requirement is of little concern to the criminal justice pragmatist. For many decades most American states have provided in their criminal statutes for enhanced minimum terms for persons convicted of certain offenses (usually, but not always, crimes against the person), when a prior felony is pleaded and proved. The "justice model" proposed by David Fogel explicitly provides for enhancement of this kind.[21] The legitimacy of "enhancement" is recognized in the salient factors of the parole and sentencing guidelines adopted by the United States Parole Commission.[22] Enhancement receives even more stress in the Minnesota Sentencing Guidelines, in which a prior felony on record adds a unit to the offender's locus on the risk axis.[23]

The clear purpose of this policy is incapacitation, and the reliance on prior offenses to determine the degree of enhancement is a continued commitment to the view that the past predicts the future—the repetitive criminal is probably going to repeat again. Interest in the use of incapacitation has become much more explicit during the last decade with the decline of lip-service to the "rehabilitative ideal." James Q. Wilson provided the momentum in his influential book, *Thinking About Crime*, published in 1975.[24] In this disquisition, Wilson observed that "most serious crime is committed by repeaters."[25] He went on to a proposition that virtually demands a policy of incapacitation: "[S]ome persons will shun crime even if we do nothing to deter them, while others will seek it out even if we do everything to reform them. Wicked people exist. Nothing avails except to set them apart from innocent people."[26]

Unfortunately, if wicked people are to be set apart, even by the most prudent definition of the terms, the criminal justice system must resort to extensive use of incarcerative penalties. To some extent, the increasing severity of new criminal legislation and judicial sentencing policies is already accomplishing this end, with the alarming consequence that the nation's prisons and jails are more crowded than ever before.

Literal adoption of Wilson's demand for incapacitation would require expansion of the prison system far beyond its present bounds. In a statistical experiment using the police and court records in Columbus, Ohio, Stephen Van Dine, John P. Conrad, and Simon Dinitz explored the effectiveness of various sentencing policies that might have been adopted to prevent street crimes committed in that city during the year 1973.[27] Van Dine and his colleagues reasoned that the persons arrested for such crimes could not have committed them had they been sentenced to five years of imprisonment on the occasion of their last previous conviction of *any* felony. Research was designed to investigate the numbers of offenders who might have been thus prevented from committing a violent offense in 1973.

The results were instructive and indicate a serious dilemma to be resolved in the formulation of any new sentencing policy calling for the prolonged restraint of violent offenders. The basic data are simple to present. There were 2,892 violent crimes reported to the Columbus police in 1973. Of this number, 638 offenses were charged against 342 persons, all of whom were arrested, and for the purposes of the experiment it was assumed that all were guilty as charged. In a review of their dossiers, it transpired that 181 had never been arrested for a felony before, and therefore the crimes for which they were arrested could not have been prevented by an incapacitative sentence imposed at the time of their last previous felony conviction. That left 161 offenders with previous felony convictions. These 161 individuals were reduced to 152, nine of whom had been convicted more than five years before 1973. These 152 offenders had committed 210 of the 2,892 violent offenses of 1973—a modest 7.3 percent of the total.

Taking into account clearances of violent crimes that could not be scored against those arrested—as for example, offenses committed by insane persons and those committed by juveniles—there were 2,100 uncleared crimes. To account for these unknowns—what used to be called the "dark figure of crime"— calls for a great leap into speculation. It was certain that many, if not most, of these crimes could be attributed to the 342 men and women who were actually arrested for similar offenses in 1973. Although some of these offenses might have been committed by persons who were never caught, and others might be attributed to transients passing through Columbus, the most probable explanation was that a very large percentage of them were committed by those who were arrested.

Making the untenable assumption that *all* the uncleared crimes could be charged to the persons who had a felony conviction between 1968 and 1973, it was calculated that 47.6 percent of the violent offenses committed in 1973 could have been prevented by the five-year term to be imposed for any felony. That speculation required that all the violence reported in 1973 was perpetrated by persons already known to the police. Imposing a distribution of the uncleared offenses that was proportionate to the distribution obtained between the repeaters and the "virgins," it was decided that the most reasonable level of prevention would be about 34.4 percent of the 2,892 crimes reported.[28]

But to maintain a sentencing policy of such stringency would increase the number of men and women to be incarcerated to unprecedented proportions. It was calculated that this increase by itself, not counting other persons to be imprisoned for other reasons, would bloat the Ohio prison population from about 9,000 in 1972 to at least 42,000.[29] Applying a methodology somewhat similar to Van Dine's to violent crime data in Denver, Joan Petersilia and Peter Greenwood concluded that preventive sentences would reduce violent crime by 31 percent, but would increase the Colorado prison population by 450 percent.[30]

Other preventive strategies were tested by Van Dine and his associates, but all fell far short of the results to be obtained by the five-year sentence to be imposed for any felony. Clearly, incapacitative sentences will prevent a substantial amount of violence, but at a social and economic cost that would propel the criminal justice system into new political, administrative, and fiscal crises. There can be no serious question of the value of enhancing the sentences of repetitive violent offenders. The data presented here show that systematic enhancement on a case-by-case basis will achieve modest reductions—far below the 30 to 35 percent sometimes claimed. We believe that prudent administration, using a system of guidelines by which terms in prison are limited to apparent necessity and available resources for control, will at least discharge the state's responsibilities for the prevention of predictable crime.

The trend toward much increased severity in sentencing violent street criminals to prison has already played an ominous part in grossly overcrowding the maximum security prisons in the more populous states. Idleness is the rule. Few prisons had enough activity to keep convicts occupied before the inundation commenced, and as the crowding has worsened educational, vocational, and psychological programs have deteriorated.

Although the "rehabilitative ideal" was never a practical objective for more than a few exceptional offenders, the disregard of programmed activity makes imprisonment an even more destructive experience than ever before. Not even the most well-balanced citizen could survive a regime of idleness featuring daily perils from predatory convicts without becoming worse for the experience. The damage to the kind of men and women sentenced as violent offenders must assure that at best on release they will be public charges, but that many of them will resume their vicious careers for want of the capability of doing anything else. Realism compels an urgency to installing a full program of educational and industrial activity in any facility designed for the confinement of violent young men and women for long terms of imprisonment.

TERTIARY INTERVENTION: CONTROL OF THE OFFENDER IN THE COMMUNITY

Necessity is the mother of invention, and a crisis hastens parturition. As already stressed in the previous section, the perceived need for more restraint for repetitively violent offenders has gravely strained the capacity of American prisons, especially those designed for the containment of convicts serving long sentences. Means must be found to reduce prison populations, the costs of construction and operation having risen to levels generally regarded as unacceptable.

Intensive Supervision

As a result, experiments are underway in several states, notably in Georgia, Alabama, and New Jersey, to create systems of probation and parole supervision so intensive that men and women under control in the community are realistically discouraged from engaging in criminal activity. The leap from the conventional administration of community corrections, usually a nominal element of criminal justice, to an effective sanction requires a redefinition of these services. The design of these programs has yet to be standardized, but the intent is a radical transformation of the traditional models of probation and parole.

The results are tentatively favorable, although not enough time has elapsed to allow a definitive evaluation. We believe that this level of surveillance should be designated as *tertiary intervention*, representing as it does a program of individual attention to serious offenders returning to normal life in the community, aimed at preventing them from choosing criminal behavior by imposing firm restrictions on their movement.

The movement for intensive control has been restricted, so far, to certifiably nonviolent felons, with the objective of keeping them out of prison, as in Georgia, or getting them out of prison earlier than would otherwise be the case, as in Alabama. We believe that good use can eventually be made of this model to improve the control of persons convicted of street felonies, whether on probation or parole. Our discussion here will focus on the Georgia model, Intensive Probation Supervision (IPS), the first in the field. The simple principles will be applicable to the post-release situation, as in Alabama.

As applied in Georgia, IPS is limited to offenders' sentences to prison for nonviolent crimes. Before the sentence is executed, IPS staff review the individual record to determine eligibility for the program. The convicted offender is interviewed to ascertain his or her willingness to submit to an intrusive system of supervision in the community. If the offender agrees, and nearly all do—with the prospect of years in prison as the sole alternative—he or she is released to a rigorous program of control.

The conditions of IPS require full-time employment, a specified number of hours a month of unpaid community service, observance of a curfew, payment of restitution to the victim of the offense, and any other special conditions imposed by the court. To assure faithful compliance, the probationer is subject to daily surveillance calls by an officer of the IPS team. The team consists of a probation officer, responsible for establishing the conditions, the plan for meeting them, and periodic reports to the court, and a surveillance officer who makes most of the field contacts and maintains liaison with local police, state criminal identification agencies, and the "client's" employer. The caseloads for these two officers are limited to twenty-five; in some localities a forty-man caseload is carried by a probation officer and two surveillance officers. The program is intended to be at least partly self-financing. Depending on ability to pay, a monthly service fee ranging from $10 to $50 is exacted from IPS probationers.

Evaluation of IPS Program

The results so far have been encouraging. Of 436 probationers tracked for six months, 41 (9.5 percent) violated the terms of probation. A twelve-month followup of 282 offenders found 65 violations, (23 percent), and of 108 offenders tracked for 18 months, 30 (27.8 percent) violated their probation.[31]

Except that intensive supervision is reserved for prisoners released in advance of scheduled parole, the Alabama program closely resembles the Georgia IPS model. Competently administered by well-trained personnel, these programs should substantially relieve population pressures in the prisons of the states that adopt them. We believe that as experience accumulates with the nonviolent offenders to which IPS is now restricted, it should become possible to apply it to all violent offenders released from prison, as well as to selected first offenders convicted of crimes against the person.

The benefits should be significant, wholly apart from the economies to be gained by reducing prison populations. Incentives would be open to prisoners to comply with rules so as to become eligible for early release. The program would increase public confidence in community corrections and at the same time assure that those released under this level of control would be under maximum preventive surveillance. Finally, individual offenders would be provided with controlled guidance, their opportunities to deviate from law-abiding conduct while in the community would be diminished, and their new careers would be encouraged.

SUMMARY AND CONCLUSIONS

No improvements in the criminal justice system can be proof against failure. The faithful adoption of the measures proposed in this chapter will not eliminate crime from the streets, nor will all the criminals arrested and convicted abstain from further crime, no matter how firmly they are controlled. The continued ineffectiveness of our present approach to dealing with street criminals reduces public confidence in the administration of justice and at the same time gives urban predators good reason to suppose that they can continue their destructive behavior with impunity.

With improvements in the quality of police patrol, more predictable sanctions imposed by the court, and more rigorous supervision of formerly violent offenders in the community, some gains in the woefully ineffective performance of the criminal justice system can be foreseen. Without change, further deterioration can be expected as stagnation becomes the general rule.

NOTES

1. The "index crimes," in current FBI usage, include murder and nonnegligent manslaughter, forcible rape, robbery, aggravated assault, burglary, larceny-theft, motor vehicle theft, and arson. Note that these categories do not allow for degrees of seriousness, as provided for murder, robbery, and burglary in all criminal statutes. Note also that arson is listed as a property crime.

2. For a summary of the work and recommendations of the President's Commission

on Law Enforcement and the Administration of Justice, see *The Challenge of Crime in a Free Society* (Washington, D.C.: U.S. Government Printing Office, February 1967).

3. For a summary of the work and recommendations of the National Advisory Commission on Criminal Justice Standards and Goals, see *A National Strategy to Reduce Crime* (Washington, D.C.: U.S. Government Printing Office, January 1973).

4. *Uniform Crime Reports, (UCR) 1977*, p. 161, *UCR, 1982*, p. 157.

5. *The Challenge of Crime in a Free Society*, pp. 262–263.

6. Nathan Glazer, "Paris—the View from New York," *The Public Interest*, no. 74 (Winter 1984), pp. 31–51, at pp. 44–45.

7. *Japan Year Book, 1982* (Tokyo: Statistics Bureau, The Prime Minister's Office), p. 618; *Uniform Crime Reports for the United States* (Washington, D.C.: Federal Bureau of Investigation, U.S. Department of Justice, 1981), p. 76.

8. William Clifford, *Crime Control in Japan* (Lexington, Mass.: D. C. Heath, Lexington Books, 1976).

9. National Advisory Commission on Criminal Justice Standards and Goals, *Police* (Washington, D.C.: U.S. Government Printing Office, 1973), pp. 154–161, 189–205.

10. Michael Banton, *The Policeman in the Community* (New York: Basic Books, 1964), pp. 127–165, 188–242.

11. Frances H. Simon, *Prediction Methods in Criminology: Including a Prediction Study of Young Men on Probation* (London: HMSO, 1971). See also John Monahan, *Predicting Violent Behavior* (Beverly Hills: Sage Publications, 1981), pp. 95–128.

12. Peter W. Greenwood, with Allan Abrahamse, *Selective Incapacitation* (Santa Monica: Rand Corporation, August 1982).

13. Ibid., p. 53.

14. John Monahan, "The Prediction of Violent Criminal Behavior: A Methodological Critique and Prospectus," in Alfred Blumstein, Jacqueline Cohen, and Daniel Nagin, eds., *Deterrence and Incapacitation: Estimating the Effects of Criminal Sanctions on Crime Rates* (Washington, D.C.: National Academy of Sciences, 1978), pp. 249–250.

15. Greenwood, *Selective Incapacitation*, p. 56.

16. Jan M. Chaiken and Marcia R. Chaiken, with Joyce E. Peterson, *Varieties of Criminal Behavior, Summary and Policy Implications* (Santa Monica: Rand Corporation, August 1982), p. 23.

17. Andrew von Hirsch. "Selective Incapacitation: A Critique," in *NIJ Reports*, January 1984, pp. 5–8.

18. Daniel P. Moynihan, "Social Science and the Courts," *The Public Interest* no. 54 (Winter 1979), pp. 16–17.

19. James Q. Wilson, "Dealing with High Rate Offender," *The Public Interest*, no. 72 (Summer 1983), pp. 52–71.

20. Stuart J. Miller, Simon Dinitz, and John P. Conrad, *Careers of the Violent* (Lexington, Mass.: D. C. Heath, Lexington Books, 1982).

21. David Fogel, "*. . . We Are the Living Proof . . .* " (Cincinnati: Anderson, 1975).

22. Don M. Gottfredson, Leslie T. Wilkins, and Peter B. Hoffman, *Guidelines for Parole and Sentencing: A Policy Control Method* (Lexington, Mass.: D. C. Heath, Lexington Books, 1978).

23. Alfred Blumstein, Jacqueline Cohen, Susan E. Martin, and Michael H. Tonry, eds., *Research on Sentencing: The Search for Reform* (Washington, D.C.: National Academy Press, 1983), Vol. 1, pp. 165–174. See also Vol. 2, pp. 184–304, passim.

24. James Q. Wilson, *Thinking About Crime* (New York: Basic Books, 1975).

25. Ibid., p. 199.

26. Ibid., p. 209.

27. Stephan Van Dine, John P. Conrad, and Simon Dinitz, *Restraining the Wicked* (Lexington, Mass.: D. C. Heath, Lexington Books, 1979).

28. Ibid., p. 122.

29. Ibid., p. 123.

30. Joan Petersilia and Peter W. Greenwood, *Mandatory Prison Sentences: Their Projected Effects on Crime and Prison Population* (Santa Monica: Rand Corporation, 1977).

31. For further particulars, see John P. Conrad, "News of the Future," in *Federal Probation* 47 (December 1983): 54–55.

BIBLIOGRAPHY

Athens, Lonnie. "Character Contests and Violent Criminal Conduct: A Critique." *Sociological Quarterly* 26, no. 3 (1985): 419–431.

    Character is a quality of a person which derives from how the person manages himself or herself during fateful activities. A character contest is voluntary interpersonal action for two or more parties that conceivably leads to violence. Athens argues that those concepts must take into account both the nature of the violent act *and* the actor.

Blau, Judith R., and Peter M. Blau. "The Cost of Inequality: Metropolitan Structure and Violent Crime." *American Sociological Review* 47 (February 1982): 114–129.

    Analysis of census data of metropolitan areas indicates that the linkage of violent crime to the relative presence of blacks stems from interracial inequality, not from poverty alone.

Block, Richard. "Community, Environment and Violent Crime." *Criminology* 17 (May 1979): 46–57.

    In community areas of Chicago, rates for homicide, robbery, and aggravated assaults were highest in neighborhoods where the very poor and middle-class lived in proximity. Gun use at the community level was negatively correlated with rates for robbery and homicide. Street crimes were less likely to involve gun use than commercial crimes.

Cocozza, Joseph J., Eliot Harstone, and Jeraldine Boaff. "Mental Health Treatment of Violent Juveniles: An Assessment Need." *Crime and Delinquency* 27 (October 1981): 487–496.

    The experience of a specialized program for diverting juveniles adjudicated for a violent crime into a mental health setting indicates that few of such offenders are appropriate candidates for that referral.

Cullen, Francis T., Bruce G. Link, Lawrence F. Travis III, and Terrence Lemming. "Paradox in Policing: A Note on Perceptions of Danger." *Journal of Police Science and Administration* 11 (December 1983): 457–462.

    Questionnaires, administered to all officers.in five suburban departments, indicated two paradoxes. First, police officers tended to see their work as safe in the sense of injuries to colleagues but unsafe in its potential for injury; second, the hazards generated vigilance but also stress.

Felson, Richard B., and Henry J. Steadman. "Situational Factors in Disputes Leading to Criminal Violence." *Criminology* 21 (February 1983): 59–74.

Incidents of homicide and assault, not part of other crimes, were analyzed in regard to behavior of offenders, victims, and third parties. Retaliation was a key element in escalation of violence.

Floud, Jean, and Warren Young. *Dangerousness and Criminal Justice*. London: Heinemann, 1981.

The book endeavors to cope with the obscurities in the definition and criteria of "dangerousness" in modern industrial societies and in assessing the merits of "protective sentencing."

Hawkins, Darnell F. "Black Homicide: The Adequacy of Existing Research for Devising Prevention Strategies." *Crime and Delinquency* 31 (January 1985): 83–103.

Doubts are expressed that proposed intervention for reducing homicide among young, black males will work because of inattention to the patterning of black homicide to etiological factors and situational correlates.

Howard, William B. "Dealing with the Violent Criminal: What to Do and Say." *Federal Probation* 44 (March 1980): 13–18.

Howard offers advice on avoiding dangerous situations, how to behave when confronted by a criminal threat, how to short-circuit a violent attack, and whether to fight back.

Liska, Allen E., Joseph H. Lawrence, and Michael Benson. "Perspectives on the Legal Order: The Capacity for Social Control." *American Journal of Sociology* 87 (September 1981): 413–426.

The author compares the number of police department employees per capita, index crime rates, and percentage of nonwhite population for most of the largest American cities over three decades. The analysis suggests that the expansion of police size after civil disorders was an effort to control a culturally and racially dissimilar population which whites associate with street crime.

Roncek, Dennis W. "Dangerous Places: Crime and Residential Environment." *Social Forces* 60 (September 1981): 74–96.

The research supports the argument that a substantial portion of the variance in urban crime depends on perils for victims related to household composition, features of the residential environment, and the interaction of the social composition and features of the residential environment.

Van Dine, Stephan, John P. Conrad, and Simon Dinitz. *Restraining the Wicked: The Incapacitation of the Dangerous Criminal*. Lexington, Mass.: Lexington Books, 1979.

The criminal histories and personal characteristics of a cohort of 342 adults charged with violent felonies in 1973 were examined. The research questions were: How much violent crime is likely to be prevented by a policy of sentencing for incapacitation? How long must sentences be if incapacitation is to have significant impact on the violent crime rate?

11

The Preventive Effects of the Family on Delinquency

JOSEPH H. RANKIN and L. EDWARD WELLS

Because the family plays a critical role in the socialization of children, parents presumably also play a critical role in determining whether or not their children misbehave.[1] This common assumption has had considerable impact in the research on the place of the family in both the etiology and prevention of juvenile delinquency. Children from broken families and families-in-conflict are thought to be psychologically "at risk" and liable to a greater incidence of undesirable behaviors and attitudes—including acute psychiatric disturbances, poor school achievement, poor sex-role identification, negative evaluations of parents, low self-esteem, lack of peer friendships, anxiety, immaturity, and depression, plus a number of behavioral problems such as juvenile delinquency.[2] Although studies in this area encompass a number of academic disciplines (e.g., psychology, psychiatry, and sociology), they share a common theme: children whose families have been disrupted by divorce, separation, or death display a greater degree of maladaptive attitudes and behaviors.

The findings from this substantial body of research are equivocal, however; they do *not* permit the general conclusion that a change in family structure (such as divorce) has any definite negative impact on children. In fact, several studies have concluded that this general psychological damage (if present) is much less than has been previously assumed or asserted. Such a conclusion has broad implications for delinquency prevention. If the specific impact of family structure on delinquency is unknown, how can we expect family-based intervention strategies (which are theoretically based) to have a preventive effect on delinquency? This suggests that the effects of family variables must be further explored before we can realistically expect positive results from family-based prevention strategies.

This chapter examines the possible etiological impact of "broken homes" and familial relations on one type of undesirable behavior—juvenile delinquency. Assuming that such a relation exists, we next explore how family variables might prevent delinquency, examining a variety of family-based intervention strategies. We conclude by arguing that existing programs are essentially inadequate for preventing serious kinds of delinquent behaviors.

THE FAMILY AS A CAUSE OF DELINQUENCY

Questions regarding the causal impact of the family on delinquency are not merely academic. Rates of divorce increased dramatically during the 1960s and 1970s, prompting some researchers to estimate that by the year 2000 more than half of all children under eighteen years of age will spend some time in a single-parent family.[3] As divorce rates increase and a greater number of children are raised in single-parent (especially father-absent) households, social scientists have only recently begun to discover its debilitating effect on children's behaviors.

After half a century of opinions, however, findings and interpretations remain contradictory. According to some researchers; the family is the single most important determinant of delinquent behavior.[4] For example:

All in all, the stability and continuity of family life stands out as a most important factor in the development of the child. . . . The relationship is strong that, if ways could be found to do it, a strengthening and preserving of family life, among the groups which need it most, could probably accomplish more in the amelioration and prevention of delinquency and other problems than any other single program yet devised.[5]

However, other researchers discount the etiological primacy of the family, arguing that:

. . . virtually none of the studies relating family variables—particularly structural ones— to delinquency produces very strong relationships . . . . it may well be that such family variables are not in fact very significant indicators of delinquent behavior. As other socializing agents, such as the peer group and mass media, become more powerful in our society, this explanation seems increasingly likely.[6]

Despite these divergent opinions, most researchers have found at least small (and statistically significant) associations between some dimension of family context and delinquency. In fact, a considerable body of research evidence exists that delinquency is related to various indicators of problematic family characteristics, either structural or relational in nature.

Family Structure

Substantial disagreement exists on the empirical significance of the broken home as an etiological factor in delinquency. Many practitioners and researchers consider it to be a strong factor,[7] while others argue that its effects are spurious or negligible.[8] Although statistically significant relations between broken homes and delinquency have frequently been found, the numerical strength of this relationship is generally small.[9]

A number of factors could possibly account for the ostensibly weak relationship between broken homes and delinquency. For example, broken homes may simply be less important than school or peer factors in the etiology of delinquency, especially for adolescents. Or broken homes may not be a significant antecedent for all *types* of delinquency. Whereas Robert Dentler and Lawrence Monroe[10] and Roy L. Austin[11] found no relation between broken homes and theft, F. Ivan Nye,[12] Karen Wilkinson,[13] and Joseph H. Rankin[14] found the highest percentage of broken homes among adolescents committing "ungovernable conduct" (e.g., truancy and running away from home). Thus, broken homes may be positively related to some delinquent acts and unrelated to others. The study of delinquency as a general concept could suppress any significantly large association between specific types of delinquent behavior and broken homes.

Not only may family breakup be differentially related to specific types of juvenile misconduct, but it may also differentially affect certain categories of juveniles. For example, the effects of broken homes may be felt more strongly by juveniles of a certain race or socioeconomic status. Roland Chilton and Gerald Markle found that broken homes may have a greater effect on the delinquency of whites than blacks and on adolescents from high-income families than from low-income families.[15] Similarly, John Johnstone's results indicate that the effect of broken homes on delinquency varies directly with the neighborhood's socioeconomic status.[16] He argues that in low-income, deteriorated areas of the city the effect of broken homes is outweighed by the negative influences of ubiquitous poverty. Only in the more affluent and stable neighborhoods will family disruption have negative behavioral effects on children. Thus, it is probably not accurate to assume that all children are equally affected by broken homes. In addition, divorce (or separation), poverty, and race are highly interrelated.[17] Until the effects of such variables are statistically controlled, we will not be able to accurately assess the effect of broken homes on delinquency.

Another problem concerns the conceptual ambiguity of the term "broken home." The most widely used definition is the absence of at least one natural (biological) parent. However, this taxonomy reduces the family structure variable to a simple dichotomy: a home is either "broken" or "intact." As Lawrence Rosen[18] and Jona M. Rosenfeld and Eliezar Rosenstein[19] have noted, this is a gross oversimplification of a rather complicated family condition. Various precipitating causes for the break (e.g., divorce, death, disability, military service), the longevity of the break (temporary or permanent), the absence of one or both parents (mother, father, or both), the presence of a stepparent, and the frequency, duration, and quality of the contact between the child and absent parent can all affect (either positively or negatively) both the psychological and behavioral risk of the child. Thus, the most common definition of a broken home—loss of at least one biological parent—conceals the fact that the difficulty in raising a child might not be the same for all types of breaks. Only recently have researchers been examining empirically the impact of different kinds and degrees of parent-absence on the child's behavior.

This brief overview of the literature on the broken home indicates its limited contribution to an understanding of what it is about parent-absence that affects the child negatively. Most research has emphasized the loss of a father as being directly detrimental to the child's development without considering other variables that may occur simultaneously with parental absence. One major exception is the research by Cynthia Longfellow, who examined the reorganization process that occurs after divorce.[20] Problems in child care, lack of a social life, apprehension in regard to visitation rights, and especially financial problems all plague the single parent. In this context, the departure of a parent is just one of many circumstances to which the child must adjust. The effect of broken homes on delinquency can be more accurately assessed only when we know more about the strains that are placed on the family as a result of a parent's departure.

Thus, it is not enough to focus only on family structure variables. The departure of the father or mother from the family unit is often characterized by a strained relationship between the parents before, during, and after the separation/divorce. Thus, a final reason for the apparently weak effect of broken homes on delinquency is that this relationship is mediated by relational variables (e.g., the *quality* of the marital or parent-child relationship). In other words, the effect of broken homes on delinquency is indirect.

Intervening Processes

Instead of a simple direct effect of family structure on the likelihood of juvenile misbehaviors, a three-step causal process is usually proposed in which structural conditions (e.g., broken homes) precipitate certain interactions or relational patterns (e.g., parent-child relationships) which in turn affect the probability of delinquency. Because this intermediate step remains implicit in most research on broken homes, its specific contribution to the causal sequence between family structure and delinquency remains implicit and ambiguous. In clarifying these intervening processes, we note that various theoretical frameworks are possible, each identifying a different set of intervening variables and providing a different interpretation of the causal process. Four general theoretical perspectives can be identified, each distinguishing a different causal dynamic between family structure and delinquency: (1) socialization, (2) social control, (3) family crisis, and (4) social structure.

The *socialization* perspective identifies the family as the primary agency for the socialization of children into cultural roles and normal adult personalities. Because socialization is a developmental process, this perspective focuses on the effects of family structure as extending over a period of years—particularly the years when children are fairly young (i.e., pre-adolescence). Structural changes in the family do not necessarily have an immediate effect on children's behaviors. Instead, the causal effects of family structure are likely to be delayed and cumulative, affecting long-term changes in behavior. Thus, the focus of this perspective is on family structure during the early, formative years of childhood which eventually precipitates unwanted behavioral changes in later adolescence.

According to this reasoning, family structural changes may differentially affect behaviors, depending on the developmental age of the child at the time of the break. This conclusion has several consequences for social policy. First, the effects of prevention strategies may be more valuable and immediate for younger children whose parents have separated/divorced in the recent past. Because the behavioral effects will be delayed and cumulative, the shorter the time frame between parental departure and preventive intervention, the less the likelihood of faulty learning of deviant behaviors, values, and concepts. Simply put, less "resocialization" will be necessary. By implication, such intervention strategies would not be expected to produce immediate, positive results for older children whose parents had separated/divorced in the distant past. Within the relatively brief time frame of most prevention programs (and evaluation research), there is a high probability that few corrective behavioral changes will be noted in these children.

A second consequence of the "cumulative" nature of this perspective is that (everything else being equal) parental breaks that occur late in the child's adolescence may have fewer developmental effects on the child. Much of the child's socialization will already have occurred by this stage. In addition, many delinquency theorists assume that by later adolescence juveniles are more strongly influenced by their peers and school than by parents. Thus, prevention strategies based on the family socialization perspective may have little effect on older children. Rather, school- and peer-oriented prevention strategies should be utilized at this stage of the child's development. The problem, of course, is that this relationship is variable; some parents may retain a great deal of influence over children at later stages of adolescence. To the degree that a child's peer and school networks contain persons that are also part of the family network, parents will remain effective in their socialization efforts throughout adolescence. Thus, age (maturation) is only one of many possible variables that make children differentially susceptible to parental influence.

As a basic proposition, the literature on the broken home generally presumes that a family structure that deviates from the Western "norm" (i.e., a nuclear family in which both biological parents are present) will retard the normal learning of proper social roles; concomitantly, broken homes will facilitate the development of behavioral problems such as delinquency. Even though they presently make up a significant proportion of family households, separated families are commonly assumed to be deviant and pathological, as exemplified in the terms by which they are commonly described—"broken," "disorganized," "disintegrated." Equation of child rearing by a single parent with a greater likelihood of delinquency is consistent with a rather "functional" view that the presence of both biological parents is the necessary minimum requirement for normal child development.[21] Because fathers generally average significantly less time per week in childcare activities relative to mothers, this functional argument may seem highly suspect.[22] Indeed, recent versions of the socialization perspective may recognize that appropriate social habits can be learned in the context of a relationship with any individual who fulfills the parenting function in a stable relationship (e.g., foster parent, guardian, grandparent, stepparent, even a single parent). The negative effects of broken homes may be neutralized if substitute structures for socialization (especially substitute role models) are provided.

A *social control* framework provides a different interpretation of the intervening causal process between family structure and delinquency. In contrast to the developmental approach, this perspective views family structure more as a synchronous cause than as a lagged, developmental cause of delinquency. Because the negative effects of family structure should be relatively immediate rather than delayed and cumulative, the social control perspective gives a potentially more optimistic view of the short-run impact of delinquency prevention. Intervention strategies should obtain relatively quick, positive results regardless of the child's current age and/or age at the point of parental breakup.

According to the social control perspective, the conventional (intact) family provides a source of basic "ties" or "bonds" to conventional social order and involvement in conventional activities and institutions. The intact family acts as a control (buffer) against deviant influences by providing a source of motivations (termed "stakes in conformity" or "attachments") to conform to social norms and rules. Thus, the properly functioning family helps to control deviant impulses, limiting the likelihood of delinquent behaviors. In this sense, social control is really a perspective on conformity rather than deviance. When the family structure breaks down, the family can lose its ability to supervise and control the behaviors of its children, thereby increasing the likelihood of delinquency.

Among the various social control perspectives, Travis Hirschi provides the most elaborated and explicit theory.[23] A central focus of his perspective is the inverse relationship between the child's bond or attachment to parents and delinquency. The greater the sensitivity to parents' wishes and concerns, the more likely the child is to consider those concerns when contemplating the commission of a delinquent act. Family bonds inhibit or control delinquency because the child does not want to jeopardize positive relationships with his or her parents. On the other hand, lack of family support is conducive to delinquency. A weak bond minimizes one's sensitivity to the opinions of parents, "freeing" the child to deviate in response to situational demands and peer encouragements. This bond between parent and child can be strengthened along three dimensions: (1) parental supervision over their child's behavior; (2) identification with or closeness to parents; and (3) intimacy of communication.

In contrast to other social control perspectives,[24] Hirschi suggests that (a) attachment to one parent can be as effective in preventing delinquency as attachment to both parents; and (b) the difference between the mother's and father's impact on a child's delinquency is negligible.[25] The implications of this suggestion are twofold. First, a broken home may have little facilitating effect on delinquency as long as the child is strongly attached to the remaining parent. Since the important consideration is whether or not *one* parent is psychologically present (providing "indirect control") when delinquent opportunities arise, it is not necessary for both parents to be present to act as a buffer against delinquency. Thus, broken homes should be associated with delinquency only when the quality of the relationship (attachment) between the child and remaining parent is poor. This reasoning contrasts with other social control approaches which suggest that the ability to supervise, punish, and generally restrain a child's behavior (providing "direct control") is substantially attenuated in a single-parent family.[26]

A second implication of Hirschi's perspective is that it does not matter to which of the parents (mother or father) the child is attached as long as the strength of this bond is high. The strength of the relation between parental attachment and delinquency is not contingent on the gender of the parent or the child. A boy raised only by his mother ought to be no more at risk than a girl raised by her mother. Hirschi's view is in contrast to some versions of the socialization perspective (especially clinical models or sex-role identification models) which have assumed that father absence has graver behavioral and psychological consequences for sons than for daughters; conversely, mother absence should have a greater adverse effect on daughters. Although research findings consistent with this latter assumption have been reported, the available evidence is very sketchy and inconclusive.[27] In fact, Joseph Rankin found no evidence to support this claim.[28] This remains an open theoretical and empirical question. Even within the socialization perspective, numerous researchers recognize that there are many others (besides biological parents) from whom gender-linked roles can be learned (e.g., peers, extended kinship relations, and stepfathers, as well as the media).

The *family crisis* perspective also views the relationship between family structure and delinquency as synchronous. Disruptions in family structure lead to temporary disturbances which must be resolved to reestablish some semblance of the pre-crisis family order and routine. In contrast to the social control perspective which emphasizes the nonmotivational, psychological aspect of parental "attachment" and the family's inability to control delinquent impulses, this approach views a change in family structure as a motivational cause of delinquency—the crisis actually "pushes" a juvenile toward misbehaving. Basically, the loss of a parent produces stress and conflict that are expressed in acting out behaviors such as parental defiance, running away from home, truancy, or general ungovernability. Thus, this approach predicts less serious, maladaptive juvenile misbehaviors (rather than serious, hard-core delinquency) that are likely to be directed against the parents themselves. Moreover, these misbehaviors are likely to be a temporary rather than a long-lasting problem, being resolved as the broken family adapts to its new conditions. By contrast, the socialization perspective and certain social control perspectives suggest that delinquency is likely to be less transient and more serious in content than the family crisis perspective suggests.

A family crisis approach does not provide a determinate model of delinquency, recognizing that several extraordinary events may be increased by the family separation—some negative, some positive.[29] The crisis could have prosocial rather than antisocial effects on the children. Conceivably, the loss of a parent could pull the remaining family closer together in a fashion similar to how relatives and friends "pitch in" to help one another after natural disasters. In a similar fashion, some children may help in the crisis by taking over the roles and responsibilities of the missing parent in such tasks as child rearing, earning an additional household income, or housekeeping. Delinquency is only one of many behavioral responses that can result from a family crisis. Future research must specify and clarify under what conditions delinquency is the most likely response.

Thus, the family crisis perspective does not necessarily imply that a change in family structure will lead to delinquency or that delinquency affects only broken homes. The quality of the relation between parent and child is not necessarily good in intact homes nor poor in broken homes. Indeed, homes that are physically intact but in a state of marital conflict may present more of a crisis than homes in which parental relationships are severed. Separation or divorce could end parental conflict and restore peace to what was already a "socially" or "psychologically" broken home.[30] Moreover, parental breakups are only one type of crisis that could initiate juvenile misbehaviors. Parental abuse (e.g., physical beatings and sexual assaults), can also motivate a child toward some type of "acting out" or "striking back" behaviors (e.g., defying parents or running away from home).[31]

The intervening causal processes discussed thus far have centered on either the characteristics of the delinquents themselves (socialization perspective) or the juvenile's family (social control and family crisis perspectives). A *social structure* perspective follows a still different approach, viewing the relationship between family structure and delinquency within the context of the larger social structure or organization of society. Broken homes affect the likelihood of delinquency by altering conditions "external" to the family. Hence, questions germane to this perspective include: What are the external characteristics of the structure or situation in which delinquent behaviors occur? Do delinquency rates vary as these situations vary?

According to this perspective, the broken home constitutes a socially and economically disadvantaged unit. Not only are the parents of lower income families more likely to divorce or separate, but many middle-income families are likely to suffer downward economic mobility as a result of a parent's departure from the family unit.[32] Less income means not only a reduction in economic and material consumption; it may also necessitate a move to poor housing accommodations in lower class neighborhoods. A low income translates into fewer educational opportunities as well as more frequent associations with delinquent values and behaviors in lower class schools and neighborhoods. Thus, legitimate opportunities for success and goal-achievement are more likely to be limited for children from broken homes.

The social structure perspective has several distinct implications for social policy. First, this approach suggests that the social forces that cause delinquency begin to affect children when they are relatively young and then continue to influence behaviors and attitudes throughout the child's life. In this sense, the social structure approach is similar to the socialization perspective. The sooner that intervention takes place after parental breakup, the more effective will be the treatment. However, there is a large difference in treatment strategies between these two approaches. Instead of focusing on the resocialization of the individual or family, the social structure approach suggests that larger scale changes must take place which attempt to reduce the socioeconomic disadvantages of the broken home (e.g., the reduction of economic discrimination against the poor or single mothers).

Second, most social structure perspectives view lower class delinquency as more violent and destructive than middle-class delinquency. Rather than assuming that delinquency is a rather mild form of "acting out" behaviors against parents (the family crisis approach), this perspective views the delinquent behavior of children from broken homes as much more serious in nature. Because the structural effects of low income are cumulative, delinquent behaviors are likely to become more serious as the child grows older.

FAMILY-BASED PREVENTION

One basic test of a theoretical perspective is its ability to predict delinquency; another equally important test is its ability to translate into practicable prevention programs. Equally predictive causal variables do not always lend themselves equally well to manipulation in actual programs of prevention.[33] Prevention strategies invariably are directed toward the intervening causal processes rather than toward the family structure per se, which is more difficult to manipulate or reform. Indeed, intervention strategies that attempt to reduce or prevent delinquency by keeping families physically intact (e.g., through modification in the economic reward structure or through welfare requirements) are probably doomed to failure.[34] Even if such programs were successful in keeping the family physically intact, all the problems associated with a conflicted, socially, or psychologically broken home (e.g., family crises, poor marital or parent-child relationships, child abuse) would remain unsolved.

Conceptualizing theoretical perspectives on the family dynamics of delinquency is an important first step toward the development and evaluation of family-based prevention strategies. However, the search for causes must be paralleled with a search for programs that can control the causal factors. Ostensibly, the perspectives outlined above may be used by criminologists and practitioners alike to assess family dynamics and the extent to which certain programs may or may not work in preventing delinquency.

Assessing the Problems

Probably the first task of the practitioner is a diagnostic assessment of families "at risk" and the causal problems associated with a child's delinquent behavior. As outlined earlier, there are at least four different causal perspectives on the relationship between home and delinquency, each with fairly unique implications for social policy. Differing perspectives describe different problems and prescribe different remedies. An assessment of the originating cause(s) of delinquency is necessary before "treatment" (whether preventive or corrective) can be prescribed. For example, delinquent behavior that is produced by social structural factors (such as economic discrimination and disadvantage) will not be responsive to programs that prescribe foster parents for children with behavior problems. Economic discrimination illustrates a "social structural" explanation, whereas reliance on foster parents is consistent with the "family crisis" orientation. In addition, the assessment aims of the two approaches will be quite different. One will be concerned only with categorically identifying families "at risk" (for eligibility to supplementary services or resources designed to reduce structural disadvantage), while the other will be concerned mainly with assessing the causal structure of each family's crisis. In the latter, the purpose of an initial diagnostic analysis is to assess the nature of the problem and thus the forms of intervention most likely to benefit a particular child in a particular family.

To systematize this initial diagnosis, objective measures may be used to identify key factors in the family situation, thus reducing the reliance on simple value judgment. Rudolf H. Moos and Bernice S. Moos have developed the Family Environment Scale (FES), which may be used to assess the "social climate" of families.[35] "Social climate" refers to the interpersonal relations among family members, the direction of personal growth emphasized within the family, and the family's basic organizational structure. Moos' FES items are grouped into ten subscales: "three assess Relationship dimensions (cohesion, expressiveness, conflict), five assess Personal Growth or Personal Development dimensions (achievement orientation, intellectual-cultural orientation, active recreational orientation, moral-religious emphasis), and the other two assess System Maintenance dimensions (Organization and Control)."[36] Among other things, their scale can be used for detailed descriptions of family social environments and for the longitudinal assessment of changes in family environments.

Where and by whom is the family assessment made? In present programs (scattered and mostly experimental), heaviest reliance is placed on the courts (particularly "family courts" responsible for mediating and resolving domestic disputes), as well as on social service agencies connected with the courts.[37] As an alternative strategy making possible wider and earlier coverage, some approaches suggest the schools as an additional point of identification and intervention.[38]

In developing intervention strategies for children from broken homes, Christine Burns and Marla Brassard argue that the school psychologist can assess the strengths of the child's environment (the school as well as the home), suggesting use of an adaptation of Kelly and Wallerstein's Divorce Specific Assessment.[39] This developmental assessment scale includes information from both the parent and school as well as direct observation of the child over a period of time. Based on the results of such an assessment, Burns and Brassard conclude that the type of intervention strategy most suitable for the child can be chosen.

Assuming that some diagnostic assessment is administered, the next step is to choose the prevention strategy best suited to the child's needs. In general, such strategies can be classified as residential, nonresidential, or family support services.

Residential Treatment

In some instances, it may be beneficial to treat the child outside the context of the family when that environment is momentarily inadequate or threatening. For example, situations of "family crisis" may dictate the temporary removal of the child from the home (for reasons of physical safety) until the crisis is resolved. Residential programs allow children to be placed outside the home without the more destructive and stigmatizing outcome of institutionalization. Generally, placements are brief because the goal is to return the children to their families as soon as possible after a period of intensive supervision.

Even though the prospect of severing family ties can be frightening, *foster family care* can serve as a temporary shelter or haven for youths (e.g., runaways, truants, ungovernables) who may need protection as well as individualized care and affection in an atmosphere that simulates a home-like environment. A number of foster homes may even work together in clusters to better develop the sense of a caring community of which the child can feel a part.[40] To insure even greater supervision and individual treatment, "intensive" foster care such as at Kaleidoscope Inc. in Chicago, Ill., usually requires that no more than two children be housed with any married couple.[41]

Temporary foster care is liable to have few positive, long-lasting effects on the child, however, unless the whole family's patterns of interaction can be changed. Parents must also learn to cope with pressures and crises. At the Baltimore Family Life Center, staff members assigned to each of the foster homes hold weekly therapeutic meetings with all family members.[42] In addition, staff members may initiate referrals to needed community services for the child and his or her parents as well as arrange recreational and social activities involving the child's family. The program's philosophy "is that a youth's natural family, his or her foster care family, and BFLC staff members are all part of the extended family and all participate in caring for the youngster."[43]

A second form of residential treatment for delinquents and "disturbed" children is the *group home*, in which approximately six to twelve children live together with houseparents. As with foster care, the purpose of the group home is to temporarily neutralize negative parental influences by placing the child in the care of adults who become temporary substitute parents in a kind of quasi-family setting.[44] During the day, the youths either attend school, hold jobs, or make use of other community resources.

Because many centers now view treatment of a child apart from his or her family as artificial or unnatural, many group homes have implemented some form of family counseling or psychotherapy as part of the treatment strategy. The purposes of such a family-oriented approach are threefold. First, parental involvement helps parents to identify the agency as being therapeutically valuable for the child.[45] Ostensibly, this may increase parent-staff cooperation which, in turn, could benefit the child's treatment. Second, it is hoped that greater contact with agency staff will make the parents themselves more responsive, empathetic, and caring. Only within the total family context can a critical understanding of the child's problems be obtained. Finally, the family's involvement in the treatment process may make the child's return to home much faster and his or her reintegration into the family and community much easier.

Nonresidential Treatment

Juvenile delinquents living in their own homes can benefit from programs developed specifically as alternatives to residential treatment or incarceration. For example, parental involvement in treatment is more likely to be realized when the treatment setting is the home rather than an office or other facility located away from the family's residence. Although residential treatment may provide short-term benefits in situations of "family crisis," since the 1960s many practitioners have believed that residential intervention strategies provide an artificial or unnatural environment in which to treat children. Because a child's behavior can be influenced by the novelty of the treatment setting, it cannot be determined whether deviant behaviors are, in fact, "normal" or an artifact of the unfamiliar treatment surroundings. Reinforcers (both positive and negative) may, for example, produce new and unwanted deviant behaviors unique to the treatment setting.

Behavior therapy applies social learning or behavior modification principles to family prevention strategies in familiar treatment surroundings—the child's own home. In this manner, the reinforcers in the child's natural environment which maintain the deviant behaviors can be directly observed and later extinguished. Whereas most traditional therapies tend to emphasize the treatment of the child only, in behavior therapy the parents are an integral part of the mechanism for change. Parents themselves are trained in noncoercive methods (e.g., positive reinforcement and negotiating skills) for recording and changing the child's deviant behaviors.[46]

Baseline observations of the child's disobedient and aggressive behaviors are taken in the period prior to therapy. This serves both as a base from which to measure changes in family interaction patterns as well as a gauge of the effect of behavior therapy on a child's behavior. Generally, the therapy itself focuses on three different aspects of parent-child interaction: stimulus control, consequation, and shaping. Parental directives (verbal and behavioral) cue the child's responses and channel behaviors. "Stimulus control" refers to changing these cues so that the child clearly understands what is expected of him or her. These cues provide clear expectations for behavior through the consistent use of appropriate verbal and behavioral reactions (termed "consequation"). The development of consistent discipline coupled with positive reinforcement for prosocial behaviors is essential. Finally, because learning is usually a gradual and incremental process, the concept of "shaping" or successive approximation is used to slowly change negative family behavioral patterns toward more positive interactions.[47]

A series of articles by Gerald R. Patterson and his colleagues illustrates the use of behavior therapy for the elimination of juvenile "conduct disorders" (i.e., "noxious" but not necessarily delinquent behaviors such as fighting, teasing, whining, and yelling).[48] Parents were trained in behavior modification principles to alter the deviant behaviors of problem children. Observational data of the children's behaviors were collected in the homes before, during, and after therapy. Their results indicated statistically significant reductions in problem behaviors from the baseline data. Moreover, followup data indicated that these family intervention effects persisted twelve months after termination of treatment. Gerald R. Patterson and M. T. Fleischman also reviewed data from comparison studies which showed that social learning procedures were more effective in reducing problem behaviors than no treatment, client-centered treatment, and traditional treatment.[49]

Unlike much of the psychoanalytic and social work literature which relies on impressionistic data to evaluate the effectiveness of delinquency prevention strategies, Patterson's conclusions were based on observable behavioral changes in both the parents and the children prior to, during, and following treatment. Nevertheless, at least two questions remain concerning the effectiveness of behavior therapy: (1) Can behavior therapy effectively reduce the frequency of more serious forms of delinquency which are committed outside the home environment? (2) Do these effects really persist after treatment is terminated?

Patterson has shown that behavior therapy seems to work well in reducing relatively mild, socially aggressive behaviors (e.g., temper tantrums, hitting, yelling) that can be identified and treated within the context of the home. However, it has yet to be shown that such a strategy can help reduce more serious delinquencies such as theft and burglary which occur outside the relatively "closed" setting of the home. J. B. Reid and A. R. Hendricks, for example, found that 57 percent of the more seriously delinquent children (e.g., those who stole, set fires, and ran away from home) were classified as failures of behavior therapy, compared to only 18 percent of the less serious, socially aggressive children.[50] It may be that behavior therapy will have its most pronounced effect on those noxious but not necessarily delinquent behaviors that tend to occur within a relatively "closed" setting, such as the home or school, where parents and teachers can closely and consistently observe and modify unwanted behaviors.

With regard to the second question, a number of authors have debated the post-termination persistence effects of behavior therapy. For example, close reexamination of Patterson's research has revealed inadequacies in the study design and data analysis. Upon reanalysis of these data, Ronald Kent argued that Patterson's conclusion regarding the persistence of treatment effects was unwarranted.[51] Other studies lend support to Kent's conclusion: there is no unequivocal evidence of post-treatment persistence effects.[52] Patterson and Fleischman have responded to this criticism by arguing that the persistence of effects is not a function of the treatment per se, but of how significant others (especially parents) react to the positive changes in the child.[53] Unless the parents continue to consistently use noncoercive means of maintaining the child's pro-social level of behavior, in the long run the child may return to baseline levels of noxious behaviors. That is, not only must treatment extinguish the coercive system of punishment, but it must also leave the family in a state where these punishments are unlikely to reassert themselves.

Difficulties experienced by single-parent families both during and following divorce/separation vary as to their frequency, duration, and magnitude. A variety of *family therapy* programs has developed as a response to these differing needs. In general, the specific counseling/casework strategies are as divergent as the number of implemented programs. For example, goal-directed counseling attempts to identify specific divorce-related problems (e.g., visitation controversies, financial planning, homemaking assistance) and fashions programs to modify these specific problems. Other strategies teach children how to deal successfully with crisis situations and cope with feelings associated with parental divorce, separation, and death. Intensive one- or two-day workshops are another family counseling strategy, the goals of which include learning to cope with feelings about marriage and divorce and developing communication skills for handling difficult situations. Trained caseworkers can also provide services in the child's home, including crisis intervention and counseling.

Although a great amount of expenditure and effort has gone into such varied and multifaceted programs, as yet little evaluative effort has been directed toward those strategies specifically involved in preventing delinquency. One exception is the study by Dennis Romig who reviewed and evaluated twelve studies of over 2,180 youth who participated in various types of family therapy prevention programs, including family crisis counseling, family communication skills programs, family casework, behavior modification, family recreation, family discussion groups, and psychodynamic family therapy.[54] He concluded that such strategies can be effective in reducing juvenile deviance when they focus specifically on teaching parents skills in communication, problem solving, and discipline. Although these counseling skills may be helpful in reducing deviance among predelinquents and status offenders, Romig cautions that this conclusion cannot be generalized to delinquents involved in more serious criminal behaviors.

Family Support Services

As an alternative to intervention programs that operate after the family situation has reached crisis proportions (thus reaching public attention and mediation), family support services aim at making basic family resources available to families in disadvantaged circumstances (generally single-parent families). Concerned with families "at risk" or "in need" rather than "in crisis," they aim at reducing the structural disadvantages attached to families rather than mediating internal family dynamics. These include a variety of volunteer or public organizations for providing a basic array of services to families, including: child care, legal assistance, informational services (on schools, other educational programs, nutrition), socio-emotional services (counseling, cooperative support groups, recreational programs), referral services (for employment, public facilities, medical care), and material assistance (emergency aid, housing supplements).

The general rationale for such programs is a structural one. Certain family structures or situations predispose to delinquency because of the socioeconomic disabilities that attach to them. Thus, reduction in this disadvantage means reduction in delinquency risks. This approach seems more clearly preventive than the treatment programs outlined earlier which are often more remedial or corrective (of extant problems) than preventive. However, at present such programs are at most experimental and suggestive. The theoretical logic of the programs, while persuasive, remains unexplicated and untested—at least with respect to delinquency prevention.

DISCUSSION AND CONCLUSIONS

Our knowledge of prevention is not very fully developed at this point, probably because we have less than complete knowledge about the causes of juvenile delinquency. It surely would be a mistake to pin all hopes on the family as a corrective or preventive instrument in delinquency. No one would regard the family as the sole determinant of delinquency. Indeed, prior research has shown that delinquency is a complex problem, consisting of a variety of different behaviors and caused by a variety of interacting factors. Even if family context caused initial delinquent behavior, other factors (e.g., peer influence) may help to maintain the delinquency, even to supplant family factors as the effective maintenance variable. Causal explanations of the origin of delinquency may not explain its persistence.[55] Thus, to be successful a program may need to offer a variety of services, only some of which may pertain directly to the family.

Because of our lack of knowledge concerning the causes of various types of delinquency, it is not surprising that its prevention and correction should prove so difficult to systematically practice and document. To date there is little existing evaluative research on the effectiveness of family-based prevention strategies, although there is no shortage of those claiming to have the solution. Unfortunately, those programs that appear to be the most successful are those that either have not been carefully evaluated or have never been implemented (i.e., recommendations set forth as "model" prevention programs). Thus, it is nearly impossible to give prevention recommendations based on known "facts" (since the latter consist of opinions and beliefs rather than verifiable data).

This chapter does suggest, however, that the broken home may not be the primary cause of serious forms of delinquency and that family-oriented prevention strategies are probably not the choice treatment for serious delinquents. Family variables generally appear to be most highly associated with less serious forms of family-related deviance (i.e., noxious but not necessarily delinquent behaviors such as general ungovernability, running away from home, and temper tantrums); concomitantly, family-oriented prevention strategies seem to be most effective in reducing family-related status offenses and "acting out" types of behaviors. Thus, prior research on both the etiology and prevention of delinquency suggests a case for specificity of family treatment. The problem of juvenile delinquency may require a host of partial solutions rather than a single, overall resolution. Shotgun approaches that treat all youth alike will probably not be as successful as those that individualize treatment.

This conclusion may be premature and should not be considered the definitive word on the viability of the family in the cause and prevention of delinquency. Little has been mentioned in this chapter about family prevention in relation to delinquency per se because, to date, little has been done in this area. To reiterate, knowledge and practice in the field of delinquency causation and prevention are not fully developed. In addition to our inability to be able to predict delinquency with any accuracy, there has been little in the way of evaluative efforts to support a claim of success for any delinquency prevention program. "Family treatment" is a jumbled mixture of conceptual models and techniques,[56] only a handful of which focus specifically on delinquency prevention. Even fewer programs have been systematically evaluated. Thus, there is a need for further consideration of the role of the family in prevention of delinquency before we can come to any firm conclusions.

NOTES

1. Walter R. Gove and Robert D. Crutchfield, "The Family and Juvenile Delinquency," *Sociological Quarterly* 23 (Summer 1982): 301–319.

2. Michael Rutter, "Parent-Child Separation: Psychological Effects on the Children," *Journal of Child Psychology and Psychiatry* 12 (1971): 233–260; Elizabeth Herzog and Cecelia Sudia, "Children in Fatherless Families," in B. Caldwell and H. Ricciuti, eds., *Review of Child Development Research*, Vol. 3 (Chicago: University of Chicago Press,

1973), pp. 141–232; Marybeth Shinn, "Father Absence and Children's Cognitive Development," *Psychological Bulletin* 85, no.2 (1978): 295–324; E. Mavis Hetherington, Martha Cox, and Roger Cox, "The Development of Children in Mother-Headed Families," in D. Reiss and H. Hoffman, eds., *The American Family: Dying or Developing* (New York: Plenum, 1979), pp. 117–145; Elaine A. Blechman, "Are Children with One Parent at Psychological Risk? A Methodological Review," *Journal of Marriage and the Family* 44 (February 1982): 179–195.

3. Richard S. Benedek and Elissa P. Benedek, "Children of Divorce: Can We Meet Their Needs?" *Journal of Social Issues* 35, no. 4 (1979): 155–169; Christine W. Burns and Marla R. Brassard, "A Look at the Single Parent Family: Implications for the School Psychologist," *Psychology in the Schools* 19, no. 4 (1982): 487–494.

4. Thomas Monahan, "Family Status and the Delinquent Child: A Reappraisal and Some New Findings," *Social Forces* 35 (March 1957): 251–258; Gove and Crutchfield, "The Family and Juvenile Delinquency."

5. Monahan, "Family Status and the Delinquent Child," p. 258.

6. David Schulz and Robert Wilson, "Some Traditional Family Variables and Their Correlations with Drug Use Among High School Students," *Journal of Marriage and the Family* 35 (November 1973): 638.

7. Monahan, "Family Status and the Delinquent Child", Roland Chilton and Gerald Markle, "Family Disruption, Delinquent Conduct and the Effect of Subclassification," *American Sociological Review* 37 (February 1972): 93–99.

8. Michael Hennessy, Pamela Richards, and Richard Berk, "Broken Homes and Middle-Class Delinquency: A Reassessment," *Criminology* 15 (February 1978): 505–527.

9. Lawrence Rosen and Kathleen Neilson, "Broken Homes," in Leonard Savitz and Norman Johnston, eds., *Contemporary Criminology* (New York: John Wiley, 1982), pp. 126–135.

10. Robert Dentler and Lawrence Monroe, "Social Correlates of Early Adolescent Theft," *American Sociological Review* 26 (October 1961): 733–743.

11. Roy L. Austin, "Race, Father-Absence, and Female Delinquency," *Criminology* 15 (February 1978): 487–504.

12. F. Ivan Nye, *Family Relationships and Delinquent Behavior* (New York: John Wiley, 1958).

13. Karen Wilkinson, "The Broken Home and Delinquent Behavior: An Alternative Interpretation of Contradictory Findings," in Travis Hirschi and Michael Gottfredson, eds., *Understanding Crime: Current Theory and Research* (Beverly Hills, Calif.: Sage Publications, 1980).

14. Joseph H. Rankin, "The Family Context of Delinquency," *Social Problems* 30 (April 1983): 466–479.

15. Chilton and Markle, "Family Disruption, Delinquent Conduct and the Effect of Subclassification," pp. 96–98.

16. John W. C. Johnstone, "Juvenile Delinquency and the Family: A Contextual Interpretation," *Youth and Society* 9 (March 1978): 299–313.

17. Ruth A. Brandwein, Carol A. Brown, and Elizabeth Maury Fox, "Women and Children Last: The Social Situation of Divorced Mothers and Their Families," *Journal of Marriage and the Family* 36 (August 1974): 498–514.

18. Lawrence Rosen, "The Broken Home and Male Delinquency," in Marvin Wolf-

gang, Leonard Savitz, and Norman Johnston, eds., *The Sociology of Crime and Delinquency* (New York: John Wiley, 1970).

19. Jona M. Rosenfeld and Eliezer Rosenstein, "Towards a Conceptual Framework for the Study of Parent-Absent Families," *Journal of Marriage and the Family* 35 (February 1973): 131–135.

20. Cynthia Longfellow, "Divorce in Context: Its Impact on Children," in George Levinger and Oliver C. Moles, eds., *Divorce and Separation* (New York: Basic, 1979).

21. Blechman, "Are Children with One Parent at Psychological Risk?," pp. 179–180.

22. Richard Berk and Sarah Berk, *Labor and Leisure at Home: Content and Organization of the Household Day* (Beverly Hills, Calif.: Sage, 1979); Joann Vanek, "Household Work, Wage Work, and Sexual Equality," in Sarah F. Berk, ed., *Women and Household Labor* (Beverly Hills, Calif.: Sage, 1980); Heidi I. Hartman, "The Family as the Laws of Gender, Class and Political Struggle: The Example of Housework," *Signs* 6 (Spring 1981): 366–394.

23. Travis Hirschi, *Causes of Delinquency* (Berkeley, Calif.: University of California Press, 1969).

24. E.g., Nye, *Family Relationships and Delinquent Behavior*; Walter C. Reckless, "A New Theory of Delinquency and Crime," *Federal Probation* 25 (December 1961): 42–46.

25. Hirschi, *Causes of Delinquency*, pp. 100–107.

26. Nye, *Family Relationships and Delinquent Behavior*, pp. 41–52.

27. John W. Santrock and Richard Warshak, "Father Custody and Social Development in Boys and Girls," *Journal of Social Issues* 35, no. 4 (1979): 112–125.

28. Rankin, "The Family Context of Delinquency," pp. 474–475.

29. Joseph Weis, *Jurisdiction and the Elusive Status Offender: A Comparison of Involvement in Delinquent Behavior and Status Offenses*, Report of the National Juvenile Justice Assessment Centers (Washington, D.C.: U.S. Government Printing Office, 1979).

30. Cf. Rankin, "The Family Context of Delinquency."

31. Dorothy Miller, Donald Miller, Fred Hoffman, and Robert Duggan, *Runaways—Illegal Aliens in Their Own Land* (New York: Praeger, 1980).

32. Brandwein et al., "Women and Children Last," pp. 500–502.

33. Hyman Rodman and Paul Grams, "Juvenile Delinquency and the Family: A Review and Discussion," in the President's Commission on Law Enforcement and Administration of Justice, *Task Force Report: Juvenile Delinquency and Youth Crime* (Washington, D.C.: U.S. Government Printing Office, 1967), pp. 188–221.

34. Blechman, "Are Children with One Parent at Psychological Risk?" p. 180.

35. Rudolf H. Moos and Bernice S. Moos, "Families," in Rudolf H. Moos, ed., *Evaluating Correctional and Community Settings* (New York: John Wiley, 1975), pp. 263–287.

36. Ibid., p. 274.

37. Benedek and Benedek, "Children of Divorce," pp. 161–163.

38. Burns and Brassard, "A Look at the Single Parent Family," Jan McCarthy, "Preventing Juvenile Delinquency Through Provision of Family-Support Services," in F. Dutile, C. Foust, and D. R. Webster, eds., *Early Childhood Intervention and Juvenile Delinquency* (Lexington, Mass.: Lexington Books, 1982).

39. Burns and Brassard, "A Look at the Single Parent Family," pp. 488–490.

40. Yitzhak Bakal and Howard W. Polsky, *Reforming Corrections for Juvenile Offenders* (Lexington, Mass.: D. C. Heath, 1979).

41. Margaret L. Woods, *Alternatives to Imprisoning Young Offenders: Noteworthy Programs* (Hackensack, N.J.: National Council on Crime and Delinquency, 1982).

42. Ibid.

43. Ibid., p. 23.

44. Morris F. Mayer, "The Parental Figures in Residential Treatment," *Social Service Review* 34 (September 1960): 273–285.

45. Alvin E. Winder, Lindo Ferrini, and George E. Gaby, "Group Therapy with Parents of Children in a Residential Treatment Center," *Child Welfare* 44 (May 1965): 266–271.

46. N. A. Wiltz, "Behavioral Therapy Techniques in Treatment of Emotionally Disturbed Children and Their Families," *Child Welfare* 52 (October 1973): 483–492; Gerald R. Patterson, "Interventions for Boys with Conduct Problems: Multiple Settings, Treatments, and Criteria," *Journal of Consulting and Clinical Psychology* 42, no. 4 (1974): 471–481.

47. Wiltz, "Behavioral Therapy Techniques," pp. 483–491.

48. Patterson, "Intervention for Boys"; Gerald R. Patterson and M. J. Fleischman, "Maintenance of Treatment Effects: Some Considerations Concerning Family Systems and Follow-up Data," *Behavior Therapy* 10 (March 1979): 168–185; Gerald R. Patterson, Patricia Chamberlain, and John B. Reid, "A Comparative Evaluation of a Parent-Training Program," *Behavior Therapy* 13 (November 1982): 638–650.

49. Patterson and Fleischman, "Maintenance of Treatment Effects," pp. 172–181.

50. J. B. Reid and A. R. Hendricks, "A Preliminary Analysis of the Effectiveness of Direct Home Intervention of Pre-Delinquency Boys Who Steal," in L. A. Hamerlynck, L. C. Handy, and E. J. Mash, eds., *Behavior Therapy: Methodology, Concepts, and Practice* (Champaign, Ill.: Research Press, 1973).

51. Ronald Kent, "A Methodological Critique of 'Interventions for Boys with Conduct Problems,' " *Journal of Consulting and Clinical Psychology* 44, no. 2 (1976): 297–302.

52. See Patterson and Fleischman, "Maintenance of Treatment Effects," pp. 183–185.

53. Ibid.

54. Dennis Romig, *Justice for Our Children* (Lexington, Mass.: D. C. Heath, 1978), pp. 87–95.

55. For an example, see McCarthy, "Presenting Juvenile Delinquency," pp. 143–148.

56. Joan M. Druckman, "A Family-Oriented Policy and Treatment Program for Female Juvenile Status Offenders," *Journal of Marriage and the Family* 41, no. 3 (1979): 627–636.

BIBLIOGRAPHY

Blechman, Elaine A. "Are Children with One Parent at Psychological Risk? A Methodological Review." *Journal of Marriage and the Family* 44 (February 1982): 179–195.

　　　　Methodological recommendations would rectify common design errors and conceptual ambiguities in empirical studies examining the relation between single-parent families and "psychological risk."

Canter, Rachelle J. "Family Correlates of Male and Female Delinquency." *Criminology* 20 (August 1982): 149–167.

Gender differences in family bonds (parent-child relationships) are examined empirically in relation to self-reported delinquency among a national sample of adolescents. Family bonds were modestly but significantly correlated with delinquency at comparable rates for girls and boys.

Gove, Walter R., and Robert D. Crutchfield. "The Family and Juvenile Delinquency." *Sociological Quarterly* 23 (Summer 1982): 301–319.

Relations between several family variables (family structure, parental characteristics, household characteristics, and parent-child relationships) and delinquency (as reported by parents) are examined empirically from a multivariate perspective. Results support the view that the family plays a significant role in whether or not juveniles misbehave, depending on interacting factors.

Haskins, Ron, and Diane Adams, eds. *Parent Education and Public Policy.* Norwood, N.J.: Ablex Publishing Co., 1983.

Parent education is addressed in terms of its history, assumptions, integration into service programs, and policy implications.

Johnstone, John W. C. "Delinquency and the Changing American Family." In David Shicor and Delos H. Kelly, eds., *Critical Issues in Juvenile Delinquency.* Lexington, Mass.: D. C. Heath, 1980, pp. 83–97.

The literature regarding the impact of the family on delinquency is reviewed, concluding that family structure per se is of little causal importance. The association was found to be ambiguous because of failures to: (a) isolate the exact causal nature of the family and how it affects behavior; (b) discriminate the types of behaviors affected by family context; and (c) examine the family within the context of larger social variables such as the community.

Lemmon, John Allen. *Family Mediation Practice.* New York: Free Press, 1985.

Mediation as a process and an arena for professional practice is analyzed for various family problems.

Mace, David R., ed. *Prevention in Family Services: Approaches to Family Wellness.* Beverly Hills, Calif.: Sage Publications, 1983.

Advocating a switch from remedial to preventative services, the authors treat the promotion of family wellness in terms of marriage enrichment, parenthood and whole family enrichment, and special services to families.

Patterson, Gerald P., and Thomas J. Dishion. "Contributions of Families and Peers to Delinquency." *Criminology* 23 (February 1985): 63–79.

The authors hypothesize that during adolescence failure of parent monitoring and deficits in social skills increase the likelihood that a youngster will associate with delinquent peers.

Patterson, Gerald R., Patricia Chamberlain, and John B. Reid. "A Comparative Evaluation of a Parent-Training Program." *Behavior Therapy* 13 (November 1982): 638–650.

Behavior therapy was randomly assigned to half of the participating nineteen "socially aggressive" children. After approximately seventeen hours, therapy was terminated and post-treatment observation data were collected. Those receiving behavior therapy showed a significantly greater reduction in the observed rates of problem behaviors than the control group.

Rankin, Joseph H. "The Family Context of Delinquency." *Social Problems* 30 (April

1983): 466–479.

The relation between broken homes and delinquency is examined empirically among two national samples of U.S. children. Neither parent-specific absence nor reason for parental breakup was significantly related to various kinds of self-reported delinquency. However, the number of absent biological parents as well as the presence of a stepparent were associated with less serious forms of juvenile misconduct.

Rosen, Lawrence, and Kathleen Neilson. "Broken Homes." In Leonard Savitz and Norman Johnston, eds., *Contemporary Criminology*. New York: John Wiley, 1982, pp. 126–135.

Fifteen studies examining the relation between broken homes and delinquency are reviewed and reevaluated. Despite variations in time, locale, sample size, nature of the populations, definitions of both delinquency and broken homes, and in research designs, the strength of the associations between broken homes and delinquency are small but significant.

Wilkinson, Karen. "The Broken Home and Delinquent Behavior: An Alternative Interpretation of Contradictory Findings." In Travis Hirsci and Michael Gottfredson, eds., *Understanding Crime: Current Theory and Research*. Beverly Hills, Calif.: Sage Publications, 1980, pp. 21–42.

The relations between father absence and various self-reported delinquencies are examined empirically while controlling for gender, ethnicity, religion, and urban-rural residence. Under some conditions and for certain types of offenses, father absence was found to be significantly related to delinquency. It is suggested that the degree of tolerance for divorce is likely to be an important variable.

12

Prevention in Business and Industry

ELMER H. JOHNSON

This chapter focuses on the kind of lawbreaking associated with industry and business. Casual observation may induce us to write off such crime as only the perverse inclination of individuals to exploit opportunities for illicit gain. Some view these individuals merely as antisocial beings separate from the organizations on which they prey. This chapter will take a different tack—arguing that organizations play a part in their victimization—in trying to understand four classes of crime—employee theft, shoplifting, burglary, and robbery—that victimize business and industry and in suggesting means of their prevention.

In trying to prevent the four classes of crime, businesses and industries are likely to assume initially that they are victims of antisocial persons who are sharply distinct from their "decent" employees or patrons. Second, the predatoriness is supposed to be outside the regular operations of the victimized company. More careful scrutiny reveals that neither assumption is sound. Most thieves are essentially like all "decent people"; it is very difficult to predict which of the "trustworthy" employees or patrons will succumb to temptation. Thievery occurs within the usual rhythm of company operations which have some influence on how the crimes are carried out.

THEFTS BY EMPLOYEES

Businesses suffer great losses from burglary, robbery, vandalism, shoplifting, employee theft, and bad checks. Addison R. Verrill presents "the cold, hard facts" that dishonesty among employees handling cash is on the increase, that the average take is growing, that collusive theft is most characteristic, and that the victimized companies are reluctant to punish managers involved in kickbacks and other dishonest acts.[1]

Internal theft, as does shoplifting, raises costs for consumers and is a drain on the viability of the enterprises. The loss of the services of apprehended and experienced employees, the possible loss or distortion of records, unfavorable publicity, and lowered morale of other employees during the investigations— all such adverse consequences must be considered. The future fate of the thieves is also part of the costs in terms of possible stigmatization and blighted careers. Adjudication imposes expenses on the defendant, the company, and the community at large.

Sources of Employee Theft

Why do apparently honest employees steal from their employing organizations? The question has fundamental implications for prevention of their transgressions. A popular explanation is that every employee is capable of stealing and that only opportunity is the missing ingredient. These people confuse need with greed, Charles R. Carson claims, and undertake theft because of a desire to enhance their social prestige or to cover expenses beyond their legitimate income.[2]

Along that line of thinking, the president of a nationwide security company reports that 95 percent of the victimization of firms is committed by trusted employees, most of whom have been with the firms for more than three years.[3] He is referring to apprehended offenders, rather than *all* employees, and he does not specify the types of offenses involved. The explanation substitutes a supposition of universal moral decay for valid evidence, but a greater deficiency is the skirting of the question "Which people steal?" in terms practical for prevention. The denial of theft opportunity to all employees, Robert C. Hollinger and John P. Clark note, could make prevention a matter of bolting everything down.[4]

A more promising beginning for identifying potential employee thieves is offered by Bob Curtis. He suggests that high-risk employees tend to live beyond their economic means, exhibit signs of emotional instability, engage in excessive drinking, drug use, or chronic gambling, make excessive efforts to ingratiate themselves with bosses, or have family problems.[5] Such tentative clues, in and of themselves, encourage snap judgments that could lead to outcomes adverse to the company. They are more useful as signals that certain persons in positions of trust merit special scrutiny.

Those clues are also useful as general criteria for preemployment screening. Civil rights legislation has limited standardized screening in regard to age, health, marital status, arrests, religion, and race. To impugn one's honesty on the basis of such status variables also risks denying employment to otherwise worthy employees. Effective screening depends on personnel interviews that test the accuracy and significance of information and on background investigations with former employers and other references, including credit institutions. Although the use and reliability of the polygraph are controversial, such testing is useful when authorized by state laws and administered competently.

The preliminary clues suggest that dishonest employees present a certain profile of personal and background conditions, but employee theft constitutes a behavior system that is linked with the conventional patterns of a given occupation and the relationships among employees as they carry out assigned tasks within the structure of the employing firm. The thefts exploit the opportunities for illicit gain within those conventional patterns and sets of assigned tasks. The profile of typical offenders in a given class of employee theft is useful in identifying which of the employees is most vulnerable to the temptation of illicit opportunities. The typical opportunities for theft within the occupational patterns and complexes of regular tasks also are worthy subjects for assessing where employee theft is likely to occur. Preventive management would match the clues of profiles of individuals with clues of where the transgressions are most likely to occur.

Embezzlement by persons in positions of trust is an especially apt illustration of the behavior system as a concept oriented toward the situational components of employee theft and its prevention. William W. McCullough denies that there is a typical embezzler and notes that they often are personable, outgoing, sociable persons. Rather, he implies that embezzlement is a behavior system in which the embezzler earns a position of trust over time and later becomes aware of the possibilities of exploiting the position for self-gain. That position and the routines of handling the company's assets insulate the thief from ready detection.[6]

Prevention of Employee Theft

Security experts usually note a pessimism among executives who recognize the problem of employee theft. Curtis, for example, quotes a manager as follows: "Sure all my people steal . . . I did the same thing years ago when I was a salesman starting out. You can't do anything about it, so you might as well forget it."[7]

That pessimism is unjustified when the toll of employee theft and the availability of preventive methods are considered. The punitive sanctions of the criminal law are available. A sophisticated security department, supported by priority on prevention in company policy, can supplement preemployment screening and inventory controls. Target-hardening devices can protect especially valuable assets. The effectiveness of those strategies, however, is dependent ultimately on the qualities of general management practices.

To obtain reliable and perspicacious information, a three-year investigation of employee theft applied several research methodologies in retailing, manufacturing, and hospital establishments of three major metropolitan areas of the United States. After assessing the effects of those strategies, Peter F. Parilla concludes that employee theft is susceptible to checks, specifically, previous work performance, reduction of inventory vulnerability, sophisticated security measures, and the apprehension and termination of culprits. However, the impact of these controls is neither uniform nor strong. In sum, although formal organizational controls negatively influence theft prevalence, those effects must be understood in combination with the other factors influencing this phenomenon.[8]

Management reactions to offenses, J. P. Martin reports, are dominated by concern for the welfare of the firm. Prosecution is avoided when the firm might experience unpleasantness, time loss, or undesirable publicity. Enforcement of the criminal law receives little concern.[9] That general attitude overlooks the environment within which employee theft appears, suggests an emphasis on post hoc reactions over prevention, and can be interpreted as evidence that the human relations elements of management are overlooked.

Market Forces and Prevention

In economic institutions, the market is defined as the place where particular services or goods are exchanged, such as a stock exchange. More broadly, the term specifies a community of specialists who engage in the transactions that form a bridge between producers and consumers. The intermediaries are in a position to regulate the flow of the given goods or services. As a form of crime prevention, Moore proposes that the regulation of a market be exploited to restrict the distribution of drugs, alcohol, and guns as criminogenic commodities.[10]

To support his case, Mark H. Moore argues that drug and alcohol users are disproportionately represented among robbers and burglars. He believes that the presence of guns in those crimes increases the likelihood of a homicide and the shifting of victimization to more lucrative targets than homes and the streets. Moore recognizes that tighter controls could increase rather than reduce crime by encouraging illicit markets and greater criminal violence. His recommendation is to concentrate on those drugs most linked to crime, on raising taxes on alcohol, and on keeping guns out of the streets and the hands of criminals.

The market for stolen goods depends on fences or private citizens who buy the loot. Joseph F. Sheley and Kenneth D. Bailey postulate that the high economic toll of thievery and burglary could be significantly reduced if the buyers no longer provided a black market.[11] They recommend an antitheft policy that would be consumer-oriented, rather than considering only the offender-victim relationship. The motivations for property crimes and for purchasing loot are economic, they say, and the threat of sanctions is unlikely to have significant long-term effect. Thus, they recommend moral appeals to the population at large in the sense of general prevention.

The practicality of prevention-oriented market control is severely tested by the great difficulties implied above. For example, the gun control issue has stirred hot debate over whether the availability of guns, especially handguns, is the fundamental cause of violence or whether the employment of guns is symptomatic of more general factors. The feasibility of targeting criminal use, without affecting legitimate gun owners from the perspective of certain constituencies in the United States, is also controversial. Objective appraisal is handicapped by the lack of proper data and the particular significance of gun ownership within the American cultural context.[12]

ENVIRONMENT OF EMPLOYEE THEFT

Effective prevention centers on proper management practices in screening new employees, supervising subordinates, and monitoring task performance. The control strategies of management depend on the support they are given by employees. Robert C. Hollinger and John P. Clark have confirmed that the attitudes of worker groups have greater influence in constraining employee deviance than do the more formal actions of bosses. Employee crime, they explain, may be deterred largely by the perception that fellow workers would not approve of such deviance.[13]

Parameters of Crimes against Companies

Employee theft is part of the workers' resistance to the pressures for conformity to management's efforts to achieve company goals. The identification of outright crime is obstructed by its concealment within the physical-social environment and organization of tasks of the employing organization. The distinction between pilfering and stealing among workers reflects a value ambivalence that also underlines management's reluctance to impose criminal justice processing on apprehended offenders. In their analysis, Hollinger and Clark found little evidence that greater economic pressure explains the bulk of employee theft or that adverse economic situations in the external community had significant influence. Factors external to the organization, they conclude, are neither the best nor the most consistent predictors of employee involvement in workplace property deviance.[14]

The prevalence of employee theft, Hollinger and Clark report, also reflects workers' perceptions of getting caught; the stronger their belief that theft would be detected, the less likely they would violate company expectations. However, worker dissatisfaction—a phenomenon that the human relations orientation of management seeks to minimize—appears to be a key element in worker resistance to management's control and in employee theft, especially in retailing organizations where desirable property is in greater quantity than in manufacturing plants.[15]

Cultural Ambivalence and Crime

Opportunities for employee theft are associated with obscurities in the right and wrong of taking company property for one's own use. Employees—and employers to a lesser extent—tend to see pilfering as rather normal behavior when the items taken are for the employee's own use, the quantities taken are small, and the act is not premeditated. In contrast, stealing is seen as taking money or other direct symbols of high value in large quantities for resale and with premeditation.[16]

In exploring that distinction among operatives in a large electronics assembly plant, Donald N. H. Horning found perception of identifiable personal property of specific individuals who purchased or produced the items at their own expense; of company property (building, fixtures, heavy machinery, and equipment); and property of uncertain ownership (screws, nails, bolts, scraps, waste, certain tools, lost money, clothing, or equipment outside an assigned work station). The work group's definition of property of uncertain ownership determined whether a worker had engaged in acceptable pilfering or in disreputable stealing. The normative distinction was dynamic, depending on the generous availability of the given item and the intensity of management's regulation of the availability. The propriety implied by the term ''pilfering'' was dependent on the work group's subculture. Taking property outside the normative boundaries deprived the culprit of the protection and approval of colleagues.[17]

Merger of Misconduct with Work Routines

Victimization of an organization is commonly regarded simply as the misconduct of individuals in violation of the behavioral standards of the organization. Employee theft in its various forms is therefore seen as something separate from the regularized and appropriate behaviors that conform with the organization's expectations. An alternative perspective is that employee theft does not necessarily oppose the purposes of the organization or stand separate from the regularized routines whereby the personnel carry out the tasks for achieving the company's purposes.

To illustrate that point, Joseph Bensman and Israel Gerver gathered data on a wing-assembly crew in an airplane factory.[18] Attention was focused on the insertion of a screw to pass through a wing plate to intersect a nut. When the nut and screw do not meet properly, the tap (a hard steel screw) cuts new threads in the nut to effect alignment, possibly distorting the wing and weakening it. Although use of the tap is officially defined as a grave offense, at least half of the mechanics had one.

The foremen were caught between pressures for production and the demand that official work rules be respected when time-consuming correction of a malaligned screw and nut was required. That conflict placed the foremen in the position of tolerating the use of the tap as a means of serving the organization's demand for production. The foremen were likely to participate in instructing new workers in the use of the tap and in the informal controls among mechanics as to who would use the device and when it was to be used.

Structural Shaping of Misconduct

The performance of employees is shaped by the general conditions set by the employing organization. Employee misconduct is influenced by conditions that affect the degree of solidarity among workers, the degree of freedom permitted, and the opportunities for interaction among workers as a means for collusive offenses.

To illustrate these variables, Gerald Mars describes four types of employee theft.[19] First, the restaurant cashier, the grocery checkout clerk, and the factory assembly-line worker have little choice in how they carry out the job; their physical movement and interactions with fellow workers are restricted. Manipulation of the cash register and cheating on piece-work rates are two typical violations of management expectations. Second, independent professional managers are less restricted, have higher prestige, and have greater opportunity to commit offenses without the collaboration of work colleagues. Third, sales representatives and delivery people enjoy considerable freedom of movement and discretion in task performance, but they share a common employer and require mutual peer support in their tasks. Fourth, longshoreworkers, miners, airplane crews, and hospital personnel belong to occupations in which work routines, at least temporary residence, and leisure activities are likely to be combined. Their work generates colleagueship and permits considerable control over work conditions that are amenable to cheating the employers when peer cooperation exists.

The patterning of work routines serves the purposes of the company, although recognition of the advantages of maintaining morale would cause management to consider the workers' selfinterests in establishing those patterns. Employee resistance to the imposed patterns may represent a simple reaction against authority, adjustments to ease boredom, or manipulation of production norms to extract prestige beyond that expected by planners of the wage system. Counterproductive employee behavior is not necessarily criminalistic.

White-Collar Crime and Employee Theft

Edwin H. Sutherland, a pioneer in the study of white-collar crime, defined it as an offense committed by a person of respectability and high social status in the course of occupational activities. As examples of such crime, he listed restraint of trade, misrepresentation in advertising, infringement of patents, unfair labor practices, rebates, financial fraud, and violations of trust. Those offenses are treated by administrative agencies rather than criminal justice agencies, Sutherland explained, because of the high prestige given those occupations and the public ambivalence about convincing such violators as criminals.[20]

In light of the great personal importance attached to work in a money economy, it is remarkable that employee theft and white-collar crime have received so little attention. A partial explanation is that traditionally the term "criminal" has been reserved for low-status persons who commit crimes against property or persons, and that victimization of businesses and industries has been seen as the acts of intruders. That conception does not fit employees whose actions would otherwise qualify as crimes according to specific legal criteria. Another explanation emphasizes that crime has traditionally been seen as the misconduct spawned in antisocial environments; that perspective tends to divert attention from the possibility that patterned relationships within the occupational sphere can play a part in the generation of offenses. A third explanation is that the basic philosophy of criminal law tends to lag behind contemporary conditions. Laws framed in the more personal age when farming and smaller cities were dominant concentrated on crimes committed by individuals. The contemporary world is characterized by much larger quantities of portable wealth, intangible property rights, and large-scale economic institutions.

Comparison of reactions against white-collar crime and employee theft, respectively, is instructive for analysis of prospects for prevention, but both the similarities and differences between the two general classes must be recognized. Such a comparison has been obstructed by the failure to distinguish corporate crime from white-collar crime. Corporate crime refers to the transgressions of economic organizations, whereas white-collar crime is perpetrated by individuals or by a group of individuals in collusive offenses. A further difference is that in white-collar crime the employing organization is the victim, whereas in corporate crime the organization is the victimizer. The distinction is suggested by Ronald R. Schmidt's definition of executive dishonesty: the misuse of authority for personal gain, to the detriment of an organization.[21]

Both white-collar crime and employee theft are involved in the regular operations of the victimized organization. Therefore, they represent a problem in human relations and are symptoms of management's attitudes and policies. There are other similarities. Few of the perpetrators have a criminal record or the philosophy and self-image of dedicated criminals in spite of their violations of management's faith in their honesty. The crimes are directed against the employing organizations rather than against individual victims. The offenses occur within the regular patterns of the occupation or the rhythms of regular task performance. The offenses are especially unlikely to be reflected in official crime statistics.

In making that kind of comparison, Gerald D. Robin also refers to differences between white-collar crime and employee theft as criminological concepts.[22] White-collar offenses are more likely to be committed against regulatory laws or against those criminal laws enacted more recently without the general moral support of public conceptions of theft. Employee theft is more vulnerable to regular criminal justice processing, but because of employer leniency fewer such cases are prosecuted than are theft cases committed outside the workplace. Many white-collar crimes reflect greater complexity and technical skill than employee theft. White-collar offenders are also are likely to occupy higher positions in the community than the employee thieves.

SHOPLIFTING: VICTIMIZING THE STORE

Unlike employee thieves, shoplifters are not part of the victimized economic enterprise. These outsiders are welcomed because their purchases are essential to profitmaking. The purchases are encouraged by merchandising practices that make the store especially vulnerable to theft. In that sense, effective prevention is hampered by the regular operations and concern of retailers that measures to deter thefts will also reduce the flow of welcome shoppers.

Relevance of Urban Conditions

The economic well-being of the retailers depends on attracting a large and heterogeneous patronage. That self-interest makes the establishment vulnerable to the conditions of urban life. Succinctly stated, urban society is characterized by massive networks of relationships among large conglomerates of people who interact with one another mechanically rather than personally. The urbanites present a variety of lifestyles and subcultural standards that undermine the unity of behaviors, especially because the large populations confer an anonymity that insulates offenders from detection.

That general environment has generated a large patronage for retailing establishments and at the same time has produced conditions favorable for shoplifting. As noted earlier, it is difficult to distinguish potential and actual shoplifters from the much larger crowd of conventional shoppers. Another consideration is that in American society there is a rather ambivalent attitude toward the morality of shoplifting; thus, some conventional shoppers hesitate to report shoplifters.

Patterns and Correlates of Shoplifting

Shoplifters are usually differentiated according to several types. The professional steals systematically as a life vocation, whereas the impulsive amateur lacks the self-image and criminal dedication of the professional. The use of special shoplifting devices has blurred some of the distinction between the two types. Amateur adults tend to be seen as predominantly females, usually middle-class housewives, who steal when an opportunity arises. However, there is greater shoplifting by adult males than is commonly acknowledged. Survey data indicate that the greatest number of incidents involve ordinary individuals using simple methods to steal small amounts of merchandise.[23]

Quantitatively, juvenile shoplifting occurs frequently, but as shown by the records of three Philadelphia department stores they usually involve items of less value than those taken by adults.[24] David May refers to the paradox of retailers being more concerned about the ''nuisance'' of juvenile shoplifting than the threats it represents to profits. He explains that, although the usual stolen item is of small value, the store management objects to the juveniles' use of the premises for meeting friends and thereby creating general disorder that possibly deters potential customers and generally impedes the business of selling.[25]

Kleptomaniacs are motivated by psychological compulsions rather than gaining economic value. Full-fledged kleptomaniacs are rare; the complex motivations involved in thefts by middle-class persons have probably invited the excessive use of this diagnosis.

Among the tools of the professional shoplifter, Harold Cohen says, are the booster box, booster bloomers, booster belts, and control of the thighs. A booster box is an empty box with an open end or a spring-action that will open it to receive stolen items. Extra large underpants of women can contain a large amount of merchandise. Men and women can wear a belt under an overcoat, hanging items on hooks. And, finally, by perfecting control of the thighs, a woman can hold an object as large as a typewriter while walking in a normal manner. Even amateurs can conceal items in the center of paper towels, on the bottom level of shopping carts, in umbrellas, coat pockets, or purses. Another method used is to switch price tags from inexpensive to more expensive items.[26]

Erhard Blankenburg points out that shoplifting can be encouraged by the physical characteristics of the store design and by its arrangements for displaying goods, by the behavior of sales personnel, and by the behavior of other customers. The physical features and arrangements of goods affect whether the theft can be observed. In his research Blankenburg employed assistants who stole items from chain supermarkets with advance agreement of the management yet without knowledge by employees. Even in shops with mirrors, his mock thieves were helped when the attention of personnel was diverted by other customers or when some unusual incident happened. The polite clerk, Blankenburg suggests, does not have the suspicious nature appropriate to theft detection.[27] The open display and mass merchandising techniques, intended to increase the shoppers' wish to possess goods, have also been offered as explanations for shoplifting. Finally, self-service has reduced the size of clerical staff but has also increased the chances that thefts will go unobserved.

Passive Barriers and Deterrence

In order to prevent shoplifting, target hardening, the design of the store's layout, packaging, and arrangement of displays are passive measures. Rather than depend solely on the persistent effort of store personnel, these measures help reduce the opportunity for theft in an automatic fashion. The usual target-hardening devices are two-way mirrors, locks, restricted display cases, alarms, closed-circuit television, and article surveillance tags. The devices function to alert store personnel. Do legitimate customers resent these devices? Question-naires administered over a 10-day period to patrons of a regional shopping center tested their awareness of and reactions to such devices. Respondents were most aware of locked display cases and observation mirrors, and reported they were most uncomfortable about checkers in dressing rooms and uniformed guards, whereas locked display cases and mirrors elicited the least discomfort. Customers who regarded shoplifting as a minor problem were most likely to consider preventive measures offensive.[28]

Store layout is important in exposing potential shoplifters to easy observation.

The arrangement of displays can be a related deterrent. The same factors that can make a store a sales powerhouse—specialty department alcoves, high-stacked displays, complete self-service in meats and produce, huge assortments and a "one-stop shopping" inventory of food, household items, drugs, sundries, even small appliances—can work in favor of the shoplifter, Len Daykin declares.[29]

Being apprehended for shoplifting may serve as a deterrent to amateurs, especially when they are exposed to the disapproval of others. Research indicates that the effectiveness of various deterrence methods depends on the likelihood of getting caught, the severity of the official sanction, and the severity of the disapproval of significant others.

In an investigation of high school students, Lloyd W. Klemke reports that respondents caught by store personnel were less likely to repeat the offense than respondents caught by their parents because store personnel were more prone to apply legal sanctions. However, Klemke notes that the disapproval of one's friends had greater influence than the perceived probability of apprehension and severe official sanctions.[30] That conclusion is consistent with the view that officially implemented punishment derives its deterrent effect not from the threat of punishment in and of itself, but from the wish to avoid social condemnation.

Preventive Effects of the Security Force

In large stores, the security unit is supervised by a person who is experienced and knowledgeable about shoplifting techniques. Allen A. Seedman believes that the presence of uniformed guards is visible evidence of concern and effort by management to do something about shoplifting.[31] The apprehension of offenders would appear to be the justification, but, since prevention depends on the commitment of the retailing management, the security unit should also mobilize other store personnel in the detection of offenders. Thus, the unit serves as a model for a personnel policy oriented to meeting the social-psychological needs of all employees.[32]

The broader conception of security functions is consistent with Harvey Burstein's caution that prosecution is rather shortsighted. Prosecution is expensive in terms of money and time and ties up the stolen property as evidence until the trial is completed.[33] Moreover, in any trial the state must demonstrate that the act was intentional, that the individuals involved actually had the article in their possession, that the merchandise was the property of the store, and that the individuals intended to convert the merchandise to their own use or to deprive the rightful owner of it.[34]

Management's reluctance to prosecute weakens the deterrent effect of security measures. The perception of certain punishment has a deterrent effect on persons who are prone to shoplifting. Some stores have undertaken tough crusades, publishing the names of apprehended shoplifters and prosecuting them, but Harold Cohen warns that such stores can be condemned as faceless corporations picking on otherwise worthy local individuals.[35]

Modifying Environmental Variables

Because retailers have developed techniques to transform potential customers into actual customers, David May asks, why not adapt the techniques to converting potential shoplifters into nonthreats? One such technique is denial of opportunity through attentive sales staff, supervised counters, passive barriers, and a security force. May also suggests further extending the situational approach to crime prevention by what he calls "manipulation of the shoplifting role."[36] May would have store personnel engage in negotiations with shoplifters early in their theft activities, placing the shoplifters in the role of regular customers rather than shoplifters per se. For example, the clerk would say: "You forgot to pay for the item in your pocket," or "You can pay at the check-out counter."[37]

The objective is to prevent individuals from becoming dedicated criminals and to cause them to recognize the ultimate meaning of unauthorized removal of property. Emphasis on apprehension presses the role of thief on amateurs before they see themselves in that role. By avoiding that imputation, the store takes advantage of the nonrecidivists' fear that they are not invulnerable to apprehension and their belief that the act will receive peer disapproval.

Similarly, M. Jerry Kallis and Dinoo J. Vanier recommend that antishoplifting campaigns avoid emphasis on the social undesirability of the conduct and instead appeal to the potential shoplifters' sense of individuality. "Make a choice on your own—don't shoplift" would be preferable to "shoplifting is a crime." The first slogan is in keeping with the shoplifters' aversion to the sickness explanation for shoplifting and with their greater respect for human confrontation tactics over passive barriers.[38]

Vincent F. Sacco has concluded that mass media campaigns have minimal effect in persuading other shoppers to get involved in apprehensions. For one thing, other shoppers are generally unlikely to be aware of shoplifting incidents. The nonpersonal messages may change public attitudes but do not increase the inclination to report shoplifters. Reporting is more likely among persons who are already morally opposed to the misconduct. Victimization of retail establishments draws less public concern than other crimes against property. Major commitment of human, financial, and other resources to large-scale antishoplifting media campaigns, Sacco suggests, is probably not justified at this time.[39] More direct public involvement in multidimensional campaigns appears to be more promising. Chok C. Hiew reports declines in apprehensions and prosecutions after a multidimensional program involving lectures in schools, an essay contest, training of store employees, and a mass media campaign.[40]

The police are highly dependent upon citizens for knowledge of criminal incidents, and lay referral to the police for shoplifting has raised several issues. Lay persons, Lundman notes, may observe shoplifting offenses but not pass on the information to the police. Second, they may base their decisions to report on extra-legal characteristics of the suspect. Third, their decisions whether or not to report gives them the power to bring the stigmatization of formal criminal proceedings. Using store security records of the midwestern branch of a department store chain during 1973–1975, Lundman found that the retail value of stolen items was the crucial variable in lay decisions to report an incident. Nonwhites, older, and, to a lesser extent, male apprehended shoplifters were more frequently reported to the police than their white, younger, and female counterparts. When the value of stolen items was also considered, race continued to be an important factor, although to a diminished degree. Gender had a weak relationship, and control for retail value eliminated that already weak distinction. Age of the shoplifters continued to be the strongest relationship even when the retail value was introduced.[41]

ROBBERY AND BURGLARY: COMMERCIAL CRIMES

Unlike employee theft, robbery and burglary victimize economic institutions without involving internal conspiracies, with the minor possibility of collusion with criminals. The regular operations of those enterprises are relevant only in the sense that insufficient preventive measures encourage criminal predatoriness. Like shoplifting, burglary and robbery represent invasions of enterprises for illegal purposes, but these two offenses qualify as traditional crimes and are not affected by the cultural ambivalence that colors the evaluation of shoplifting.

Burglary and robbery stir particular moral abhorrence. Invasion of private premises, especially of the home, by burglars, violates the owner's right to control events in those premises and carries with it the possibility of injury to the legitimate occupants. Relatively few robberies involve loss of life, but some injury occurs in about a third of such incidents, depending on the sex, age, and racial status of the victim.[42] Even when no injury is suffered, there is slight comfort to the citizen who is suddenly confronted by a gun or a knife. The risk of death or serious physical injury is, of course, of greater concern to the victim than loss of money.

In addition to arousing fear, burglary and robbery exact an economic toll in loss of property and expenditure of personnel resources of economic institutions in remedying the physical damages. The prosecution of apprehended criminals also imposes fiscal costs and the expenditure of staff effort.

Robbery is largely a crime of the big cities, whereas burglary is more widely distributed. Economic loss is significantly greater for all kinds of burglaries than for all robberies; and businesses do not necessarily recover losses through insurance.[43] Although fencing the stolen business property gives burglars substantially less return than business robbers, the greater risk of police intervention and longer prison sentences makes robbery less attractive.

Patterning of Commercial Crimes

As is true of shoplifters, there are several types of robbers and burglars, with the main distinction being that between professionals and amateurs. Amateurs do not often plan their thefts, they usually work alone, may well have no police record, are generally successful in committing the robberies, and probably steal to satisfy a personal need, often to obtain money to buy drugs, Daykin says. In contrast, professional robbers will find a successful method and generally stick to it.[44]

According to Peter Letkemann, burglary is a surreptitious crime in which direct confrontation of the victim is avoided, whereas robbery is an overt crime entailing victim confrontation. They also differ in the procedures of assessing the crime setting in advance (casing), gaining access (making the in), and the act of theft itself. In casing, the burglar is likely to prefer cash; if goods are the objective, a means of carrying the goods away must be planned. "Making the in" entails evading alarms and gaining access by picking locks, obtaining keys, or breaking windows or skylights. Tools may be used to extract money from cash registers, safes, or vending machines. In robbing commercial enterprises, criminals plan the place and time of the robbery to minimize the chances of unwelcome intervention and to expedite escape. Unlike the burglar, the robber is more concerned about getting out than making the in because it is a crime of speed. Victim management is crucial in the act of robbery that depends on surprise; specifically, the robber seeks to effect the momentary mental paralysis of victims and to establish authority over them.[45]

In Letkemann's interviews with convicted robbers, he was told that experienced robbers avoid firing guns in a crime because guns are intended only for intimidation of victims, along with loud commands and physical violence; a shootout with police in order to escape is another matter.[46] The gun is an effective tool, Philip J. Cook points out, because it enhances the robber's power by threatening deadly harm from a distance, creating a buffer zone between the robber and victim, and permitting control of several victims simultaneously. Cook finds that the gun is more frequently used in commercial robberies than in residential and other robberies.[47]

Letkemann reveals that because of night depositories, credit cards, and complex alarm systems burglaries of major business establishments are most often committed by the most skilled burglars, using weapons.[48] John E. Conklin and Egon Bittner provide evidence that burglary in the suburbs tends to be predominantly of residences, with victimization of commercial establishments accounting for only a quarter of all burglaries in these areas.[49]

In his study of professional armed robbers, Werner J. Einstadter reports that three persons usually make up the loosely organized robbery team, depending on the size and complexity of the robbery, and that three tactics are used. The three persons are the automobile driver who stays outside at the wheel, the leading robber, and the backup man, who covers those in the building while the take is collected. The three tactics are as follows: the unsophisticated ambush which takes all robbers into the victimized establishment with the least planning; the selective raid which involves some casing and advance planning in choosing a target; and the planned operation, which is carefully cased and well structured.[50]

Interviews with prisoners and the writings of other robbers have provided Neal Shover with information about professional burglars. He describes these prisoners as technically competent, accepted by colleagues as trustworthy, tending to specialize in burglary, and relatively successful in that crime. A team, usually made up of two or three members, is selected in those terms through contacts at a favorite bar or other hangout. Tipsters—friends or other persons with knowledge about a promising target—provide information on the existence of loot and the place to be burglarized, usually for a fee. Fences provide the means of disposing of stolen merchandise; they, along with corrupt bondspersons and attorneys, are part of the social matrix of professional burglars.[51]

Victimization surveys indicate that three out of four burglaries of businesses take place at night, but are less numerous than all residential burglaries which usually occur in the day when homes are more likely to be unoccupied. On the average, the economic loss from business burglaries is greater than that from business robberies but less than that from residential burglaries. Robberies are most likely to occur on streets and highways (about half of all robberies). Some 11 percent are residential. Among commercial robberies, major businesses are the primary target, with convenience stores second, gasoline or service stations third, and banks a distant fourth.[52]

Types of Preventive Measures

The surreptitiousness of burglary and the sudden attack of robbery deprive businesses and industries of the advantages of managerial techniques that can reduce employee theft and can help cope with shoplifting. The presence of amateurs among robbers and burglars lends relevance to the view that the crimes are situationally determined by the combination of unfulfilled personal needs and an opportunity for illicit gain perceived by the potential offenders. Perhaps for them, the strategies of primary and secondary prevention have long-term significance for turning the quest for personal satisfaction into legitimate courses of action, but, for commercial and industrial enterprises, more direct and immediate means of prevention are in demand.

Broadly speaking, the preventive measures fall into three general categories. First, the physical design of facilities, target hardening, and the methods of situational crime prevention help reduce opportunities for predatory offenses and to avoid the initiation of burglary and robbery. Alarms, electronic detectors, and stress alarms are among target-hardening devices. Reduction of opportunity appears to be the most promising practical answer, Mike Maguire believes, when there are a limited number of potential targets, when the targets can be equally well protected, and when the impulse to commit an offense is more likely to be spontaneously created by the situation.[53] Situational crime prevention rests on the premises that the decision to steal is shaped by the individual's immediate situation, that the decision is precipitated by the opportunities presented, and that, among the possibilities for prevention, reduction of opportunities will narrow the choices to undertake burglary or robbery.[54] The idea is to avoid the initiation of crimes against *this* facility.

Second, at the casing stage of the behavioral system of crimes previous to execution, robbers and burglars may be persuaded that a given target poses excessive difficulties. According to Eleanor Chelimsky et al., the robbers look for every entry, exit, and control opportunity within the facility. An automobile driving past slowly several times or parked with the motor running are cues that a robbery is contemplated. Visible deterrents signal that the target is not worthwhile for burglary.[55] Limiting the availability of cash blunts the attractiveness of a given target. Cash can be limited by frequent and irregularly scheduled bank deposits, by holding down the amount of cash kept in all-night operations, and by restricting information on safe combinations. Expensive and portable merchandise may be removed from easy observation.

Third, increased chances of capture serve as a form of deterrence. The physical features of the building, its layout, and its immediate environs can at least delay the perpetration of robberies and burglars. Chelimsky and associates recommend that the best rule of thumb is to discreetly observe the criminals for later identification, record any license numbers or description of automobiles, and quickly report the robbery to the police.[56] An internal silent alarm may signal a break-in in progress. To give police the opportunity to collect evidence, the space of intrusion should be left undisturbed. The disposal of stolen goods can be handicapped by sales tags and by recording serial numbers and trademark emblems.[57] Mark H. Moore's idea about controlling the market for illicit goods for the sake of crime prevention is particularly relevant to providing identification of stolen goods to complicate fencing.[58]

PRIVATE SECURITY AND PREVENTION

The growth of the private security industry has been remarkable in recent decades, encompassing 1.1 million employees in 1982 and an estimated expenditure of $20 billion in 1980. In spite of the expansion of public police in response to suburban and urban crime rates, the number of personnel and expenditures in the private sector have become greater.[59] That growth reflects in part the increasing concern of private enterprises about the crimes discussed above and unprecedented recognition of the importance of crime prevention.

Development and Functions

The history of private security may be traced as far back as the guarding of animals against marauders before the rise of Christianity, but organized police departments made their first appearance with the establishment of London's Metropolitan Police in 1830, breaking with previous uses of military personnel, unpaid constables, and privately employed watchmen or guards. The rise of private security in the United States was marked by the early work of Allan

Pinkerton and his agents during the latter half of the nineteenth century, by railroad and iron-and-steel police forces, and by the emergence of primitive forms of various bodies of federal agents.[60]

The recent burgeoning of private security is the result of the higher level of crime, greater public concern about crime, and more general trends. James S. Kakalik and Sorrel Wildhorn have summarized the general trends. Space and defense activities and need for security against violent demonstrations, bombings, and hijackings have expanded the demands for security within governmental agencies. Insurers have raised their rates or require the use of certain private security systems as the condition for rate discounts. Businesses and industries have introduced more specialization of all services; security work has been part of that trend. Higher corporate and private income has added to the property to be protected and the economic means to pay for protection. Scientific advances in electronic and other target-hardening devices have sparked new branches of protection companies. Underlying the increased reliance on private security has been a conviction that the regular police forces are so burdened in coping with crime that private security measures are necessary.[61]

Private security personnel carry out a variety of services. They may be contracted by businesses specializing in security services, or they may be in-house forces employed by business, industry, or the private individual. Contract agencies may perform services such as guarding, roving patrol, armored-car escort, central alarm station, and investigative work for preemployment screening, credit or insurance matters, or court proceedings. A small share of the personnel may be deputized or otherwise granted police powers appropriate to specific duties. The services, broadly speaking, are information gathering, maintaining order and monitoring access to private property, and preventing and detecting crime on the premises.[62]

Involvement in Crime Prevention

Victimization by employee theft, shoplifting, robbery, or burglary places private economic enterprises in the position of safeguarding their property and their personnel. The private security industry has expanded its services to that end, but it has been argued that this preventive role also provides public benefits. The activities prevent and reduce the crimes that are the workload of public police agencies and frees them somewhat to deal with other responsibilities. Private security has the advantage of working within private space in dealing with employee theft and shoplifting that are likely to elude the usual police net. Proactive measures, such as those of target-hardening devices and employee screening as considered above, are available in contrast to the usual reactive strategy of regular law enforcement.[63]

Because the major contributions of security personnel are to protect assets and to prevent losses, they are engaged in the reduction of theft, fires, and other forms of losses that would threaten the profitability of the company. Within the scope of those functions, private security can fill some of the discrepancies between the crime prevention mission assigned to public law enforcement bodies and the realities of the heavy emphasis placed on those bodies to cope with active criminality in public space.

Objective appraisal must incude an evaluation of the efficiency of private security personnel. A survey of private guards in 1969 reported that they typically were aging white males with poor education, poor pay, and little experience in private security. The typical private investigator was a somewhat younger white male, had completed several years of high school, had eight to ten years of experience in private security, and probably earned between $6,000 and $9,000 a year.[64] Another survey conducted ten years later found a more favorable set of characteristics among guards, especially among in-house security personnel who have higher levels of training, education, and compensation.[65]

The use of security guards poses several problems: abuse of authority, such as unnecessary use of force, false arrest, improper search and interrogation, impersonation of a public police officer, illegal bugging and wiretapping, and improper surveillance. For incidents managed through criminal prosecution, the obscurity about the powers and prerogative of private police officers and questions about the quality of their training became problematic.[66] William C. Cunningham and Todd H. Taylor report that the number of contract personnel carrying firearms is small and is decreasing, and that detention, searches, and use of force are discouraged by the policies of security companies and client companies.[67]

The authority of private security, Clifford D. Shearing and Philip C. Stenning point out, derives from the ordinary powers and privileges of private property owners to control access to, use of, and conduct on their property. Thereby, conditions for entry to or departure from the premises include random searches, surrender of property while on the premises, and insistence on certain information for credit or other legitimate purposes of the owners. Since victim-controlled policing is involved, private security does not have to rely primarily on the criminal justice system and can avoid the legal entanglement of prosecution by using the sanctions of firing employee thieves or denying future access to apprehended shoplifters.[68]

SUMMARY

The growth of private security has been stimulated by the victimization of enterprises by employee theft, shoplifting, burglary, and robbery. Efforts to reduce losses have involved victim-oriented private policing that is especially oriented toward prevention.

Employee thefts are crimes against business and industry committed within the regular operations and behavior patterns of those enterprises. Crimes should be examined not as symptoms of the pathological behavior of antisocial persons, but as the expressions of cultural beliefs and aspirations of the main society. In that sense, prevention takes us into topics of study beyond crime per se.

Shoplifting is also fraught with the cultural ambivalence of contemporary society which complicates the identification and treatment of apprehended offenders as clearcut criminals. The psychology of the various kinds of shoplifters is important to effective prevention, but the sociocultural milieu is crucial to prevention, as are mercantile practices that fuel the consumerism essential to company success.

Burglary and robbery represent the most visible intrusions of traditional criminals into the private space of businesses and industries. Again, the conditions of society in general shape the perpetration of these crimes, but here the difficulties of coping with predatory crime raise problems for prevention different from those for employee theft and shoplifting. Prevention involves knowledge of the typical patterns of perpetration and use of physical design, target hardening, and situational crime prevention to convince potential criminals that the risks of unsuccessful intrusion and capture are excessive.

NOTES

1. Addison H. Verrill, "Confronting the Growing Problem of Employee Theft," in Sheryl Leininger, ed., *Internal Theft: Investigation and Control—An Anthology* (Los Angeles: Security World Publishing Co., 1975), pp. 6–8.

2. Charles R. Carson, *Managing Employee Honesty* (Los Angeles: Security World Publishing Co., 1977), p. 14.

3. "Who's Doing the Stealing?" *Management Review* 61 (May 1972): 34–35.

4. Robert C. Hollinger and John P. Clark, *Theft by Employees* (Lexington, Mass.: Lexington Books, 1983), p. 8.

5. Bob Curtis, *Security Control: Internal Theft* (New York: Lebhar-Friedman, 1973), pp. 35–41.

6. William W. McCullough, *Sticky Fingers: A Close Look at America's Fastest Growing Crime* (New York: AMACOM, 1981), pp. 11–13.

7. Curtis, *Security Control*, p. 7.

8. Peter F. Parilla, "Formal Organizational Controls and Property Deviance," in Hollinger and Clark, *Theft By Employees*, p. 117.

9. J. P. Martin, *Offenders as Employees* (New York: St. Martin's Press, 1962), pp. 127–128.

10. Mark H. Moore, "Controlling Criminogenic Commodities: Drugs, Guns, and Alcohol," in James Q. Wilson, ed., *Crime and Public Policy* (San Francisco: ICS Press, 1983), pp. 125–144.

11. Joseph F. Sheley and Kenneth D. Bailey, "New Directions for Anti-Theft Policy: Reductions in Stolen Goods Buyers," *Journal of Criminal Justice* 13, no. 5(1985); 399–415.

12. For further reading on the gun control issue, see Don B. Kates, Jr., ed., *Firearms and Violence: Issues of Public Policy* (Cambridge, Mass.: Ballinger, 1984); David Lester, *Gun Control: Issues and Answers* (Springfield, Ill.: Charles C Thomas, 1984); James D. Wright, Peter H. Rossi, and Kathleen Daly, *Under the Gun: Weapons, Crime and Violence in America* (Hawthorne, N. Y.: Aldine, 1983); Philip J. Cook, "The Influence of Gun Availability in Violent Crime Patterns," in Michael Tonry and Norval Morris, eds.,

Crime and Society, Vol. 4 (Chicago: University of Chicago Press, 1983); William R. Tonso, *Guns and Society: The Social and Existential Roots of the American Attachment to Firearms* (Latham, Md.: University Press of America, 1982); Edward F. Dolan, *Gun Control: A Decision for Americans* (New York: Franklin Watts, 1977).

13. Hollinger and Clark, *Theft By Employees*, p. 128.

14. Ibid., pp. 60–61.

15. Ibid., pp. 120, 126, 84–85, 146.

16. Martin, *Offenders as Employees*, pp. 125–126.

17. Donald N. H. Horning, "Blue-Collar Theft: Conceptions of Property, Attitudes Toward Pilfering, and Work Group Norms in a Modern Industrial Plant," in Erwin O. Smigel and H. Laurence Ross, ed., *Crimes Against Bureaucracy* (New York: Van Nostrand Reinhold Co., 1970), pp. 46–64.

18. Joseph Bensman and Israel Gerver, "Crime and Punishment in the Factory: The Function of Deviance in Maintaining the Social System," *American Sociological Review* 28 (August 1963): 588–598.

19. Gerald Mars, *Cheats at Work: An Anthropology of Workplace Crime* (London: George Allen and Unwin, 1982). The relationships between affiliations among employees and their offenses are analyzed by Richard C. Hollinger and John P. Clark, "Formal and Informal Social Controls of Employee Deviance," *Sociological Quarterly* 23 (Summer 1982): 333–343 and by Richard C. Hollinger and John P. Clark, "Deterrence in the Workplace: Perceived Certainty, Perceived Severity, and Employee Theft," *Social Forces* 62 (December 1983): 398–418.

20. Edwin H. Sutherland, *White Collar Crime* (New York: Holt, Rinehart and Winston, 1961), pp. 9, 12, 18, 46.

21. Ronald R. Schmidt, "Executive Dishonesty: Misuse of Authority for Personal Gain," in Leininger, *Internal Theft*, pp. 68, 75.

22. Gerald D. Robin, "White-Collar Crime and Employee Theft," *Crime and Delinquency* 20 (July 1974): 251–262.

23. "Shoplifting Keeps Pace with Inflation," *Security Management* 22 (July 1978): 27.

24. Gerald D. Robin, "Patterns of Department Store Shoplifting," *Crime and Delinquency* 9 (April 1963): 163–172.

25. David May, "Juvenile Shoplifters and the Organization of Store Security: A Case Study in the Social Construction of Delinquency," *International Journal of Criminology and Penology* 6 (May 1978): 144–155.

26. Harold Cohen, *The Crime That No One Talks About* (New York: Progressive Grocer Co., 1974), pp. 41–46.

27. Erhard Blankenburg, "The Selectivity of Legal Sanctions: An Empirical Investigation of Shoplifting," *Law and Society Review* 11 (Fall 1976): 117–118.

28. Hugh J. Guffey, Jr., James R. Harris, and J. Ford Laumer, Jr., "Shopper Attitudes Toward Shoplifting Preventive Devices," *Journal of Retailing* 55 (Fall 1979): 81–89.

29. Len Daykin, *Loss Prevention: A Management Guide to Improving Retail Security* (New York: Progressive Grocer Co., 1981), p. 63.

30. Lloyd W. Klemke, "Does Apprehension for Shoplifting Amplify or Terminate Shoplifting Activity?" *Law and Society Review* 12 (Spring 1978): 391–403.

31. Allen A. Seedman, "Retail Security," in Lawrence J. Fennelly, ed., *Handbook of Loss Prevention and Crime Prevention* (Boston: Butterworths, 1982), p. 644.

32. Daykin, *Loss Prevention*, pp. 10–11.

33. Harvey Burstein, *Industrial Security Management* (New York: Praeger Publishers, 1977), p. 187.

34. Dorothy B. Francis, *Shoplifting: The Crime Everybody Pays For* (New York: Elsevier/Nelson Books, 1980), pp. 31–33.

35. Cohen, *The Crime That No One Talks About*, p. 63.

36. See Chapter 1, pp. 16–17.

37. May, "Juvenile Shoplifters and the Organization of Store Security," pp. 146–149.

38. M. Jerry Kallis and Dinoo J. Vanier, "Consumer Shoplifting: Orientations and Deterrents," *Journal of Criminal Justice* 13, no. 5 (1985): 470.

39. Vincent F. Sacco, "Shoplifting Prevention: The Role of Communication-Based Intervention Strategies," *Canadian Journal of Criminology* 27(January 1985); 23–26.

40. Chok C. Hiew, "Prevention of Shoplifting: A Community Action Approach," *Canadian Journal of Criminology* 23(January 1981): 59–67.

41. Richard J. Lundman, "Shoplifting and Police Referral: A Re-examination," *Journal of Criminal Law and Criminology* 69(Fall 1978): 395–398.

42. *Criminal Victimization in the United States, 1983* (Washington, D.C.: Bureau of Justice Statistics, U.S. Bureau of Justice, August 1985), Table 72.

43. Ibid., Table 83.

44. Daykin, *Loss Prevention: A Management Guide to Improving Retail Security*, p. 138.

45. Peter Letkemann, *Crime As Work* (Englewood Cliffs, N. J.: Prentice-Hall, 1973), pp. 49–57, 107–109.

46. Ibid., pp. 114–115.

47. Philip J. Cook, "The Role of Firearms in Violent Crime: An Interpretative Review of the Literature," in Marvin E. Wolfgang and Neil Alan Weiner, eds., *Crime Violence* (Beverly Hills, Calif.: Sage Publications, 1982), pp. 252–253.

48. Letkemann, *Crime as Work*, p. 89.

49. John E. Conklin and Egon Bittner, "Burglary in a Suburb," *Criminology* 11(August 1973): 212.

50. Werner J. Einstadter, "The Social Organization of Armed Robbery," *Social Problems* 17 (Summer 1969): 74–76.

51. Neal Shover, "The Social Organization of Burglary," *Social Problems* 20(Spring 1973): 499–514.

52. *Sourcebook of Criminal Justice Statistics, 1984* (Washington, D.C.: Bureau of Justice Statistics, U.S. Department of Justice, 1984), pp. 425–431.

53. Mike Maguire, "Burglary as Opportunity," *Research Bulletin* (British Home Office), no. 10(1980): 7.

54. In regard to residential burglary, the principles of situational crime are applied by Trevor Bennett and Richard Wright, *Burglars on Burglary* (Aldershot, England: Gower Publishing Co., Limited, 1984).

55. Eleanor Chelimsky, Frank C. Jordan, Jr., Linda Sue Russell, and John R. Strack, *Security and the Small Business Retailer* (Washington, D.C.: National Institute of Law Enforcement and Criminal Justice, Law Enforcement Assistance Administration, February 1979), pp. 8–11.

56. Specific preventive measures involving personnel are described by John W. Kennish, "Responding to the Robbery Threat," *Security Management* 29(July 1985): 77–80.

57. Chelimsky et al., *Security and the Small Business Retailer*, pp. 8–11.
58. Moore, "Controlling Criminogenic Commodities: Drugs, Guns, and Alcohol," pp. 130–133.
59. William C. Cunningham and Todd H. Taylor, *Private Security and Police in America* (Portland, Oreg.: Chancellor Press, 1985), pp. 105–108.
60. Milton Lipson, *On Guard: The Business of Private Security* (New York: Quadrangle/New York Times Book Co., 1975), pp. 20–40; Robert R. J. Gallati, *Introduction to Private Security* (Englewood Cliffs, N. J.: Prentice-Hall, 1983), pp. 14–22.
61. James S. Kakalik and Sorrel Wildhorn, *The Private Police: Security and Danger* (New York: Crane Russak, 1977), pp. 19–20.
62. Ibid., pp. 8–9.
63. *Private Security: Report of the Task Force on Private Security* (Washington, D.C.: National Advisory Committee on Criminal Justice Standards and Goals, 1976), pp. 18–19.
64. James S. Kakalik and Sorrel Wildhorn, *The Private Police Industry: Its Nature and Extent*, Vol. 11 (Washington, D.C.: National Institute of Law Enforcement and Criminal Justice, Law Enforcement Assistance Administration, February 1972), p. 67.
65. Cunningham and Taylor, *Private Security and Police in America*, p. 260.
66. The complex legal issues are considered in Kakalik and Wildhorn, *The Private Police*, pp. 303–372.
67. Cunningham and Todd, *Private Security and Police in America*, p. 103.
68. Clifford D. Shearing and Philip C. Stenning, "Private Security: Implications for Social Control," *Social Problems* 30 (June 1983): 497–501.

BIBLIOGRAPHY

Albrecht, W. Steve, et al. *How to Detect and Prevent Business Fraud*. Englewood Cliffs, N.J.: Prentice-Hall, 1982.
    Designed to advise auditors and managers, the book outlines strategies for reducing fraud in management and by employees.
Anderson, R. E. *Bank Security*. Boston: Butterworths, 1981.
    Anderson concentrates on the victimization of banks through robbery, fraud, and computer crime. He considers security devices and protective services from that perspective.
Berger, David L. *Security for Small Business*. Boston: Butterworths, 1981.
    Technical information on security equipment and methods is provided; prevention of shoplifting and employee theft receive special attention.
Brodsky, Stanley L., Martha L. Bernatz, and William B. Beidleman. "The Perfect Crime: An Investigation of the Gasoline Station Drive-Away." *British Journal of Criminology* 21(October 1981): 350–356.
    The motorists who pump gasoline into their automobile's tank and drive away are analyzed as a version of shoplifting.
Cleary, James J., Jr. *Prosecuting the Shoplifter: A Loss Prevention Strategy*. Stoneham, Mass.: Butterworths, 1986.
    Arguing that prosecuting shoplifters is a deterrent when convictions are obtained, Cleary discusses the means and issues of the gathering and evaluation of evidence.
Collins, James J. "Can Criminologists Measure Deterrence?" *Security Management* 27

(June 1983): 73–74.

After a brief review of what research has shown about the deterrent effect of punishment, Collins urges an ongoing dialogue between criminologists and security personnel and between the public and private security worlds.

Conklin, John E. *Robbery and the Criminal Justice System*. Philadelphia: J. B. Lippincott Co., 1972.

This particularly worthy treatise examines why robbery rates have increased, the behavior of robbers, types of robbers, use of force, police force, police reactions, and court disposition of cases.

Griswold, David B. "Crime Prevention and Commercial Burglary: A Time Series Analysis." *Journal of Criminal Justice* 12, no. 5 (1984): 493–501.

The effects of security and greater street lighting on commercial burglary in a section of Portland, Oregon, were traced over a four-year period. Griswold reports a significant and persistent decrease of commercial burglaries.

Schrager, Laura Shill, and James F. Short, Jr. "Toward a Sociology of Organizational Crime." *Social Problems* 25(April 1978): 407–419.

The authors suggest the difficulties of crime prevention within legitimate organizations. They cite the organizations' tendency to overlook a large share of serious offenders and the difficulty of placing responsibility for organization-induced misconduct.

Wesley, Roy L., and John A. Wanat. *A Guide to Internal Loss Prevention*. Stoneham, Mass.: Butterworths, 1986.

Managerial and administrative controls are examined for security against internal theft.

13

Public Facilities

SIDNEY E. MATTHEWS and
ELMER H. JOHNSON

Crime is a major problem facing many, if not most, American cities and towns, and much of it takes place in public access areas: parks, museums, libraries, hospitals, zoos, mass transit facilities, schools, theaters, restaurants, and recreational areas whether under public or private ownership. These diverse settings share the characteristics of public facilities. This chapter will consider the issues of crime and delinquency prevention in five of those settings: libraries, museums, public hospitals, parks, and mass transit.

THE CONCEPT OF PUBLIC FACILITY

Libraries, museums, hospitals, parks, and mass transit facilities differ from one another in many ways, but they present many common features when the parameters of crime and delinquency prevention are under scrutiny. The concept of public facility is a useful vehicle for analysis of those common features in regard to prevention. The words "public" and "facility" symbolize the bringing together of a number of ideas.

Implications of "Public"

"Public" opens the way for an examination of two separate but interrelated phenomena involving patronage and patrons: first, the qualities of the group relationships that are related to patronage, that characterize the tenuous interaction among patrons as a social group, and that characterize the interaction of the patrons within the formal organization of the given facility.

Second, a *public* facility exists to serve a vast aggregate of persons who, other than those interests that bring them to the facility, are of great diversity and do

not otherwise qualify as an organized group with a defined leadership, a sense
of involvement in the persistent affairs of the facility, and a feeling of responsibility for assuming the preservation and further development of the facility.
The patrons form a transitory collectivity of individuals with a constant turnover
of members who happen to be together for a brief time because their immediate
self-interests make the facility's services useful. They lack the elements of social
solidarity because they bring a great variety of biographies, standards of behavior,
and social experience. Their transitory and brief presence in the facility and their
relatively large number make for anonymity that shields the individual from a
responsibility for the conduct of others.

The public *facility* is expected to offer access to the people at large with
minimal restriction on patronage. In that sense, it is a vehicle for equalitarian
participation in the benefits of an advanced civilization. There are restrictions
implied by the requirement that an entrance fee be paid to a museum, a library
card be obtained, or evidence be provided that a hospital bill be satisfied, but
the official rhetoric of a public facility is that the services are available to all.
That rhetoric and the values it expresses complicate determination of who belongs
and who does not and of who is a potential deviant and who is not.

"Facility" is sometimes used as a synonym for a building or set of buildings
as physical structures. The word is a specialized extension of the verb "to
facilitate" referring to making something easier to accomplish or to make more
convenient. Thus, "facility" as used here refers to the means of accomplishing
facilitation. The implication is that physical structure is the setting within which
relevant resources and a staff organization are mobilized to serve purposes for
specified patrons.

Here the word is employed to focus attention on, first, the dimensions of the
physical environment within which prevention activities are undertaken and,
second, the formal organization of resources and staff that are part of the etiology
of and preventive responses to crime and delinquency in the settings portrayed
in this chapter. Those settings are similar in that the facilitation of specified
services occurs within the social-psychological aspects of the organization's
orientation to the public as an amorphous group.

The facilities are *public* in two senses. They are maintained by or for the
people at large, and they must remain open to those persons with reason to make
use of their services. Some public facilities, such as hospitals, operate around
the clock to expose their staffs to the unorthodox events and crises that are
characteristic of "night society." Other public facilities, such as parks and
metropolitan subways, extend beyond the boundaries of buildings per se and
add complexities to preventive activities. The public facilities have drawn an
increasing volume of patrons and have developed highly differentiated staffs as
their functions have become more complex and have generated more elaborate
organizations that also complicate the mounting of preventive programs.

Public facilities existed in earlier eras, but the conditions of urban society
have increased the volume and spread of their patronage. The democratization

of the delivery of services as implied by the term "public facilities" has added to the volume and has made the facilities accountable to a broader range of constituencies. Measures to differentiate between potential offenders and regular patrons are inhibited by the necessity to provide access to the broadly defined public.

AN EXAMPLE: IMPACT ON LIBRARIES

Those who regard the library only as a place of quiet and tranquility, isolated from the troubles of the world outside its walls, are likely to be surprised to learn that librarians must carry on a persistent struggle against human transgressors and the threats of nature. The metropolitan libraries probably face the greatest threat.

New York City's librarians are struggling to preserve not only their traditional peace and quiet, but also their very safety as they fend off drug addicts, vandals, thieves, derelicts, and teenagers who curse and even threaten the staff: "We've lost the subways and most of the parks and we just can't afford to lose our libraries," said Thomas E. Slade, the assistant public commissioner for legal affairs. "We've got to control those problems before the scale tips."[1]

The type of serious crimes are arson, as when Hollywood Regional Library in Los Angeles was torched, the library demolished, and three-quarters of its 90,000 volumes destroyed;[2] murder, as seen in the slaying and wounding of two staff members of the Norfolk, Virginia, Public Library System's Barron F. Black Branch;[3] and the wounding of University of Florida Library Director by a former employee.[4] However, the most frequent crimes are theft and mutilation of the collections.

Librarians are facing pressures from all directions—financial, technological, legal, and natural disasters that cause loss of all or part of a library's collection: water, humidity, fire, insects, and earthquakes. None of these, however, has caused as much loss or insidious consequences to as many libraries as theft and mutilation of collections by some of the very patrons those libraries seek to serve. Theft and mutilation are not recent problems and can be traced in the history of books and libraries, but reports of collection losses and annual loss rates just began to appear in the mass media in the late 1960s. A 1963 report estimated that the national cost of such thefts was $5 million each year.[5] A worse consequence, in the opinion of librarians and library patrons, is the denial of books to other uses.

The Carnegie Council on Policy Studies in Higher Education released *Fair Practice in Higher Education* in 1979 and concluded that book theft is a serious problem for most college libraries.[6] Princeton University's Harvey S. Firestone Memorial Library revealed the following losses: 12.5 percent of the 40,000 titles essential to teaching programs, and more than 4.3 percent of the almost 2 million volumes in Firestone's open stacks, with replacement expenses calculated at $3 million.[7] In September 1983 *The Chronicle of Higher Education* reported: "all but 25 percent of incidents estimated to be 'inside jobs' and libraries urged to close stacks to halt the 'epidemic of theft'."[8]

WHY THEFTS FROM LIBRARIES?

More than 18 years ago, the former director of the Free Library of Philadelphia wrote: "Prevention of book thefts is one of our most urgent problems facing our library and others."[9] His early warning, however, has not forestalled major losses. For example, in 1984 about 37,400 books were missing from the City University of New York's collection of 516,000 volumes, with a replacement value of a million dollars. In addition, more than 19,400 books belonging to the seven community college libraries of that university system were so long overdue that there was no hope of recovering them. Most of the books had been legally charged out to students.[10]

The latter point suggests that the analysis of the varied motives of library theft include those of casual offenders who do not see themselves as criminals, who do not engage in systematic unauthorized removal of books, and who are trying to evade library rules on circulation. "The largest percentage of stops with our electronic security system is with an ordinary patron, the run-of-the-mill patron who proclaims a multitude of excuses for unauthorized removal of library materials, ranging from 'I forgot my library card' to 'I needed a longer loan period'," according to the librarian of the Evanston (Illinois) Public Library.[11] Those excuses may be evaluated as the desire to fulfill the legitimate obligations of the student and scholar, but those transgressions complicate the ready identification of the full-fledged thief.

The bibliomaniac, another type, acquires a large number of books and papers out of his or her love for books or scholarship. In effect, a personal library is acquired through systematic theft. In 1981 a former history student at Princeton was asked to leave, and a cache of up to 4,000 stolen books valued at hundreds of thousands of dollars was found in his apartment.[12] In 1979 an English instructor at the University of California at Riverside was arraigned for the theft of more than 10,000 books. The estimated cost of the stolen materials was between $100,000 and $200,000.[13]

The withholding of criminal prosecution from the casual offender appears appropriate in light of the stigmatizing effects of arrest and the probability that usually initial apprehension is a sufficient deterrent. The noneconomic purpose and scholarly motive of the bibliomaniac raises greater doubts because of the systematic nature and volume of the illegitimate withdrawals. After all, the bibliomaniac aggravates the impact on the library mission and on the denial of access to patrons to irreplaceable books, rare manuscripts, historic documents, reference materials, and technical equipment. As we have seen, hardships are exposed in budget-tight libraries required to replace the material.

The social values of the library work against criminal prosecution of the acts of persons who appear to be regular patrons—acts that are legally defined as crimes and that have those adverse consequences. In addition to humane considerations, libraries are usually unwilling to prosecute because of the prospect of unfavorable publicity for the library itself. Furthermore, most libraries are unlikely to recognize that those acts detected account for only a fraction of the total losses. Librarians are quick to point out that a yearly inventory is virtually impossible in most large libraries today. Besides quantity, there is the tactical problem of recording books in and out of circulation.

In making their own contributions to the theft problem, libraries open the way for the calculated and systematic raids of professional criminals, the third type. Here the thefts are those of persons who know the marketable value of the books and manuscripts they selectively steal and who have access to an illicit market for their loot. They prefer libraries to bookstores principally because the chances of apprehension and prosecution are less, books are more accessible, and a greater variety of books is available.

Early in 1984 the University of Maryland and the Federal Bureau of Investigation reported the theft of 150 rare leather-bound volumes, most of which were quarto and octavo European editions dating from the sixteenth, seventeenth, and eighteenth centuries from a locked special-collections area of the institution's library. These items had not been listed in the library's catalog and had a value of up to $75,000.[14]

In 1983 the *York County Coast Star* reported that two thieves specializing in expensive editions of art and photography books were arrested and held on a federal detainer and were wanted for twenty-six counts of felony in Philadelphia, grand theft in California, and probation violation in McLean, Virginia.[15] In 1982 *The Houston Post* reported that Rice University had recovered $100,000 in prints that had been razored out of 1800s editions of architecture, engineering, and natural science books following the arrest of a Dallas book dealer who had been caught stealing at the University of Illinois at Champaign/Urbana.[16]

PREVENTIVE STRATEGIES OF LIBRARIES

In undertaking preventive actions against theft, libraries are caught between the wish to protect holdings and the insistence of the modern library philosophy that making library resources available to patrons is the basic mission. That dilemma was less pressing in the earlier days of "chained" books and book chests. Chained books were developed at a time when the medievalist was interested in acquisition and possession rather than use. This concern was carried to its extreme in many small countries. In India, where control of loss was seemingly guaranteed by making the librarian financially responsible for his collections, this was considered a deterrent to service and called for balancing service against the risk of loss.[17]

Mobilizing Staff and Target Hardening

The size and availability of resources, of course, affect the nature of the security procedures that are appropriate for adequate protection. However, essential actions are the taking of an up-to-date inventory to make possible the detection of losses, a clear and accurate marking of all items, and alerting the staff that security consciousness is vital. The education of a staff involves more than showing films, circulating articles and reports, and meeting with security officers. One university initiated preparedness courses for librarians on handling security problems and emergencies. The program at the University of California, Berkeley, in 1982 offered seven courses. In eight-hour courses, staff were trained to act quickly and appropriately.

Libraries combat the theft problem with exit guards, turnstiles, special patrons, closed stacks, restricted access, strict registration, building design, circulation systems, badges, moratoriums on fines, and legal action as most state laws provide a legal definition of library theft and a legal basis for dealing with thieves. Laws have been passed in Virginia in 1975,[18] in Mississippi in 1978,[19] in Iowa in 1979,[20] and in Wisconsin in 1980. Similar statutes have been debated in Illinois, California, and New York.

Only a handful of libraries employ closed circuit television or other monitoring devices. However, use of electronic security systems since early 1970 has been widespread and successful. It was estimated in 1980 that more then 2,500 electronic detection systems were in American libraries and that 500 were leased or sold annually.[21] Worldwide installations are estimated even higher at 6,600 as of 1979.[22]

All electronic security systems operate in the same basic way with a treated target placed in the material. The two basic systems are: bypass and full-circulating. The systems have been tested for health safety involving pacemakers, hearing-aids, and radiation. Only one major incident involving electronic-security-system interference with cardiac pacemakers has even been reported, and this was in England in 1978. Hearing-aid interference seems to be even less of a problem, whereas the question of radiation is more difficult.[23] Most of the systems use less than the maximum power allowed or use none at all.

Electronic security systems for book theft detection have undergone some changes in the last few years, primarily as a result of their increased use in retail and supermarket sales. The public is probably most familiar with these systems through the hard plastic tags attached to merchandise in many clothing stores. They are becoming increasingly visible in hard goods retail operations. One new product is particularly suitable for use in drugstores, supermarkets, and bookstores; it can be used on cassette tapes, audiovisual equipment, and magazines. Current estimates of annual loss are $16 million; however, less than 2 percent of bookstores around the country have implemented electronic security systems.[24]

An electronic security system is less costly than augmentation of staff, gives a high degree of security, increases staff and patron sense of security, prevents theft, reduces the possibility of civil suits, and reduces time in court. The chief disadvantages are the difficulty of justifying high first-time cost; maintenance costs may tend to decrease patronage; failure may occur at critical instances; and such a system may call attention to theft problems and actually inspire theft behavior to beat the system. Even an electronic security system may fail: "another 18,000 books are believed to have been stolen" as the libraries' theft-detection system missed 13 percent of all unauthorized withdrawals.[25]

Collecting and Disseminating Information

In spite of the serious problems described above, libraries as a whole have not given sufficient attention to the need for preventive action. A recent survey by the Association of Research Libraries, covering 89 of the 117 member libraries, found that few libraries have collection security policies, and of the ones that do most prescribe what to do about thefts after the fact.[26] Those conditions have stimulated a number of conferences and workshops attended by librarians, booksellers, lawyers, and law enforcement agents to discuss their common concerns about book theft and to develop a unified approach to prevention.

Guidelines have been offered for dealing with the problems of security. The Association of College and Research Libraries, Committee on Security, Rare Books and Manuscripts Section, published a second draft of its "Guidelines for the Security of Rare Books, Manuscripts and Other Special Collections" in *College and Research Libraries News* in March 1982. Also published in 1982 was *Rare Books and Manuscript Thefts: A Security System for Librarians, Booksellers, and Collectors* by John H. Jenkins. Two issues of *Library and Archival Security* (formerly *Library Security Newsletter*) in 1982 are relevant. The first issue was entitled "Protecting Your Collection: A Handbook, Survey, and Guide for the Security of Rare Books, Manuscripts, Archives, and Works of Art." The second issue described the nature of book thieves; told what to do when the thief is caught, when the books are recovered, and when librarians are offered suspicious books; and offered advice on how to avoid book thefts.

One of the major problems in assessing crime in libraries has been the lack of national analysis. A three-year study of crime and disruption in public libraries in the fifty states, as reported in the Library Crime Research Project, gives basic data. The project measured the evidence of eighteen different types of crime and disruption and classified them as vandalism, theft, problem patron behavior, assault, and arson. Faced with the potential crimes, what can library administrators do to best secure facilities? The development of a library crime index provides a reasonable way for libraries, especially public libraries, to assess how serious their problems may be in relationship to what other libraries are experiencing. Such an assessment makes it possible to develop and design a program. "Designing a good security program involves a five-step approach, devising a security checklist, making a risk assessment study, monitoring crime patterns, establishing a reporting procedure, and implementing the program."[27]

The computer-assisted alerting service has moved into the arena to alert the book trade and others to theft of unique items. "Bookline Alert: Missing Books and Manuscripts" (BAMBAM) is a not-for-profit program on the computer facilities of *American Book Prices Current*, the New York-based annual record of the prices of books and manuscripts at auctions. BAMBAM consists of two parts: an on-line database, which will also be available as published hard copy; and a hard-copy supplement.[28]

MUSEUMS: CULTURE FOR THE "MASSES"

In previous centuries, the audience for the arts and consumers of leisure-time activities were largely confined to a selected elite. Relatively few people were literate or were in a position to cultivate a taste for "high culture" before formal education was extended to all segments of the population. Technological advances have reduced the proportion of total human energy that must be devoted to producing sustenance needs and have made leisure time available to a greater share of the population. In short, general changes in the society as a whole help us understand the tremendous upsurge in museum attendance.

New Popularity of Museums

The trend toward a "cultural democracy" has stimulated a debate between those critics who see a debasement of aesthetic values through the rewarding of triviality and debased tastes and those observers who applaud an unprecedented distribution of the fruits of an advanced civilization. Regardless of the merits of either side of the argument, the upsurge in attendance exposes museums and other cultural institutions to the criminogenic conditions of public facilities.

Greater museum attendance is symptomatic of an expanding interest in cultural objects which, in turn, has produced an unprecedented market for the sale of those objects. The popularity of museums, along with publicity on the sale of the rare works of master artists for fabulous sums of money, attracts professional thieves and unscrupulous dealers. However, predatory behavior is stimulated by a variety of motives; as Renata Rutledge notes: "Aside from personal greed or the desire for an individual to acquire a particular object, some of these crimes are committed for ransom, for personal publicity, or as an expression of political protest."[29] Hans Urbanski tells of a theft in 1974 of fourteen paintings owned by a South African millionaire and the ransom demand for food for starving people in the Congo and the release of four imprisoned terrorists.[30]

Attempts to Deal with Offenders

Since libraries and museums share a number of common characteristics, the previous discussion of library security measures is relevant here. However, for museums, perimeter and space control security is particularly important. Perimeter devices include step or pressure mats, foil tape, and magnetic switches that provide an electrical barrier against intrusion. Step mats are placed under carpeting at doorways or in prohibited areas to alert employees. Magnet switches sound an alarm when a window or door is opened. Metallic tape around windows and in walls performs the same function. Within the museum space control is maintained by closed circuit television, ultrasonic detectors, capacitance alarms (electronic protection of an especially vulnerable object or area), audio detectors, microwave alarms, and electric eyes.

In spite of the usefulness of mechanical electric devices, Robert C. Tillotson regards an efficient and alert guard force to be the basis of museum security. Traditionally, security personnel have been recruited from the unskilled, unemployed, and retired. They then suffer from low pay and prestige. Tillotson urges strict recruitment standards to obtain physically fit and intelligent guards, provision of distinctive uniforms and adequate remuneration, and proper training.[31]

HOSPITALS: MEDICAL CARE AND PREVENTION

The general hospital has become the focal point of medical care as it has changed from a custodial institution where death was common to a complex multipurpose institution applying progress in anatomy, physiology, cellular pathology, bacteriology, endocrinology, biochemistry, and other sciences supporting medicine. Medical practice has developed an increasing range of specialties illustrated by the medical team of physician, nurse, and laboratory technician. With greater prevalence of specialization, affiliation with a hospital is essential if the physician is to have access to, and the patient is to benefit from, the more sophisticated medical technology. The typical site of diagnosis and treatment has been shifted away from the patient's home or the physician's office to the hospital where a team of specialists is mobilized.

A hospital is faced with the security problems of a hotel, an industrial complex, and an office building, Gion Green and Raymond C. Farber point out, but many hospital administrators fail to recognize the problems of theft from patients, vandalism, employee theft, dishonest vendors, and even armed robbery and arson.[32] Furthermore, the hybrid nature of the hospital's organization and the crisis nature of its service delivery color the security problem.

As an organization, the public hospital combines the work of a professional staff of doctors, surgeons, nurses, and technicians in the delivery of medical services and the work of a variegated staff that carries out the duties of administration, maintenance, and other forms of supportive activities. The physicians usually are engaged in private practice and are not regular members of the hospital's staff. Since they are highly autonomous as a profession and are the fundamental decision makers in medical care, hospital administrators are handicapped in imposing routines on them for the sake of security. The relative irregularity of their presence in the hospital raises the problem of their identification and the possibility of intruders gaining access by displaying the appearance of being physicians. Since the nurses and technicians are employees, the usual security measures can be employed more effectively: identification cards and name badges, package inspection, time clocks, background investigations, and in-service security education.

The patients are involuntary consumers who are admitted in medical crises, usually for relatively brief periods. Their abrupt appearance initiates tentative relationships with staff on whom they are dependent for specialized and routine services. Here there is a similarity to the transitory nature of hotel patronage, but the medical crisis places patients under the authority of personnel who impose normative demands under conditions not familiar to the patients. Conversely, the personnel lack biographic knowledge of the patients, the patient's need for supportive responses is met by the impersonality of the medical bureaucracy and the depersonalization inherent in the management of patients. Routinization of daily hospital life exposes private areas of the body and otherwise the individuality of habits of eating, dress, making beds, and even taking medication.

Visitor control and building security loom large in prevention activities in hospitals, and both entail architectural design. Walter M. Strobl notes that hospitals may have so many entrances that control of intruders is very difficult at best. In design of hospitals, he recommends that the number of entrances be restricted, emergency doors be equipped with alarms or signals to the guard headquarters, and closed circuit television be installed. Passes, color coded for the given day of the week, are means of visitor control, especially when the authorized area is specified. Parking areas require illumination in order to protect against vandalism and theft from vehicles and against attacks on the nursing staff on the night shift. Pharmacy departments on the first floor are especially vulnerable to theft of narcotics.[33]

PUBLIC PARKS AND VANDALISM

As for libraries and museums, the remarkable expansion of parks and playgrounds in economically advanced societies reflects a democratization of leisure-time activities. That development is the culmination of technological progress over recent centuries, which has enabled a greater proportion of the population to meet their basic sustenance needs of food, shelter, and clothing and have time left over for recreation. Public parks are part of a revolutionary expansion of leisure activities that began in the nineteenth century as a result of the shortened work week, the inclusion of women in those activities through the introduction of labor-saving techniques in the home as well as industry, improvements in the efficiency of transportation, and increased recognition of the functions of recreation for sustaining social order and serving personal interests.

Vulnerability of Public Parks

The emergence of commercialized recreation is a remarkable modern phenomenon, but our concern is with the similarly remarkable emergence of public parks and playgrounds. Those public facilities serve a vast aggregate of persons with diversified backgrounds and status positions drawn together by the particular recreational interest served. In other words, the general crime prevention issues of the public facility are relevant in that they contribute to the rise of the problem of vandalism.

Although statistics on crime in public parks are fragmentary, a study of twenty parks in five major cities published in 1972 provides some insights.[34] The amount of reported index crimes was substantially less than popularly assumed. Of the 7,853 criminal acts reported in the neighborhood areas, only 2,633 were on the streets adjacent to the parks and only 108 in the parks themselves. The offenses were most frequent in the larger parks, which also had the lowest security measures, and when the served population was undergoing racial, ethnic or class change. Most of the offenses were victimless.

Vandalism: Its Nature and Impact

A sign above a window in the Bronx Zoo says: "See the most destructive animal alive!" Looking in, the people see themselves reflected in a mirror. Thereby, George A. Kenline makes the point that vandalism in parks, zoos, and outdoor recreational areas represents the misconduct of a variety of persons motivated by a desire for property or souvenirs, for revenge or the expression of more general frustrations, for malicious mischief, and for graffiti. Aside from acts committed by children unsupervised by parents, destructive acts include nailing equipment to trees, gathering wood for campfires, driving vehicles into vegetated areas for convenience, dumping trailer sanitary tanks, and starting forest fires inadvertently. Basically responsible people can be temporarily inconsiderate.[35]

From the perspective of delinquency and crime, vandalism is simple property destruction. The word has been traced to the Vandals, an East German tribe that sacked Rome in 455 and came to be viewed as barbaric destroyers of civilization. The lumping of all destructive behavior in this way, as Stanley Cohen shows, overlooks the complexity of motives. He presents five types of vandalism to illustrate his point.[36] *Acquisitive vandalism* includes stripping metal from buildings to sell to junk dealers, collecting street signs and similar items for display as trophies, or looting coins from parking meters and vending machines. *Tactical vandalism* serves to gain publicity for a cause or to attract attention and help solve a personal problem. In *vindictive vandalism*, property destruction is a form of revenge against individuals or social institutions. *Malicious vandalism* expresses hatred and enjoyment that the victim of destruction suffers discomfort.

Play vandalism stems from curiosity, demonstrating a skill, or engaging in competition with other persons without being malicious.

It has been estimated that vandalism costs the United States more than a billion dollars a year through destruction, defacement, or defilement of property. Robert E. Sternloff and Roger Warren summarized evidence in regard to parks. The 150 city parks of San Jose, California, suffered $114,000 in damage in eighteen months. A survey of 171 park recreation departments reported that vandalism repair cost 10.3 cents per capita for the population served. The Vicksburg District of the U.S. Army Corps of Engineers spent $63,000 in 1980 to remedy 460 acts of vandalism. Those costs do not cover the lasting effects on the national features and irreplaceable cultural artifacts of parks.[37]

Preventive Measures

Preventive measures that are standard for other public facilities are appropriate to combat vandalism: public and staff education, effective law enforcement as a deterrent, and denial of free access to crucial areas. Sternloff and Warren suggest other measures for parks. Volunteer hosts in the parks and campgrounds offer assistance to visitors, and their presence reduces vandalism. Vandal-proof facilities and equipment—restrooms, shelters, drinking fountains, benches, signs, electric outlets, and so on—have been recommended. User fees, especially vandalism surcharges, are supposed to give patrons a sense of protective ownership. Prompt repair or replacement appears to deter further destructive behavior.[38]

Target hardening is a contest, Jack Howley notes. He refers to the use of polycarbonate in Baltimore schools. Vandals removed the glazing compound before it was set. Since the glazing strips were secured with sheet metal screws, the vandals carried screwdrivers. Pop rivets stopped them temporarily, but the vandals sprayed the windows with lighter fluid and set them afire.[39]

A variety of empirical experiments have been carried out to prevent vandalism. Deerfield, Illinois, for example, requires parents to pay the cost of damages to parks made by their children. Plainclothes police officers use bicycles in Richardson, Texas, to patrol vulnerable areas inaccessible by automobile. Stillwater, Oklahoma, had neighborhood children paint a mural of favorite animals on a water tower that had been the target of paint spray-can graffiti. The strategy was successful until one piece of graffiti initiated the progressive marring of the mural.[40]

TRANSIT SYSTEMS: CRIME AND VANDALISM

The vulnerability to street crime felt in metropolises is especially evident among patrons of mass transit systems. It is therefore not surprising that a large segment of the public conferred hero status on Bernhard H. Goetz after he wounded four teenagers who accosted him on December 22, 1984, in a New

York subway car. According to police, three of the shooting victims had arrest records and three were armed with sharpened screwdrivers. Goetz's act was compared with that in the movie *Death Wish*, in which an honest citizen became a vigilante stalking muggers. Hundreds of phone calls flooded police stations cheering Goetz for "only protecting himself" and suggesting that he run for mayor.[41]

Rising Concern about Crime

The spontaneity of that response demonstrates the conviction of many subway riders that predatory criminals lurk among the transitory and anonymous collectivity of persons assembled in physical proximity but without social intimacy in a closed space for rapid transportation. That conviction is coupled with a lack of confidence that police can either prevent crimes there or provide essential assistance. The "subway vigilante" symbolized the belief of some persons that individuals have to depend on themselves for protection.

Until the 1950s transit crime primarily involved offenses against property, but an upsurge in crimes against persons and violence in the 1950s and 1960s brought public concern and an expansion of the transit police. Because of the shortage of reliable and relevant data, a conclusive answer cannot be given to the question of whether or not subway riders have a greater risk of criminal victimization than the average urbanite. However, subway patrons run a greater risk than bus patrons, and the risk is greatest in those locales where the neighborhood crime rates are highest.[42]

A review of research on transit robberies shows the following general conclusions: Most robberies occur in the evening, especially on Fridays and Saturdays and when the victims are alone. Most robberies occur on station platforms; when committed on trains, robberies occur while the train is in motion. Very few witnesses report the crimes; most crimes are reported by victims. Most victims are not injured. Most patrons would feel more secure if they knew emergency assistance could be readily obtained.[43]

Urban mass transit systems are vital to the maintenance of the commercial and cultural life of metropolises because they move large numbers of patrons through space in a relatively short time. Crime is a serious problem for many of those systems because the fear of potential riders reduces revenue, further aggravating the fiscal difficulties already created by the popularity of private automobiles. Differential patronage affects relative vulnerability to fare increases and criminal victimization. Residents of the inner city are captives of public transit, for few can avoid its use. The young, old, and minorities tend to be the predominant users.

A study of a metropolitan transit system by Carnegie-Mellon University delineated the major dimensions of the problem.[44] In a ten-year period ridership dropped 22 percent in the 1960s and per capita automobile registration increased 20 percent. Ridership shifted from evening use to the hours from 9:00 AM to

3:00 PM. Robberies were predominant among transit crimes, and they were most likely to occur on elevated station platforms at times of low patronage. The risk was greater on rapid transit than on buses. The transit stations with high ridership and crimes were in areas with high unemployment and high crime rates. Criminal predators tended to work in territories familiar to them and were not likely to use public transit to extend their crimes outside their own neighborhood.

The older subway systems present features that security consultants find conducive to crime: multiple entrances, a maze of connecting tunnels, poor lighting, and many areas denying observation. The use of routine patrol is expensive and is more reactive than proactive. In examining the effectiveness of saturation patrol in the New York subway system, researchers concluded that felonies were reduced but at a cost of $35,000 for each deterred felony.[45] However, the visibility of patrol officers reassures the public that assistance will be rapidly provided. Thus, Robert Shellow and his associates recommend security devices for that purpose: emergency telephones, closed-circuit television monitoring, movable barriers that narrow the accessible platform areas during periods of low ridership, public address systems, and monitoring centers where television observation and telephone communication are coordinated.[46]

Vandalism and Public Transit

Vandalism generally is legally defined as the willful or malicious destruction, injury, disfigurement, or defacement of property without the consent of the owner or persons in authority. Transit vandalism is largely that of juveniles and involves damage to equipment and facilities and graffiti. Although damage entails only a small fraction of operating expenses, it imposes indirect social and economic costs. Patrons are disturbed by dilapidated and disfigured vehicles and are inconvenienced by reductions in service when the vehicles are being repaired. Passengers and employees may be injured because of the effects of vandalism; the transit system must bear insurance and legal costs. Revenue suffers from the withdrawal of damaged vehicles from service.

Those of us who have seen the subway cars of New York City can attest to the remarkable extent of graffiti. Is it simply vandalism or expressions of latent artistic talent? The transit system bears the heavy costs of repetitively removing the defacement and attempting prevention. As for all forms of vandalism, patrons are disturbed and ridership rates suffer. A more favorable assessment is that the subway cars are the moving palettes that carry the nicknames, initials, and "artistic" messages throughout the city.

Psychologists have evaluated graffiti activity as expressions of fear and hate and, sometimes, as a form of clique behavior. Dorothy B. Francis reports that the cliques carry names such as Acid Writers, WAR (Writers Already Respected), and CIA (Criminals In Action) and are selective in conferring membership status. Graffiti expeditions are carefully organized to sneak into tunnels or car yards and carry out preconceived designs. The transit authority is responding to graffiti in several ways. Apprehended vandals or their parents are required to pay part of the cost of repainting the car. A vandalism squad, plus guard dogs, are assigned to areas of high graffiti activity.[47]

To counter vandalism, public transit organizations have experimented with public education, especially in schools, and with prosecution of apprehended vandals to serve as deterrent examples. Resistant materials are one resource for preventing vandalism; acrylic and polycarbonate glass is especially appropriate for vulnerable windows. Hard seats, usually of fiberglass, resist cutting.

FINAL SUMMING UP

The multifaceted sources of crime and vandalism in public transit and the special difficulties of prevention are another example of the effects of open access to a diverse patronage that is characteristic of the various public facilities. As is true of libraries, museums, hospitals, and parks, public transit serves a vast aggregate of patrons who are momentarily placed together but without the elements of social solidarity that motivate conformist behavior. The patrons are dependent on the public facility for needed services, but those qualities of their brief and tenuous contacts offer opportunities for perpetrating delinquency and crime because of the difficulty of identifying the potential lawbreaker.

Although means of prevention are available, their implemention is made especially problematic by the conditions found in public facilities. As we have seen, libraries, museums, hospitals, parks, and transit systems possess some unique features and conditions, but they share the qualities of public facilities and thereby symbolize the effects of mass society on the field of prevention.

NOTES

1. *New York Times*, July 11, 1981, p. 1.

2. "Hollywood Regional Library Destroyed in Arson Fire," *Library Journal* (June 1, 1982): 1034.

3. "Knife Wielding Youth Slays Public Library Staff Member," *American Libraries* 14 (April 1983): 174.

4. "University of Florida Library Director Shot by Former Employee," *American Libraries* 14 (June 1983): 334.

5. *Protecting the Library and Its Resources: A Guide to Physical Protection and Insurance*, Report on a Study Conducted by Cage Babcock & Associates, Inc. (Chicago: Library Technology Project, American Library Association, 1963), p. 21.

6. "Security in Libraries," *Library Journal* 103 (June 1, 1979): 1206.

7. "Princeton Cuts Acquisitions; Theft on the Upswing," *Library Journal* 103 (May 1, 1978): 97.

8. Beverly T. Watkins, "Libraries Urged to Close Stacks to Halt 'Epidemic of Theft'," *Chronicle of Higher Education* 27 (September 28, 1983): 1.

9. "To Test Book Theft Prevention," *American Library Association Bulletin* 62 (April 1968): 337.

10. "Books Worth $1 Million Are Missing from CUNY," *Chronicle of Higher Education* 27 (February 1, 1984): 2.

11. Alice Harrison Bahr, *Book Theft and Library Security Systems, 1981-1982* (White Plains, N. Y.: Knowledge Industry Publications, 1981), p. 123.

12. "Princeton Catches a Thief; Ex-student Faces Trial," *Library Journal* 107 (April 15, 1982): 767.

13. "Grand Larceny," *Wilson Library Bulletin* 53 (May 1979): 617.

14. "150 Rare Volumes Missing from University of Maryland Library," *Chronicle of Higher Education* 27 (February 8, 1984): 3.

15. "Book Thieves Caught in Maine with Loot from Several Libraries," *Library Journal* 108 (September 1, 1983): 1642.

16. "Following Theft, Rice University Will Sell Recovered Prints," *Library Journal* 107 (December 1, 1982): 2212.

17. "Losses of Books from Libraries" (Letter), *India Library* 22 (December 1967): 157.

18. Edmund Berkeley, Jr., "Code of Virginia Revised to Benefit Libraries and Archivists," *Virginia Librarian* 21 (May 1975): A.

19. "Bedeviled Libraries—Is It Bibliomania?" *Mississippi Library News* 42 (June 1978): 75.

20. "Iowa Throws the Book at Thieves, Delinquent Patrons," *Library Journal* 104 (August 1979): 1510.

21. Richard W. Boss, "The Library Security Myth," *Library Journal* 54 (March 15, 1980): 683.

22. Nancy H. Knight, "Theft Detection Systems for Libraries Revisited: An Updated Survey," *Library Technology Reports* 15(May-June 1979): 211–409.

23. Ibid., p. 334.

24. "Books Worth $1-Million Are Missing From CUNY," p. 2.

25. David Tuller, "Electronic Surveillance Systems in Bookstores," *Publishers Weekly* 225 (May 25, 1984): 45.

26. Association of Research Libraries, Office of Management Studies, Systems and Procedures Exchange Center, *Collections Security in ARL Libraries Kit 100* (Washington D.C.: SPEC Center, OMS/ARL, 1984).

27. Alan Jay Lincoln, *Crime in the Library* (New York: R. R. Bowker Co., 1984), p. 156.

28. J. L. Chernofsky, "Computerized System to Alert Trade to Thefts [Bookline Alert: Missing Books and Manuscripts]," *AB Bookman's Weekly* 67 (June 29, 1981): 5058.

29. Renata Rutledge, "The Many Facets of a Museum Security Director's Job," in Lawrence J. Fennelly, ed., *Museum, Archive, and Library Security* (Boston: Butterworths, 1983), p. 26.

30. Hans Urbanski, "The Insurance of Objects of Art," in Fennelly, *Museum, Archive, and Library Security*, p. 42.

31. Robert G. Tillotson, *Museum Security* (Paris: International Council of Museums, 1977), pp. 17–26.

32. Gion Green and Raymond C. Farber, *Introduction to Security* (Los Angeles: Security World Publishing Co., 1975), pp. 241–243.

33. Walter M. Strobl, *Crime Prevention Through Physical Security* (New York: Marcel Dekker, 1978), pp. 289–293.

34. Harold Lewis Malt, "An Analysis of Public Safety as Related to the Incidence of

Crime in Parks and Recreation Areas in Central Cities'' (Washington, D.C.: Harold Lewis Malt Associates, January 1972), pp. iv, 100–102.

35. George A. Kineline, "Vandalism: An Overview," in *Vandalism and Outdoor Recreation: Symposium Proceedings* (Berkeley, Calif.: Pacific Southwest Forest and Range Experiment Station, U.S. Department of Agriculture, Forest Service, General Technical Report PSW–17, 1976), pp. 6–7.

36. Stanley Cohen, "Property Destruction: Motives and Meanings," in Colin Ward, ed., *Vandalism* (London: Architectional Press, 1973), pp. 42–48.

37. Robert E. Sternloff and Roger Warren, *Park and Recreation Maintenance Management* (New York: John Wiley and Sons, 1984), pp. 302–303.

38. Ibid., pp. 304–309.

39. Jack Howley, *Reducing Park Vandalism* (Bismarck, N. D.: Upper Plains State Innovative Group, June 1981), p. 19.

40. Ibid., pp. 27–28, 29, 37.

41. *St. Louis Post Dispatch*, December 24, 1984, p. 9A, and December 25, 1984, p. 10C.

42. L. Siegel, M. Molof, W. Moy, J. Strack, and F. Jordon, Jr., "An Assessment of Crime and Policing Responses in Urban Mass Transit Systems" (Technical Report MTR 7497) (McLean, Va.: Mitre Corporation, April 1977), pp. 9–10, 47–48.

43. Transportation Research Institute, "Subway Crime," in Leonard D. Savitz and Norman Johnston, eds., *Crime in Society* (New York: John Wiley and Sons, 1978), pp. 949–950.

44. Robert Shellow, James P. Romualdi, and Eugene W. Bartel, "Crime in Rapid Transit Systems: An Analysis and a Recommended Security and Surveillance System," in *Crime and Vandalism in Public Transportation* (Transportation Research Record 487), (Washington, D.C.: Transportation Research Board, 1974), pp. 2–5.

45. Alan M. Chaiken, Michael W. Lawless, and Keith A. Stevenson, *The Impact of Police Activity on Crime: Robberies in New York Subway System* (Santa Monica, Calif.: Rand Corporation, 1974), pp. 22, 63.

46. Shellow, Romualdi, and Bartel, "Crime in Rapid Transit Systems," pp. 7–11.

47. Dorothy B. Francis, *Vandalism: The Crime of Immaturity* (New York: Lodestar Books, 1983), pp. 17–26.

BIBLIOGRAPHY

Bannon, Joseph J. *Problem Solving in Recreation and Parks*. Englewood Cliffs, N. J.: Prentice-Hall, 1981.
    A problem-solving model for managers of recreational facilities is illustrated by case histories.
Christiansen, Marty L. *Vandalism Control Management for Parks and Recreation Areas*. State College, Pa.: Venture Publishing, 1983.
    The manual for control management of vandalism outlines a record system, social and physical strategies, and means of implementation and evaluation.
Gallati, Robert R. J. *Introduction to Private Security*. Englewood Cliffs, N. J.: Prentice-Hall, 1983.
    Chapter 18 applies physical security principles to education institutions, health-care facilities, hotels and motels, museums, and libraries.
Healy, R. J. *Design for Security*. 2d ed. Somerset, N. J.: John Wiley, 1983.

Planning, design, and modern technologies are related to physical security in businesses, industries, and institutions.

Kirkpatrick, John T. "Explaining Crime and Disorder in Libraries." *Library Trends* 33 (Summer 1984): 13–28.
Criminological theories are reviewed as background for understanding victimization of libraries.

Lincoln, Alan Jay. *Crime in the Libraries*. New York: R. R. Bowker Co., 1984.
In addition to a general review, the book presents findings of a major study of library crime patterns.

Thayer, Ralph E., and Fritz W. Wagner. *Vandalism: The Menace to Leisure Resources in the 1980's*. Arlington, Va.: National Recreation and Park Association, 1981.
The authors endeavor to pull together a fragmented literature to guide recreational professions on the meaning of vandalism and the means of dealing with it.

Ungarelli, Donald L. "Insurance and Prevention: Why and How?" *Library Trends* 33 (Summer 1984): 57–67.
Insurance against libraries is assessed as one of the means of risk management.

14

Evaluation: How Does It Work?

JIM C. HACKLER

Whenever a program is launched which claims to reduce crime or delinquency, we obviously would like to know if it worked. A large body of expertise has developed to try to provide intelligent answers to this question. Evaluation research is an old tradition, but it blossomed during the 1960s. More government support for crime prevention programs became available, along with the requirement that these programs would be evaluated. To some extent, evaluation is taken for granted.

It is fairly easy to find entire books devoted to the evaluation process itself.[1] One can also find more abbreviated guides to evaluation in books dealing with broader aspects of criminal justice planning.[2] The books, manuals, and articles that tell researchers how to do evaluations are so numerous that the reader will find that the references included in this chapter will quickly lead anyone interested to many others. Therefore, this chapter will not repeat the various steps required for doing an evaluation. Instead, the main thrust will be to ask much more basic questions. Which programs should be evaluated? Should we attempt to evaluate every crime prevention program? Are there some negative consequences which have not been considered? Does an evaluation really provide us with "usable knowledge"?[3] Would some other knowledge-gathering procedure be preferable to the experimental design typically used for project evaluations? What are the conditions under which an evaluation is most likely to provide meaningful information? Under what conditions can an evaluation cause problems or lead us astray? These issues need to be addressed *before* one moves headlong into the process of evaluating crime prevention programs.

EVALUATING THE EFFECTIVENESS OF PROGRAMS

Many social scientists argue that good methodology, such as the careful use of the experimental design, should be able to separate out those programs that reduce criminology and those that do not. On the surface, this seems to be a reasonable task; and yet, there is considerable disagreement over the ability of prevention programs to achieve even the most modest of goals. This chapter will argue that the potential advantages of doing evaluations have been oversold. We have hoped for too much. I am not going to argue against evaluations, but rather against the unrealistic expectations that some policy makers and some evaluation researchers have claimed.

This chapter will not provide a thorough review of evaluation strategies. Instead, it will review selective illustrations of attempts to assess crime prevention programs. The evaluation of any prevention program must operate within a variety of organizational and other constraints. I wish to examine a few of those constraints that are frequently ignored when the validity of claims are assessed and when those same claims are used as the basis for policy recommendations in the reduction of crime. Let us first begin with our traditional obsession with the experimental design.

Obsession with Experimental Design

When any of us are asked to review a manuscript about a delinquency prevention program, we always look to see if an experimental design was used. Was there a very carefully selected control group that matched the treatment group? We check to be sure that the evaluator assigned treatment and control group participants in a random fashion in order to permit the use of powerful statistical techniques. Frequently, we try to ignore the many difficulties that arise in trying to assign people to experimental and control groups. If they were white rats, they might cooperate more readily, but human subjects can give you more trouble.

When we were launching the Opportunities for Youth project in Seattle in the early 1960s, our first group of boys arrived at a gymnasium to complete the initial questionnaire. The payment of money provided some incentive, but the main reason the boys were there was the possibility of a job.[4] Of course, there were only enough jobs for half of the boys. We had to have a control group. We put all the names in a hat, and half of the boys were randomly selected. This procedure would satisfy the purists, but what about the boys who did not get jobs? Was it ethnical to hold up the possibility of a job when we knew there were not enough for all? Would the disappointment change the control group from a true control group to a group of boys who had received a different type of stimulus?

Random assignment in experimental and control groups is one of the basic procedures for the evaluation researcher, but the ethical and practical issues that arise are numerous. In addition, random assignment can camouflage important findings.[5] We may be interested in certain individual characteristics. For example, white boys and black boys may respond to our job program in a different way. With random assignment, the relationship between the program and this particular group may be masked. With huge samples, random assignment may solve such problems, but typically our groups are small and crucial characteristics are not equally distributed. Of course, there are ways of getting around this problem. *If one knows* which characteristic to search for, one can always analyze the data in an appropriate way afterwards, but random assignment can still camouflage characteristics that were not recognized.

In addition, the random assignment may not work. Eager to show our sophistication at experimental design, those of us responsible for the Opportunities for Youth project created sixteen experimental settings and four different types of control groups. Unfortunately when our subjects were randomly assigned, there were some significant differences among the various experimental and control groups. Those in one type of treatment group were considerably more delinquent than those in another type of treatment group. We could have stuck with the theoretical purity with our random assignment, but we found that if we collapsed our sixteen original experimental groups into four groups, the experimental groups became much more comparable to the control groups. Of course, with huge samples random assignment usually yields comparable groups; but most experimental programs in areas such as delinquency prevention deal with a modest number of subjects. As a result, random assignment can easily lead to problems.[6]

Ethical Implications

Some researchers argue that there are a number of ways of resolving these practical problems, using statistics and techniques. Donald T. Campbell, probably the best-known name in evaluation research today, has solved many of these technical problems. However, when we look at some of the other ideas Campbell offers, it is clear that he is warning us of various pitfalls. His 1971 lecture on the experimenting society at the American Psychological Association contained many disquieting thoughts. As far as this author knows, the widely distributed manuscript has never been published. (Campbell continues to believe the paper needs revision.) Leonard Saxe and Michelle Fine have reprinted an overview of his ideas in the introduction of their book on social experiments.[7]

In his comments on random assignment, Campbell notes that when a social experiment is testing a proposed governmental policy, such as crime prevention, it is a political process. It should be characterized by openness, honesty, and voluntarism, and it cannot be justified on the grounds of expediency. At present, researchers do not tell their subjects if they are in the treatment or the control group. That would contaminate the experiment. But if we are launching a program designed to prevent crime, is there a moral obligation to inform the subjects about how they are being used?

Barry Latzer and Michael P. Kirby argue that the experimental design is so desirable that one should try to overcome the criticisms.[8] They offer eight arguments in defense of the method, but these arguments may not make people like Donald Campbell more comfortable. In fact, random assignment is only an illustration of one type of problem created by the evaluation process. Another set of questions begins to plague us if we review some of the basic assumptions inherent in evaluations.

Questioning Some Basic Assumptions

How is knowledge used? Many policy makers assume that the purpose of evaluation research is to provide guidance for choosing the best programs that are available. Unfortunately others have concluded that knowledge gathering, and possibly evaluation research in particular, is used primarily for the benefit of those who are in power. In his introduction to the study by Robert Rich, which analyzes the use of a major research project, Kenneth Prewitt argues that "policy makers accept information not because it gives focus to a given policy choice but because it sustains the interest of the agency or advances a career."[9] Rich contends that good quality research is not a sufficient condition for the effective use of that knowledge by policy makers. Furthermore, social scientists do not have much impact on the use of such information. The probability of information being used depends less on its appropriateness for a substantive policy and more on its utility for bureaucratic interests. Information is more likely to be used if bureaucratic interests are enhanced. And, too, the information is more likely to be used if it is passed on to superiors by trusted aides rather than by less trusted aides. Similarly, the form in which the information is passed through the bureaucracy is more important than the content of the information.

Campbell makes a similar observation about other types of data. In recent years we have witnessed a growing interest in "social indicators." This includes all sorts of public records of crimes, diseases, and so on, as well as opinion surveys. Social scientists are great advocates of social indicators. Campbell warns us that there is a discouraging law that seems to be emerging: *the more any social indicator is used for social decision-making, the greater the corruption pressures upon it.*[10] There are few social indicators that attract attention as much as crime rates. Thus, we would be naive to believe that evaluations of crime prevention programs will not be subject to tremendous distorting pressures.

Evaluators Examine Themselves

Evaluation research involves the close examination of others. We have extended that skill to an examination of agents of social control, such as the police and the courts, who may be involved in some sort of crime prevention program, and we have also questioned the way social science knowledge is actually being used by social bureaucrats and other policy makers. But what about ourselves? What motivates our work? Why do we take on the task of evaluating a particular program? Karin Knorr points out that scientists are concerned with "success," a concept similar to what some other authors have called "making out." The type of success, however, depends a great deal on the local context of the scientist.

What counts as success is determined by the field and by the agent's position in the field ... the notion of success is an *indexical* expression which refers us to the context of a local, idiosyncratic situation ... success is *by and for* an agent at a particular *time and place*, and carried by local *interpretations*.[11]

Bill Harvey has studied a group of physicists and argues that these physicists' aims and motivations can only be satisfactorily accounted for if we include detailed discussion of their local social context.[12] It is beyond this chapter to explore the sociology of how knowledge is created, but we would be naive to believe that evaluation researchers are motivated only by the desire to find the best solution to a problem, that policy makers are driven to accomplish the best for the people whose lives they can influence, and so forth. It is important to realize that evaluating problems has been a rewarding sideline for social scientists for the past couple of decades and will continue to be rewarding in the future. It is not comfortable to doubt the utility of these activities.

Problem Attacking, Not Problem Solving

Social scientists frequently argue that problem solving, or at least sensible policy choices, cannot be made without careful analysis of the advantages and disadvantages of each course of action.[13] In addition, Herbert J. Gans tells us that "the distinctive quality of social policy is its aim for what might be called programmatic rationality; it seeks to achieve substantive goals through instrumental action programs that can be proven logically or empirically to achieve these goals."[14]

These views express a fairly typical theme from social science and possibly even more so from evaluation researchers. However, Charles E. Lindblom and David K. Cohen warn us that information and analysis constitute only one route among several to social problem solving or, rather social problem attacking.[15] Gathering information and doing sophisticated analyses is one way to proceed. However, a great deal of problem attacking is accomplished through various forms of social interaction that substitute action for thought, understanding, or analysis. Sometimes this other action is better for social problem attacking. For example, voting is a social interaction that attacks certain problems. Elections substitute action for thought. The problem is how to reconcile many diverse preferences into a collective decision. It is possible that a scientific investigation and careful analysis could help us to choose the "best" president. One could argue that "solving" this "problem" is equal in importance to attacking the crime problem, but we do not do it scientifically.

Use of the rules of voting, counting ballots, and following other rules to determine who will win is a different type of strategy from science, but it "works." It solves, or at least, attacks the problem. It is solved in large part by an elaborate ceremony of action.

Problems connected with crime and delinquency are attacked with action as well as with evaluation and other forms of analysis. We deceive ourselves when we argue that these other actions are less effective than those devised by scientific evaluations. When we confidently state that we are adding to a greater body of scientifically valid knowledge, we ignore the possibility that scientific inquiry may be forever destined to do no more than reshape or refine ordinary knowledge.[16]

At present we approach the evaluation of crime prevention programs in a naive and somewhat arrogant manner. We assume that we can guide policy simply by being technically competent. In her study of scientists working in the "harder" sciences, Karin Knorr-Cetina argues for a more sensitive—in contrast to a frigid—methodology.[17] In the pages that follow, I would like to think that I am being sensitive to suggestions offered by Knorr-Cetina and many others who examine the way researchers work when I look at the way various evaluators have dealt with the question, "do crime prevention programs work?"

Debate Over Correctional Effectiveness

Although other disciplines have debates over scientific questions, there are large areas of agreement on factual information. In crime prevention there seems to be less agreement on the facts. The current disagreement over whether or not delinquency prevention or correctional programs "work" has strong advocates on either side.[18] Reviews of the literature also lead to different conclusions suggesting that there really is no clear answer to the question as it is presently formulated.[19] David Greenberg reviewed a number of findings in relation to individual therapy, group counseling, behavior modification, and so on, and concluded that most of these treatment programs were not reducing crime to any appreciable extent.[20] There were occasional favorable results, but most of them were modest and those claiming favorable results used evaluations that were seriously lacking in rigor.

By contrast, Paul Gendreau and Bob Ross (1979) reviewed studies that presumably should have been dealing with similar questions.[21] They concluded that several types of intervention programs have proven successful. How is it that comprehensive reviews of the research can arrive at such diametrically opposite conclusions? Focusing on the specific argument itself may not be as important as the larger question of the sociology of knowledge and the very nature of scientific enterprise. Something else besides the nature of the phenomenon under study seems to be operating. By focusing on correctional programs, we may be ignoring the dynamics of research activities and the institutional forces that influence the way social scientists work, the conclusions they reach, and the policies they recommend.

FACTORS INFLUENCING OUTCOMES OF EVALUATION: THREE LEVELS OF QUESTIONING

A review of a few factors that influence the outcome of evaluation research may illustrate some organizational arrangements that mold the policy-making environment. These arrangements structure the entire strategy of identifying, studying, and trying to "solve" social problems. For convenience these factors can be grouped at three levels: global, intermediate, and specific. At the *global* level we consider influences that are fairly pervasive in society. At the *intermediate* level, we note influences related to specific disciplines and the subcultures in which academics work. At the *specific* level, we describe some unique and personal factors that make generalization difficult.

A number of authors have examined how social problems and other social issues are conceived and how this has consequences for proposed solutions.[22] Others have focused on the relationship between social research and social policy and on the disappointment experienced by social scientists who feel their work is not appreciated.[23] These issues raised by the authors referred to above might be viewed as "global" because they influence not only the evaluation researchers, but also policy makers and the rest of society in general. In one sense, the first portion of this chapter dealt with global issues. One more illustration of a global issue is offered to introduce the discussion of the three different levels.

Global Questions and Assumptions

Some correctional researchers seldom question the definition of the problem or the wisdom behind the process that develops that definition.[24] We assume that the individual coming into conflict with the justice system needs correcting. "Prevention" refers to individual deviants, rarely to social institutions. These ideas are reinforced by dominant societal values which cherish individual motivation and responsibility.[25] This naturally leads to a person-centered causal attribution bias and a "victim blaming" ideology.[26] Once tied into these assumptions, it is difficult even to question the relationship between powerful and weak members of the society and see those relationships as a possible source of the problem. Organizations, responding to funding sources, resist policies that look outside the individual and focus on the system. By contrast, programs such as behavior modification fit the needs of agencies because they maintain authorities in a position of dominance and keep the prisoner or juvenile in his place.[27] In addition, a complete panoply of scientific respectability buttresses behavior modification practices. This does not necessarily make the ideas wrong, but it does suggest that research issues respond to larger societal pressures.

This brief presentation obviously oversimplifies the issue and focuses on a limited aspect of behavior modification, but the specific program strategy is not the primary concern here. Rather, certain types of explanations, such as those that emphasize "personal blame," are convenient and useful from the standpoint of those who must make policy decisions. Edward Seidman points out that the self-interests of organizations, individuals who would view a change in altered role relationships as a threat, and dominant societal values all converge to restrict the research questions an agency is willing to ask.[28] In addition, government policy, funding agencies, and the training of social scientists are part of a system that limits conceptual thinking and hence the questions that are asked.[29] These "global" biases are not necessarily bad, but they need to be recognized and made explicit so that evaluations can be assessed with an awareness of the assumptions of which they are based.

The next section focuses on a specific illustration at the intermediate level: why do psychologists tend to say that various correctional programs "work" while sociologists tend to argue that they do not? Is it possible that the factors mentioned above impinge on psychologists and sociologists in a different manner? In addition to general factors, are there intermediate "subcultural" factors within the social sciences that influence outcomes?

Intermediate Level: Which Discipline?

The debate over whether or not "something works" may have little to do with the real merits or demerits of correctional programs. The scientific social-ization of those doing the research, combined with pressures that influence disciplines differently, may more adequately explain the conclusions defended so vigorously in academic journals. Researchers may deny that *they* are part of the problem, just as professionals in social control agencies were initially sur-prised when sociologists began studying *them* and the dynamics of their agency (while ignoring the behavior of their clients). Such research was on the wrong track; the problem clearly lies with the behavior of the deviants. Judges, probation officers, psychiatrists, and the rest of the people working in the social control system were simply responding in a rational and humane manner to the actions of clients. Some researchers have been advised to abandon this folly of studying the obviously reasonable and intelligent behavior of professionals and to get back to the basic problem of explaining just why those deviants act the way they do.

Researchers have nonetheless persisted in looking at people who staff the criminal justice system, pursuing the possibility that their behavior follows certain sociological principles and hence may make a difference in the systems where they work (Richard V. Ericson for example, in his study of the police[30]). Fol-lowing the same strategy, we should step outside of the debate on correctional treatment and analyze the behavior of the debaters themselves as the products of institutional patterns. If studying the behavior of judges, lawyers, parole officers, and prison guards yields insights, then studying the behavior of program evaluators might be rewarding. For example, why is it that the two reviews by Greenberg[31] and by Gendreau and Ross,[32] which examine approximately 100 studies, show an overlap of only six studies that were common to both bibliographies? Another assessment of delinquency prevention projects reported in the literature by Richard J. Lundman, Paul T. McFarlane, and Frank R. Scarpitti also reviews a large number of delinquency prevention programs and concludes that none of these projects successfully prevented delinquent behavior.[33] Again, if we compare the bibliography of the Lundman, McFarlane, and Scarpitti article or the review by Charles H. Logan[34] with the Gendreau and Ross paper, we see very little overlap. A sociologist might look at the Gendreau and Ross work and ask how they could ignore the thirty-year followup of the Cambridge-Somerville program by Joan McCord.[35] On the other hand, if Ross and Gendreau were to look at some of these literature reviews by sociologists, they would probably be aghast that these reviews neglect certain psychological studies that are obviously crucial, at least to most psychologists.

We should not be surprised that reviewers of different sets of literature come to different conclusions; but when the question appears to be identical, why do they select different research to review? Robert Scott and Arnold R. Shore note that scholars, at least sociologists, approach problems in a way that is molded by the discipline.[36] The training of psychologists and sociologists will naturally influence their methodology and could lead to different conclusions.

The work by Joan Brockman, C. D'Arcy, and L. Edmonds suggests that the training of researchers may be related to the conclusions they reach.[37] Brockman and her colleagues analyzed studies that focused on changes in public attitudes toward the mentally ill and noted that the studies conducted by social scientists tended to be negative, whereas evaluations by medical personnel were positive. In addition, open-ended interviews (with vignettes) and self-response questionnaires tended to give negative results, whereas closed-ended interviews led to positive results. Finally, there was a definite preference on the part of each discipline for different data-collecting techniques.

Perhaps we should consider the following hypothesis: *the success or failure of any social program designed to change peoples' attitudes or behavior can best be predicted by knowing the discipline or profession of the evaluator and the methodology used.* This hypothesis may be a bit unfair, but available evidence from delinquency prevention programs is suggestive.

Brockman et al. concluded that attitudes toward the mentally ill are multifaceted and highly complex.[38] Therefore, it is difficult to evaluate changes. This description also fits the evaluation of correctional research or delinquency prevention; they are multifaceted and the variables complex. Hence, attempts to assess the effectiveness of programs will remain inconclusive until we also take into account the dynamics of the evaluation process and the organizational arrangements in which it takes place.

One should not say that "nothing works." Rather, nothing seems to work *reliably.* The personalities of staff and situational factors that surround every prevention program seem to overwhelm any of the theoretical variables that were part of the experimental design. Even if the factors under our control operate in a systematic manner, they may be rather puny compared to the situational characteristics surrounding the project. However, biases created by professional training and the subculture of various disciplines might operate in a systematic way. Thus, these variables might be studied more profitably than those that appear to be linked more directly to delinquency prevention.

One challenge might be to try to identify the specific variables that distinguish sociologically and psychologically oriented evaluators of correctional programs. There are a few obvious features of the two disciplines that are worth considering. In the 1960s and early 1970s sociologists entered an expanding job market. It was relatively cost-free to be a revolutionary or a reformer. The intellectual influence of symbolic interaction, the labeling perspective, Marxism, and so on, made it possible, in fact profitable, to question "value-free" science and a number of other conventional ideas. This cohort of sociologists was also not free from the constrictions mentioned earlier; they were under pressure from a new conformity. At times the new radical environment created a conformity in thought that was equally constricting, such as at the National Deviancy Conference in England in the early 1970s where it was fashionable to refer to that "positivistic shit" and use a ritualized rhetoric that showed disdain for traditional social science. Although many sociologists of this period took part in dialogues that exposed them to a variety of perspectives, others became rigidly aligned to an alternate orthodoxy. Evaluations done by scholars wedded to this new orthodoxy could also suffer from intellectual blinders, just as conventional scholars did not always recognize the limitation in their thinking.

During this same period of the 1960s and 1970s less radical sociologists had the opportunity to put some of their ideas into action. Not having had much practice at modifying opportunity structures, reforming prisons, and revising social institutions, it is not surprising that these reform-minded scholars failed to produce dramatic results. By contrast, the psychologically trained researcher, given a chance to apply behavior modification, for example, could rely on a much better developed body of techniques that could be applied to an area limited in scope and more amenable to manipulation.

It is not that psychologists were untouched by the radical ideas of the 1960s and 1970s, but changes and expansions within psychology during this period did not affect the basic assumptions of social science to the same degree as they did in sociology. Organizationally speaking, psychologists were more likely to be part of the system, whereas sociologists were more inclined to be outside the system (or attacking it vigorously). In addition, psychologists were more skilled in doing experimentation and attempted more modest changes. Sociologists were trying to save cities from crime, while psychologists knew they were fortunate if they could get juveniles to clean up the litter in their institution.

These rather casual comparisons between psychologists and sociologists should not be viewed as a definitive attempt to explain outcomes of evaluation research. The task in this chapter is simply to call attention to the more general point: *researchers will reflect the culture of their discipline and will relate to institutions and agencies in a manner that will differ from discipline to discipline.* The organizational arrangements that characterize a discipline (or some other "group") will be manifested in the way they work.

Let us turn from this generalization to the more specific topic of reviews of correctional programs. In addition to the broader influences imposed by a discipline, and its traditions for training researchers, there are some very idiosyncratic dynamics that may at times seem trivial but that may influence larger issues. In the reviews of delinquency prevention and correctional programs, we noted that the conclusions differed from writer to writer. We should inquire into the selection process that seems to operate in any review of the literature as well as the reasons why a particular study becomes widely quoted.

Specific Level: What's Popular?

Idiosyncratic factors can affect the selection process that influences any "review" of the literature. There is usually a rational reason for the selection of research reviewed, but why is it that one comprehensive review chooses criteria that includes one body of literature and neglects another? Why did Robert Martinson's "What works?" article become so popular in 1974 when similar arguments were being made for several years?

The merits or demerits of crime prevention or its evaluation are influenced by idiosyncratic dynamic conditions surrounding academics and policy makers. For example, our reaction to specific reviews of the literature can be emotional rather than objective. Scholars quote sources for a variety of reasons. We quote our thesis advisors, friends, those who agree with us, and, in certain areas, we must quote Durkheim and Weber and those who might be reviewing the research proposal. Although the quality of ideas influences which source gets quoted, other factors play a role. For example, Walter Gove's well-known article questioning societal reaction as an explanation of deviance, which appeared in 1970, is neither his most tightly reasoned nor his most convincing argument against the labeling perspective.[39] (Gove has agreed with this statement in conversation.) However, its timing and its appearance in a prestigious journal were probably important for its impact.

Similarly, when Martinson's "nothing works" article appeared in 1974, it reflected work that was done in the 1960s because publication of the larger work was delayed for several years. The ideas were not necessarily new, but they were presented forcefully, in an influential journal, and at an appropriate time. None of this detracts from Martinson, since his monumental work with Douglas Lipton and Judith Wilks is obviously a major contribution; but would that larger volume be well known without the appearance of the earlier, more publicized paper?[40]

The point of this section is to emphasize the idiosyncratic aspect of what we sometimes claim to be an objective and rational process. Although quality ideas will probably endure in the long run, in the short run exciting arguments between colorful writers, personal friendships or animosities, and various fads will in-

fluence not only what gets published but also what gets cited. These phenomena
are one part of a larger category of events that are more or less random and
usually unpredictable. Although these dynamics are understandable, they are
difficult to explain with more general powerful principles. We appreciate the
importance of chance discoveries, the principle of serendipity; but when we
come to conclusions about evaluations of correctional programs, we cannot
accept something so haphazard as chance as influencing our reasoning.

Important breakthroughs can result from the fortuitous meeting of minds. For
example, the well-known double helix molecular-structure of DNA was discovered when a geneticist and a biochemist were able to utilize new techniques of
X-ray diffraction developed by a crystallographer for determining molecular
structure. Although this may illustrate serendipity, or favorable outcomes, the
interaction of ideas and techniques also generates useless activity. The application
of factor analysis or some other new statistical technique has undoubtedly led
to many unnecessary pages in journals. Many applications of new techniques
are inappropriate, but debates are generated and careers are made as scholars
play with their newfound tools. Because this process does occasionally produce
major breakthroughs, the inappropriate and less productive work can be written
off as the normal cost of exploring ideas. The point to be emphasized here is
that we all recognize the principle of serendipity, but we pay little attention to
the chance interactions that generate heated debates that do not necessarily produce breakthroughs.

I have applied the word "idiosyncratic" to these phenomena because the long-
range impact may be minimal, but in the short term the mole hills *appear* to be
mountains. Occasionally, a few of them actually turn out to be mountains.
Evaluation research, and the writings concerning this topic, may be somewhat
more susceptible to these idiosyncratic phenomena than other areas of scientific
endeavor.

Summary. The debate over correctional research will probably continue because: (1) at a *global* level the basic assumptions held by the scientific community
and dominant institutions of society may inhibit asking appropriate questions.
Those asking different questions frequently have different assumptions, and it
is unlikely that a "correct" picture can be created that will bridge these differing
perspectives in the near future; (2) at an *intermediate* level the culture and
organizational arrangements of individual disciplines, such as psychology and
sociology, will continue to train and socialize their respective members into
methodologies that will generate different conclusions. For example, the greater
emphasis on tight experimental design will encourage psychologists to work in
institutions where tighter controls of variables are possible, as illustrated by some
of the work in behavioral modification. Sociologists, by contrast, will probably
get more experience and training working with programs in the community.
Larger samples and attempts to randomize variables will characterize their efforts
to control variation. Although there is much overlap in the tools used, we should
not be surprised if the different emphasis leads to contrasting inferences; and

(3) at the *specific* level the idiosyncratic characteristics of situational dynamics, personalities, and local societal pressures will be difficult to predict and will resist "rationalization." We need to recognize the role of fads and chance elements, even though we may be able to do very little about them.

WHERE DO WE STAND?

The preceding pages have tried to suggest that many factors influence the "evaluation business" and that viewing evaluation from within the traditional social science perspective may not provide the necessary insights. In fact, our compulsion to evaluate social programs is part of our positivistic mentality. It is one of the global level factors similar to those discussed earlier. Our desire to know the impact of proposed changes is a Western trait. In some areas of the world people accept change more fatalistically. These desires and compulsions are part of the dynamics of the evaluation debate.

This next section offers some concrete illustrations of the factors described earlier at the global, intermediate, and specific levels and tries to suggest how these conditions could be utilized to achieve certain policy goals. At the global level, for example, many have great faith in science as a cure for evil. Such thinking pervades much policy thinking. Although this approach may have its strengths, it could also become a barrier, as illustrated by our love affair with measuring devices.

Search for Better Measuring Devices

One aspect of our rational-positivistic orientation toward planned social change is a continuing faith that scientific tools, such as better measuring devices, will lead to more definitive results in evaluations. In some studies sophisticated methods and statistical techniques have led to meaningful insights. The Transitional Aid Research Project (TARP), which provided unemployment benefits to released prisoners in Georgia and Texas, is an illustration of an evaluation that made effective use of sophisticated analytic techniques.[41] Their findings suggest that unemployment benefits can be helpful, but programs of this nature should be careful not to reward ex-inmates for not working.

The TARP experiment illustrates a situation in which a number of factors coincide which permitted the researchers to take advantage of sophisticated research tools. An extensive body of theoretical and empirical work was utilized to build a conceptual framework, large samples were available, the variance of potentially confounding variables was reduced by the design, the variance of important predictor variables was increased, and so on. To summarize, in many situations sophisticated measurement can make a contribution, but some evaluation researchers have argued that the improved methodology alone will lead to adequate evaluations.[42]

Misplaced Faith in Science

An illustration of this faith in the "better measuring device" approach to improved evaluations was provided at the 1980 sessions of the American Sociological Association by James Q. Wilson. He noted that some studies simply used recidivism as the criterion for judging the success or failure of a crime prevention program. Wilson cited the work by Charles A. Murray and Louise Cox, *Beyond Probation* (1979), as an illustration of a program that demonstrated success if you looked at the frequency of the crime committed rather than simply using recidivism as an indicator of success.[43] With the conventional rate, there may be no success, Wilson argued, but with frequency as the criterion, there may be success. But Wilson's underlying logic is faulty if he thinks it is likely that recidivism rates would be similar if one group of ex-offenders were to commit crime with great frequency while a comparison group were to commit few crimes. If this were to happen, we simply know that something is wrong. The conditions that could lead to such illogical differences in findings suggest that researchers have more difficulties on their hands than a simple measurement problem. It is interesting that researchers respond with glee when they find that one of their indicators "worked" even though other indicators failed. In fact, this might still be more evidence that our ability to assess should be questioned or the variables being measured are puny.

This line of reasoning should not be viewed as a condemnation of all evaluations. The Murray and Cox study generated a discussion of methodology that will warn future researchers that certain statistical techniques might generate results that could be interpreted as success.[44] The point is the necessity of more programs than evaluated so far, more precise measurement, by itself, will not lead to great breakthroughs.

Admittedly, one indicator may be cruder than the other, but if in fact there were some powerful principles operating in these crime prevention programs, even our crude efforts should have uncovered them by now. Many great breakthroughs in science were made without highly refined instruments. Insights into the movement of heavenly bodies, the meaning of air pressure, and the significance of gravity were not discovered with precise measurement. The principles were consistent and powerful, and hence were revealed to investigators in spite of their imprecise methods. The very fact that findings from correctional evaluation are so inconsistent and so puny suggests that there simply isn't very much there. There may be hope, but the impact of most efforts will be modest, and, as a result, the use of more careful experimental procedures or sophisticated techniques of analysis will not provide much more in the way of guidance than less rigorous but perhaps more insightful examinations.

Scott and Shore point out that an emphasis on methodology may impress academic colleagues without being particularly helpful to policy makers.[45] If influencing policy is our primary goal, "soft" or nonempirical data may be just as persuasive.[46] Academics may also emphasize the importance of science as a factor in influencing policy. "In many cases, the findings of social science seemed to come after, rather than before, changes in policy, which suggests that political events may influence scholars more than research influences policy."[47]

The sophistication of the work may be secondary to the compatibility of the research with other trends. In the famous *Brown* case, decided by the Supreme Court in 1954, social science opinion was clear about the equality of races and the disadvantages of segregated schools, but the evidence available was less than precise.[48] The social science community had influence, but not because of sophisticated methodology. Policy makers may utilize social science research but in a manner that is not always obvious, contributing to the notion that policy makers ignore research findings.[49]

Arrogance of Social Scientists

Our exalted view of science, or rather the techniques and procedures which we sometimes confuse with science, makes us unappreciative of the contribution of others who use what we might call "common sense."[50] As we watch dramatic changes taking place in juvenile justice systems, such as the dramatic shift in thinking illustrated in Canada by the new Young Offenders Act, we see a tendency for scholars to ignore the "local wisdom" that might provide insight into the workings of those systems.[51] It is possible that we are so hung up on our methodology that we ignore the insights of those working closer to everyday problems.

The above illustration suggests that the very nature of doing science is a global characteristic of the way we ask questions. At the intermediate level, we have earlier noted that psychologists tend to find more evidence of success in prevention programs than do sociologists. Could this be influenced by certain traditions?

Traditions and .05 Level of Significance

Psychologists may be like the medical personnel who found positive results in efforts to change public attitudes toward the mentally ill.[52] Working in highly controlled experimental settings in prisons, they may be able to bring about moderate changes in these restricted environments, but there is also the possibility that editors of psychological journals have a tendency to accept only studies at the .05 level or better. This could influence the sort of findings that get published. If psychologically oriented editors continue their bias against those experiments that show that nothing happened, it is distinctly possible that successful programs will be reported more frequently than those that showed no change. In contrast, editors of sociological journals may get a certain perverse pleasure out of documenting programs that fail. Obviously, the point is overstated, but we still should be alert to differences in intellectual traditions and publishing patterns in various disciplines as an illustration of the type of influence that can influence the reporting and interpretation of findings.

The specific illustrations given above are of minor importance. The main point is that we should not be surprised to get different conclusions from different disciplines. This should not be reduced to general prejudices in various disciplines; that is, lawyers see problems in the criminal code, geneticists blame crime on heredity, while sociologists find fault with the social structure. That is too simple. The more subtle differences in disciplinary subcultures need to be identified. This should enable us to utilize these disciplines more effectively and apply them to policy questions such as: "can correctional programs succeed?" Assuming we have become aware of the global and intermediate level factors influencing the way we are doing evaluation, what factors have to be considered when we are faced with the creation or assessment of a specific crime prevention program? For example, is it possible that the very nature of launching prevention programs means creating situations that are inherently unique?

Uniqueness of Each Program

Not many reviewers of correctional programs argue that nothing works at all. Rather, they point out that there isn't consistent success for any particular treatment strategy that can be replicated reliably from one place to another.[53] Sometimes things work in some places but fail elsewhere. This should suggest to us that the personality of the individuals concerned, the social settings, or a variety of other factors interact in such a way that it is almost impossible to transplant a successful program from one place to another. Seidman provides a particularly interesting illustration of how a successful program was carefully transplanted but a change in the situation modified outcomes extensively.[54] Theoretically, one should be able to measure all of the meaningful interacting variables and transplant them all, but in actual practice these conditions are too varied and are simply not replicable.

There is some reason, then, to take seriously the recommendations of the report published by the National Academy of Sciences by L. Sechrest, O. White, and E. Brown.[55] These authors concluded that the evidence for the effectiveness of rehabilitation appears to be weak or nonexistent. There was no evidence that any treatment or intervention with criminal offenders could be relied on to produce decreases in crime.

In those exceptional programs, such as TARP, the variables used were easier to control in a uniform manner. Payments of money are more uniform than the personalities of social workers. In addition, the settings were not greatly different from those facing others on parole. For example, ex-inmates in the TARP program were in contact with regular civil servants who had a range of duties.[56] In an earlier study (LIFE), ex-prisoners were in almost daily contact with a research staff that was devoted solely to the experiment.[57] Kenneth J. Lenihan's experience with the LIFE study probably led to a later experiment that was more like the real world. That is, with TARP there was a reduction in uniqueness, in idiosyncratic characteristics. When skilled researchers and program planners can launch programs in stages, they may be able to make them less unique and more transferable. They may also be able to specify the settings needed for certain types of programs. However, most programs are smaller and less sophisticated, and have less continuity of experience than TARP. Smaller programs are characterized by energetic, possibly charismatic, leaders who come and go and circumstances that change over time. Such programs are meaningful, but should they be evaluated with an experimental design? Do they provide insights rather than models to imitate?

If uniqueness is what characterizes most evaluation efforts, then the whole logic of rigorous evaluation doesn't make sense. Not only are the treatment programs themselves somewhat unique, but the way in which researchers analyze data could be somewhat unique. For example, when Roy Austin reanalyzed data from the Preston study, which utilized the Interpersonal Maturity Level Theory, he came up with a quite different line of reasoning.[58] These exercises and reanalyses are meaningful, but the combination of the uniqueness of the projects, the uniqueness of the settings, and finally the uniqueness of the investigators will combine to produce continually unique findings. Only rather powerful forces would lead to consistency, and these tend to be rare.

At this point, should the reader conclude that evaluations of prevention or correctional programs are a complete waste of time? No, but perhaps we should be asking what sort of projects merit evaluation or what situations make evaluations more meaningful. There is a difference between choosing selected areas where evaluation may be profitable in contrast to evaluating every program. We may be persisting in an unprofitable enterprise when we emphasize the evaluation of so many different types of programs. Many projects have unrealistic expectations, and hence an evaluation will add very little to either knowledge or policy. Assuming that evaluations of correctional effectiveness will continue, selective choice, taking into account the general, intermediate, and specific factors mentioned above, might yield a better return.

CONCLUSION: EVALUATING EVALUATORS

One could argue that scientific knowledge plays a minor role in policy making in the criminal justice area.[59] When knowledge is used, how do we deal with conflicting findings? The evaluation of correctional programs offers an illustration of this confusion, but if we look at the various factors that impinge on the scientific enterprise surrounding this area, the discrepancies are not surprising. Such factors were discussed at a global or pervasive level, at an intermediate or disciplinary level, and at a specific or idiosyncratic level. If one is able to assess those factors that impinge on the research that is done, the methodologies that are chosen, and the conclusions we reach, we would be in a more advantageous position to make use of the tools available to the social scientist.

At this time, most correctional programs may not be appropriate for systematic evaluation. Occasionally, projects such as TARP may permit the control of enough important confounding variables to use traditional tools in a way to suggest a policy that could make modest improvements. For most correctional evaluations, however, inconsistent findings will probably continue to be the rule. In other areas as well, where science is called on to guide legislation and policy, we may be expecting too much clarity from social science endeavors. When those endeavors are viewed within the setting described above, their contributions may be more meaningful.

Positive Contribution of Evaluation

The reader could come to the mistaken impression that I am opposed to evaluations. In fact, evaluations are essential to intelligent program development. Even when they run into some of the difficulties described above, they frequently tell us a great deal. Future evaluations will be of greater value if they can avoid some of the naive assumptions used in the past. Evaluations are too often seen as a task that is separate from other basic research. In actuality, good evaluations do more than ask: did the program succeed? In these final illustrations, one can see that evaluation might be viewed as research that analyzes the way people attack problems. More is involved than simply deciding whether or not the attack succeeded.

Longitudinal Research on Crime

Most programs are evaluated after a relatively short period, since policy makers are eager to know the results. Some evaluations follow cases, usually juveniles, for twenty years or more and provide greater insights into the actual impact of programs and into the natural history of delinquent behavior and the way detected offenders progress through the criminal justice system. In the Cambridge-Somerville study, the impact of the program itself seems to be negative, but the insights coming from the thirty-year followup of the juveniles make this evaluation unique.[60]

In England, a research team at Cambridge University has been following the life history of 400 boys since 1961.[61] Although many would argue that this is not a conventional evaluation of a program, we might do better to dispense with many superficial evaluation attempts and concentrate instead on selected longitudinal studies. The fact that two scholars have recently questioned the value of studying careers in this manner only adds spice to the debate.[62]

Neighborhood Watch. In recent years, we have seen the implementation of a variety of Neighborhood Watch programs. Evaluations in Seattle and Detroit suggest that there has been a positive impact.[63] One could argue that these successes are due to the increased cohesiveness that results in the community, or that crooks have moved to other areas, but we do not have to explain every set of dynamics before making use of this information. When the body of accumulated knowledge is assessed, policy guidelines emerge that increase the likelihood of reducing crime.[64]

Changing Individuals

Sociologists tend to be suspicious of programs that attempt to alter individuals without modifying the social surroundings. However, several recent studies have demonstrated successful attempts to modify individuals. One program reduced drug abuse by developing skills that included resisting persuasion.[65] Another utilized martial arts training to modify the behavior of chronically disruptive students.[66] A more conventional program used a preemployment skills training program to increase the success of adolescents in finding and keeping employment.[67] The skeptical sociologist could argue that some of these changes have occurred because the surroundings have altered as well as the individual subjects, but a policy maker is now in a better position to make a decision as a result of these evaluations.

Living with Crude Indicators

Because of the difficulty of finding valid indicators of success, researchers tend to reject cruder indicators of program success. In France there has been growing concern over crime, which seems to increase during the hot summers when the French typically go on vacation. Swimming pools and other recreational facilities are closed because of the widespread pattern of leaving the cities for the mountains and beaches during this period. Lower class youth tend to remain in the cities with less to do than usual. Since 1982 many communities have attempted "anti-été chaud" programs, that is, programs to cool out the hot summers by sending these lower class youth on vacations as well.[68] Although I am not aware of any systematic evaluations, the police in some areas report a 20 to 40 percent reduction in property crimes.[69] Should we accept these figures as appropriate evidence for the success of these programs? On the other hand, should conflict between local youth in a tourist area and visiting youth from the city be seen as evidence that the program failed?[70] Impressionistic accounts and official statistics certainly have their limitations, but policy makers will notice them. Given the faults that arise when sophisticated researchers attempt to develop refined indicators of success, perhaps we should be generous when it comes to interpreting changes in police statistics. In many situations, where the political climate is highly charged, sophisticated evaluations are unlikely, and using readily available information makes good sense.

Applying Theory to Prevention

In Seattle, a group of scholars at the University of Washington launched a delinquency prevention program based on social control and cultural deviance theories.[71] Although others have used theories in the past, Joseph Weis and his colleagues felt there was a great deal of consensus in certain areas. Therefore, programs that involved the cumulative influence of family, school, peers, and community on the social development of youths would increase the likelihood of changing delinquent behavior. The project was launched in schools in six different cities. Although the range of programs used in this program is not necessarily new, few attempts to prevent delinquency have coordinated available knowledge so extensively or have attempted to implement the program in a manner that is consistent with available knowledge.

Not surprisingly, the project met resistance in a variety of forms in the various school systems, but initial findings suggest that the range of activities is having a positive impact on juveniles and on the teachers in these schools.[72] Obviously, well-articulated, well-funded prevention programs such as this one require a systematic evaluation. However, it is important to do more than simply ask if delinquency has been reduced. We need to know why some schools resisted, how administrators manipulated the program, what changes took place among teachers, and so forth. Fortunately, questions like these are being asked in this project.[73]

In conclusion, evaluation should not be viewed as simply a technical process that determines whether a program achieved its stated goal. One must see evaluation as part of the social fabric surrounding the issues that are the focus of attention. In some cases a genuine evaluation may be unattainable, and it may be more reasonable to live with estimates of changes in the crime rate, as illustrated by the French summer programs mentioned above. The question is not whether we should evaluate or how we should evaluate. Of course, we must; but we must also be aware of the many factors that will nullify and distort evaluation efforts. These last illustrations did not show us how to prevent crime, but they may illustrate situations where evaluations do or do not make sense. Policy makers will still have difficulty reducing crime, but evaluation plus the other knowledge we have gained about the way programs are launched can increase the odds.

Perhaps it is appropriate to end a chapter on evaluation as Douglas Kerr ended a review of the difficulties of preventing delinquency.[74] He cited P. Berman's analogy of a "house of cards":

Successful processes do not seem robust, but rather consist of fragile concatenations of the events, people, and idea at the right times in the right places. A single, misplaced, or mistimed element seems likely to collapse the delicate "assembly" leading to success. Consequently, there are many ways to fail and few ways to succeed.[75]

NOTES

1. Charles M. Judd and David A. Kenny, *Estimating the Effects of Social Interventions* (Cambridge: Cambridge University Press, 1981).

2. See Chapter 13 in Donald T. Shanahan and Paul M. Wisenand, *The Dimensions of Criminal Justice Planning* (Boston: Allyn and Bacon, 1980).

3. Charles E. Lindblom and David K. Cohen, *Usable Knowledge* (New Haven and London: Yale University Press, 1979).

4. James C. Hackler, "Boys, Blisters, and Behavior: The Impact of a Work Program

in an Urban Central Area," *Journal of Research in Crime and Delinquency* 3 (July 1966): 155–164.

5. Leonard Saxe and Michelle Fine, *Social Experiments: Methods for Design and Evaluation* (Beverly Hills, Calif.: Sage Publications, 1981).

6. LaMar Empey and Maynard Erickson, *The Provo Experiment* (Lexington, Ky.: Lexington Books, 1972); James C. Hackler, "The Dangers of Political Naivete and Excessive Complexity in Evaluating Delinquency Prevention Programs," *Evaluation and Program Planning* 1 (Spring 1979): 273–283.

7. Saxe and Fine, *Social Experiments*, pp. 13–18.

8. Barry Latzer and Michael P. Kirby, "Is Experimental Design Constitutional?" in Barbara Raffel Price and Phyllis Jo Baunach, eds., *Criminal Justice Research: New Models and Findings* (Beverly Hills, Calif.: Sage, 1981).

9. Robert F. Rich, *Social Science and Public Policy Making* (San Francisco: Jossey-Bass, 1981), p. xi.

10. Saxe and Fine, *Social Experiments*, p. 17.

11. Karin D. Knorr, "Producing and Reproducing Knowledge: Descriptive or Constructive? Towards a Model of Research Production," *Social Science Information* 16 (1977): 670–74.

12. Bill Harvey, "The Effects of Social Context in the Process of Scientific Investigation: Experimental Tests of Quantum Mechanics," in Karin D. Knorr, Roger Krohn, and Richard Whitley, eds., *The Social Process of Scientific Investigation* (Dodrecht: D. Reidel, 1980).

13. Edith Stokey and Richard Zeckhauser, *A Primer for Policy Analysis* (New York: W. W. Norton, 1978).

14. Herbert J. Gans, "Social Science for Social Policy," in Irving Louis Horowitz, ed., *The Use and Abuse of Social Science*, 2d ed. (New Brunswick, N. J.: Transaction Books, 1975), p. 4.

15. Lindblom and Cohen, *Usable Knowledge*, pp. 20–29.

16. Ibid., p. 38.

17. Karin D. Knorr-Cetina, *The Manufacture of Knowledge* (Oxford: Pergamon Press, 1981).

18. Robert Martinson, "What Works?—Questions and Answers About Prison Reform," *The Public Interest* 35 (Spring 1974): 22–54; Ted Palmer, "Martinson Revisited," *Journal of Research in Crime and Delinquency* 12 (July 1975): 133–152.

19. Helen Annis, "Treatment in Corrections: Hoax or Salvation?," unpublished manuscript (Toronto: Addiction Research Foundation, 1980).

20. David Greenberg, "The Correctional Effects of Corrections: A Survey of Evaluations," in D. Greenburg, ed., *Corrections and Punishment* (Beverly Hills, Calif.: Sage Publications, 1977).

21. Paul Gendreau and Bob Ross, "Effective Correctional Treatment: Bibliography for Cynics," *Crime and Delinquency* 25 (October 1979): 463–490.

22. Malcolm Spector and John Kitsuse, *Constructing Social Problems* (Menlo Park, Calif.: Cummings, 1977: Edward Seidman, "Justice, Values and Social Science: Unexamined Premises," *Research in Law and Sociology* 1 (1978): 174–200; N. Caplan and S. D. Nelson, "On Being Useful: The Nature and Consequences of Psychological Research on Social Problems," *American Psychologist* 28 (1973): 199–211; I. Mitroff and M. Turoff, "Technical Forecasting and Assessment: Science and/or Mythology," *Technical Forecasting and Social Change* 5 (1973): 113–134; Gideon Sjoberg and Paula

Miller, "Social Research on Bureaucracy: Limitations and Opportunities," *Social Problems* 21 (Summer 1973): 129–143.

23. Robert A. Scott and Arnold R. Shore, *Why Sociology Does Not Apply: A Study of the Use of Sociology in Public Policy* (New York: Elsevier, 1979); Carol H. Weiss, *Social Science Research and Decision-Making* (New York: Columbia University Press, 1980); Lindblom and Cohen, *Usable Knowledge*, pp. 21–29; Nathan Caplan, Andrea Morrison, and Russell J. Stambaugh, *The Use of Social Science Knowledge in Policy Decisions at the National Level: A Report to Respondents* (Ann Arbor, Mich.: Institute for Social Research, 1975).

24. Caplan and Nelson, "On Being Useful," p. 206.

25. Seidman, "Justice, Values and Social Science," p. 182.

26. Howard Ryan, *Blaming the Victim* (New York: Random House, 1972); John Galliher and James McCartney, "The Influence of Funding Agencies on Juvenile Delinquency Research," *Social Problems* 21 (Summer 1973): 77–90.

27. Seidman, "Justice, Values and Social Science."

28. Ibid., p. 185.

29. Galliher and McCartney, "The Influence of Funding Agencies," pp. 83–88.

30. Richard V. Ericson, *Reproducing Order: A Study of Police Patrol Work* (Toronto: University of Toronto Press, 1982).

31. Greenberg, "Correctional Effects of Corrections," pp. 111–148.

32. Gendreau and Ross, "Effective Correctional Treatment," pp. 463–490.

33. Richard J. Lundman, Paul T. McFarlane, and Frank R. Scarpitti, "Delinquency Prevention: A Description and Assessment of Projects Reported in the Professional Literature," *Crime and Delinquency* 22 (July 1976): 297–308.

34. Charles H. Logan, "Evaluation Research in Crime and Delinquency: A Reappraisal," *Journal of Criminal Law, Criminology, and Police Science* 63 (September 1972): 378–387.

35. Joan McCord, "A Thirty-year Follow-up of Treatment Effects," *American Psychiatrist* 33 (March 1978): 284–289.

36. Scott and Shore, *Why Sociology Does Not Apply*, ch. 2.

37. Joan Brockman, C. D'Arcy, and L. Edmonds, "Facts or Artifacts? Changing Public Attitudes Toward the Mentally Ill," *Social Science and Medicine* 13A, no. 6 (1979): 673–682.

38. Ibid.

39. Walter R. Gove, "Societal Reaction as an Explanation of Mental Illness: An Evaluation." *American Sociological Review* 35 (October 1970): 873–884.

40. Douglas Lipton, Robert Martinson, and Judith Wilks, *The Effectiveness of Correctional Treatment* (New York: Praeger, 1975).

41. Richard A. Berk, Kenneth J. Lenihan, and Peter H. Rossi, "Crime and Poverty: Some Experimental Evidence from Ex-offenders," *American Sociological Review* 45 (October 1980): 766–786.

42. Ronald Roesch, "The Evaluation of Pretrial Diversion: A Response," *Crime and Delinquency* 25 (October 1979): 503–508.

43. Charles A. Murray and Louise A. Cox, *Beyond Probation: Juvenile Correction and the Chronic Delinquent* (Beverly Hills, Calif.: Sage Publications, 1979).

44. Ibid.

45. Scott and Shore, *Why Sociology Does Not Apply*, ch. 2.

46. Caplan, Morrison, and Stambaugh, *The Use of Social Science Knowledge*, p. 49.

47. Henry Aaron, *Politics and the Professors: The Great Society in Perspective* (Washington, D.C.: Brookings Institution, 1978), p. 9.

48. Paul Rosen, "Social Science and Judicial Policy Making," in C. H. Weiss, ed., *Using Social Research in Public Policy Making* (Lexington, Ky.: D.C. Heath, 1977).

49. Karin D. Knorr, "Policymakers' Use of Social Science Knowledge: Symbolic or Instrumental?" In Weiss, ed., *Using Social Research in Public Policy Making*, pp. 177–179.

50. Lindblom and Cohen, *Usable Knowledge*, pp. 12–18.

51. James C. Hackler, "Interpreting Meaning in Juvenile Court," *Journal of Juvenile and Family Courts* 34 (1983): 71–82.

52. Brockman et al., "Facts or Artifacts?"

53. Edward Seidman, "The Myths and Realities of Utilizing Social Experiments as a Foundation for Policy Formation," paper presented to the meetings of the American Society of Criminology in San Francisco, November 1980.

54. Ibid.

55. L. Sechrest, O. White, and E. Brown, *The Rehabilitation of Criminal Offenders: Problems and Prospects* (Washington, D.C.: National Academy of Sciences, 1979).

56. Berk et al., "Crime and Poverty," pp. 768–770.

57. Kenneth J. Lenihan, *Unlocking the Second Gate* (Washington, D.C.: U.S. Government Printing Office, 1977).

58. R. L. Austin, "Differential Treatment in an Institution: Reexamining the Preston Study," *Journal of Research in Crime and Delinquency* 14 (July 1977): 177–194.

59. James C. Hackler, *The Great Stumble Forward: The Prevention of Youthful Crime* (Toronto: Methuen, 1978), ch. 6.

60. McCord, "A Thirty-year Follow-up," p. 288.

61. David Farrington, "Longitudinal Research on Crime and Delinquency," in Norval Morris and Michael Tonry, eds., *Crime and Justice: An Annual Review of Criminal Justice Research* (Chicago: University of Chicago Press, 1979).

62. Travis Hirschi and Michael Gottfredson, "Age and the Explanation of Crime," *American Journal of Sociology* 89 (November 1983): 552–584.

63. Paul Cirel, Patricia Evans, Daniel McGillis, and Debra Whitcomb, *An Exemplary Project: Community Crime Prevention Program, Seattle, Washington* (Washington, D.C.: U.S. Department of Justice, 1977).

64. Rick Linden, Irwin Barker, and Doug Frisbie, *Working Together to Prevent Crime: A Practitioner's Handbook* (Ottawa: Solicitor General Canada, 1984).

65. Elias Duryea, Michael Hammes, and Gene Romo, "Preventing Substance Abuse in Adolescents from a Rural, Isolated Hispanic Community: The Mora Risk Project," Presentation at the International Conference on Prevention, May 1985, University of Montreal.

66. John Myers and David Armor, "Innovative Corrections: Martial Arts Training for Chronically Disruptive Youth," Presentation at the International Conference on Prevention, May 1985, University of Montreal.

67. Chok Hiew and Greg MacDonald, "Promoting Competence in Adolescents Through Pre-employment Skills Training and the Development of a Support System," Presentation at the International Conference on Prevention, May 1985, University of Montreal.

68. *Le Monde*, "Le debat sur la delinquance et la securite," July 13, 1984; *Le Matin*, "Delinquance: pour que l'été soit moins chaud," July 9, 1984.

69. *Liberation*, "Plan anti-été chaud: la gauche rejoue et gagne," June 6, 1984.

70. *Le Monde*, "Une bouffee de colere estival à Belle-Ile." August 2, 1984.

71. Joseph Weis and John Sederstrom, *The Prevention of Serious Delinquency: What to Do?* (Submission to the National Institute for Juvenile Justice and Delinquency Prevention) (Seattle: Center for Law and Justice, University of Washington, 1981).

72. Joseph Weis, Presentation at the International Conference on Prevention, May 1985, University of Montreal.

73. Douglas Kerr, "Changing Schools to Prevent Delinquency," Prepared for the American Psychological Association Annual Convention, Toronto, 1984.

74. Ibid.

75. P. Berman, "Toward an Implementation Paradigm," in R. Lehming and M. Kane, eds, *Improving Schools* (Beverly Hills, Calif.: Sage Publications, 1981), p. 270.

BIBLIOGRAPHY

References on how to do evaluations are numerous and easy to find in any library. The book by Saxe and Fine listed below and the journal *Evaluation and Program Planning* will lead the reader to the appropriate part of the library. Most of this bibliography refers to sources that raise questions about the evaluation process.

Berk, Richard A., Kenneth J. Lenihan, and Peter H. Rossi. "Crime and Poverty: Some Experimental Evidence for Ex-offenders." *American Sociological Review* 45 (October 1980): 766–786.

    This evaluation illustrates some of the characteristics of a crime prevention project that increase the likelihood of a genuine evaluation.

Blomberg, Thomas G. "Diversion's Disparate Results and Unresolved Questions: An Integrative Evaluation Perspective." *Journal of Research in Crime and Delinquency* 20 (January 1983): 24–38.

    This review of the literature on evaluation of diversion traces a record of reports of positive results, the expanding net of the juvenile system, and other detrimental results. As a corrective of those inconclusive evaluations, Blomberg calls for specification of youth types that are targets, of the characteristic ways they are to be handled, and of expected and unexpected outcomes.

Hackler, James C. "The Dangers of Political Naivete and Excessive Complexity in Evaluating Delinquency Prevention Programs." *Evaluating and Program Planning* 1 (Spring 1979): 273–283.

    This paper describes some of the pitfalls that can frustrate an evaluator, especially if the design is complex and certain political factors are ignored.

Knorr-Cetina, Karin D. *The Manufacture of Knowledge*. Oxford: Pergamon Press, 1981.

    This study of the way some "hard" scientists work illustrates areas of concern for evaluators of crime prevention programs that are usually ignored.

Krisberg, Barry. *The National Evaluation of Delinquency Prevention: Final Report*. San Francisco: Research Center, National Council on Crime and Delinquency, 1981.

    Examination of over 100 programs leads to the conclusion that, regardless of type of program or of intervention technique, little positive evidence of effectiveness was found.

Lindblom, Charles E., and David K. Cohen. *Usable Knowledge*. New Haven and London: Yale University Press, 1979.

The authors question the effectiveness of social science research, including evaluations, as a means of solving problems. They suggest that we "attack" problems rather than solve them. Many other strategies might be more effective than evaluations.

Rich, Robert F. *Social Science and Public Policy Making*. San Francisco: Jossey-Bass, 1981.

Rich questions the assumption that quality evaluations will lead directly to improvements. The needs of bureaucracy, not the needs of the public, will determine what knowledge is used.

Ross, Robert, and Paul Gendreau, eds. *Effective Correctional Treatment*. Toronto: Butterworths, 1980.

This collection of studies argues that correctional treatment has been successful.

Rutman, Leonard, and George Mowbray. *Understanding Program Evaluation*. Beverly Hills, Calif.: Sage Publications, 1983.

This primer defines evaluation and its purposes, presents the steps in a simple evaluation process, and offers case examples.

Saxe, Leonard, and Michelle Fine. *Social Experiments: Methods for Design and Evaluation*. Beverly Hills, Calif.: Sage Publications, 1981.

This is one of many recent books on evaluation but also includes a summary of the often discussed presidential address by D. T. Campbell to the American Psychological Association where he raises moral and practical questions about social experiments.

Scott, Robert A., and Arnold R. Shore. *Why Sociology Does Not Apply: A Study of the Use of Sociology in Public Policy*. New York: Elsevier, 1979.

These authors note that many of the sophisticated methodological tools that sociologists have developed to assess programs may in fact be of little consequence when it comes to influencing public policy.

APPENDIX A:
Supplementary Selected Bibliography

Delinquency and crime prevention are related directly or indirectly to a far-ranging array of topics. The items in the following bibliography were selected to be representative of major topics but are not intended to be comprehensive. The sheer volume of articles and books and the continuous addition of new insightful items denies a comprehensive compendium.

This bibliography supplements, rather than duplicates, the specialized bibliographies prepared by authors of the chapters. The bibliographies collectively provide the reader with entry points for exploring the particular literature of special interest. The items suggest where to look for other references.

A very valuable resource is the National Criminal Justice Reference Service (NCJRS), National Institute of Justice, Box 6000, Rockville, Maryland 20850; see the listing in Appendix B of this book. NCJRS gave us indispensable services in the preparation of this handbook.

PREMISES AND PRINCIPLES

Bloom, Martin. *Primary Prevention: The Possible Science*. Englewood Cliffs, N.J.: Prentice-Hall, 1981.

> Bloom strives to convince us that, in spite of many difficulties, primary prevention is a systematic and creative enterprise.

Clarke, Ronald V. "Opportunity-Based Crime Rates." *British Journal of Criminology* 24 (January 1984): 74–83.

> The paper considers methodological problems of refining opportunity-based crime rates as a means of demonstrating the infrequency of crime. Situation-based rates are seen to be useful for denoting the potentiality of preventive actions.

Lipsey, Mark W. "Is Delinquency Prevention a Cost-Effective Strategy? A California Perspective." *Journal of Research in Crime and Delinquency* 21 (November 1984): 279–302.

A cost-benefit model is applied to Los Angeles County prevention programs to support the contention that local and state government saves money under certain conditions.

Lundman, Richard J. *Prevention and Control of Juvenile Delinquency.* New York: Oxford University Press, 1984.

Predelinquent intervention is discussed in terms of individual treatment and area projects, preadjudication intervention as diversion, and postadjudication intervention as probation and parole, "Scared Straight," community treatment, and institutional treatment.

O'Brien, Robert M. *Crime and Victimization Data.* Beverly Hills, Calif.: Sage Publications, 1985.

The historical development of crime statistics in the United States is traced in an analysis of Uniform Crime Reports, the National Crime Surveys on victims, and self-reports by offenders.

Smith, Richard A., and Richard E. Klosterman. "Criminal Justice Planning: An Alternative Model." *Criminology* 17 (February 1980): 403–417.

In lieu of the general planning process model, the authors prefer restricting analysis of only policy alternatives that differ incrementally from each other and from existing programs; concurrent, as opposed to sequential, analyis of problems and alternatives; and dispersal of the planning process among planning bodies in the relevant area.

Vito, Gennard F., Dennis R. Logmine, and John P. Kenney. "Cracking Down on Crime: Issues in the Evaluation of Crime Suppression Programs." *Journal of Police Science and Administration* 11 (March 1983): 38–41.

The authors were involved in an evaluation of a program utilizing a task force, multijurisdictional, and proactive approach to suppressing a specific crime, in most cases, burglary. From their experiences, they present the methodological issues and practical problems raised in evaluative efforts.

CRIME CONTROL AND DETERRENCE

Buckner, John C., and Meda Chesney-Lind. "Dramatic Cures for Juvenile Crime: An Evaluation of a Prisoner-Run Delinquency Prevention Program." *Criminal Justice and Behavior* 10 (June 1983): 227–247.

The authors examine the effects of the "Stay Straight" program at Hawaii's major prison on previously arrested youths. Subjects were later arrested at a significantly higher rate than controls, but the outcomes may reflect their preexisting involvement in delinquency.

Grasnick, Harold G., and Donald E. Green. "Deterrence and the Morally Committed." *Sociological Quarterly* 22 (Winter 1981): 1–14.

A popular hypothesis is that the threat of legal sanctions influences only those not morally committed to a norm. Grasnick and Green offer evidence of effects at all levels of moral commitment.

Ross, H. Lawrence. *Deterring the Drinking Driver: Legal Policy and Social Control.* Rev. ed. Lexington, Mass.: Lexington Books, 1984.

An evaluation of drunk-driving laws concludes that perceived certainty of punishment produces only short-lived reduction of death rates and perceived severity of punishment has negligible results.

Toby, Jackson. "Deterrence Without Punishment." *Criminology* 19 (August 1981): 195–209.

The article considers the feasibility of symbolic redefinition of criminal acts so as to make social disapproval and self-condemnation more probable.

ENVIRONMENTAL FACTORS

Booth, Alan. "The Built Environment as a Crime Deterrent: A Reexamination of Defensible Space." *Criminology* 18 (February 1981): 557–570.

Matched samples of victimized and nonvictimized household were compared. Booth reports that defensible space has slight impact on feelings of responsibility for public space. Crime was deterred in indoor areas, but not in outdoor areas.

Davidson, R. N. *Crime and Environment.* London: Croom Helm, 1981.

British and American data are used in an analysis of the spatial patterning of crime. One of the conclusions is that three issues—ideology, displacement, and choice of coping strategy—must be considered before policy prescriptions.

Duffala, Dennis C. "Convenience Stores, Armed Robbery, and Physical Environmental Features." *American Behavioral Scientist* 29 (November-December 1976): 227–246.

Vulnerability to armed robbery of convenience stores, Duffala concludes, is increased by proximity to major transportation routes, light vehicular traffic, location in a residential or vacant area, and isolation from surrounding commercial activities.

Gillis, A. R., and John Hogan. "Density, Delinquency, and Design: Formal and Informal Control and the Built Environment." *Criminology* 19 (February 1982): 514–529.

This review of the literature on the general impact of the physical environment centers on two perspectives on control: the impairment of informal control and the attraction of the police as agents of formal control.

Ruth, Mary Jo. "Strategies for Crime Reduction in Public Housing." *Journal of Sociology and Welfare* 8 (September 1981): 587–600.

This literature review finds frequent citation of these potential contributions to crime in public housing projects: restricted surveillance of certain areas, insufficient target hardening against burglary, failure to control access, lack of controlled pedestrian routes, and insecure facilities for awaiting public transportation.

Insel, Paul M., ed. *Environmental Variables and the Prevention of Mental Illness.* Lexington, Mass.: Lexington Books, 1980.

The impact of environmental variables on individual behavior is examined to undergird the prevention, as well as treatment, of mental illness.

O'Donnell, Clifford R., and Tony Lydate. "The Relationship of Crimes to Physical Resources." *Environment and Behavior* 12 (June 1980): 207–230.

Honolulu police beats were classified according to physical resource categories and patterns of selected crimes.

INTERVENTION: TREATMENT AND SERVICES

Blomberg, Thomas G. "Diversions, Disparate Results and Unsolved Questions: An Integrative Evaluation Perspective." *Journal of Research in Crime and Delin-*

quency 20 (January 1983): 24–38.

Evaluations of diversion, Blomberg says, have been mixed, fragmented, and have failed to deal simultaneously with negative and positive effects. He proposes a multi-goal approach as a means of reducing those deficiencies.

Braukmann, Curtis J., Kathryn A. Kirigin, and Montrose M. Wolf. "Group Home Treatment Research: Social Learning and Social Control Perspectives." In Travis Hirschi and Michael Gottfredson, eds., *Understanding Crime: Current Theory and Research*. Beverly Hills, Calif.: Sage Publications, 1980, pp. 117–130.

Three studies of community-based group homes for delinquents provide data to test social learning and social control theories. Since the results were consistent with both postures, the authors see a basic complementarity.

Feldman, Ronald A., Timothy E. Caplinger, and John S. Wodarski. *The St. Louis Conundrum: The Effective Treatment of Antisocial Youths*. Englewood Cliffs, N.J.: Prentice-Hall, 1983.

The book describes and reports outcomes of a three-year project that integrated antisocial and prosocial youth in an experimental design differentiating level of experience of staff, method of group treatment, and mode of client-group composition.

Garrett, Carol J. "Effects of Residential Treatment on Adjudicated Delinquents: A Meta-Analysis." *Journal of Research in Crime and Delinquency* 22 (November 1985): 287–308.

Over one hundred studies of juvenile institutional or community residential settings were selected for using a comparison group or pre-post design. The general conclusion was that treatment in residential setting does work.

Gordon, James S. "Alternative Human Services in Crisis Intervention." *Victimology: An International Journal* 2 (Spring 1977): 22–30.

The research psychiatrist lists premises of alternative services—drop-in centers, free clinics, self-help groups, and so on—that make them a superior instrument for primary prevention.

Henshelwood, R. D., and Nick Manning, eds. *Therapeutic Communities: Reflections and Progress*. London: Routledge and Kegan Paul, 1979.

A collection of essays explores the tension between discovery and management, as a dilemma for therapeutic communities.

Kaplan, Louise J. *Adolescence: The Farewell to Childhood*. New York: Simon and Schuster, 1984.

The psychoanalytic literature is arranged to bear on the "invention" of adolescence and the dilemmas and solutions of the adolescents engaged in active revision of an infantile past.

Lemert, Edwin M. "Diversion in Juvenile Justice: What Has Been Wrought." *Journal of Research in Crime and Delinquency* 18 (January 1981): 34–46.

Lemert traces the origin, meaning, and various rationales of diversion. He sees it as a solution to the dilemma of the police posed by pressure for control and decarceration of status offenders. The future of diversion is questioned.

Loeber, Rolf, and Thomas J. Dishion. "Early Predictors of Male Delinquency: A Review." *Psychological Bulletin* 94 (July-November 1983): 68–99.

Recommendations for improvement of prediction studies were derived from assessment of studies. The principal predictors of delinquency were parents' family management, the child's conduct problems, parental criminality, and the child's poor academic performance.

Martin, Susan E., Lee B. Sechrest, and Robin Redner, ed. *New Directions in the Rehabilitation of Criminal Offenders*. Washington, D.C.: National Academy Press, 1981.

This report from the Panel of Research on Rehabilitative Techniques focuses on developing more effective treatment programs and evaluation procedures through a client-selector process.

Meichenbaum, Donald, and Matt E. Jaremko, eds. *Stress Reduction and Prevention*. New York: Plenum Press, 1983.

Consumers of a wide variety of programs are the intended audience of this analysis of the premises and mechanisms of a variety of programs for the prevention and management of stress in many settings.

McCord, Joan. "A Thirty-Year Follow-Up of Treatment Effects." *American Psychologist* 33 (March 1978): 284–289.

In 1939–1944 the Cambridge-Somerville youth project boys, aged five and thirteen years, were exposed to a treatment program, with a control group receiving no treatment. Forty years later McCord administered questionnaires to 253 of the experimental group and 253 of the control group. She reports that treatment failed to prevent adult crimes and to have negative side effects in terms of greater incidence of alcoholism and mental disturbance, lower occupational status, and less job satisfaction.

McMurtry, Steven L. "Secondary Prevention of Child Maltreatment: A Review." *Social Work* 30 (January-February 1985): 42–48.

Before secondary prevention of child abuse is effective, McMurtry concludes, better criteria for identifying abusive parents and better means of intervention must be developed.

Orsagh, Thomas, and Mary Ellen Marsden. "What Works When; Rational-Choice Theory and Offender Rehabilitation." *Journal of Criminal Justice* 13, no. 3 (1985): 269–277.

The authors argue that treatment will be effective if addressed to specific offender groups. In that vein, they advocate motivating offenders through programs that would increase their taste for income or for work and would enhance their income.

Roskin, Michael. "Integration of Primary Prevention into Social Work Practice." *Social Work* 25 (May 1980): 192–196.

The potential for primary prevention through social work practice is illustrated, but why has only lip-service been offered? Roskin offers an explanation.

Rutter, Michael. *Maternal Deprivation Reassessed*. New York: Penguin Books, 1981.

Rutter reviews the qualities of mothering needed for normal personality development and the differential effects of "maternal deprivation."

Selke, William L. "Diversion and Crime Prevention: A Time-Series Analysis." *Criminology* 20 (November 1982): 395–406.

Evaluation of seven youth service bureaus found they had little effect. Selke sees potential in diversion, but the small size of the bureaus and the emphasis on systems-level change weaken outcomes.

Sieber, Sam D. *Fatal Remedies: The Ironies of Social Intervention*. New York: Plenum Press, 1981.

"Social intervention" is defined as any deliberate effort to alter a human situation in some desired direction. Sieber concentrates on the possibilities that intervention will render the original goal less attainable because of functional disruption, exploitation, goal displacement, arousal of opposition, faulty classification of clients, excessive goal ambition, relative availability of resources, and deterioration of effectiveness through compromise with supporting parties or with the practical realities encountered.

INVOLVING THE COMMUNITY

DuBow, Fred, and David Emmons. "The Community Hypotheses." In Dan A. Lewis, ed., *Reactions to Crime*. Beverly Hills, Calif.: Sage Publications, 1981, pp. 167–181.

The evolution and concepts of the community anticrime program (LEAA) are reviewed. The CACP experience is that the organizations undertaking prevention projects are not derived from primary concern about crime, that the relationship between informal control and crime reduction is not sufficiently understood, but that the community crime prevention movement is promising in drawing more attention to the need to address broader social conditions that affect crime at the local level.

Hale, Donna C., and Robert G. Leonik. "Planning Community-Initiated Crime Prevention." *Journal of Police Science and Administration* 10 (March 1982): 76–82.

What can be done through planning to facilitate citizen involvement in that process? Hale and Leonik concentrate on the general systems and organizational behavioral theories in assessing a neighborhood foot patrol officer program as a tool of crime prevention.

Marx, Gary T., and Dave Archer. "Community Police Patrols and Vigilantism." In H. John Rosenbaum and Peter C. Sederberg, eds., *Vigilante Politics*. Philadelphia: University of Pennsylvania Press, 1976, pp. 129–157.

Marx and Archer describe and assess twenty-eight "self-defense" groups that were found to be heterogeneous in being either supplementary or adversarial toward the police and either encouraged or opposed by the police. The groups differed in the legitimacy accorded by the communities they wished to serve, recruitment and management, chosen operations, and qualities essential to group survival.

Ostrowe, Brian B., and Rosanne DiBiase. "Citizen Involvement as a Crime Deterrent: A Study of Public Attitudes Toward an Unsanctioned Civilian Patrol Group." *Journal of Police Science and Administration* 11 (June 1983): 185–193.

Questionnaires were administered to civilians, transit authority police officers, and New York City police officers about the Guardian Angels. The civilians were more favorable than either police group.

Percy, Stephen L. "Citizen Coproduction of Community Safety." In Ralph Baker and Fred A. Meyer, Jr., eds., *Evaluating Alternative Law-Enforcement Policies*. Lexington, Mass.: Lexington Books, 1979, pp. 125–134.

The active participation of citizens in the production of community security and safety is conceived according to two distinctions: individual-household activity versus group activity and direct cooperation with police versus little or no cooperation with police.

Piliavin, Jane Allyn, John F. Dovidio, Samuel L. Gaertner, and Russell D. Clark III. *Emergency Intervention*. New York: Academic Press, 1981.

Will individuals intervene in a crisis situation involving other people? The authors deal with the process of deciding to intervene.

Rosenbaum, Dennis P., ed. *Community Crime Prevention: Does It Work?* Beverly Hills, Calif.: Sage Publications, 1986.

This collection of papers evaluates four typical community crime prevention programs: citizen initiatives to prevent residential crime; programs against commercial crime; police initiatives against residential crime; and media strategies.

Washnis, George J. *Citizen Involvement in Crime Prevention.* Lexington, Mass.: Lexington Books, 1976.

After delineating the rationale for citizen participation, Washnis analyzes block associations, mobile patrols, special units, police-community councils, and citizen anticrime crusades.

Woodson, Robert L. *A Summons to Life: Mediating Structures and the Prevention of Youth Crime.* Cambridge, Mass.: Ballinger Publishing Co., 1981.

Mediating structures are identified as the family, neighborhood, and community-based organizations that stand between the identity needs of inner-city youth and the large-scale institutions of the society at large. Control and treatment models of prevention, Woodson argues, are inferior in outcomes to summoning the potentialities of the mediating structures.

SOCIALIZING INSTITUTIONS

Brown, Stephen E. "Social Class, Child Maltreatment, and Delinquent Behavior." *Criminology* 22 (May 1984): 259–278.

Data from 110 high school freshmen reveal that emotional abuse and neglect were correlated positively with all forms of delinquency but physical abuse was not.

Casserly, Michael D., Scott A. Bass, and John R. Garrett. *School Vandalism.* Lexington, Mass.: Lexington Books, 1980.

The authors review research, analyze major options for prevention, and describe selected prevention programs for schools.

Griffiths, Curt Taylor. "Police School Programs: The Realities of the Remedy." *Canadian Journal of Criminology* 24 (July 1982): 329–340.

Programs in schools are a common strategy for alleviating favorable images of the police among juveniles. Griffiths questions the usual premises of such programs.

Lavrakas, Paul J. "On Households." In Dan A. Lewis, ed., *Reactions to Crime.* Beverly Hills, Calif.: Sage Publications, 1981.

A telephone survey of a sample of Chicago households finds that some households use a variety of protective measures, that others employ few or none, and that homeowners are much more likely than renters to take such measures.

Ouston, Janet. "Delinquency, Family Background and Educational Attainment." *British Journal of Criminology* 24 (January 1984): 2–26.

An investigation of twelve inner-London secondary schools shows a relationship between delinquency and family background. Parental occupation and intelligence test scores together have a strong relationship to delinquency. Since schools with lower proportions of disadvantaged and less able pupils have lower delinquency rates, the development of schools with mixed-ability classes and suitable curricula appeared to have preventive effects.

Pink, William T. "Schools, Youth, and Justice." *Crime and Delinquency* 30 (July 1984): 439–461.

Effective schools, orchestrated with changes in the occupational arena, are seen as a promising preventive strategy. Pink offers a reform agenda for school districts.

Roncek, Dennis W., and Donald Faggiani. "High Schools and Crime: A Replication." *Sociological Quarterly* 26, no. 4 (1985): 491–505.

Proximity to public high schools, the author's data indicate, only increases crime on Cleveland city blocks which are immediately adjacent to the schools. The size of enrollment has little effect.

Thornberry, Terence P., Melanie Moore, and R. L. Christensen. "The Effect of Dropping Out of High School on Subsequent Criminal Behavior." *Criminology* 23 (February 1985): 3–18.

Does dropping out of high school increase chances of subsequent criminal behavior? In general, the article says "yes." Two theoretical perspectives are tested.

Toby, Jackson. "Crime in the Schools." In James Q. Wilson, ed., *Crime and Public Policy*. San Francisco: ICS Press, 1983, pp. 69–88.

The sources of crime in schools are outlined, and the means of reducing school violence are assessed. Toby recommends that all states set age fifteen as the upper limit of compulsory attendance.

Wilson, Harriett. "Parental Supervision: A Neglected Aspect of Delinquency." *British Journal of Criminology* 20 (July 1980): 203–235.

Families in the inner city and suburbs were compared in terms of degree of social handicap, parental supervision, and delinquency. Wilson concludes that parents who are lax in supervising children are highly likely to produce delinquents in high-delinquent areas and that lax parenting methods are often the result of social handicaps.

CRIMINAL JUSTICE AND PREVENTION

Balkin, Steven, and Pauline Houlden. "Reducing Fear Through Occupational Presence." *Criminal Justice and Behavior* 10 (March 1983): 13–33.

A questionnaire administered to university students provides evidence that persons in uniform reduce fear of crime in public areas.

Berg, Ian, Alison Goodwin, Roy Hullen, and Ralph McGuire. "The Effect of Two Varieties of the Adjournment Procedure on Truancy." *British Journal of Criminology* 23 (April 1983): 150–158.

The city of Leeds, England, brings juvenile truants before courts that follow either of two procedures: "Flexible" adjournment of one, two, three, or four weeks and then monthly adjournments; or "inflexible" adjournment of only every four weeks. The two procedures did not have significantly different effects in reducing school attendance problems.

Clarke, Steven H., and Gary F. Hoch. "Juvenile Court: Therapy or Crime Control, and Do Lawyers Make a Difference?" *Law and Society Review* 14 (Winter 1980): 263–308.

Two North Carolina juvenile projects were studied to determine their degree of concern about rehabilitation, crime prevention, and adversarial procedure. The intake of less serious offenders had been reduced, but punitive management of the remaining cases remains.

Davis, Robert C. "Victim/Witness Noncooperation: A Second Look at a Persistent Phenomenon." *Journal of Criminal Justice* 11, no. 4 (1983): 287–299.

Programs dedicated to increasing the participation of victims and witnesses in adjudication are relevant to deterrence as a form of prevention. Davis reviews empirical studies to conclude that their noncooperation is not a serious obstacle to prosecution.

Forer, Lois G. *Criminals and Victims: A Trial Judge Reflects on Crime and Punishment.* New York: W. W. Norton and Co., 1980.

In drawing on her experiences as lawyer, law teacher, and judge in commenting on a variety of issues, Forer offers a critique of deterrence as the central philosophy in the court as a vehicle for crime prevention.

Greenberg, Martin Alan. *Auxiliary Police: The Citizen's Approach to Public Safety.* Westport, Conn.: Greenwood Press, 1984.

The voluntary participation of citizens in police activities is one of the favored ideas for prevention of crime and delinquency. Drawing on the history of auxiliary police in New York City, Greenberg analyzes the issues of legal and authority implications. Special attention is devoted to subway patrol and the Guardian Angels.

Kelling, George L. "Police Field Services and Crime: The Presumed Effects of a Capacity." *Crime and Delinquency* 24 (April 1978): 173–184.

Since research has indicated that police emphasis on crime-related activities has failed to reduce crime, Kelling calls for improvement of police-citizen interaction and developing approaches that reduce citizen fear.

McCarthy, John J. "Dispute Resolution: Seeking Justice Outside the Courtroom." *Corrections Magazine* 8 (August 1982): 33–40.

Mediation centers are described as alternatives to adjudication that are intended to reduce tensions that can lead to violence and criminal behavior.

Pearce, Jack B., and John R. Snortum. "Police Effectiveness in Handling Disturbance Calls: An Evaluation of Crisis Intervention Training." *Criminal Justice and Behavior* 10 (March 1983): 71–92.

In crisis intervention, trained officers were found to rate their handling of cases more positively than untrained officers and to be rated more highly for service by clients.

Sherman, Lawrence W. "Patrol Strategies for Police." In James Q. Wilson, ed., *Crime and Public Policy*. San Francisco: ICS Press, 1983, pp. 145–163.

The history and nature of watching as one of the major prevention strategies are sketched as background for noting that the burgeoning growth of private policing may reflect the public's declining faith in the effectiveness of the private police. Sherman suggests an altered police policy governing both public and private watching for prevention.

Smith, Douglas A., and Jody R. Klein. "Police Control of Interpersonal Disputes." *Social Problems* 31 (April 1984): 468–481.

Observation of police-citizen encounters leads to the conclusion that arrest decisions in disputes depend on certain situational variables, as screened by type of neighborhood, and the organizational characteristics of police agencies.

Szynkowski, Lawrence J. "Preventive Patrol: Traditional Versus Specialized." *Journal of Police Science and Administration* 9 (June 1981): 167–183.

Traditional preventive patrol is the routine movement of uniformed officers by vehicle or on foot through delineated geographial areas. Specialized patrol includes plainclothes units, uniformed tactical units that supplement traditional units and saturated areas for specific periods of time, use of mechanical devices, and team policing. Example programs and difficulties of implementing specialized patrol are described.

Teplin, Linda A., ed. *Mental Health and Criminal Justice*. Beverly Hills, Calif.: Sage Publications, 1984.

The interface of the mental health and criminal justice systems is examined from the perspective of "law in action" and the dynamics of the growing interdependence of the two systems.

Trojanowicz, Robert C. "An Evaluation of a Neighborhood Foot Patrol Program." *Journal of Police Science and Administration* 11 (December 1983): 410–419.

The Flint, Michigan, Foot Patrol Program, Trojanowicz concludes, contributed to a greater sense of safety, greater participation in crime prevention, and respect for the police among citizens. He also believes that foot patrols are more economical and efficient than other police units.

Turner, David. "The Probation Officer and Community Delinquency Prevention: The Shift Out of Reactive Casework." *Canadian Journal of Criminology* 26 (January-February 1984): 75–95.

A Canadian probation officer describes actions taken to prevent delinquency in a subsidized housing complex. He applies a systems model for the practitioner's involvement in change processes associated with the proactive stance of prevention.

Zeisel, Hans. *The Limits of Law Enforcement*. Chicago: University of Chicago Press, 1982.

On the basis of his study of the New York City Police Department, Zeisel concludes, because the power of law enforcement comes too late, that crime control must develop its preventive arm.

PRACTICAL GUIDES

Barefoot, J. Kirk. *Employee Theft Investigation*. Los Angeles: Security World Publishing Co., 1979.

The business manager is alerted to means of detecting and investigating employee theft.

Barnard, Robert L. *Intrusion Detection Systems: Principles of Operation and Applications*. Boston: Butterworths, 1981.

Elements for designing intrusion detection systems are presented, including exterior detectors, interior detectors, and central station monitoring.

Fennelly, Lawrence J. *Handbook of Loss Prevention and Crime Prevention*. Boston: Butterworths, 1982.

Vulnerability assessment, technical details on target-hardening devices, and management are emphasized in this handbook for physical security programs.

Fike, R. A. *How to Keep from Being Robbed, Raped and Ripped Off—A Personal Crime Prevention Manual for You and Your Loved Ones*. Washington, D.C.: Acropolis

Books, 1983.

This practical guide is organized around the principles: avoid hostile situations, be able to apply defensive tactics as a last resort, and continually assess vulnerabilities to crime in one's lifestyle.

Howard, William B. "Dealing with the Violent Criminal: What to Do and Say." *Federal Probation* 44 (March 1980): 13–18.

Howard offers advice on avoiding dangerous situations, how to behave when confronted by a criminal threat, how to short-circuit a violent attack, and whether to fight back.

Linenberg, A. "Explosive Detectors." *Assets Protection* 5 (November-December 1980): 38–41.

A technical expert describes devices used to locate explosive devices.

Sklar, Stanley L. *Shoplifting: What You Need to Know About the Law.* New York: Fairchild Publications, 1982.

Setting out to avoid "gobbledygook," Sklar would help merchandising organizations combat shoplifting while guiding them to stay within the law.

Sloane, Eugene A. *The Complete Book of Locks, Keys, Burglar and Smoke Alarms, and Other Security Devices.* New York: William Morrow and Co., 1977.

This profusely illustrated handbook describes a wide variety of target-hardening devices and gives instructions on their installation and use.

APPENDIX B:

Directory of Selected Organizations Involved in Delinquency and Crime Prevention

Where may expert counsel be obtained for implementing a new program in the prevention of delinquency and crime? Which particular strategy is most appropriate to the purposes and target population of the proposed program? What difficulties lurk in ambush that could be avoided by careful planning and intelligent implementation based on the experiences of those groups already undertaking prevention? Where can essential resources be obtained? To provide answers to such practical questions, a selected number of organizations involved in prevention programs were approached for fundamental information. Their answers are the substance of this directory.

To identify those organizations, three sources were used. First, the National Institute of Law Enforcement published a directory: James L. Lockard, J.T. Skip Duncan, and Robert N. Brenner, *Directory of Community Crime Prevention Programs: National and State Levels* (Washington, D.C.: National Institute of Law Enforcement and Criminal Justice, December 1978). Second, the International Society of Crime Prevention Practitioners publishes the *International Crime Prevention Directory*. Third, we consulted the National Crime Prevention Institute of the University of Louisville in Kentucky.

Our purposes were to produce a directory that would be current by excluding organizations no longer operating in 1984, that would be representative of the various kinds of organizations, and that would be manageable within the space limitations of this handbook. A remarkable number of organizations emerged when federal funding was available; the sharp contraction of that support has ended many of the programs. Prevention has been undertaken by a variety of public and private agencies, of voluntary and formal organizations, of law enforcement and social service agencies, and of organizations operating at the municipal, state, or national levels. Rather than attempting comprehensive coverage of all existing organizations, this directory is selective in representing that array of programs.

For each organization represented here, a summary description reports the reply of the given respondent to the mailed questionnaire. The statements should be interpreted in terms of the following questions:

1. What is the major function(s) of your organization?
    (a) Encouraging other groups to develop prevention programs.
    (b) Coordinating prevention programs.
    (c) Establishing and operating programs.
    (d) Public education.
    (e) Increasing public participation.
    (f) Clearinghouse for information.
    (g) Providing referral services.
    (h) Another function (please specify).
2. Which of the following best describes your program?
    (a) Wide range of approaches are used.
    (b) Only certain approaches are used (specify in item 3).
    (c) Wide variety of constituencies are served.
    (d) Only a particular constituency is served.
        (1) Juveniles only.
        (2) Elderly only.
        (3) A particular ethnic group only.
        (4) Another group (please specify).
3. What types of specific programs are utilized?
    (a) Operation identification.
    (b) Public education.
    (c) Court watch.
    (d) Neighborhood watch.
    (e) Target hardening.
    (f) Victim assistance.
    (g) Crime blockers.
    (h) Prevention vans.
    (i) Against commercial crime.
    (j) Against burglary.
    (k) Against substance abuse.
    (l) Against arson.
    (m) Against vehicle theft.
    (n) Against vandalism.
    (o) Against rape/assault.
    (p) Other (please specify).
4. Is accessibility to your service limited to only certain professionals in prevention?
    (a) No, there are no limitations.
    (b) Yes, only to residents of the given state.
    (c) Yes, these limitations are imposed (please specify).
5. On what topics is technical information available in print (purchase, free, or loan)?
    (a) On program planning.
    (b) On program operations.
    (c) On training.
    (d) On program content.
    (e) On program evaluation.
6. Are these kinds of resources available on request (purchase, free, loan, or rental)?
    (a) Films.
    (b) Video cassettes.

   (c) Slide presentations.
   (d) Training plans/manuals.
   (e) Library on prevention topics.
   (f) Clearinghouse for information.
   (g) Referral services.
   (h) Public education brochures.
   (i) Mass media materials.
7. Add any comments or further information you consider important for an accurate and clear report on your organization.

NATIONAL ORGANIZATIONS

American Association of Retired Persons
Criminal Justice Services
1909 K Street N.W.
Washington, D.C. 20049

Contact Person: George Sunderland, Senior Coordinator, (202) 728–4363

Summary Description: Functions are service to AARP units in establishng and operating programs, public education, increasing public participation, clearinghouse, referral, and providing course materials for police training. A wide range of approaches are used for serving its elderly constituency. Specific programs used are operation identification, public education, court watch, neighborhood watch, target hardening, against burglary, against vehicle theft, against vandalism, against rape/assault, against rural crime, and against abuse of elderly. There are no limitations except availability of materials. All topics on technical information in print are available free; slides are available by loan or purchase. Free resources are training plans/manuals, clearinghouse, referral, public education brochures, and mass media materials.

Comment of Agency: AARP is a membership organization that also maintains a gerontological resource center for materials on aging, research studies, and other subjects related to older persons.

American Society for Industrial Security
1655 North Ft. Myer Drive
Suite 1200
Arlington, Va. 22209

Contact Person: Chairman of Crime Prevention Committee (changes annually)

Summary Description: The function of this professional association, through its crime prevention committee, is to encourage other groups to develop prevention programs. A wide range of approaches are used primarily for the association's members. Specific programs utilized are public education and target hardening directed against all types of crime. The committee endeavors to respond to all appropriate inquiries. Technical information in print may be purchased on program planning, training, and content. Referral services are free; training plans/manuals and library items may be borrowed.

Comment of Agency: The library being developed is expected to offer interlibrary loans in 1985. The association's magazine, *Security Magazine*, carries a column on crime prevention programs.

Center for Women Policy Studies
2000 P Street N.W.
Suite 508
Washington, D.C. 20036

Contact Person: Nancy R. King, Deputy Director, (202) 812–1770

Summary Description: Functions are public policy and public education on a variety of issues affecting women. The primary current focus is on the victimization of women and children, including wife and child battery, child sexual abuse, sexual assault, elder abuse, pornography, sexual harassment in the workplace, and related issues. Social Security and other issues affecting older women are also being examined. Resources on a variety of issues are available through the publication department, including a quarterly journal, *Response to the Victimization of Women and Children*.

Comment of Agency: The center develops information and analyses on family violence, sexual assault, and other forms of victimization of women and children. A quarterly journal and a variety of materials are disseminated.

Institute of Criminal Justice Studies
Southwest Texas State University
San Marcos, Tex. 78666

Contact Person: George A. Landry, Director, (512) 245–3030

Summary Description: Functions are clearinghouse and training in all specific programs. A wide variety of approaches are used, and a wide variety of constituencies are served. The only limitation is that non-Texas residents pay a fee for training. No technical information in print is available. Slides and training plans/manuals may be purchased; library and clearinghouse are free.

Comment of Agency: The institute sustains a broad range of adult training programs for citizens and professionals engaged in work with crime and delinquency, including prevention.

National Association of Town Watch, Inc.
P.O. Box 769
Havertown, Pa. 19083

Contact Person: Matt A. Peskin, Executive Director, (215) 649–6662

Summary Description: All functions are served except establishing and operating programs. A wide variety of constituencies are served without limitations. Specific programs used are public education, neighborhood watch, against commercial crime, against burglary, against vehicle theft, against vandalism, and against rape/assault. Technical information in print on program planning and operations is free. Resources available free are clearinghouse, referral, public education brochures, and mass media materials. The association is a nonprofit membership organization, with the classifications: law enforcement/professional member, crime watch group member, and associate-individual member. (Crime watch groups must be affiliated and cooperating with local police.) Members receive the association's "New Spirit" newsletter.

Comment of Agency: The association was established in 1981, in the face of rising crime rates and municipal budgetary cutbacks, to involve "the people" in a nationwide prevention effort through local voluntary organizations and social institutions.

National Center for the Prevention and Control of Rape
Parklawn Building, Room 6C–12
5600 Fishers Lane
Rockville, Md. 20857

Contact Person: Eunice Raigrodski, Technical Information Assistant, (301) 443–1910

Summary Description: Concentrating on crimes of rape/sexual assault, the center encourages other groups to develop prevention programs, conduct public education programs, maintain clearinghouses, and operate victim assistance referral services, in addition to supporting research on rape and sexual assault of adults and children. A wide variety of constituencies are served without limitations. Technical information in print on training is free. Resources available on loan are films, training plans/manuals, clearinghouse, referral, and public education brochures.

National Crime Prevention Institute
School of Justice Administration
College of Urban and Public Affairs
University of Louisville, Shelby Campus
Louisville, Ky. 40292

Contact Person: Milton E. Brown, Director, (502) 588–6987

Summary Description: All functions are served except coordinating prevention programs, establishing and operating programs, and increasing public participation. The institute trains law enforcement, military, public officials, and citizens in crime prevention and security. A wide range of approaches are used, and a great variety of constituencies are assisted in all types of specific programs. Accessibility to services is unlimited. Topics on technical information in print are available free or on loan. Referral services and single-copy public education brochures are free, and the clearinghouse information is either free or on loan.

National Clearinghouse for Drug Abuse Information
National Institute on Drug Abuse
P.O. Box 416
Kensington, Md. 20795

Contact Person: Correspondence preferred.

Summary Description: The only function is the clearinghouse on substance abuse serving a wide variety of constituencies for public education. There are no limitations on accessibility of services otherwise. Technical information in print is available free on program planning, operation, and evaluations. Public education brochures are free.

National Council on Crime and Delinquency
760 Market Street, #433
San Francisco, Calif. 94102

Contact Person: Dr. Barry Krisberg, President, (415) 956–5651

Summary Description: Functions are public education and conducting criminal justice research for a wide variety of constituencies. Technical information is available in print by purchase on program planning, program operation (some items are free), training (some items free), program content, and evaluation (some items free). Training plans and manuals as well as public education brochures may be purchased.

National Crime Prevention Council
805 15th Street N.W.
Washington, D.C. 20005

Contact Person: John A. Calhoun, Executive Director, (202) 393–7141

Summary Description: All functions except establishing, operating, and coordinating prevention are performed. A wide range of approaches are used, and many constituencies are served. All types of specific programs are used except court watch, crime blockers, and against substance abuse. Technical information in print on all topics, except program evaluation, is available. Resources for purchase are training plans/manuals and library materials. Those available free are clearinghouse, referral, public education brochures, and mass media materials.

Comment of Agency: The council manages the National Crime Prevention Coalition (which is composed of ninety-four groups, including federal government agencies, statewide crime prevention organizations, and the Advertising Council) and the McGruff media campaign. The Coalition supplies prevention materials on a limited basis. The council can provide technical assistance and training to strengthen and reinforce existing and new programs. A computerized index of crime prevention programs and resources is available.

The National Exchange Club
3050 Central Avenue
Toledo, Ohio 43606

Contact Person: James A. Schnoering, Executive Vice President, (419) 535–3232

Summary Description: Functions are establishing and operating programs, as well as increasing public participation and education. Through local organizations, a wide constituency is served utilizing such specific programs as neighborhood watch and operation identification. There is no limitation on accessibility to services. Technical information in print may be purchased on program planning and operations. Resources available for purchase are slides, training plans/manuals, public education brochures, and mass media materials.

U.S. Department of Justice
Community Relations Service
5550 Friendship Boulevard, Third Floor
Chevy Chase, Md. 20901

Contact Person: Wallace Warfield, Associate Director, (301) 492–5939

Summary Description: Functions are encouraging other groups to develop programs, providing public education, increasing public participation, and providing referral services. A wide range of approaches are used, and a wide variety of constituencies are served. ("Agency's mandate, under Title X of 1964 Civil Rights Act, specifies problems of race, color, or national origin.") Programs utilized are public education, neighborhood watch, and target hardening.

National Institute of Justice
Community Crime Prevention Division
633 Indiana Avenue N.W.
Washington, D.C. 20531

Contact Person: Fred Heinzelmann, Director, (202) 724–7684

Summary Description: Functions are research and evaluation on prevention and control of crime, public education, increasing public participation, and clearinghouse. A wide variety of constituencies are served without limitations. Technical information and other resources are available from the National Criminal Justice Reference Service (described in this appendix).

National Institute of Justice
National Criminal Justice Reference Service
Box 6000
Rockville, Md. 20850

Contact Person: Leonard A. Sipes, Jr., Senior Crime Prevention Specialist, (301) 251–5500

Summary Description: The national constituency is served through clearinghouse information, referral, a free bimonthly justice journal, data base searches, and free and cost-recovery documents. Information is available without limitation on all types of specific programs. All types of technical information in print are offered by purchase, loan, or free. Films, video cassettes, and slides may be rented. Available through purchase, loan, or free distribution are training plans/manuals, library, clearinghouse, and public education brochures. Referral is free. Mass media materials may be borrowed.

Comment of Agency: The Reference Service covers all criminal justice topics, including prevention in the 78,000 document base; more than 5,000 titles deal specifically with prevention. To gain access to the extensive free referral service and other information, letters should include a phone number.

National Organization for Victim Assistance
1757 Park Road N.W.
Washington, D.C. 20010

Contact Person: Marlene A. Young, Executive Director, (202) 232–8560

Summary Description: Functions are encouraging other groups to develop programs, public education, increasing public participation, clearinghouse, referral services, direct service to victims, and national advocacy. Specific programs are public education and victim assistance. Crime prevention is an integral part of primary focus on victims as constituency. Accessibility to services is unlimited. All types of technical information in print are available through purchase or are free. Resources available on loan are video cassettes, slides, library, and mass media materials. Training plans/manuals are free or may be purchased. Free resources are clearinghouse, referral, and public education brochures.

National Rural Crime Prevention Center
2120 Fyffe Road
The Ohio State University
Columbus, Ohio 43210

Contact Person: Joseph F. Donnermeyer, Director, (614) 422–1467

Summary Description: All functions are performed except establishing and operating programs and increasing public participation. A wide variety of approaches and specific programs are used, except victim assistance and program against arson; agricultural security is a special interest. A wide variety of constituencies are served. Accessibility to services is unlimited. Technical information in print is available for purchase, except on program evaluation. Available for purchase are: video cassettes, slides, training plans/ manuals, and public education brochures; for rental: video cassettes and slides; for loan: slides; free: library, clearinghouse, and referral.

National Sheriff's Association
1450 Duke Street
Alexandria, Va. 22314

Contact Person: Ben Gorda, Director, Crime Prevention Programs, (793) 836–7827

Summary Description: All functions except establishing and operating programs are performed. A wide range of approaches are used, and many constituencies are served. Programs are directed to operation identification, public education, neighborhood watch, target hardening, victim assistance, commercial crime, burglary, substance abuse, and vandalism. Accessibility to services is not limited. Technical information in print may be purchased on program planning, operations, and content. Films and similar resources are not available.

U.S. Postal Inspection Service
475 L'Enfant Plaza
Washington, D.C. 20260

Contact Person: W. J. Maisch, General Manager, (202) 245–5317

Summary Description: Functions are encouraging other groups to develop prevention programs; establishing operating and coordination prevention programs within the Postal Service; public education; and increasing public participation against fraud and mail theft.

A wide variety of approaches are used, and a wide variety of constituencies are served. Specific programs used are public education, target hardening, and victim assistance; for the Postal Service prevention is directed against burglary, substance abuse, vehicle theft, vandalism, mail fraud, and mail theft. No limitations are placed on services. Technical information in print on program content is available. Films, video cassettes, and slides are available on loan. Public education brochures and mass media materials are free.

STATE OR LOCAL ORGANIZATIONS

Airport Security Council
P.O. Box 30705
JFK International Airport
Jamaica, N.Y. 11430

Contact Person: Edward J. McGowan, Executive Director, or William Schulman, Staff Advisor, (516) 328–2990

Summary Description: Functions are establishing and coordinating cargo theft prevention programs for airlines. In addition to serving as a clearinghouse for information, the council analyzes specific types of cargo thefts to determine preventive measures. A limited supply of printed material is available on request. Manuals and slide presentations are offered on loan to security professionals.

School of Justice
University of Alaska, Anchorage
3211 Providence Drive
Anchorage, Ak. 99508

Contact Person: Steve Edwards, Director of Research, (907) 786–1812

Summary Description: Functions are encouraging other groups to develop prevention programs, public education, increasing public participation, clearinghouse, and referral. A wide variety of constituencies are served, but no specific programs are operated. There are no limitations on accessibility to services. Technical information in print is available on program planning and evaluation. Video cassettes and mass media materials are available on loan; referral services are free.

California Attorney-General's Office
Crime Prevention Center
1515 K Street, Suite 383
Sacramento, Calif. 95814

Contact Person: John E. Dugan, Director, (916) 324–7863

Summary Description: All functions are performed except establishing and operating program, plus technical assistance. A wide range of approaches are used, and a wide variety of constituencies served. The following programs are used: operation identification, public education, neighborhood watch, target hardening, victim assistance, school safety, and programs for the prevention of commercial crime, burglary, vandalism in business or schools, and rape/assault. Accessibility to services is limited to not-for-profit organizations. Technical information in print is free on program planning and training. Resources available are films on loan, video cassettes on loan or purchase, and the following are free: training plans/manuals, library, clearinghouse, referral, public education brochures, and mass media materials.

California Crime Prevention Officers Association
P.O. Box 12249
Santa Ana, Calif. 92712

Contact Person: David A. Parsons, President, (415) 231–2099

Summary Description: Functions are encouraging other groups to develop prevention programs, public education, and training prevention officers. A wide variety of constituencies are served. All programs are utilized except court watch, victim assistance, and crime blockers. Accessibility to services is not limited. No technical information is available in print. The association will coordinate requests for resources by referral to appropriate members.

Colorado Springs Police Department
Crime Prevention Unit
2334 Robinson Street
Colorado Springs, Colo. 80904

Contact Person: Officer Charles Pizzitola, Crime Prevention Officer; Ms. Joan Reber, Crime Prevention Specialist, (303) 578–6707 or 6498

Summary Description: All functions are performed except encouraging other groups to develop prevention programs plus school resources for the twelfth grades. A wide variety of approaches are used, and many constituencies are served. Programs used are operation identification, public education, neighborhood watch, target hardening, against commercial crime, burglary, substance abuse, and vandalism. There are no limits on accessibility to technical information in print on program planning, operations, and content. Films may be borrowed. Services are free for clearinghouse, referral, and (in limited supply) public education brochures.

Connecticut Law Enforcement Crime Prevention Association
430 Boston Post Road
Milford, Conn. 06460

Contact Person: Officer Ed Kelly, Vice President, (203) 878–6551 ext. 213

Summary Description: All functions except providing referral services are served by this membership organization for prevention practitioners. The association conducts a basic crime prevention school for police personnel at the State Police Academy for Police Officers. A wide range of approaches are used in regard to specific programs other than court watch, victim assistance, crime blockers, prevention vans, and against substance abuse. Accessibility to services is not limited, but no technical information in print is now available. Clearinghouse and public education brochures are free.

HELP STOP CRIME!
Office of the Attorney General

The Capitol
Tallahassee, Fla. 32301

Contact Person: Jim T. Murdaugh, Program Director, (904) 487–3712

Summary Description: This organization functions as the state coordinating agency in crime prevention. It develops programs, provides training and technical assistance, and stimulates activities at the local level. Specific programs are: residential burglary, business burglary, commercial armed robbery, retail theft, operation identification, neighborhood watch, sexual assault, crimes against the elderly, and agricultural crime. Printed and audiovisual materials are available free for the above topics.

Idaho Department of Law Enforcement
6081 Clinton Street
Boise, Id. 83704

Contact Person: Shannon Pound, State Coordinator, (208) 334–2909

Summary Description: Functions are coordinating prevention programs, clearinghouse, and referral. There is a wide range of approaches and of constituencies. The following programs are used: operation identification, public education, neighborhood watch against commercial crime, against burglary, against substance abuse, against vehicle theft, against vandalism, and against rape/assault. Accessibility is not limited. Technical information in print is available free on program planning and operations. Resources available on loan are: slide, library, and clearinghouse; a sample copy of public education brochures is free.

Comment of Agency: This office is the resource center for Idaho local prevention programs. Idaho has an active Crime Prevention Association that conducts forty-one school hours in prevention.

Illinois Criminal Justice Information Authority
120 South Riverside Plaza, Suite 1016
Chicago, Ill. 60606

Contact Person: Kevin P. Morison, Public Information Officer, (312) 793–8550

Summary Description: Functions are public education, clearinghouse, referral, and providing detailed crime statistics and other data. There are no limitations on answering requests for information about the incidence of crime in Illinois as a whole or in selected parts of the state.

Comment of Agency: This agency is part of the executive branch of Illinois government. It develops and operates computerized criminal justice information systems and conducts research/analysis of criminal justice data. Although prevention is not the primary function, the staff can provide information on prevention programs and referrals to appropriate agencies.

Illinois Department of Law Enforcement
Office of Training

3700 Lake Shore Drive
Springfield, Ill. 62707

Contact Person: John F. Janssen, Chief of Academic Services Bureau, (217) 786–6902

Summary Description: Functions are public education, clearinghouse, referral, and prevention training of state police cadets. Approaches are public education, victim assistance, and actions against burglary and vehicle theft. Services are limited to residents of Illinois. Technical information in print on training is available free. Films, video, and slide presentations are available on loan; public education brochures are free.

Sangamon County Sheriff's Department
Crime Prevention Bureau
800 East Monroe, Room 209
Springfield, Ill. 62701

Contact Person: Sergeant Ronald Ellis, Director of Crime Prevention, (217) 753–6845

Summary Description: All functions are served, plus a prevention training curriculum. A wide range of approaches are used in serving the county constituency. All types of specific programs (forty-two programs), except court watch, are used, plus law-focused school programs and activities against rural crimes, extortion/kidnapping, and crimes against the elderly. Services are for the locality, but inquiries from elsewhere will be accepted. Free technical information in print is available on training and program content. Central Illinois police agencies or civic groups may borrow films, video cassettes, and slides. Training plans/manuals may be borrowed.

Iowa State Patrol Crime Prevention Center
Department of Public Safety
Wallace State Building
Des Moines, Iowa 50319

Contact Person: Beverly Richardson, Coordinator, (515) 281–8395

Summary Description: All functions are served except establishing and operating programs. A wide variety of approaches are used, and wide constituencies are served. All types of programs are used except court watch, target hardening, victim assistance, and prevention vans. Accessibility to services is not limited. Technical information in print is available free on program operations and content. Available on loan are films, slides, and library; clearinghouse and public education brochures are free.

Comment of Agency: Special troopers in each of the fourteen patrol districts are Community Services Officers who conduct programs with children, stimulate prevention programs, and conduct training. The coordinator, a civilian, also conducts programs, coordinates technical assistance, stimulates a wide variety of crime prevention programs, and does some training.

Maryland Crime Watch
Department of Public Safety and Correctional Services
One Investment Place, Suite 700
Towson, Md. 21204

Contact Person: Patricia Sill, Program Coordinator, (301) 321–3686

Summary Description: All functions are served except establishing and operating programs. A wide variety of approaches is used, and a wide variety of constituencies is served. Specific programs used are operation identification, public education, neighborhood watch, target hardening, against commercial crime, against burglary, and against rape/assault. Services are primarily for residents of Maryland, but exceptions are considered case by case. Technical information in print on program operations is available on loan. The following resources are available on loan or by purchase: video cassettes, slides, training plans/manuals, library, and clearinghouse. Public education brochures and mass media materials are available free or by loan.

Maryland State Police Headquarters
1201 Reisterstown Road
Pikesville, Md. 21208

Contact Person: Second Lieutenant Robert L. McWhorter (or Corporal Danny Shell) Commander, Crime Prevention Unit, (301) 486–3101 ext. 377 or 251

Summary Description: All functions plus agency policy development on prevention activities are served. A wide variety of approaches are used, and wide constituencies are served; all programs are used except court watch, crime blockers, and arson. Accessibility is limited to not-for-profit organizations. Program information in print is available free (not in quantity). Library resources are available on loan statewide: films, video cassettes, slides, and training plans/manuals.

Comment of Agency: The unit advises staff on related policy and procedures; develops and recommends new programs for statewide implementation; coordinates agency crime prevention efforts throughout the department and with other organizations; and evaluates existing programs and manages change.

Massachusetts Crime Watch
1 Ashburton Place
Room 1310
Boston, Mass. 02108

Contact Person: Thomas J. Chuda
Program Director, (617) 727–7827

Summary Description: All functions are served using a wide range of approaches for many constituencies. Specific programs are operation identification, public education, neighborhood watch, target hardening, prevention vans, and prevention of the following offenses: commercial crime, burglary, vehicle theft, vandalism, rape/assault, and child abuse. Accessibility is unlimited for borrowing technical information in print on program planning, operations, training, and contents. All kinds of resources may be borrowed.

Crime Prevention Association of Michigan
1300 Beaubien, Room 207
Detroit, Mich. 48226

Contact Person: Sergeant James Knittel, Secretary, (313) 244–4030

Summary Description: All functions are served except establishing and operating programs for a wide variety of constituencies. Public education is emphasized without limitation on free resources for clearinghouse, public education brochures, and mass media materials.

Minnesota Crime Watch
318 Transportation Building
St. Paul, Minn. 55155

Contact Person: Charles H. Rix, Coordinator, (612) 297–7541

Summary Description: Functions are establishing and operating programs, public education, increasing public participation, and clearinghouse. Approaches are illustrated by specific programs: operation identification, neighborhood watch, target hardening, against commercial crime, against burglary, against vehicle theft, and against rape/assault. The constituency is limited to law enforcement agencies of Minnesota. No technical information in print is available. Films, video cassettes, and mass media material are loaned. Free materials are slides and public education brochures.

Missouri Department of Public Safety
P.O. Box 749
Harry S Truman State Office Building
Jefferson City, Mo. 65102

Contact Person: David E. Rost, Program Analyst, (314) 751–4905

Summary Description: Functions are encouraging other groups to develop prevention programs, increasing public participation, clearinghouse, and referral. A wide range of approaches are used with the exception of court watch, crime blockers, prevention vans, and against vandalism. Services are limited to Missouri residents, but special exceptions can be made. Technical information in print is available free on program planning. Films, video cassettes, and slides are available on loan; clearinghouse, referral, and public education brochures are free.

Comment of Agency: The Department also oversees the State Fire Marshal's Office (arson awareness), Division of Highway Safety (alcohol abuse/DWI programs), Peace Officer Standards and Training Program, victim assistance program, and the distribution of federal prevention funds.

Montana Crime Prevention/Crimestoppers Association
303 North Roberts
Room 463, Scott Hart Building
Helena, Mont. 59620

Contact Person: John L. Strandell, President, (406) 444–4444

Summary Description: All functions are served through a wide range of approaches. All specific programs are utilized except court watch. Accessibility to technical information in print is unlimited through loan; topics are program planning, operations, training, and content evaluation. All kinds of resources may be borrowed.

New Jersey Crime Prevention Officer's Association, Inc.
Box 464
Madison, N.J. 07940

Contact Person: Detective David R. Green, President, (201) 377–7928

Summary Description: All functions except establishing and operating programs are served. A wide range of approaches is recognized in serving active prevention practitioners. All programs are represented except court watch, victim assistance, crime blockers, and against arson. Accessibility is limited only by volunteer time available to members. Technical information in print is available free on neighborhood watch and training. Resources are available on loan on training plans/manuals and public education brochures; services for clearinghouse and referral are free.

New Jersey Department of Community Affairs
Crime Prevention Unit
363 West State Street
Trenton, N.J. 98625

Contact Person: Michael J. Renahan, Supervising Program, Development Specialist, (609) 292–6110

Summary Description: All functions are served except directly operating programs. A wide range of approaches are used. All types of programs are used except court watch, victim assistance, and crime blockers. Accessibility to services is not limited. All types of technical information in print are available free. Video cassettes and slides are available on loan; these resources are available free: training plans/manuals, library, clearinghouse, referral, public education brochures, and mass media materials. The agency does not provide funding for activities at this time.

New York State Division of Criminal Justice Services
Office of Crime Prevention
Executive Park Tower
Stuyvesant Plaza
Albany, N.Y. 12203

Contact Person: Susan Jacobsen, Director, (518) 457–3700

Summary Description: Functions are encouraging other groups to develop programs, public education, and coordinating funding for community groups, and training law enforcement personnel. Only certain approaches are used: operation identification, public education, and neighborhood watch. A wide variety of constituencies are served but only within New York State. Training materials are distributed only to trainees. Technical information in print is available free on program operations and content. The following resources are available on loan: films and slides; public education brochures and mass media materials are free.

Division of Crime Prevention
P.O. Box 27687
Raleigh, N.C. 27611

Contact Person: Bruce E. Marshburn, Director, (919) 733–5522

Summary Description: Functions are encouraging other groups to develop programs, public education, and clearinghouse. There is a wide range of approaches and constituencies. All programs are used. There are no limitations on accessibility to services; technical information in print is available free on program content. The following resources are free: newsletters, limited films, video cassettes, slides, and public education brochures.

Crime Prevention Association of Oregon
P.O. Box 13718
Salem, Oreg. 97309

Contact Person: Hugh Wilkinson, Executive Secretary, (503) 378–3674

Summary Description: All functions are served for a wide range of constituencies through main approaches. All types of specific programs are utilized, except prevention vans. Accessibility to services is unlimited. Technical information in print is available free on program planning, operations, training, and content. Films, video cassettes, slides, and library resources may be borrowed. Free resources are training plans/manuals, library materials, clearinghouse, referral, public education brochures, and mass media materials.

Oregon Crime Watch
Board on Police Standards and Training
325 13th Street, NE
Suite 404
Salem, Oreg. 97310

Contact Person: Hugh Wilkinson, Crime Prevention Coordinator, (503) 378–3674

Summary Description: All functions are served other than directly establishing and operating programs. One major function is to assist in establishing programs at the local level. Referral services are emphasized. A wide range of approaches are used, and many constituencies are served. All types of specific programs are used except court watch, victim assistance, crime blockers, prevention vans, and against arson, plus youth programs. Services are limited to residents of Oregon. Technical information in print is available on loan on program planning, operations, and training. Resources available on loan are films, video cassettes, and library; free resources are clearinghouse, public education brochures, and mass media materials.

Comment of Agency: This statewide agency was formed in 1979 to support local law enforcement and other crime prevention programs through technical assistance, and training, and counsel on establishing and maintaining programs.

Bureau of Crime Prevention, Training and Technical Assistance
Pennsylvania Commission on Crime and Delinquency
P.O. Box 1167
Federal Square Station
Harrisburg, Pa. 17108

Contact Person: Herbert C. Yost, Director, (717) 787–1777

Summary Description: The commission coordinates the state's law enforcement efforts in order to establish and operate localized prevention programs. It provides training, consultative services, technology transfer, and resources identification to state and municipal government organizations developing prevention efforts. The commission utilizes a wide variety of program approaches via a coalition of resources. All specific program areas except court watch, crime, blockers, prevention vans, and substance abuse are addressed. Printed technical information, training curricula, and public education brochures are available for purchase, while films, slides, and library materials are provided on a loan basis. Referrals and mass media items are available at no cost.

Division of Public Safety Programs
Governor's Office, State of South Carolina
1205 Pendleton Street
Columbia, S.C. 29201

Contact Person: Vachel Jones, Acting Deputy Director, (803) 758–8940

Summary Description: Functions are coordinating programs, public education, and funding delinquency prevention programs. Only these are programs used: public education and allocation of action grant funds. Accessibility is limited to South Carolina. No technical information is in print. Films on loan and free public education brochures are available.

Comment of Agency: The primary activities are conferences for police and social service practitioners involved in problems of criminal behavior. Training is provided for police agencies without prevention officers.

Criminal Justice Division of the Governor's Office
P.O. Box 12428
Capitol Station
Austin, Tex. 78711

Contact Person: Gilbert Pena, Executive Director, (512) 475–3001

Summary Description: Functions are encouraging other groups to develop prevention programs, clearinghouse, and providing grant funds for criminal justice projects, especially in delinquency and crime prevention and increased security. Wide varieties of constituencies, limited to Texas, are served through all types of specific grant-funded programs. Technical information in print is free for program planning and on loan for program operations, content, and training. Training plans/manuals, library, and public education brochures may be borrowed. The clearinghouse is free.

Comment of Agency: This agency has a primary role in criminal justice planning for Texas. Its activities also include providing grants and disseminating information about successful criminal justice programs.

Utah Council for Crime Prevention
Utah Department of Public Safety
4501 South 2700 West
Salt Lake City, Utah 84199

Contact Person: Tibby Milne, Executive Director; John Phelon, Jr., Program Coordinator, (801) 965–4591 or (801) 295–7866

Summary Description: All functions are served, and there is a wide range of approaches and constituencies. All types of programs are used except crime blockers and prevention vans, plus against abduction/kidnapping. There are no limitations on accessibility to services. Technical information in print is available free on program planning, operation, and content. All resources are available free or on loan except for library.

Comment of Agency: The agency is volunteer owned and operated; this feature is believed to be advantageous. A board of forty volunteers coordinates efforts through the Utah Department of Public Safety which provides office facilities and support services.

TIPS Program
Jefferson Annex
Fourth Street, N.W.
Charlottesville, Va. 22901

Contact Person: Loreli Damron, Project Director, (804) 293–5179

Summary Description: Function is public education through classroom instruction in grades kindergarten through eight. "TIPS" reflects two goals of the program: Teaching Individuals Protective Strategies (in avoiding victimization) and Teaching Individuals Positive Solutions (in dealing with conflict). TIPS office services are generally provided to schools without charge. An instructional manual is available for purchase by teachers, guidance counselors, or volunteer personnel. A program evaluation report is available in short supply.

Virginia Crime Prevention Center
Department of Criminal Justice Services
805 East Broad Street, 10th Floor
Richmond, Va. 23219

Contact Person: Patrick Harris or Harold Wright, Crime Prevention Specialists, (804) 786–4000

Summary Description: Functions are encouraging other groups to develop prevention programs, public education, clearinghouse, and referral. A wide range of approaches are used for many constituencies. Types of specific programs are operation identification, public education, neighborhood watch, target hardening, victim assistance, and CPTED. Accessibility to services is unlimited. Technical information is available free on program planning and content. Library materials may be borrowed. Clearinghouse and referral services and newsletter are free.

Comment of Agency: The center staff serves the Governor's Business and Industry Committee on Crime Prevention and the Public Safety Secretary, Crime Prevention through Environmental Design Committee.

Greater Washington Board of Trade
Retail Bureau
1129 20th Street N.W.
Washington, D.C. 20036

Contact Person: Garry R. Curtis, Manager, Retail Bureau, (202) 857–5980

Summary Description: Functions are coordinating prevention programs and public education. A wide range of approaches are used, and many constituencies are served. Programs are public education, support of neighborhood watch, and actions against commercial crime. An anti-shoplifting campaign is the focus, but extension to broader community program is being considered. Accessibility is unlimited for technical information in print (free) on program content. In the Washington, D.C., area only, the following resources are available free: films, video cassettes, training plans/manuals, clearinghouse, public education brochures, and mass media materials.

Washington Crime Watch
2450 South 142nd Street
Seattle, Wash. 98168

Contact Person: Brooks P. Russell, Director, (206) 764–4002

Summary Description: All functions are served except establishing and operating programs and increasing public participation. A wide range of approaches are used, and the broad constituency is limited to residents of the state of Washington. All specific programs are used except court watch, crime blockers, prevention vans, against substance abuse, and against arson. Technical information in print is free on all topics. Films and video cassettes may be borrowed and slides purchased. Other kinds of resources are free.

Fox Valley Technical Institute
Police Science/Security and Loss Prevention Department
1825 North Bluemound Drive
Appleton, Wis. 54913

Contact Person: Edward J. Krueger, Coordinator, (414) 735–5600

Summary Description: The department serves as a crime prevention training center for police and other interested persons as part of its service to law enforcement agencies of Wisconsin. Usually in conjunction with the Wisconsin Crime Prevention Officers' Association, several training courses in crime prevention are offered annually.

Wisconsin Council of Criminal Justice
30 West Mifflin Street, Suite 1000
Madison, Wis. 53702

Contact Person: Patrick Riopelle, Program Planning Analyst, (608) 266–3323

Summary Description: All functions are served except establishing and operating programs. A wide range of approaches are used, and wide constituencies are served. Specific programs are operation identification, public education, neighborhood watch, victim assistance (with Wisconsin Department of Justice), against commercial crime, and against burglary. Services are accessible only to residents of Wisconsin. Technical information in print is available on loan in all topics except program operations. Loan of the following resources is available: training plans/manuals, clearinghouse, referral, and mass media materials. The Department of Justice, Training and Standards Bureau, provides films and video cassettes.

Wisconsin Crime Prevention Officers' Association
President Don Perretz
c/o Grafton Police Department
1981 Washington Street
Grafton, Wis. 53024

Contact Person: Don Perretz, President, (414) 377–2220

Summary Description: Objectives include development of various crime prevention programs with an emphasis on public education and awareness. In addition, the association serves as a clearinghouse for individuals interested in crime prevention. A wide range of services are available, and many constituencies are involved. Accessibility to technical information in print is not limited, but only clearinghouse and referral services are free. The association collaborates with the Fox Valley Technical Institute (listed in this appendix) in training courses and with the Training and Standards Division, Wisconsin Department of Justice.

About the Editor and Contributors

MAURICE M. BELL is the originator and present coordinator of the Seattle Police Department Business Watch program. He previously was responsible for the United Church of Christ's Urban Ministry program in the City of New York. During that period he was instrumental in developing a bail reform program operated by the New York City Board of Corrections. He was the first Director of Human Resources for the Puget Sound Council of Governments. He graduated from the University of Oregon with a B.S. in History and Harvard University with an S.T.B.

MERLYN M. BELL is a writer and consultant, specializing in criminal justice issues. She was the Director of the King County Department of Rehabilitation Services which included the county jail and adult social services. She was Director for Assessment to the Alternative to Incarceration Project. Earlier in her career she was the Research Director for the Federal Offender's Rehabilitation Program. She graduated from the University of Kansas with a B.A. in Sociology and from the University of Washington with an M.A. in sociology.

ROBERT B. COATES is Professor at the Graduate School of Social Work, University of Utah. He was awarded a Ph.D. in Sociology by the University of Maryland in 1972. His previous experience includes Research Director, PACT Institute of Justice, Valparaiso, Indiana; Associate Professor, School of Social Service Administration, University of Chicago; and Associate Director, Center for Criminal Justice, Harvard Law School. Among his numerous publications, he has been co-author of *Diversity in a Youth Correctional System: Handling Delinquents in Massachusetts* (1978); *A Theory of Social Reform: Correctional Change Processes in Two States* (1977); and *Indeterminate and Determinate Approaches to Institution Release Decision-Making in Juvenile Justice: A Cross-State Analysis* (1985).

JOHN P. CONRAD, a prolific author, was a leader in correctional research for more than two decades. As a lecturer and researcher, he has been on the faculties of numerous universities and criminological institutes, including the American Justice Institute in

Sacramento, the Academy for Contemporary Problems in Columbus, the London School of Economics, the United Nations Asia and Far East Institute for the Prevention of Crime and Treatment of Offenders in Tokyo, the National Institute of Justice in Washington, D.C., the University of Pennsylvania, Sam Houston State University, and Simon Fraser University in British Columbia. His most recent book, with Ernest Van den Haag, is *The Death Penalty: A Debate* (1983).

GERALD E. DAVIDSON is Medical Director, Elan One, Poland Springs, Maine, and Consultant in Psychiatry, Massachusetts General Hospital. His career includes Commonwealth Fund Fellow in Psychiatry and Fellow in Child and Community Psychiatry, Beth Israel Hospital/Harvard Medical School; instructor in psychiatry, Harvard Medical School; Assistant Psychiatrist, Massachusetts General Hospital; and Psychiatrist, City of Boston Drug Program, Boston City Hospital.

JIM C. HACKLER, Professor at the University of Alberta obtained his Ph.D. in Sociology at the University of Washington in 1965. Active in many professional associations, Hackler has been President of the Western Association of Sociology and Anthropology (1973), Canadian Association for Criminological Research (1973–1975), and Section on Deviance and Social Control, International Sociological Association (1974–1978). Among his numerous publications is *The Prevention of Youthful Crime: The Great Stumble Forward* (1978).

J. DAVID HAWKINS received his Ph.D. in Sociology from Northwestern University in 1975. He is Director, Center for Social Welfare Research and Associate Professor of Social Work at the University of Washington. His extensive professional publications have expressed his multifaceted interests in delinquency prevention, program evaluation, drug abuse, schools, and the family.

ELMER H. JOHNSON, Ph.D. in Sociology, University of Wisconsin (1950), is Distinguished Professor of SIU, Center for the Study of Crime, Delinquency and Corrections, Southern Illinois University (1966 to date). Previously, he taught at North Carolina State University at Raleigh. His considerable publications in criminology and criminal justice include *Crime, Correction, and Society*, 4th ed. (1978); *Social Problems of Urban Man* (1973); and *International Handbook on Contemporary Developments in Criminology* (two volumes) (1983).

JAMES L. LEBEAU is Assistant Professor, Center for the Study of Crime, Delinquency, and Correction, Southern Illinois University at Carbondale. Previously, he was a member of the faculty of the Department of Criminology, Indiana State University. He was awarded a Ph.D. in Geography in 1978 by Michigan State University. He has conducted research and evaluative studies in police operations. His publications reflect a special concern with the relationship between criminology and geography.

DENISE M. LISHNER, Master's of Social Work, University of Washington (1978), is research consultant with the Center for Social Welfare Research, University of Washington. Her professional career placed her with the Center for Law and Justice, University of Washington; Center for Addiction Services, Seattle; and the Alcohol Research Group, University of California, Berkeley. Her publications have emphasized delinquency prevention as related to aggression, prediction, substance abuse, schools, employment, and program models.

ROBERT A. LORINSKAS is Associate Professor at the Center for the Study of Crime, Delinquency, and Corrections, Southern Illinois University at Carbondale. He was awarded a Ph.D. in Political Science by the University of Georgia in 1973. Earlier, he taught at Michigan State University, the University of Wisconsin at Oshkosh, and the Public Services Institutes of Chicago City Colleges which involved him directly with the Chicago Police Academy. His professional publications and research interests, especially oriented to private security, have concentrated on the interface of political science and law enforcement.

SIDNEY E. MATTHEWS, Master's of Science in Library Science, University of Illinois (1952), is Assistant Director of Library Services, Southern Illinois University at Carbondale. His publications and consultations have drawn on his expertise in library affairs. His career services also have been at the University of Illinois, the Ohio State University, and Virginia Military Institute.

JOSEPH H. RANKIN, Ph.D. in Sociology, University of Arizona (1978), is Associate Professor of Sociology, Eastern Michigan University. Previously, he was on the faculty of the Department of Sociology, Purdue University. In addition to his research on the family and delinquency, his publications and special interests are in the areas of criminology, the sociology of law, social control, and social change.

ROBERT P. WEISS received his Ph.D. in Sociology at Southern Illinois University in Carbondale in 1980, and he now teaches criminology and corrections within the Department of Sociology, State University of New York at Plattsburgh. He has also taught at the University of Houston-Clear Lake, and the University of Minnesota-Twin Cities. Dr. Weiss has published on the topics of radical criminology, and his articles on penal history and the historical development of private policing institutions have appeared in professional journals in the United States, Canada, and Great Britain.

L. EDWARD WELLS, Ph.D in Sociology, University of Wisconsin (1975), and post-doctoral fellow, Stanford University (1976–1977). Dr. Wells is on the faculty of Illinois State University; previously he was at Purdue University (1977–1983) and Indiana University (1983–1985). He is co-author of *Self-Esteem: Its Conceptualization and Measurement* (1976). His research interests and publications are in the area of the criminological implications of social psychology, social control, and research methods.

NANCY TRAVIS WOLFE is Associate Professor, College of Criminal Justice, University of South Carolina. She holds a Ph.D. from the University of Delaware, specializing in American constitutional history. Her scholarly interest in the judicial process within the criminal justice system has taken her to the Federal Republic of Germany and the Democratic Republic of Germany under research grants to study courts.

Index